Digital Humanities and Religions in Asia

Introductions to
Digital Humanities – Religion

Edited by
Claire Clivaz, Charles M. Ess, Gregory Price Grieve,
Kristian Petersen and Sally Promey

Volume 3

Digital Humanities and Religions in Asia

—

An Introduction

Edited by L.W.C. van Lit and James Harry Morris

DE GRUYTER

ISBN 978-3-11-074725-6
e-ISBN (PDF) 978-3-11-074760-7
e-ISBN (EPUB) 978-3-11-074775-1

Library of Congress Control Number: 2023943634

Bibliographic information published by the Deutsche Nationalbibliothek
The Deutsche Nationalbibliothek lists this publication in the Deutsche Nationalbibliografie;
detailed bibliographic data are available on the Internet at http://dnb.dnb.de.

© 2024 Walter de Gruyter GmbH, Berlin/Boston
Cover image: Social network visualization. With friendly permission of Martin Grandjean.
Typesetting: Integra Software Services Pvt. Ltd.
Printing and binding: CPI books GmbH, Leck

www.degruyter.com

J.H. Morris and L.W.C. van Lit
The Digital Humanities and the History of Religion in Asia: An Introduction

Opening the pages of Edmund A. Bowles's 1967, *Computers in Humanistic Research*,[1] one is greeted with a sense of optimism and a feeling that the contributors have been swept up in the excitement of the possibilities that the digital humanities can offer. Though the book is far from uncritical, there is not a great deal of discussion throughout its chapters about the potential limitations and challenges of digital methods. Today things feel much the same — the same optimism and sense of progress leaps off of the pages of the recently published *Ōbeiken dejitaru hyūmanitīzu no kiso chishiki* 欧米圏デジタルヒューマニティーズの基礎知識[2] or the *Jinbungaku no tame no tekisuto dēta kōchiku nyūmon* 人文学のためのテキストデータ構築入門[3] which followed it. Any reader will realize that huge technological developments have taken place between 1967 and 2023, but how many will also notice the increasing centrality of the non-English speaking world? Though *Ōbeiken Dejitaru Hyūmanitīzu no kiso chishiki* is squarely focused on digital humanities in Europe it was written by Japanese scholars in Japanese with a lengthy portion devoted to Middle Eastern studies. Other recently published works have also encapsulated this turn away from Europe including L.W.C. van Lit's *Among Digitized Manuscripts*,[4] as have projects such as *The Digital Orientalist* — an online magazine focusing on the interface between the digital humanities and African, Asian, and Middle Eastern Studies which has worked over the past ten years to reach 50,000 unique visitors annually. This platform is of particular note since it acted as a sort of incubator for this volume bringing together not only the editors, but also several of the contributions.

Despite the ongoing turn away from Europe, the traditional focus of the digital humanities on texts written in European languages and Latin script has meant that

---

1 Edmund A. Bowles, ed. *Computers in Humanistic Research: Readings and Perspectives* (Englewood Cliffs, NJ: Prentice-Hall Inc., 1967).
2 Kogaze Naoki 小風尚樹, Kogawa Jun 小川潤, Oda Sōki 纓田宗紀, Nagano Sōichi 長野壯一, Yamanaka Mitsuo 山中美潮, Miyagawa Sō 宮川創, Ōmukai Ikki 大向一輝, and Nagasaki Kiyonori 永﨑研宣, eds., *Ōbeiken dejitaru hyūmanitīzu no kiso chishiki* 欧米圏デジタルヒューマニティーズの基礎知識 (Tokyo: Bungaku Tsūshin, 2021).
3 Ishida Yuri 石田友梨 and Ōmukai Ikki 大向一輝, eds. *Jinbungaku no tame no tekisuto dēta kōchiku nyūmon* 人文学のためのテキストデータ構築入門 (Tokyo: Bungaku Tsūshin, 2022).
4 L.W.C. van Lit, *Among Digitized Manuscripts: Philology, Codicology, Paleography in a Digital World* (Leiden: Brill, 2020).

https://doi.org/10.1515/9783110747607-001

most digital tools have been designed to work with documents of European origin and not those from other geographical and historical spaces. Those of us engaged in the study of the histories and religions of different parts of Asia use sources that are written in non-Latin scripts and composed using different conventions than those we find in the "Latinsphere."[5] The critical differences between European and Asian manuscripts and printed texts are based on "the materials used, the shape and the method of usage of the codex, and the climate in which they were produced and stored [. . .] we may encounter different directions of writing, different number systems, different calendars, and different naming conventions."[6] We may also encounter the use of different writing implements such as brushes rather than pens, pencils, and quills in the composition of manuscript sources, and the use of different printing techniques in the creation of printed materials. It comes as no surprise then that the texts we encounter in Asia pose a different set of questions and challenges. This chapter outlines the *modus operandi* of this volume outlining the challenges that scholars of Asian religions face when applying digital tools and methods to our subject area and provides a brief introduction to the essays that form the volume.

The Challenge of Studying Asian Histories and Religions Digitally

Paul Vierthaler notes the long history of the involvement of those engaged with East Asian studies with the digital world, its tools, methods, and infrastructures, but also notes that "East Asian digital humanities lags behind digital practice in other parts of the world. Some of this relates to the linguistic nature of the material and the historically Eurocentric focus of software development."[7] As Vierthaler's comments suggest not all contexts and fields are created equal. Pointing to the Eurocentric nature of the digital humanities and software development is a useful point of departure for understanding disparity between the field in Asia and Europe,

---

5 We use this term to refer to those places that where the prominent languages are rendered in Latin scripts which today includes most of Europe, North and South America, Oceania, and parts of Africa and Southeast Asia, but historically formed a much more geographically limited space aligning with Central, Northern, and Western Europe.
6 L. W. Cornelis van Lit, James H. Morris and Deniz Çevik, "A Digital Revival of Oriental Studies," *Revue de l'Institut des langues et cultures d'Europe, Amérique, Afrique, Asie et Australie* 39 (2020): 6.
7 Paul Vierthaler, "Digital humanities and East Asian studies in 2020," *History Compass* 18, no. 11 (2020). DOI: https://doi.org/10.1111/hic3.12628.

Acknowledgments

The genesis of this volume dates back to 2020, when we discussed with several colleagues the merits of bringing together our experience in a more formal manner. We were all members of *The Digital Orientalist* (ISSN: 2772-8374), an online magazine dedicated to publishing short articles on the theory and practice of applying computer technology to premodern history of cultures and civilizations from the continents of Africa and Asia. Our working title for the joint volume was *Across Ancient Asia: Studying Religions Electronically*. With this title we wished to convey that we wanted to focus on the commonalities in the issues and opportunities that digital methods provide when applied to premodern religions from all parts of Asia. Since the aim of our magazine is to provide accessible and easy instructions for people who are completely new to digital humanities, we wanted to make the volume serve as an introduction. We thank Kristian Petersen, editor of the series *Introductions to Digital Humanities — Religion* at De Gruyter for engaging with us early on and guiding us to pitch our idea, the peer-reviewers who helped to improve the volume, De Gruyter's Aaron Sanborn-Overby and Katrin Mittmann, and Integra Software Services's Kowsalya Perumal for their help during the project.

With a core team of colleagues from *The Digital Orientalist* already in place, we spent much of 2021 searching for other scholars to get a balanced group in this volume, according to many factors such as religions, source materials, technical methods and of course a diverse representation of the global scholarly community. Some people withdrew, while others were brought in at a late stage. In October 2022 the editors met at Waseda University (Tokyo) and finalized their discussion of all the contributions, slightly altering the scope and focus of the volume, most notably by explicitly including modern religious practice insofar as it has ties with premodern religions. A meeting a few days later overlooking Nikko's Kegon Falls pinned down elements of the introduction and conclusion. The completion and forthcoming release of the volume was informally announced at *The Digital Turn in Early Modern Japanese Studies: A Conference* held at Cambridge University from December 2–4, 2022, and organized by Laura Moretti, Yuta Hashimoto, James Morris, and Joseph Bills, as well as at *The Digital Orientalist*'s 2023 Conference on June 3, 2023. The volume took shape as our own lives radically changed — moments before our first meeting with Aaron at De Gruyter, James's wife entered labor with their first child; a second was on the way (though not quite so imminently) when the editor's met in Japan in 2022; both editors changed jobs and moved houses; and they met in-person for the first time. So, of course, it goes without saying that we would like to extend our thanks to all of those who were directly or indirectly part of this journey including our families and loved ones, our colleagues, and each other.

https://doi.org/10.1515/9783110747607-202

We also wish to thank all contributors for their generosity and most of all their patience. We also thank Daigengna Duoer and Maddalena Poli who, with the help of Rachel Griffiths, Jonathan Robker, and Mariana Zorkina, took the reins of and guided *The Digital Orientalist* to further successes as we turned to focus on this volume and other projects. We are also incredibly grateful to current and previous members of *The Digital Orientalist*: Maksim Abdul Latif, Fatma Aladağ, Joanne Bernardi, Elizabeth Bishop, Mark Boersma, Zachary Butler, Guilia Buriola, Alice Casalini, Deniz Çevik, Rohan Chauhan, Christopher Diamond, Michele Eduarda Brasil de Sá, Elene Giunashvil, Julie Hanlon, Matthew Hayes, Bryce Heatherly, Ephrem Ishac, Henry Jacobs, Sarah Ketchley, Tyler Kynn, Elizabeth Lee, Megan Lewis, Alex Mallett, Shiva Mihan, So Miyagawa, Thomas Newhall, Anna Oskina, Aleksandra Piskunova, Adrian Plau, Claudia Simonelli, Charles Riley, Lu Wang, Anaïs Wion, Yusuf Yuksek, Wang Yingda, and Theodora Zampaki.

We would also like to acknowledge the use of a Waseda University Grant for Special Research Projects for post-publication corrections.

Contents

Acknowledgments —— V

J.H. Morris and L.W.C. van Lit
The Digital Humanities and the History of Religion in Asia: An Introduction —— 1

Temples

Alberto González Pons
BulgyoLoc, a Geographical Approach to Korean Buddhism: From the Three Kingdoms Period to Current Koreas through Korean Buddhist Temples —— 27

Elizabeth Lee
Rock-Carved Buddhist Images on Mt. P'algong: An Exploration of the Utility of GIS Analysis in Art Historical Research —— 47

Manuscripts

Dick van der Meij and Jan van der Putten
DREAMSEA Digital Repository of Endangered and Affected Manuscripts in Southeast Asia. A Multiple Religious and Cultural Digitization Experience —— 73

L.W.C. van Lit
Getting Ready for the CV Revolution —— 97

Jonathan Miles Robker
The (Hyper)Text of the Hebrew Bible / Old Testament: Digital and Online Environments — Their Impact on Considerations on the Text, Its Reconstruction, and Its History —— 111

Adrian Plau
Digital Orientalism? Philology, Digital Methodologies, and Reflections on the Study of Primary Sources to North Indian Religions —— 139

Texts

Peter Flügel
The Jaina Prosopography Database: A New Tool for the Humanities —— 157

Mariana Zorkina
Daoist Immortals as a Poetic Image in the Tang Dynasty: A Corpus Study —— 177

James Harry Morris
Missiology in the Digital Age: Challenges and Opportunities for the Study of Pre-Modern Christianity in Japan —— 205

Social Media

Kusumita Datta
***Gonojagoron Monchos* of the 2013 Shahbag Protests in Bangladesh: "Religions" and Digital Media** —— 233

Paula R. Curtis
On Kami and Avatars: Social Media Literacy and Academics as Public Intellectuals —— 257

Kaitlyn Ugoretz
Consuming Shinto, Feeding the Algorithm: Exploring the Impact of Social Media Software on Global Religious Aesthetic Formations —— 289

L.W.C. van Lit and J.H. Morris
Conclusion: Surprising Effects of the Digital Turn —— 317

Subject index —— 329

which we have already employed at the beginning of this chapter and elsewhere.[8] However, the terms "Eurocentric" and "Eurocentrism" prove potentially problematic and indeed must be problematized — what exactly is it that we mean by these terms? The terms when applied to computing and the digital humanities seemingly refer to both the development of computing, software, and the digital humanities within "Europe" and the "Europe"-facing tendencies of scholars and research, but this is not all that is captured through use of the term. Ella Shohat and Robert Stam write that:

> Endemic in present-day thought and education, Eurocentrism is naturalized as "common sense." Philosophy and literature are assumed to be European philosophy and literature. The "best that is thought and written" is assumed to have been thought and written by Europeans. (By Europeans, we refer not only to Europe *per se* but also to the "neo-Europeans" of the Americas, Australia, and elsewhere.) History is assumed to be European history [...] Standard core courses in universities stress the history of "Western" civilization, with the more liberal universities insisting on token study of "other" civilizations. And even "Western" civilization is usually taught without reference to the central role of European colonialism within capitalist modernity. So embedded is Eurocentrism in everyday life, so pervasive, that it often goes unnoticed. The residual traces of centuries of axiomatic European domination inform the general culture, the everyday language, and the media, engendering a fictious sense of the innate superiority of European-derived cultures and peoples.[9]

Nevertheless, "Eurocentrism" is a convenient and potentially arbitrary term. Like the concept of "culture" which "has come to stand for all manner of contestatory differentiations between groups"[10] and thus may impede the study of the complexity of social realities due to its homogenizing tendencies, the term "Eurocentrism" is often lazily applied as a descriptor for a wide array of challenge-worthy points of differentiation between "Europe" (or the knowledge of "Europe") and other spaces (or the knowledge of those spaces), and often risks homogenizing these spaces. Unlike the term "culture," however, which is often used "in defence of something that is 'ours' [...] or as a term that props up the false superiority of one group over another,"[11] the concept of "Eurocentrism" is primarily critical and seeks to

---

[8] Van Lit, Morris and Çevik, "A Digital Revival of Oriental Studies."
[9] Ella Shohat and Robert Stam, "Introduction," in *Unthinking Eurocentrism: Multiculturalism and the Media* (London: Routledge, 2014), digital version with no page numbers.
[10] Alissa Jones Nelson, *Power and Responsibility in Biblical Interpretation: Reading the Book of Job with Edward Said* (London: Routledge, 2014), 82. Alissa Jones Nelson is describing: Mario I. Aguilar, "Changing Models of the 'Death' of Culture: A Diachronic and Positive Critique of Socio-scientific Assumptions," in *Anthropology and Biblical Studies: Avenues of Approach*, ed. L. J. Lawrence and M. I. Aguilar (Leiden: Deo, 2004), 299–313.
[11] Jones Nelson, *Power and Responsibility in Biblical Interpretation*, 82.

challenge the false superiority of "Europe." Despite this, it isn't always clear exactly what is meant by the term — authors oft employ it rather than provide a detailed exploration of the historical, political, or economic contexts of that which they are describing. What is Europe? Do we also include North America and Australasia and perhaps elsewhere? What about Eastern Europe? Are we referring to former colonial nations? Are we referring to the First World? Are we referring to the Global North? Are we referring to whiteness? Perhaps we are referring to several of these things at once. The problem is that when we employ the term "Eurocentrism" we don't show much concern for these questions — we propose a boogey man representing "successful" (wealthy) capitalist economic centers with some vague geo-political positioning in Europe, North America and perhaps Oceania, in which some of the nations have a history of colonialism and some are predominantly white. In doing so we homogenize not only "European," but also non-"European" spaces. We don't acknowledge, for example, that Eastern Europe only began organized efforts to develop digital humanities in the 2010s "at least 10–15 years after similar developments in Western Europe"[12] and around the same time as South Asia. We come to ignore these sorts of inter-European disparities by looking almost exclusively at Western Europe and the USA. Perhaps this suggests that the term really refers to Western Eurocentrism and Americentrism. Similarly, through a pre-occupation with the divide between "Europe" and that which is not-"Europe" we also come to see Asia as a homogenous block (or blocks such as South Asia and East Asia) overlooking inter-Asian disparities in and outside of the digital humanities. For instance, whereas Roopika Risam and Rahul K. Gairola note that the first concerted efforts to develop the field in South Asia began in the 2010s,[13] in East Asia scholars have been using digital tools and methods since the 1970s[14] and in Syriac studies the digital humanities took off with the publication of George Kiraz's *Computer-Generated Concordance to the Syriac New Testament* in 1993.[15] A further risk is that we homogenize history by overlooking the historically complex encounters and exchanges between Europeans and Asians, their contexts, and ideas. This is something that

---

[12] Ephrem Aboud Ishac, "From Ancient Manuscripts to Digital Screens: Syriac Liturgy in Digital Humanities," in *Empowering the Visibility of Croatian Cultural Heritage through the Digital Humanities*, ed. Marijana Tomić, Mirna Willer and Nives Tomašević (Newcastle upon Tyne: Cambridge Scholars Publishing, 2020), 150.
[13] Roopika Risam and Rahul K. Gairola, "South Asian Digital Humanities Then and Now," *South Asian Review* 40, no. 3 (2019): 141–154.
[14] Vierthaler, "Digital humanities and East Asian studies in 2020."
[15] Mădălina Chitez, Rozana Rogobete, and Alexandru Foitoș, "Digital Humanities as an Incentive for Digitalisation Strategies in Eastern European HEIs: A Case Study of Romania," in *European Higher Education Area: Challenges for a New Decade*, ed. Adrian Curag, Ligia Deca, and Remus Pricopie (Cham: Springer, 2020), 549.

some of the chapters in this volume seek to address with Morris, Robker, and Ugoretz in particular exploring themes that cross continental borders and histories. In quite a tautologous fashion then our attempts to criticize "Eurocentrism" become Eurocentric,[16] and we begin to overlook real-world diversity. This homogenizing tendency is dangerous, spurring the creation of inaccuracies and perpetuating colonial narratives. It is akin in many ways to the employment of the problematic and perhaps even meaningless categories of "Eastern" and "Western" which have long been challenged in our respective fields.[17]

None of this means that we reject the potential usefulness of criticisms against the Eurocentrism of the digital humanities — such a challenge lies at the heart of this work — but these criticisms must show specificity and recognize the possible existence of multiple centers, peripheries, and semi-peripheries on global, regional, national, local and institutional levels. There is a global economic divide between Western Europe/North America and Asia grounded in the legacies of colonialism, globalization, and capitalist discourses. This has had a huge effect in some Asian spaces resulting in poor funding for research and education and a lack of popular access to digital technology which is in turn reflected in a comparatively less developed digital humanities infrastructure.[18] There are also inter-Asian (regional) disparities (not

---

[16] This criticism has been made by critics of postcolonial studies. See description in: Roopika Risam, "Breaking and Building: The Case of Postcolonial Digital Humanities," in *The Postcolonial World*, ed. Jyotsna G. Singh and David D. Kim (London: Routledge, 2017), 346.

[17] Kiri Paramore, referring to common scholarly understandings of anti-Christian discourses in Edo Period (1601–1868) Japan, notes that the conceptualization of history in terms of an "Eastern" and "Western" clash narrates "the flow of history as a determined function of an essentialized conception of 'culture'" (Paramore 2009, 5) and is both inaccurate and politically dangerous. Indeed, these sort of conceptualizations, which are at the root of many scholarly and popular attempts to understand Asia vis-à-vis Europe, have been challenged in a broad array of literature including Chiara Bottici and Benoît Challand's *The Myth of the Clash of Civilizations*, Martin W. Lewis and Kären Wigen's *The Myth of Continents*, and Ella Shohat and Robert Stam's *Unthinking Eurocentrism*, which challenge the existence of the "East" and "West" as civilizational, cognitive, cultural and geographical categories, and question their usefulness in scholarship. Kiri Paramore, *Ideology and Christianity in Japan* (London: Routledge, 2009), 5, 11–12; Chiara Bottici and Benoît Challand, *The Myth of the Clash of Civilizations* (London: Routledge, 2010); Martin W. Lewis and Kären Wigen, *The Myth of Continents: A Critique of Metageography* (Berkeley, CA: University of California Press, 1997); Ella Shohat and Robert Stam, *Unthinking Eurocentrism: Multiculturalism and the Media* (London: Routledge, 1994).

[18] See critical discussions in: Dhanashree Thorat, "Digital Infrastructures and Technoutopian Fantasies: The Colonial Roots of Technology Aid in the Global South," in *Exploring Digital Humanities in India: Pedagogies, Practices, and Institutional Possibilities*, ed. Maya Dodd and Nidhi Kalra (London: Routledge, 2001), digital version with no page numbers; Massimo Ragnedda and Anna Gladkova, eds. *Digital Inequalities in the Global South* (Cham: Springer Nature, 2020); Massimo Ragnedda and Glenn W. Muschert, eds., *Theorizing Digital Divides* (London: Routledge, 2018).

necessarily grounded in Eurocentrism) — economically successful nations such as Japan have much more opportunities to develop computing and the digital humanities than poorer economies. Disparities within single nations (not necessarily grounded in Eurocentrism) right down to the institutional level also exist — Morris has much greater access to research funding at Waseda University than he might at another institution. On one level then, Western Eurocentrism and Americentrism is perhaps best understood in terms of a description of the global economic system and the history of this system, and may be particularly helpful for explaining the historico-economic causes of the digital divide or why the digital humanities are less advanced in South Asia than in Western Europe or North America. However, it is not possible to employ it as a singular explanation of economic disparities especially when considering regional, national and local contexts. Eurocentrism is not only an economic descriptor — it is also a way of conceiving the world and creating knowledge, which has acted to peripheralize Asian spaces regardless of their economic status. Alongside contextual specificity and the recognition of global diversity, criticisms of Eurocentrism must be outward looking highlighting the many voices of those working in the digital humanities outside of Europe and on projects focusing on non-European histories, languages, peoples, texts, and spaces[19] — to do otherwise breeds only more Eurocentrism. As important a question as it is, it isn't enough to ask, "Why are the digital humanities so white?"[20] rather we must ask how we can best highlight and include non-white voices. Perhaps this will require new questions reflecting not only global, but regional disparities — "Why are digital humanities in Asia so East Asian?" "How can we include South Asian voices?" "What are the barriers to entry and how do we break these down?" etc., but these are topics to be broached at another time.

We have suggested that the Eurocentric nature of computing and the digital humanities and the linked disparities between Europe/North American and Asian digital humanities infrastructures are firmly grounded in economic divide. But how can we talk of such a divide as a cause of disparity in computing and the digital humanities when, for example, Japan and the Republic of Korea have long been economic powerhouses (both nationally and on a per capita basis)? When both these countries are known for their technology and electronics industries?

---

[19] Titilola Babalola Aiyegbusi and Langa Khumalo's "Digital Humanities Outlooks beyond the West" strikes the balance of critical engagement with the Eurocentrism of the digital humanities and highlighting non-European voices well. See: Titilola Babalola Aiyegbusi and Langa Khumalo, "Digital Humanities Outlooks beyond the West," in *The Bloomsbury Handbook to the Digital Humanities*, ed. James O'Sullivan (London: Bloomsbury Academic, 2023), 29–40.
[20] We refer here to: Tara McPherson, "Why are the digital humanities so white? Or thinking the histories of race and computation," in *Debates in the Digital Humanities*, ed. Matthew K. Gold (Minneapolis, MN: University of Minnesota Press, 2012).

Or when there is a divide in the development of the digital humanities between different parts of Asia? It is clear that economic disparity and a history of European colonialism have suppressed advancement (digital and otherwise) in South Asia and less economically developed areas. Although this economic divide and history of colonialism may not be present or may play a diminished role in the case of more economically developed countries (Japan, for example, exhibits neither this economic disparity nor the history of colonialism), these countries may still find themselves in (geographically, politically, economically) peripheral or semi-peripheral positions vis-à-vis European and North American centers which shape their technological development. The gap between the development of computing in Europe and North America on the one hand and Japan on the other has traditionally been explained as a problem of linguistics and computing culture. For example, the Nihon Hōsō Kyōkai 日本放送協会's *Konpyūtā wa kotoba no kabe o koerareru ka: IBM e no chosen* コンピューターは言葉の壁を越えられるか: IBMへの挑戦 notes that:

> IBM [the world leader in computing during much of the second half of the twentieth century] was a global company with diverse racial and religious backgrounds, but also a shared sense of American national identity and a common cultural foundation in the English language making the company itself analogous to the United States of America.
> Computers were originally born and raised in the USA. The process of the spread of computer "culture" around the world was also the process of the spread of American computer culture.[21]

As such, until around 1980 "Japanese computers were little different from those of American manufacture, in that [they] also used English programmes."[22] IBM was able to secure a place amongst the top three market suppliers in Japan despite government protection and promotion policies that limited the ability of foreign companies to enter the market.[23] It released the IBM 2245 Kanji Printer in 1970 and the Nihon Hōsō Kyōkai presents this as evidence that IBM was leading the way in developing technology for use with the Japanese language.[24] Conversely,

---

[21] Nihon Hōsō Kyōkai 日本放送協会, ed. *Konpyūtā wa kotoba no kabe o koerareru ka: IBM e no chosen* コンピューターは言葉の壁を越えられるか: IBMへの挑戦 (Tokyo: Kadokawa Shoten, 1988), 39.
[22] Christopher Seeley, *A History of Writing in Japan* (Honolulu, HI: University of Hawai'i Press, 2000), 185.
[23] See historical exploration in: Marie Anchordoguy, *Computers Inc.: Japan's Challenge to IBM* (Cambridge, MA: Council on East Asian Studies, Harvard University, 1989); Dennis J. Encarnation, *Rivals beyond Trade: America versus Japan in Global Competition* (Ithaca, NY: Cornell University Press, 1992).
[24] Nihon Hōsō Kyōkai, ed. *Konpyūtā wa kotoba no kabe o koerareru ka*, 87.

however, it seems that most major innovations in technology and computing were being undertaken by Japanese companies and organizations. Toshiba introduced the first Japanese language word processor with an input system for Chinese characters in 1978,[25] the first Japanese Industrial Standards character encoding (JIS C 6226) was also introduced that year,[26] and Fujitsu introduced the Japanese Language Information System JEF (Japanese processing Extended Feature) in 1979 allowing Japanese language to be processed on any system.[27] It wasn't until 1991 when IBM released its DOS/V operating system that other foreign companies using IBM's software were able to introduce their own computers into the market.[28] In other words, although we can't overlook the role that IBM played in Japanese computing, innovation came primarily from within. When we observe that the development of Chinese input methods were also an internal affair linked directly to the history of the Chinese typewriter[29] or that Syriac fonts were innovated by George A. Kiraz at Alaph Beth Computer Systems,[30] we may posit that the lack of development of technology for the Asian market has as much to do with a general disregard for Asian spaces as it does with some unrequited desire, thwarted by the action of Asian governments, to enter and develop technology for Asian markets. This peripheralization of Asia continues — despite the fact that Arabic is the third most widely used script in the world, Windows software still didn't offer support for Arabic fonts until the mid-2000s and Microsoft products for Mac continue to exhibit issues when writing with Arabic.[31] In other words, a combination of economic disparities and the peripheralization of Asian spaces has and continues to limit the development of computing and the digital humanities in Asia to different degrees dependent on a given location's contextual circumstances. Whilst this is not the space to flesh out this discussion, it is enough

---

[25] Nanette Gottlieb, *Word-Processing Technology in Japan: Kanji and the Keyboard* (London: Routledge, 2000), 33, 39.
[26] Seeley, *A History of Writing in Japan*, 186.
[27] IPSJ Computer Museum, "[Fujitsu] The Japanese Language Information System JEF," http://museum.ipsj.or.jp/en/computer/main/0048.html.
[28] Martin Campbell-Kelly and Daniel D. Garcia-Swartz, *From Mainframes to Smartphones: A History of the International Computer Industry* (Cambridge, MA: Harvard University Press, 2015), 143.
[29] Thomas S. Mullaney, *The Chinese Typewriter: A History* (Cambridge, MA: The MIT Press, 2017), 237–281.
[30] George A. Kiraz, "Challenges in Syriac Text Editions using the DOS-Based Word Processor Multi-Lingual Scholar," in *The Letter before the Spirit: The Importance of Text Editions for the Study of the Reception of Aristotle*, ed. Aafke M.I. van Oppenraay (Leiden: Brill, 2012), 448.
[31] Andrea Stanton, "Broken is Word," in *Your Computer is on Fire*, ed. Thomas S. Mullaney, Benjamin Peters, Mar Hicks, and Kavita Philip (Cambridge, MA: The MIT Press, 2021), 222–226.

to note that both sorts of divide have positioned the Asian digital humanities on the back foot vis-à-vis North America and Europe. Although different geographic locations within Asia and the fields associated with those locations (e.g., India and Indology) may be at different stages, there may also be factors that act to unite the Asian digital humanities and provide scope for inter-Asian dialogue and collaboration.

It is not only economic disparities and the peripheralization of Asia that play a major role in influencing the development of and approaches to the digital humanities, practical issues facing those engaged in interface between the digital humanities and Asian studies are also of key importance. Although the Chinese, Indian and Islamic worlds played an important role in the history of early computing and mathematics,[32] the digital humanities and modern computing more generally have been built for and by those using languages that are written in Latin script and more specifically in the English language. This is linked to the history of modern computing. Henry M. Walker notes that:

> In the early days of electronic computing (in the 1960s and 1970s, or perhaps even in 1980), much of the experimentation with and development of technology occurred in America and Great Britain. In these environments, researchers typically used English as their primary (or only) language, and therefore developed text-based systems for computers with the 26-letter Latin alphabet in mind. Other computer development occurred in Europe, but most of these people also used the Latin alphabet. Further, because most hardware came from U.S. manufacturers, researchers in non-European countries often began with equipment based on the Latin alphabet and basic English punctuation.[33]

Although Walker suggests that demand for the ability to type and display non-Latin alphabets and characters is a recent phenomenon associated "with the expansion of international communication and the advent of the Internet,"[34] it is important to highlight that the dominance of Anglophone, Latinate and alphabetical[35] computing reinforced the aforementioned economic and technological disparities, and created difficulties for those seeking to develop computing for use with non-Latin scripts. Purbasha Auddy notes, for example, that whilst optical character recognition (OCR)

---

32 See descriptions in: Victor Katz, ed. *The Mathematics of Egypt, Mesopotamia, China, India, and Islam: A Sourcebook* (Princeton, NJ: Princeton University Press, 2007); Gerard O'Regan, *Introduction to the History of Computing: A Computing History Primer* (Cham: Springer, 2016), 13–36.
33 Henry M. Walker, *The Tao of Computing*, 2nd edition (London: CRC Press, 2013), 48.
34 Ibid., 49.
35 Alphabetical scripts (Latin, Cyrillic, Greek) are mostly used within European languages and the languages of some of Europe's former colonies, whereas Asian languages tend to exhibit the use of different systems; logographic (Chinese and Japanese), abjad (Arabic and Hebrew), and abugida (Indic).

technology functions well with Latin scripts, it has not been satisfactorily developed for non-Latin scripts.[36] Auddy summarizes the disparity between Latinate and non-Latinate digital humanities aptly when noting "Bengali is amongst the five most common languages in the Global South. It is also the seventh most widely spoken language in the world. However, its representation on the internet and in DH is not proportional to its number of speakers."[37] There is significant overlap and a causational linkage between the peripheralization of Asia and practical limitations. Indeed, practical issues are not inherent to Asian languages and scripts, but exist only in so far as computing and software development is Latin-centric. As Andrea Stanton writes "Our assumptions about technology and its relationship to the Roman alphabet, and to the unidirectional scripts it supports, have led us to ask the wrong questions — and to seek the wrong solutions [...] Arabic is not the problem — thinking of Arabic script as a problem is."[38] The same may be true of other scripts also. Peripheralization of Asian digital spaces refers then primarily to the propensity of European and North American technological giants to trivialize, overlook, and refuse to cater to the needs of Asian markets, whereas our use of the term practical issues refers to challenges grounded in combination of Latin-centrism, computing history, and the (potentially imagined) difficulties inherent in the characteristics of our objects of our study.

The focus on some (alphabetical) scripts over others within the history and present of computing, software development, and the digital humanities is a key determinant in limiting the development of and creating the practical challenges at the very foundations of these fields in Asia. Whereas "the word processor was a natural progression from the typewriter"[39] for those in the Anglophone world, this was not necessarily the case for people in Asia. Typing in Japanese created significant issues in the age of typewriting and as such there was a need to develop a way to input Japanese writing, which consists of the logographic script known as *kanji* (Chinese characters), two types of syllabic scripts known as *hiragana* and *katakana* (collectively *kana*) and occasionally Latin script (*rōmaji*), with a total of around 3,000–3,500 characters needed to be able to read everyday texts,[40] into a computer. Resolution came when Toshiba developed the first system that was able

---

36 Purbasha Auddy, "Mining Verbal Data from Early Bengali Newspapers and Magazines: Contemplating the Possibilities," *Global Debates in the Digital Humanities*, ed. Domenico Fiormonte, Sukanta Chaudhuri, and Paola Ricaurte (Minneapolis, MN: University of Minnesota Press, 2022), digital version with no page numbers.
37 Ibid.
38 Stanton, "Broken is Word," 213.
39 Gottlieb, *Word-Processing Technology in Japan*, 27.
40 Seeley, *A History of Writing in Japan*, 2.

to deal with this writing system and which allowed for the conversion of *kana* into *kanji* in 1978.⁴¹ As Nanette Gottlieb notes this was a revolutionary advancement:

> No longer was it necessary to search for one character among several thousand in the bulky trays of the traditional typewriter. Instead, the operator could type in the word in kana and then press the conversion button to bring the kanji for that word up from the internal dictionary onto the screen. Where there was more than one possibility, the correct one could be selected from the alternatives on offer [. . .] [Moreover] the text [. . .] could be edited, parts deleted, other parts added, all done on the screen without printing out.⁴²

Similar issues exist with the input of abjad scripts which, like logographic scripts, require conversion by the computer's software into the correct form.⁴³ We may observe then that Asian scripts and languages may produce difficulties in comparison to Latin script when considering even the most elementary questions i.e., how to input text.

There are also issues linked to how characters can be displayed once they are input into a computer. Word processing is in many ways a successor to moveable type printing, but what is inherited — the standardization of script through specific typefaces and formatting — may be at divergence with the way that Asian texts have been printed and rendered. In the case of Japan, woodblock printing was prevalent until the modern period. This involved printing copies of handwritten texts.⁴⁴ The boundaries between handwritten and printed sources are, therefore, blurred — for example, a printed text might feature cursive script and the appearance of single characters may vary radically with each usage. These features cannot be replicated in moveable type printing or on a word processor since the printing of Latin script (upon which these technologies are based) has been guided by uniforming principles that limit scriptal diversity. The appearance of characters may be key in some types of writing. Helen Magowan notes that with some Japanese writing styles such as *nyohitsu* 女筆 the way in which the characters are rendered, the thickness or thinness of brush strokes etc., may have played an important role for helping readers to determine how to read a character.⁴⁵ These features can be retained through wood-

---

41 Gottlieb, *Word-Processing Technology in Japan*, 33, 39.
42 Ibid., 39–40.
43 Tsuguya Sasaki and Kumiko Tanaka-Ishii, "Text Entry in Hebrew and Arabic Scripts," in *Text Entry Systems: Mobility, Accessibility, Universality*, ed. I. Scott MacKenzie and Kumiko Tanaka-Ishii (San Francisco, CA: Morgan Kaufmann Publishers, 2007), 256, 259.
44 Alex Lamb, Tarin Clanuwat, and Asanobu Kitamoto, "KuroNet: Regularized Residual U-Nets for End-to-End Kuzushiji Character Recognition," *SN Computer Science* 1: 177 (2020): 2.
45 Here we draw upon the work of Helen Magowan who has explored some of the limitations of transcribing and representing *nyohitsu* digitally. We draw particularly on Magowan's lecture at the 8ᵗʰ Cambridge Summer School in Japanese Early Modern Palaeography (2021): Helen

block printing, but are completely lost when we transcribe a text on a computer. There are now increasing efforts to address the imbalance between Latin and non-Latin scripts, issues associated with the display of characters and particularly the inability to input or display certain scripts due to a lack of character encoding or the use of encodings that are not widely supported. For example, the realization that ASCII (American Standard Code for Information Interchange), a commonly used character encoding standard, was Anglo- and Latin-centric led to efforts to design an encoding system that could be used for all languages (the Unicode Standard).[46] Nevertheless, the Anglo-, Latin- and alphabet-centric nature of computing remains. Martin Paul Eve notes that English-language Latinate characters appear first in Unicode and thus the supposed internationalization at the heart of Unicode implies "a spread outwards from a centered English to other 'peripheral' cultures, demonstrating a strong Anglocentrism."[47] This Anglo- and Latin-centrism remains present in other ways. The Unicode Standard has driven an increase in the inclusion of Asian scripts both modern and historical. For instance, the Kana Supplement and Kana Extended-A blocks allow for the input of historically used variant *kana* when writing in Japanese. Nevertheless, these characters represent standardized ideals and remain dependent on a typeface meaning that much of the information captured in the original text is still likely to be lost through computerized input.[48] The issue of standardization is at the heart of Unicode's efforts to unify Chinese, Japanese, and Korean (CJK) characters in an effort known as "Han unification." Since a large number of CJK characters have a shared origin and exist across pre-existing code sets, it was decided to assign these characters shared code points (in order to avoid duplication) with the localized display depending on the user's chosen font.[49] This created a number of controversies. Jing Tsu notes that some Japanese commentators objected that:

Magowan, "Reading ~~Between~~ the Lines," presented at the *8th Cambridge Summer School in Japanese Early Modern Palaeography*, (12/08/2021). Problems of this nature are also briefly discussed in: Lamb, Clanuwat, and Kitamoto, "KuroNet: Regularized Residual U-Nets for End-to-End Kuzushiji Character Recognition," 6–7.

[46] V. Rajaraman and Neeharika Adabala, *Fundamentals of Computers*, 6th edition (Delhi: PHI Learning Private Limited, 2015), 18–19.

[47] Martin Paul Eve, *The Digital Humanities and Literary Studies* (Oxford: Oxford University Press, 2022), 99.

[48] For discussion, see: James Harry Morris, "Japanese Texts in the Digital Age: Thoughts on New Possibilities in the Transcription of Pre-Modern Japanese," *Practicing Japan. 35 years of Japanese Studies in Poznań and Kraków*, Forthcoming.

[49] Andrew Deitsch and David Czarnecki, *Java™ Internationalization* (Sebastopol, CA: O'Reilly & Associates, 2001), 155–157.

> [. . .] an international standard should be predominantly determined by American corporate interests [. . .]
>
> Others felt the same. South Korea thought unification ignored the fact that written Han script traditions had in essence evolved into separate cultural systems in East Asia. One basic question was what would be included as a most common character in Unicode's official character set [. . .] and "common" for whom. Unicode purported to represent all human scripts, but some characters are more frequently used in Japan than in China or Korea. Moreover, Korea's own history of Han script use, going back to the fourth century, predated the PRC's simplification campaigns in the twentieth century. From Korea's perspective, traditional — not simplified — characters should, if anything, be the basis of the unified character set.[50]

This is not only an issue of linguistic and cultural identities, and potentially regional geo-politics, but also relates to the universalizing nature of the Latinate episteme. Asian scripts are still being made to conform to digital standards that are built on Anglo- and Latin-centric assumptions. Whilst supporters have noted, for example, that "Han Unification does not prevent a computer program from displaying the correct national glyphs [. . .] [it] is simply a matter of choosing a font that contains the [appropriate] glyphs,"[51] historians will be keenly aware of the difficulties this has created with inputting and displaying variant characters.

The issue of script extends beyond the question of characters and may have a direct impact on our use of digital tools and methods. The characteristics of handwriting, cursive script, and different calligraphic styles, for example, may influence the efficacy and application of digital tools and methods to Asian sources. Mohamed Cheriet records the difficulties associated with creating OCR technology for use with handwritten Arabic texts categorizing these difficulties as linked to the script itself, individual writing styles and calligraphy, and the quality of document images.[52] He writes:

> Given the complexity, anomalies and inherent specificities of the Arabic handwriting, approaches and techniques used in other language contexts cannot apply directly to the context of Arabic [. . .] using the approach of segmentation of words into letters first, followed by recognition of the resulting characters afterwards, does not operate well for Arabic handwritten text. Consequently, many issues in Arabic handwriting still constitute important questions [. . .][53]

---

[50] Jing Tsu, *Kingdom of Characters: The Language Revolution that made China Modern* (New York, NY: Riverhead, 2022), 263–264.
[51] Deitsch and Czarnecki, *Java™ Internationalization*, 157.
[52] Mohamed Cheriet, "Visual Recognition of Arabic Handwriting: Challenges and New Directions," in *Arabic and Chinese Handwriting Recognition: SACH 2006 Summit, College Park, MD, USA, September 2006, Selected Papers*, ed. David Doermann and Stefan Jaeger (Berlin: Springer-Verlag, 2008), 4–5.
[53] Ibid., 5.

Text direction is another major point of divergence with Latin script. In Japanese text can be aligned vertically or horizontally running right-to-left or left-to-right and sometimes without sequential order. Abjad scripts also tend to diverge from Latin script running from right-to-left and in addition to this may lack the presence of verbs. Text direction causes issues for word processing software. Microsoft Word has struggled with bi-directional text and the formatting of Arabic,[54] and some word processing applications such as Google Docs do not support vertical text alignment. Furthermore, whereas texts written in Latin script can be easily segmented into meaningful parts due to the white space that exists between words (excluding some styles such as *scriptio continua*), some Asian languages such as Chinese, Japanese, and Thai do not feature spaces between words. In the case of Japanese, this means that text segmentation and morphological analysis have to be conducted together because in the absence of white space morphological information becomes essential for tokenization.[55] Thus even major word processing software such as Microsoft Word and Google Docs struggle with simply counting the number of Japanese terms in a text. This issue is explored at greater length in the chapter by Morris included in this volume. Thus, practical challenges associated with Asian scripts created by the Latin-centric nature of computing and the digital humanities influence our interaction with the digital world at every step.

We must be careful not to reduce the practical challenges we face to a matter of scripts alone. There are other fundamental differences between our objects of study and those that a historian of the Latinsphere on almost every level. We have mentioned, for example, the prevalence of woodblock printing in Japan and that its usage meant that printed texts retained some of the characteristics of handwritten texts. The characteristics of Japanese woodblock printed texts, which also include variant characters, interlinear gloss, and illustrations, shape tasks such as OCR.[56] Across Asia there are also different types of binding methods including scrolls, "concertina" style texts, and stitched bindings amongst others; different types of materials used in writing including papyrus, parchment, different types of paper, bamboo, wood, and silk; and different implements used to write such as brushes. We can see a huge divergence between the Latinate printed texts around which computers are designed and the materials that we work with. Our documents may not come in pages or standardized paper sizes or even on paper. How do we translate a silk scroll (scrolls don't come on A4 or US letter sized

---

54 Stanton, "Broken is Word," 222–225.
55 Paul McCann, "fugashi, a Tool for Tokenizing Japanese in Python," *Proceedings of Second Workshop for NLP Open Source Software (NLP-OSS)* (2020): 45.
56 See the summary of some of these features and the issues they pose in: Lamb, Clanuwat, and Kitamoto, "KuroNet: Regularized Residual U-Nets for End-to-End Kuzushiji Character Recognition," 6.

paper) written with a brush into the digital world of page-based Microsoft Word documents? Perhaps these issues also mean that the boundaries between texts and artifacts are blurred. This may influence how we think about digitization — is it enough to make a keyboarded transcription? It goes without saying that key differences in materials and composition or construction are also present in the worlds of architecture and art. Yet, differences run much deeper than aesthetics — they exist on an epistemological level. Even questions of how to measure date and time are called into question: in Japanese history we might find the use (sometimes in combination) of the Gregorian calendar and/or the lunisolar calendar, the Japanese regnal era system (*nengō* 年号), Japanese imperial year (*kōki* 皇紀), and sexagenary cycles (*kanshi* 干支), as well as calendrical notes such as the *rokuyō* 六曜, *jūnichoku* 十二直, *nijūhasshuku* 二十八宿 and others. Thus, ultimately all the basic assumptions of the Latinsphere are called into question — How does a person open a door? How do people consume food? What is the color blue?[57] These questions have different answers in different contexts — and this variety is the crux of the problem with studying Asian religious history digitally — the variety of the world does not fit a Latinspherical mold unless, as we touched on above, it is forced to do so.

A focus on religion can prove to be a complicating factor. As well as using specialized vocabulary which may not appear within digital tools and resources, religious materials may be composed according to particular conventions and written in special scripts. For example, East Asian Buddhist texts are likely to be written in Classical Chinese and may feature the presence of other scripts such as Siddhaṃ.[58] In other words, a scholar of Japanese Buddhism may be engaging with texts written in languages and scripts other than Japanese. This would likely mean that the scholar would need to engage with and employ multiple tools and methods designed for use with the different languages and scripts that they encounter in their research. Religion can also influence binding and printing. For instance, printed Buddhist scriptures in Tangut tend to be "concertina"-bound, "butterfly"-bound, or scrolls,[59] whilst Christian

---

[57] These questions are inspired by a question I (Morris) was asked when I was an undergraduate by Mario I. Aguilar – "How many legs does a chair have?" – and why the answer "four" might not necessarily reflect human experience in some parts of the world. Here I chose questions where I could conceive of variety based on my own experiences and whilst I think the first two are quite clear (in East Asia there are sliding doors and chopsticks amongst other methods, for example), the last question deserves a little exploration — naming conventions for colors may vary based on what is considered to be significant in a given context, see discussion in: Azby Brown, "Foreword," in *The Colors of Japan*, by Sadao Hibi (New York, NY: Kodansha America, 2000), 6.
[58] Peter Francis Kornicki, *Languages, Scripts, and Chinese Texts in East Asia* (Oxford: Oxford University Press, 2018), 44–46.
[59] Jinbo Shi, *Tangut Language and Manuscripts: An Introduction* (Leiden: Brill, 2020), 113.

missionaries to Japan introduced and used moveable type printing rather than the prevalent woodblock printing methods.[60] A scholar may, therefore, need to work with texts of a completely different type of composition than those prevalent in the field and for which digital tools have likely been designed. Calligraphic styles or artistic motifs may also be employed or even reserved for religious texts or art. In Islam, for example, calligraphy plays a particularly important role. Seyyed Hossein Nasr notes that:

> [. . .] calligraphy provides the external dress for the Word of God in the visible world but this art remains wedded to the world of the spirit, for according to the traditional Islamic saying, 'Calligraphy is the geometry of the Spirit.' The letters, words and verses of the Quran are not just elements of a written language but beings or personalities for which calligraphic form is the physical and visual vessel [. . .]
>
> [. . .] calligraphy as the visible embodiment of the Divine Word aids the Muslim in penetrating and being penetrated by that Presence in accordance with the spiritual capabilities of each person.[61]

This description also highlights the fact that religion is something that shapes beliefs including those that center on the historical objects that we study. This vitality of religious subject matter is something that is apparent within some of the essays collected in this volume. When we think about religious sources we are considering a narrower set of documents and artefacts bound together by particular rules, conventions, and language, however, when these features diverge from prominent types within the wider field (e.g. the use of movable type printing in a context where only woodblock printing is used or the use of "concertina"-bound books in a context where stitched bindings are prominent) this may reduce the efficacy of or even render useless the tools developed to deal with other sources in said field. We, therefore, risk facing a triple challenge represented by both the Eurocentric and Latin-centric nature of the digital humanities, and the "Asiatic" and religious composition and content of our sources — we must deal with each of these challenges to build and develop the tools, projects and resources that address our needs.

Although there is also great variety within Asia, those of us working on and within Asian contexts are united by the divergence of our sources from those of the "Latinsphere" and discrepancies in the techno-economic development of our fields vis-à-vis the centers of Western Europe and the USA. It is necessary to create diversified digital humanities infrastructures that address our contextual needs,

---

60 Peter Kornicki, *The Book in Japan: A Cultural History from the Beginnings to the Nineteenth Century* (Honolulu, HI: University of Hawai'i Press, 2001), 125–127.
61 Seyyed Hossein Nasr, *Islamic Art and Spirituality* (Albany, NY: State University of New York Press, 1987), 18–19.

however, on the path to this goal we may learn how to address shared problems by entering into dialogue with scholars working on other Asian histories and religions. This is a concept central to this volume.

Breakdown of Chapters

This book is divided into four sections featuring a total of twelve chapters. We have grouped these around the themes of temples, manuscripts, texts, and social media. These categorizations represent one aspect of the thematic content — the object of study — of the chapters with the order also marking a general movement from the more practical to the more conceptual (both broadly over the course of the whole work and within each section). They are, of course, idealized representations of the chapters — in reality there are many converging aspects and themes. Kaitlyn Ugoretz's chapter, for example, has been positioned within the section on social media, but it might equally find home alongside the pieces on temples through its focus on places of worship (though the moniker "temple" would not adequately describe the chapter's focus on shrines). There are numerous other ways that we could have chosen to categorize the chapters: a geo-religious categorization may have explored Abrahamic, South Asian, and East Asian traditions; a technological focus may have seen categorizations such as geographic information systems (GIS), digitization, and text encoding initiative (TEI) used; and a focus on theoretical or conceptual approach may have seen chapters categorized according to whether they were analyses, technical explanations, or project-based. We hope, however, that the current presentation is the most inviting for newcomers to the subject.

Opening the volume are two chapters exploring geographic information systems (GIS) and temples in Korea. Alberto González Pons's "BulgyoLoc, a Geographical Approach to Korean Buddhism: From the Three Kingdoms Period to Current Koreas through Korean Buddhist Temples," focuses on the BulgyoLoc project — an accessible interactive map that provides a visual representation of the presence of Buddhism on the Korean Peninsula and information on individual temples. He provides a critical introduction to the project and the key decisions in its creation and development e.g., how he decided which sources to use for data collection. He also offers a brief outline and contextualization of the insights that the project has provided in relation to the unequal spatial and temporal distribution of Buddhist temples on the Korean peninsula. Elizabeth Lee's "Rock-Carved Buddhist Images on Mt. P'algong: An Exploration of the Utility of GIS Analysis in Art Historical Research," asks how a GIS assisted analysis may aid in exploring the environmental factors that influenced the creation of medieval Buddhist stone sculptures on Mt. P'algong.

Rather than positing digital methods in terms of absolutes, something to be used instead of analogue methods, Lee's chapter skillfully illustrates how digital methods can be used alongside classical research to fill the gaps that are left by the textual record. The chapter provides two case studies based on two different methods — a Least Cost Path analysis and a Viewshed analysis — and illustrates how these analyses support the hitherto unsubstantiated conclusions of earlier scholarship on Mt. P'algong's Buddhist statues. In one sense these two chapters encapsulate two possible approaches to using GIS — the development of large scope visualization projects on the one hand, and the use of GIS methods to supplement more localized research on the other. We hope, therefore, that they offer an interesting introduction to the different scales of and the different sorts of insights one can garner from digital humanities projects.

The second section of the book focuses on manuscripts and contains four chapters. Opening this section is Dick van der Meij and Jan van der Putten's "DREAMSEA Digital Repository of Endangered and Affected Manuscripts in Southeast Asia. A Multiple Religious and Cultural Digitization Experience." The chapter explores the digitization of endangered Southeast Asian (principally Indonesian, Laotian, and Thai) manuscripts through the DREAMSEA project. The chapter explains the importance of digitizing Southeast Asian manuscripts — though the reasons undoubtedly apply to other manuscript cultures — whilst also engaging with the question of how digitization missions have influenced understandings of manuscripts amongst their owners. Much like Pons's opening chapter Van der Meij and Van der Putten's contribution is practical in focus and provides a detailed critical analysis of the development of DREAMSEA, the challenges that the researchers faced, the outcomes of the project, and how it might be used. The project's challenges are a central theme that run throughout the chapter. Van der Meij and Van der Putten ask their readers — how does one go about digitizing Asian manuscripts when the processes of digitization are designed for Western books? How does one do this in the field? How does one collect adequate metadata? In turn, these questions and Van der Meij and Van der Putten's reflections challenge us to think about the way that we approach digitization in our own projects. Next is L. W. Cornelis van Lit's "Getting Ready for the CV Revolution" — a chapter which advocates for and highlights the growing importance of the use of computer vision (CV), an increasingly accessible technology that "allows computers to detect cohesion between pixels." At the base of the chapter's argument is Van Lit postulation of the *sitz im leben* of the digital humanities as the adaptation of technology. CV fills a technological gap, Van Lit argues, directing us to explore how we use digital photographs, the basic unit of digitization, in the text-centric field of the digital humanities. Van Lit skillfully illustrates what we need (improved quality of data), how the CV revolution will fit into digital humanities methodologies, and how CV is applicable to those on the fringes of the digital humanities, whilst also including practical notes on how to become an early adopter of the technology. Following this is "The (Hyper)Text of the Hebrew Bible/Old Testament: Digital and Online Environments — Their Impact on Considerations on the Text, its Reconstruction, and its History," by Jonathan Robker, which focuses on the benefits, limits, and opportunities created by the transition of the Bible into digital environments. Robker provides a critical overview of different digitized versions of the Hebrew Bible/Old Testament and tools for their study, before exploring the potential advantages and disadvantages of accessing biblical texts digitally. As with Lee's chapter, Robker's contribution shows a dialogue between analogue and digital scholarship with the focus here being on the limits of text history. The use of digital versions of the Hebrew Bible/Old Testament may, Robker argues, help to move the field beyond a focus on text-critical questions and help to deepen understandings of the transmission of the biblical text in both analogue and digital epochs. Closing the second section of the book is Adrian Plau's "Digital Orientalism? Philology, Digital Methodologies, and Reflections on the Study of Primary Sources to North Indian Religions." Plau's chapter explores both the practical — how he developed a critical edition of Vaidyaraja Nainsukh's *Vaidyamanotsava* using TEI-based methodologies — and the theoretical — how the digital humanities risks replicating Orientalizing tendencies. Thus, the first part of the chapter provides a critical overview of Plau's study of *Vaidyamanotsava* and the methods that he employed, whilst the second part investigates what Plau terms "twenty-first century technology powered by nineteenth-century thinking" — the belief that digital methodologies divorces researchers from their context(s). He argues that without critical reflection at every step one will inevitably commit this Digital Orientalism. A potential resolution, he argues, is to liberate source materials from both him and his research to make them more accessible to those outside of scholarship including the communities to whom the objects of his research rightfully belong. This section then offers an insight into the breadth that exists in doing manuscript studies digitally — the practical act of digitizing documents, the use of these materials to advance a given field, and the theoretical challenges that digital methods imply. The chapters are, in our eyes, blueprints for different kinds of work. In need of doing a survey of the state of the art in a field engaged with ancient religious texts? Robker shows how to do it. Preparing for field work? Van der Meij and Van der Putten will help you out. In need of thinking about the future development of your field? Van Lit provides an example. Wanting to find ways of nuancing or criticizing one's own approach? Plau points in the right direction. In all these chapters, issues specific to Asian religions will come to the fore, showing the need to do this kind of work ourselves, instead of depending on others who are technically skilled but not religiously schooled.

The third section of the book features three chapters focusing on texts. As is the case with the first and second sections of the book, the first chapter of the third section focuses on the digital humanities in practice. Peter Flügel opens this section with his "The Jaina Prosopography Database: A New Tool for the Humanities," which introduces the Jaina Prosopography Database — a database that allows for the sociological investigation of various aspects of Jaina mendicant orders and the relationships between different individuals, places, events, and works. The chapter opens with a description of the project and its conception through different phases. Reflection on the difficulties faced during the development (past and future) of the project are covered as the chapter progresses. Flügel's chapter is not about editing full-length texts, but about extracting information from them to compile a database. Following Flügel's chapter is Mariana Zorkina's "Daoist Immortals as a Poetic Image in the Tang Dynasty: A Corpus Study," Zorkina's approach is also practical, but reflecting the makeup of the book's first section focuses on a small-scale, personal project, rather than the sort of a large-scale project based on global collaboration that was the basis of Flügel's chapter. Zorkina investigates the usage of the term *xian* (immortals) in Tang dynasty poetry through a structuralist computational analysis exploring the syntagmatic and paradigmatic relationships of the term. This allows her to analyze how immortals were perceived, their relationships, and the aspirations of the poets. The chapter walks the reader through the steps of the project and its problems by describing and critically reflecting on the corpus, pre-processing, and the analysis itself, before offering an interpretation of the results. Whereas the first two chapters of this section illustrate the possibilities presented by the use of digital methods in large and small scale projects (though not without critical reflection on the challenges that these methods present), the final chapter, James Morris's "Missiology in the Digital Age: Challenges and Opportunities for the Study of Pre-Modern Christianity in Japan," focuses squarely on the limitations presented by sixteenth- and seventeenth-century texts created by missionaries to and Christians present in Japan known as *Kirishitan-ban*. Morris argues that the diversity present in these texts including the use of multiple languages and scripts, their compositional divergence from other texts of the period, and the limits of accessible digital tools provides challenges, not insurmountable for a trained digital humanist, but a barrier to access for casual users, for those wishing to apply digital analyses even on the most fundamental levels. The chapter is peppered with small experiments as Morris attempts to check what tools might function with *Kirishitan-ban* and to what extent, and although he is skeptical about the current state of the field, he notes that *Kirishitan-ban* may provide an important point of possible collaboration between scholars of Japanese and Iberian history. Notably absent from this section is a discussion on digital editing, such as in TEI-XML (which is mentioned in a previous chapter, by Plau). This third section is about what to do with texts, how to handle those texts that are already out there digitally. Each chapter covers some essential skills to become digitally fluent.

The final section consists of three chapters on topics relating to digital media. These chapters which illustrate the vitality of religion in the digital world and indeed the interface between religion in its analogue and digital varieties commence with Kusumita Datta's *"Gonojagoron Monchos* of the 2013 Shahbag Protests in Bangladesh: 'Religions' and Digital Media." Datta's chapter focuses on the use of digital media during the 2013 Shahbag protests. She illustrates how perceived religious distinctions between the supporters and opponents of the Shahbag movement, the religio-political narratives of these people, and their real world actions were carried into and represented within digital spaces, whilst also exploring the closing urban-rural technology gap present in Bangladesh. Datta extends her study beyond social media by also probing into music and short stories related to the movement shared online, thus highlighting important aspects of online activity that have been missed by other studies. Like Datta's chapter, the following "On Kami and Avatars: Social Media Literacy and Academics as Public Intellectuals" by Paula R. Curtis also focuses on the role of digital media within conflict, however, here the conflict takes place between academics and online antagonistic voices. Curtis reflects on her own experience observing engagements with an anonymous Twitter user in order to outline both the potentialities and challenges inherent in public engagement on social media. Curtis provides a detailed description of how antagonist users craft their online identities, how they write, and how they are connected to wider networks, before presenting the case for a measured engagement with antagonistic voices online within the limits of a given scholar's personal context. This section is closed with "Consuming Shinto, Feeding the Algorithm: Exploring the Impact of Social Media Software on Global Religious Aesthetic Formations," by Kaitlyn Ugoretz which whilst moving away from the conflict encapsulated in the foregoing chapters retains a focus on tensions that surface within the digital world. The chapter explores how members of online Shinto communities engage with and share digital representations of ritual objects. Ugoretz argues that members use digital representations and engagement with them on social media as an attempt to both gain recognition of their belonging and increase their social and Shinto capital. In Ugoretz determination these actions are informed by notions of value and capital as well as internet culture and the Facebook algorithm. The chapters combined show the remarkable vitality of ancient religions, finding new modes of being in the digital world. More importantly, as they adopt these new modes, scholars need to adopt new methods to adequately analyze them. All chapters, but especially Curtis's, speak of the urgency to become proficient in the new episteme which religions take on. Even for those working merely with temple ruins of many centuries ago, these chapters are still important to understand not only how we can present our findings in new ways, but also to prepare for antagonistic encounters.

The book closes with concluding reflections by Van Lit and Morris which seek to critically engage with the chapters and the gap between editors' plan for the volume and the finished project. In it, we pick up the theme of Orientalism once more and focus on what it means that ancient religions from Asia find all kinds of new ways of remaining relevant and alive in the digital realm.

Bibliography

Aguilar, Mario I. "Changing Models of the 'Death' of Culture: A Diachronic and Positive Critique of Socio-scientific Assumptions." In *Anthropology and Biblical Studies: Avenues of Approach*, edited by L. J. Lawrence and M. I. Aguilar, 299–313. Leiden: Deo, 2004.

Aiyegbusi, Titilola Babalola and Langa Khumalo. "Digital Humanities Outlooks beyond the West." In *The Bloomsbury Handbook to the Digital Humanities*, edited by James O'Sullivan, 29–40. London: Bloomsbury Academic, 2023.

Anchordoguy, Marie. *Computers Inc.: Japan's Challenge to IBM*. Cambridge, MA: Council on East Asian Studies, Harvard University, 1989.

Auddy, Purbasha. "Mining Verbal Data from Early Bengali Newspapers and Magazines: Contemplating the Possibilities." In *Global Debates in the Digital Humanities*, edited by Domenico Fiormonte, Sukanta Chaudhuri, and Paola Ricaurte. Minneapolis, MN: University of Minnesota Press, 2022.

Bottici, Chiara and Benoît Challand. *The Myth of the Clash of Civilizations*. London: Routledge, 2010.

Bowles, Edmund A., ed. *Computers in Humanistic Research: Readings and Perspectives*. Englewood Cliffs, NJ: Prentice-Hall Inc., 1967.

Brown, Azby. "Foreword." In *The Colors of Japan*, by Sadao Hibi, 6–7. New York, NY: Kodansha America, 2000.

Campbell-Kelly, Martin and Daniel D. Garcia-Swartz. *From Mainframes to Smartphones: A History of the International Computer Industry*. Cambridge, MA: Harvard University Press, 2015.

Cheriet, Mohamed. "Visual Recognition of Arabic Handwriting: Challenges and New Directions." In *Arabic and Chinese Handwriting Recognition: SACH 2006 Summit, College Park, MD, USA, September 2006, Selected Papers*, edited by David Doermann and Stefan Jaeger, 1–21. Berlin: Springer-Verlag, 2008.

Chitez, Mădălina, Rozana Rogobete, and Alexandru Foitoș. "Digital Humanities as an Incentive for Digitalisation Strategies in Eastern European HEIs: A Case Study of Romania." In *European Higher Education Area: Challenges for a New Decade*, edited by Adrian Curag, Ligia Deca, and Remus Pricopie, 545–564. Cham: Springer, 2020.

Deitsch, Andrew and David Czarnecki. *Java^{TM} Internationalization*. Sebastopol, CA: O'Reilly & Associates, 2001.

Encarnation, Dennis J. *Rivals beyond Trade: America versus Japan in Global Competition*. Ithaca, NY: Cornell University Press, 1992.

Eve, Martin Paul. *The Digital Humanities and Literary Studies*. Oxford: Oxford University Press, 2022.

Gottlieb, Nanette. *Word-Processing Technology in Japan: Kanji and the Keyboard*. London: Routledge, 2000.

IPSJ Computer Museum. "[Fujitsu] The Japanese Language Information System JEF," http://museum.ipsj.or.jp/en/computer/main/0048.html.

Ishac, Ephrem Aboud. "From Ancient Manuscripts to Digital Screens: Syriac Liturgy in Digital Humanities." In *Empowering the Visibility of Croatian Cultural Heritage through the Digital Humanities*, edited by Marijana Tomić, Mirna Willer and Nives Tomašević, 148–159. Newcastle upon Tyne: Cambridge Scholars Publishing, 2020.

Ishida Yuri 石田友梨 and Ōmukai Ikki 大向一輝, eds. *Jinbungaku no tame no tekisuto dēta kōchiku nyūmon* 人文学のためのテキストデータ構築入門. Tokyo: Bungaku Tsūshin, 2022.

Jones Nelson, Alissa. *Power and Responsibility in Biblical Interpretation: Reading the Book of Job with Edward Said*. London: Routledge, 2014.

Katz, Victor, ed. *The Mathematics of Egypt, Mesopotamia, China, India, and Islam: A Sourcebook*. Princeton, NY: Princeton University Press, 2007.

Kiraz, George A. "Challenges in Syriac Text Editions using the DOS-Based Word Processor Multi-Lingual Scholar." In *The Letter before the Spirit: The Importance of Text Editions for the Study of the Reception of Aristotle*, edited by Aafke M.I. van Oppenraay, 447–461. Leiden: Brill, 2012.

Kogaze Naoki 小風尚樹, Kogawa Jun 小川潤, Oda Sōki 纓田宗紀, Nagano Sōichi 長野壮一, Yamanaka Mitsuo 山中美潮, Miyagawa Sō 宮川創, Ōmukai Ikki 大向一輝, and Nagasaki Kiyonori 永﨑研宣, eds. *Ōbeiken dejitaru hyūmanitīzu no kiso chishiki* 欧米圏デジタルヒューマニティーズの基礎知識. Tokyo: Bungaku Tsūshin, 2021.

Kornicki, Peter Francis. *The Book in Japan: A Cultural History from the Beginnings to the Nineteenth Century*. Honolulu, HI: University of Hawai'i Press, 2001.

Kornicki, Peter Francis. *Languages, Scripts, and Chinese Texts in East Asia*. Oxford: Oxford University Press, 2018.

Lamb, Alex, Tarin Clanuwat, and Asanobu Kitamoto. "KuroNet: Regularized Residual U-Nets for End-to-End Kuzushiji Character Recognition." *SN Computer Science* 1: 177 (2020): 1–15.

Lewis, Martin W. and Kären Wigen. *The Myth of Continents: A Critique of Metageography*. Berkeley, CA: University of California Press, 1997.

Lit, L. W. Cornelis van. *Among Digitized Manuscripts: Philology, Codicology, Paleography in a Digital World*. Leiden: Brill, 2020.

Lit, L. W. Cornelis van, James H. Morris and Deniz Çevik. "A Digital Revival of Oriental Studies." *Revue de l'Institut des langues et cultures d'Europe, Amérique, Afrique, Asie et Australie* 39 (2020): 1–15.

Magowan, Helen. "Reading ~~Between~~ the Lines." Presented at the 8th Cambridge Summer School in Japanese Early Modern Palaeography, (12/08/2021).

McCann, Paul. "fugashi, a Tool for Tokenizing Japanese in Python." *Proceedings of Second Workshop for NLP Open Source Software (NLP-OSS)* (2020): 44–51.

McPherson, Tara. "Why are the digital humanities so white? Or thinking the histories of race and computation." In *Debates in the Digital Humanities*, edited by Matthew K. Gold. Minneapolis, MN: University of Minnesota Press, 2012.

Morris, James Harry. "Japanese Texts in the Digital Age: Thoughts on New Possibilities in the Transcription of Pre-Modern Japanese." *Practicing Japan. 35 years of Japanese Studies in Poznań and Kraków*, Forthcoming.

Mullaney, Thomas S. *The Chinese Typewriter: A History*. Cambridge, MA: The MIT Press, 2017.

Nasr, Seyyed Hossein. *Islamic Art and Spirituality*. Albany, NY: State University of New York Press, 1987.

Nihon Hōsō Kyōkai 日本放送協会, ed. *Konpyūtā wa kotoba no kabe o koerareru ka: IBM e no chosen* コンピューターは言葉の壁を越えられるか: IBMへの挑戦. Tokyo: Kadokawa Shoten, 1988.

O'Regan, Gerard. *Introduction to the History of Computing: A Computing History Primer*. Cham: Springer, 2016.

Paramore, Kiri. *Ideology and Christianity in Japan.* London: Routledge, 2009.

Rajaraman, V. and Neeharika Adabala. *Fundamentals of Computers.* 6th edition. Delhi: PHI Learning Private Limited, 2015.

Ragnedda, Massimo and Anna Gladkova, eds. *Digital Inequalities in the Global South.* Cham: Springer Nature, 2020.

Ragnedda, Massimo and Glenn W. Muschert, eds., *Theorizing Digital Divides.* London: Routledge, 2018.

Risam, Roopika. "Breaking and Building: The Case of Postcolonial Digital Humanities." In *The Postcolonial World*, edited by Jyotsna G. Singh and David D. Kim, 345–363. London: Routledge, 2017.

Risam, Roopika. and Rahul K. Gairola. "South Asian Digital Humanities Then and Now." *South Asian Review* 40, no. 3 (2019): 141–154.

Sasaki, Tsuguya, and Kumiko Tanaka-Ishii. "Text Entry in Hebrew and Arabic Scripts." In *Text Entry Systems: Mobility, Accessibility, Universality* edited by I. Scott MacKenzie and Kumiko Tanaka-Ishii, 251–268. San Francisco, CA: Morgan Kaufmann Publishers, 2007.

Seeley, Christopher. *A History of Writing in Japan.* Honolulu, HI: University of Hawai'i Press, 2000.

Shi, Jinbo. *Tangut Language and Manuscripts: An Introduction.* Leiden: Brill, 2020.

Shohat, Ella and Robert Stam. "Introduction." In *Unthinking Eurocentrism: Multiculturalism and the Media*, edited by Ella Shohat and Robert Stam. London: Routledge, 2014.

Stanton, Andrea. "Broken is Word." In *Your Computer is on Fire*, edited by Thomas S. Mullaney, Benjamin Peters, Mar Hicks, and Kavita Philip, 213–230. Cambridge, MA: The MIT Press, 2021.

Thorat, Dhanashree. "Digital Infrastructures and Technoutopian Fantasies: The Colonial Roots of Technology Aid in the Global South." In *Exploring Digital Humanities in India: Pedagogies, Practices, and Institutional Possibilities*, edited by Maya Dodd and Nidhi Kalra. London: Routledge, 2001.

Tsu, Jing. *Kingdom of Characters: The Language Revolution that made China Modern.* New York, NY: Riverhead, 2022.

Vierthaler, Paul. "Digital humanities and East Asian studies in 2020." *History Compass* 18, no. 11 (2020). DOI: https://doi.org/10.1111/hic3.12628.

Walker, Henry M. *The Tao of Computing.* 2nd edition. London: CRC Press, 2013.

Temples

Alberto González Pons
Bulgyoloc, a Geographical Approach to Korean Buddhism: From the Three Kingdoms Period to Current Koreas through Korean Buddhist Temples

Introduction

The study of religions is a field of knowledge that has sometimes been accused of lacking its own methodology,[1] or an object of study that is exclusive to it,[2] but the truth is that specialists in the study of religions have managed to be pioneers in many of their approaches, precisely because many of them are engaged in the study of religious phenomena enrooted in ancient and distant civilizations. This area of study, given that it has finite and already established direct sources, often leads to reaching dead ends if only traditional methodologies are applied. That is, if researchers specialized in ancient religions limited themselves to repeatedly reading direct sources, the future of the study of religions would not be very bright. This is when digital humanities (DH) help prove the endless knowledge that can be drawn from the study of religions. Especially during the last two decades, the methodologies used in the digital humanities have proven their efficiency and resourcefulness, so it is only natural that specialists in the study of religions turn to this approach to achieve dynamic, efficient and creative research in order to make new connections and understand new layers of the objects of study we have always researched.

The case of Korean Buddhism serves as a great example of this. Although it is by no means a new area of knowledge, the digital approach has revived the way in which it is studied. It can now be seen how this approach has allowed for new projects and publications that expand the current paradigm of study of this topic and for the gradual creation of a wide corpus of DH projects pivoting around Buddhism and its materialization.[3] Within this broad field of knowledge, temples are of

---

[1] Michael Stausberg and Steven Engler, "Introduction: Research methods in the study of religion's," in *The Routledge Handbook of Research Methods in the Study of Religion*, eds. Michael Stausberg and Steven Engler (London: Routledge, 2011), 4.
[2] Michael Stausberg and Mark Gardiner, "Definition," in *The Oxford Handbook of the Study of Religion*, eds. Michael Stausberg, and Steven Engler (Oxford: Oxford Academic, 2017), 11.
[3] Marcus Bingenheimer, "Digitization of Buddhism (Digital Humanities and Buddhist Studies)," in *Oxford Bibliographies Online* in *Buddhism*, 2020, https://www.oxfordbibliographies.com/view/

https://doi.org/10.1515/9783110747607-002

enormous interest, because, although the place of worship is not as important in Buddhism as it may be in other religions, as devotion can be shown both in temples or at home, temples are indeed the heart of the Buddhist community.[4] Hence, they allow both Buddhists and, in this case, researchers to enter further into the Buddhist consciousness as well as its precepts and principles.

When setting the location of temples as the core of a research project, it should be kept in mind that Buddhism arrived in Korea being an already established system with a specific doctrine and particular needs.[5] Therefore, when it penetrated Korean territory in the fourth century CE, Buddhism did not have to face a period of growth and adaptation that would affect its immediate material expression, as had happened in China, and therefore Buddhist monks made a conscious use of the available places and resources that best suited their needs. This resulted in a minimal number of Buddhist communities with no religious architecture of their own, which is something that only occurred in the very early stages of the settlement of Buddhism in Korea. The location of temples, therefore, provides us with highly valuable information, since they are found where they were intended to be, whether it was at the time of original construction or during reconstruction.

There are also other aspects about the foundation of temples beyond their location that are relevant to the Buddhist history of Korea and that, in fact, are actually available in different records and sources. These sources provide inestimable information regarding the chronology of the foundation of the temples, the Buddhist order they belong to, who founded them and much more information that would fall under the "Miscellaneous" category but is definitely useful for different research projects on Korean Buddhism. All these data are, in fact, interconnected, so what is needed is an appropriate way of displaying them. If they are presented in a dynamical way, it will be possible to link different pieces of information regarding temples, such as the province they are located in or their date of foundation. The options are really endless, but there is a need for an organized system, and the digital humanities allow us to develop that system. This is the background that has led to BulgyoLoc.

---

document/obo-9780195393521/obo-9780195393521-0265.xml; Kiyonori Nagasaki, Toru Tomabechi, and Masahiro Shimoda, "Towards a digital research environment for Buddhist studies," *Literary and Linguistic Computing* 28, no. 2 (2013): 296–300; Daniel Veidlinger, ed., *Digital Humanities and Buddhism: An Introduction* (Berlin: De Gruyter, 2019).

4 Sung-woo Kim, *Buddhist Architecture of Korea* (Elizabeth, NJ: Hollym, 2007).

5 Ingyu Hwang, "Bukanjiyeong goguryeowa balhaeui bulgyo sachal -goguryeowa balhaeui sachal balgul bogwon" [Buddhist temples in Goguryeo and Balhae, North Korea — excavation and restoration of temples in Goguryeo and Balhae], *Bulgyoyeon-gu* 32 (2019): 139–170.

BulgyoLoc

The Project

BulgyoLoc[6] is a digital interactive project based on cartographic representation of information about Korean Buddhist temples. In more simple words: it is an interactive map that shows the location of Buddhist temples throughout Korean territory and that contains further information about each one of them. The name itself is quite simple, but effective, and that is the spirit of the project too. *Bulgyo* means "Buddhism" in Korean and *Loc* is just an abbreviation for "location."

Buddhism has had a great impact on Korean culture and history, and that is why it can be observed in many spheres of life and many places throughout Korea. The construction of temples is just an aspect of Buddhist tradition in Korea, but it is one that can serve as a catalyzer for the rest of the information that is available on Korean Buddhism.

Thus, the first objective to be achieved with the development of BulgyoLoc is the simplification of direct access to information. Although it may seem that it is *just a map*, it is intended to be more than that. This project contains information on different aspects of the temples apart from their location, such as the eras of foundation, the names of the founders, or the Buddhist order they currently belong to.

As can be seen, the cartographical representation is the way of displaying just two pieces of information (location and era of foundation) and the navigation system and BulgyoLoc is, rather than *just a map*, a cartographically displayed database. Given the information contained in the dataset, it is meant to be used by all types of researchers, ranging from experienced senior researchers who may already have much of the information herein contained but would like to keep that information made dynamically visible in one place to junior researchers who might just be searching for a new research topic and are looking for inspiration — in between, all the researchers that might be specialized in only one or two of the topics covered in BulgyoLoc. However, not only researchers might make use of it. Given the simple navigation system and the easy access to information that the digital humanities promote, it is, in the end, suitable for any individual that may be interested in Korean Buddhism.

Figure 1 shows the main page of BulgyoLoc. The minimalist design allows the viewer to focus on the information without losing its geographical context. It also includes a retractable map legend that shows the classification to which the color pattern of the location points correspond, two zoom buttons, a GitHub button that

---

6 BulgyoLoc, http://www.bulgyoloc.com/.

Fig. 1: BulgyoLoc's main page. (BulgyoLoc).

redirects the user to the dataset repository in the platform and two "share" buttons. Simplicity and accessibility are key aspects in the development of BulgyoLoc, since the goal is to provide direct, easy to understand information.

As can be observed, the temples are marked with circles of different colors. These colors are not arbitrary by any means. As the map legend indicates, each color represents the era of Korean history in which each temple was founded. There are a total of 11 colors, each representing an era. The navigation system allows the user to select specific eras to visualize only the temples that correspond to that era. The visualization of the whole territory with the temples displayed by eras alone can help the viewer make connections, reach conclusions or become inspired in their search for a research topic. But BulgyoLoc has more to offer:

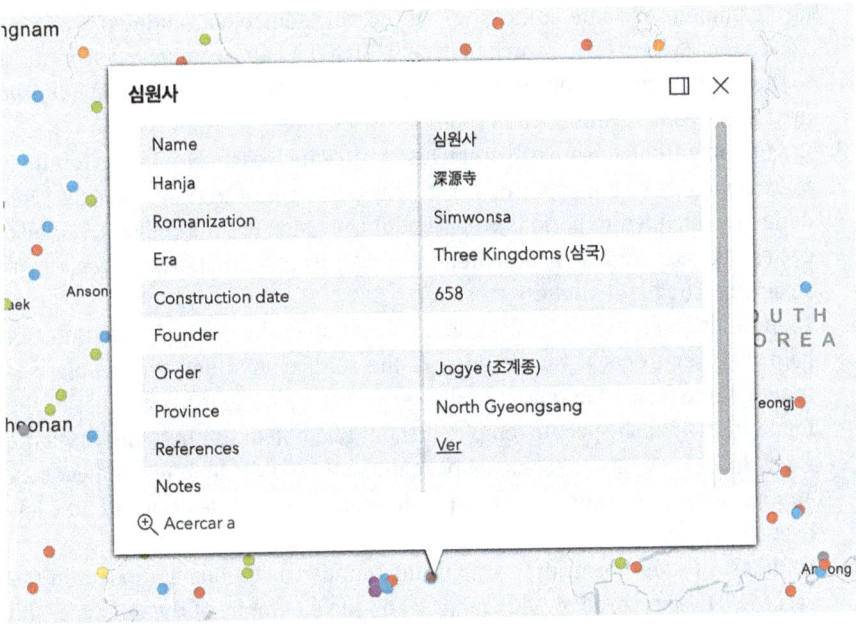

Fig. 2: Temple information tab. (BulgyoLoc).

Figure 2 shows the information tab which displays the data of each temple.
In the tab of each temple, ten information sections can be found:
a) Name: the name of the temple in *hangeul* (the Korean writing system), as it appears on Korean literature, governmental reports, maps, etc.
b) *Hanja*: the name of the temple in *hanja*, that is, the Chinese characters that were used as the writing system for the Korean language before the invention of *hangeul* in 1443. Although temples before that date could only be named

using *hanja*, the continued use of this writing system overtime as part of the Buddhist tradition means that even today, Chinese characters hold a particular relevancy. Knowing the name in *hanja* is important mainly for two reasons. In the first place, it is the way in which temples are referred to in ancient records, so the *hanja* is needed to be able to identify any possible mention to the temple historically; secondly, each *hanja* holds a meaning, which provides the full name of the temple with a particular meaning too, and knowing this can be convenient for the researcher.

c) Romanization: the representation of the temples' names in Latin script is also added in order to help researchers refer easily to the temples in projects that are written in languages that use Latin script. For this project, the official Revised Romanization of Korean (RR) has been used, however, it is also common for some authors to use the now somewhat outdated McCune-Reischauer System (MR), which may not match the name romanized according to the RR. To facilitate consensus, it is advisable to include the name in *hangeul* next to the romanization when referring to a temple.

d) Era of foundation: the era of Korean history in which each temple was founded is extremely relevant too. Buddhism was perceived differently during each dynasty, which led to periods when Buddhism was the state religion, but also cycles of persecution against Buddhism. Buddhist temples, however, were constructed throughout all these eras.

e) Foundation date: the year of foundation. Although the era of foundation can help the user to get a general idea of the context in which the temple was founded, the exact date allows a deeper understanding of the context of the foundation of each specific temple. It should be noted that in many cases the exact date of construction has not been preserved, while in others not even an approximate time is known. When possible, an approximate period of time has been provided.

f) Founder: in some cases, the name of the founder or founders appears in the records. These records provide material on the biography of the monks or the different authorities who founded the temples.

g) Order: the Buddhist order to which each temple belongs to currently is also indicated. This allows researchers to delve deeper into the history of these orders.

h) Province: the province in either South Korea or North Korea where the temple is currently located. This provides a clearer representation of the current state of the Buddhist landscape in the two Koreas.

i) References: every digital humanities project grows stronger when it can establish connections with other initiatives. That is why, when available, the information tabs includes links to external projects' entry on the temple. Currently, only projects in Korean are available. The difference between this external entry and the information tab in BulgyoLoc is the amount of information. As previously stated, BulgyoLoc intends to present only concise and clear key data but other projects offer more extensive descriptions of the temples and their history. Additionally, some of these projects include networks linking the temple to other elements of its history. The three linked projects are: 한국민족문화대백과사전 (*Encyclopedia of Korean Culture*), 조선왕조실록 전문사전 위키 (*Sillok Wiki*) and *Encyves Wiki*.[7]

j) Notes: this last section of the information tab is designed to provide information primarily about the temple in relation to BulgyoLoc. That is, it does not include detailed information about the temple, which can be found in the links provided in the "References" section, but rather comments about issues or specifications of the temple on the BulgyoLoc map, such as "approximate coordinates."

All this information is highly relevant in that, although all of it is directly mentioned in some source or another, it has also contributed to Korean cultural production, not necessarily with explicit mention. For instance, there are known cases of writers who retired to temples to write their works, and that is just one example of the link between Buddhism and Korean history and culture. Thus, the digital humanities' methodologies provide us with endless opportunities that can result in projects of immense specialized knowledge that are of great value to the international academic community, of which BulgyoLoc aims to be part of.

In fact, it should be noted that one key aspect of BulgyoLoc is collaborative work. Through the project's GitHub repository, the user is able to download the dataset in a convenient CSV file so they can comfortably work with the data. Hence, the website allows for direct visualization and quick extraction of key information, but it is also important to allow users who wish to work with the data contained therein to manipulate them easily, giving them the option to be more selective with the data they wish to handle. Not only is it important to help researchers work on their own projects with BulgyoLoc's data, but it is also crucial to let them get involved in the project as well. A relatively high amount of key information can be found on BulgyoLoc, but it is far from being completely comprehensive. Therefore, BulgyoLoc can benefit from the work of other researchers to grow and develop overtime.

---

7 Encyclopedia of Korean Culture, https://encykorea.aks.ac.kr; Sillok Wiki, http://dh.aks.ac.kr/sillokwiki; Encyves Wiki, http://dh.aks.ac.kr/Encyves.

Sources

In deciding which sources to use for the data collection in this project, given BulgyoLoc's commitment to open-access, the ideal choice from the outset has been academic sources also published in open-access and official data made publicly available by state, provincial and local government authorities.

The information on each temple has been extracted from very specific sources: the reports 전통사찰 현황 (972개소, 2021.1.31. 기준)[8] (lit. "Status of traditional temples [based on 972 locations, 2021.1.31.]") and 전통사찰 보존·정비 사업평가 및 중장기 발전방안[9] (lit. "Preservation of traditional temples. Evaluation of maintenance projects and mid- to long-term development plans"); the Jogye Order official website's temple database;[10] and, lastly, the digital humanities projects mentioned earlier: the *Encyclopedia of Korean Culture*, *Sillok Wiki*, and *Encyves Wiki*. Each one of these sources indicate the resources from which the information has been extracted for each temple.

Many of these sources focus on temples that are still standing, as they are administrative documents related to present-day Buddhist cultural heritage management, so the information they provide is only useful for certain pieces of information provided in BulgyoLoc. It is also necessary to turn to sources that speak about Buddhist heritage in historical terms, that is, that provide information about the foundation of Buddhist temples in Korean history, including those that may have disappeared or may have been relocated but whose former location is known, or even those whose existence cannot be proved with certainty. All this, although not immediately cognizable in an empirical way, is part of the Buddhist tradition and, therefore, it is necessary to keep it in mind and provide a space for it within our studies.

It should also be noted that one of the most common obstacles in Korean Studies has been present in the development of this project: most research projects and academic literature are carried out or published in Korean. Although there is a vast amount of specialized literature written in a large number of languages, it is naturally outnumbered by what is written in Korean. In the case of very specific cultural or historical assets, as is the case of BulgyoLoc, it is not easy to find prolific, updated and high-quality literature written in languages other than Korean.

---

[8] Status of Traditional Temples [based on 972 Locations, 2021.1.31.], https://www.mcst.go.kr/kor/s_policy/dept/deptView.jsp?pCurrentPage=1&pType=03&pTab=01&pSeq=1450&pDataCD=0417000000.
[9] Preservation of Traditional Temples. Evaluation of Maintenance Projects and Mid- to Long-term Development Plans, https://mcst.go.kr/kor/s_policy/dept/deptView.jsp?pSeq=157&pDataCD=0406000000&pType=.
[10] Jogye Order of Korean Buddhism, http://www.buddhism.or.kr/jongdan/main/index.php.

Despite the fact that it has not been an insurmountable obstacle in this specific scenario, it should be pointed out, since Korean Studies are becoming increasingly prominent in the international scene, and as mentioned earlier, not many projects focus on the study of Buddhist temples in Korean territory and history, and it is not common to find them written in English.

Nevertheless, one key issue is that it has not been possible to accurately find all the information about all the temples. As can be seen in the web application, there are three aspects in which this lack of information affects the data presentation: (a) in some cases the abbreviation "n/i" ("no information") has been added because there is no record of that information; (b) in other cases, the exact date of foundation cannot be known, so an approximate period of time is provided; and (c) the exact location of many temples is also unknown, especially for temples in the territory now belonging to North Korea, although there are also cases of temples in South Korea that are no longer standing and whose former location is not known with accuracy — in these cases the observation "Approximate location" has been added in the "Notes" section of the information tab.

Development

As usual with DH projects, BulgyoLoc has not been developed in its final presentation, but has gone through a series of stages. The project has had three main stages of development: the creation of the dataset, the configuration of the cartographical representation, and the development of the web application.

The first step in the development of the project has been, naturally, the extraction of quantitative information. Although the above-mentioned sources offer a high amount of qualitative information, the extraction of quantitative data has not been a particularly complex task since the key points of BulgyoLoc are easily recognizable and their extraction only requires knowledge of the Korean language and some key aspects of Korean history and Buddhism.

Thus, the objective in the first phase of development was to create a spreadsheet in which all this information would be progressively collected and organized under the following categories: "Latitude," "Longitude," "Name," "Hanja," "Romanization," "Era of foundation," "Foundation date," "Order," and "References." As can be seen, most of these categories coincide with the sections of the information tab discussed above. It is not fortuitous: this spreadsheet is not only used to concentrate the information, but, by converting it into a CSV dataset, it becomes the main structure of the project.

The elaboration of this initial spreadsheet has also presented certain obstacles or, at least, concrete decisions have had to be made in regard to certain situations.

First of all, although the RR system of romanization is the official system of South Korea and the most widely used in the current academic environment, it has not been adopted in North Korea. Therefore, the RR system has primarily been used in the romanization of the names of temples and provinces in South Korea, Buddhist orders, and the names of eras in Korean history, while the Romanization of Korean (RK) system, the official system in North Korea, has been used for the names of North Korean provinces.

The processing of coordinates has also been a key point. As mentioned above, it has not been possible in all cases to obtain the exact location of the temple. In these cases, only information pertaining to which village, town or city the temple is or was located in has been found. However, as the map development system requires the inclusion of specific coordinates, the central location of the most restrictive administrative unit known has been chosen for each of these temples. These cases have been marked with "Approximate coordinates" in the "Notes" section of the information tab.

Regarding the technical aspects of the project's development, the base structure is a CSV file, which the ArcGIS software, developed by Esri, allows to be transformed into a map. In addition, ArcGIS technology allows the conversion of the map into a web application, which has been migrated to an independent server and modified with HTML and CSS.

Figure 3 shows the basic structure of the CSV file that serves as the base for the application:

In this case, the GIS (Geographical Information System) mapping software used was ArcGIS,[11] one of the most popular GIS tools, but the task of importing information from a CSV file to a point layer on a map can be executed with other software, such as QGIS,[12] an Open Source GIS software, and the basemap can be obtained from other projects, such as OpenStreetMap.[13]

The transfer of information is done automatically in ArcGIS, so special attention must be paid to the representation of the data. Thus, we opted for the representation in colored points on a grayscale background to help in the visualization of the information. Of course, the color distribution on the map is not arbitrary. The map legend has been organized by era of foundation, since it was necessary to select a value that would allow the temples to be grouped in their presentation on the map, the era of foundation being the most coherent. Organization by provinces was not valid because the location points on the map already indicate the province

---

11 ArcGIS, https://www.arcgis.com/index.html.
12 QGIS, https://www.qgis.org/en/site/.
13 OpenStreetMap, https://www.openstreetmap.org/.

#	Latitude	Longitude	Name	Hanja	Romanization	Province	Era	Construction date	Order	References	Fo
253	38.58577685255754	128.16491559810282	유점사	楡岾寺	Yujeomsa	Kangwon (NK)	Three Kingdoms (삼국)	4	n/i	http://encykorea.aks.ac.kr/Contents/Item/E0041802	n/i
794	35.44917862047369	128.84188164060777	만어사	萬魚寺	Maneosa	South Gyeongsang	Three Kingdoms (삼국)	46	Jogye (조계종)	http://encykorea.aks.ac.kr/Contents/SearchNavi?keyword=만어사&ridx=0&tot=5	
301	36.54712397990329	127.85978478304217	상환암	上歡庵	Sanghwanam	North Chungcheong	North and South States (남북국)	70	Jogye (조계종)	http://encykorea.aks.ac.kr/Contents/Item/E0027426	
402	35.95886809569789	127.94189236953802	봉곡사	鳳谷寺	Bongguksa	North Gyeongsang	Goryeo (고려)	92	Jogye (조계종)	http://encykorea.aks.ac.kr/Contents/Item/E0023803	
771	36.77119429166554	126.3140254118425	흥주사	興住寺	Heunjusa	South Chungcheong	Three Kingdoms (삼국)	222	Jogye (조계종)	http://encykorea.aks.ac.kr/Contents/Item/E0066054	흥
430	35.42631865270916	128.95122305599378	신흥사	新興寺	Sinheungsa	North Gyeongsang	Three Kingdoms (삼국)	301	Jogye (조계종)	http://encykorea.aks.ac.kr/Contents/Item/E0033616	신
776	35.531891035471354	128.55350934049844	관룡사	觀龍寺	Gwanryongsa	South Gyeongsang	Three Kingdoms (삼국)	349	Jogye (조계종)	http://encykorea.aks.ac.kr/Contents/SearchNavi?keyword=관룡사&ridx=0&tot=14	n/i
231	37.63231179754325	126.48498732720353	전등사	傳燈寺	Incheonsa	Incheon	Three Kingdoms (삼국)	381	Jogye (조계종)	http://encykorea.aks.ac.kr/Contents/Item/E0049355	아
920	35.20068574797798	126.54982514253885	불갑사	佛甲寺	Bulgabsa	South Jeolla	Three Kingdoms (삼국)	384	Jogye (조계종)		
921	34.908446396634126	126.8229260...	불회사	佛會寺	Bulhwesa	South Jeolla	Three Kingdoms (삼국)	384	Jogye (조계종)	http://encykorea.aks.ac.kr/Contents/Item/E0025048	마
355	35.83108087363006	129.02440019817504	금강암	金剛庵	Geumgangam	North Gyeongsang	Three Kingdoms (삼국)	385	Jogye (조계종)	http://encykorea.aks.ac.kr/Contents/SearchNavi?keyword=금강암&ridx=0&tot=915	도
646	37.47358995356882	127.0466706271521	대성사	大聖寺	Daeseongsa	Seoul	Three Kingdoms (삼국)	385	대각회		
628	39.091551733690466	125.82652066927744	광법사	廣法寺	Gwangbeobsa	Pyongyang (NK)	Three Kingdoms (삼국)	392	n/i	http://encykorea.aks.ac.kr/Contents/Item/E0005131	
630	39.04885111166297	125.75440851160667	영명사	永明寺	Yeongmyeongsa	Pyongyang (NK)	Three Kingdoms (삼국)	392	n/i	http://dh.aks.ac.kr/sillokwiki/index.php/영명사(永明寺)	
224	37.75109944734523	126.43741846394425	백련사	白蓮寺	Baekryeonsa	Incheon	Three Kingdoms (삼국)	416	Jogye (조계종)	http://encykorea.aks.ac.kr/Contents/Item/E0022066	
230	37.73733187976639	126.41008665789235	적석사	積石寺	Jeokseoksa	Incheon	Three Kingdoms (삼국)	416	Jogye (조계종)	http://encykorea.aks.ac.kr/Contents/Item/E0049165	
233	37.746332436579365	126.44789982905658	청련사	青蓮寺	Cheongryeonsa	Incheon	Three Kingdoms (삼국)	416	Jogye (조계종)	http://encykorea.aks.ac.kr/Contents/Item/E0056399	
887	34.63920978055296	127.41435539641364	능가사	楞伽寺	Neunggasa	South Jeolla	Three Kingdoms (삼국)	417	Jogye (조계종)	http://encykorea.aks.ac.kr/Contents/SearchNavi?keyword=능가사&ridx=0&tot=4881	n/i
347	36.051613536973726	128.18295412701465	고방사	古方寺	Gobangsa	North Gyeongsang	Three Kingdoms (삼국)	418	Jogye (조계종)	http://encykorea.aks.ac.kr/Contents/SearchNavi?keyword=고방사&ridx=0&tot=1580	아
461	36.11677325314236	128.004043268...	직지사	直指寺	Jikjisa	North Gyeongsang	Three Kingdoms (삼국)	418	Jogye (조계종)	http://encykorea.aks.ac.kr/Contents/Item/E0054538	아
346	36.17270406237772	128.18151232331695	계림사	鷄林寺	Gyerimsa	North Gyeongsang	Three Kingdoms (삼국)	419	Jogye (조계종)	http://encykorea.aks.ac.kr/Contents/SearchNavi?keyword=계림사&ridx=0&tot=1	아
701	36.365728877848014	127.18750322820995	갑사	甲寺	Gamsa	South Chungcheong	Three Kingdoms (삼국)	420	Jogye (조계종)	http://encykorea.aks.ac.kr/Contents/Item/E0000898	아
891	34.476385769239286	126.61688522709902	대흥사	大興寺	Daeheungsa	South Jeolla	Three Kingdoms (삼국)	426	Jogye (조계종)		정
374	35.9861442800302	128.59910829828868	도덕암	道德庵	Dodeokam	North Gyeongsang	Three Kingdoms (삼국)	435	Jogye (조계종)		
947	35.040399429223925	126.88412157503019	죽림사	竹林寺	Jokrimsa	South Jeolla	Three Kingdoms (삼국)	440	Jogye (조계종)		
362	36.33584046436233	128.24199481179025	대둔사	大芚寺	Daedunsa	North Gyeongsang	Three Kingdoms (삼국)	446	Jogye (조계종)	http://encykorea.aks.ac.kr/Contents/SearchNavi?keyword=대둔사&ridx=0&tot=20	
394	36.27279332912691	128.4386141559668	법주사	法住寺	Beobjusa	North Gyeongsang	Three Kingdoms (삼국)	480	Jogye (조계종)	http://encykorea.aks.ac.kr/Contents/Item/E0022717	n/i
418	35.987512304773254	128.73882480022695	선본사	禪本寺	Seonbonsa	North Gyeongsang	Three Kingdoms (삼국)	491	Jogye (조계종)	http://encykorea.aks.ac.kr/Contents/Item/E0028721	
32	35.99293652189084	128.70397534061874	동화사	桐華寺	Donghwasa	Daegu	Three Kingdoms (삼국)	493	Jogye (조계종)	http://encykorea.aks.ac.kr/Contents/SearchNavi?keyword=동화사&ridx=0&tot=68	
787	35.08339506414247	127.9197976559426	다솔사	多率寺	Dasolsa	South Gyeongsang	Three Kingdoms (삼국)	503	Jogye (조계종)	http://encykorea.aks.ac.kr/Contents/SearchNavi?keyword=다솔사&ridx=0&tot=4850	
890	34.96132842199292	127.13280106943344	대원사	大原寺	Daewonsa	South Jeolla	Three Kingdoms (삼국)	503	Jogye (조계종)	http://encykorea.aks.ac.kr/Contents/SearchNavi?keyword=대원사&ridx=0&tot=23	
965	39.3009021410106	125.82657557723982	안국사	安國寺	Anguksa	South Pyongan (NK)	Three Kingdoms (삼국)	503	n/i	http://encykorea.aks.ac.kr/Contents/Item/E0034535	
519	35.51244454604096	127.45554701166219	귀정사	歸政寺	Gwijeongsa	North Jeolla	Three Kingdoms (삼국)	515	Jogye (조계종)	http://encykorea.aks.ac.kr/Contents/SearchNavi?keyword=귀정사&ridx=0&tot=4859	현
251	38.68365472976337	128.19487096926963	신계사	神溪寺	Singyesa	Kangwon (NK)	Three Kingdoms (삼국)	519	n/i	http://encykorea.aks.ac.kr/Contents/Item/E0032646	보

Fig. 3: BulgyoLoc's database. (BulgyoLoc).

in which they are located; neither was the Buddhist order to which the temples belong because it is not the key information concerning Buddhist temples in Korea from a historical perspective. All other options were immediately discarded as they were individual for each temple. However, all the networks that were not selected for the map legend can be explored externally with the dataset provided. In fact, some of these networks are included as graphs made in RAWGraph from the GitHub repository.

Not only is the representation system significant, but so is the navigation system. Being key to the project's simplicity and in order to access knowledge quickly and directly, the manner the user makes use of the application is crucial. ArcGIS offers a whole variety of applications, each focused on a different functionality. For BulgyoLoc, the most convenient option was a simple and minimalist application that allows a wide navigation frame.

Starting from this base of free map exploration, the various additions have been inserted in the margins of the web application. The peripheral elements of the project are: contact form or entry proposal form, GitHub repository link for data download, and sharing options. Although these are not specific to the development of digital humanities projects, they can be key aspects for the diffusion and development of DH tools as well as for the dissemination and enlargement of the project's content. Although ArcGIS does not offer the function of adding HTML or CSS elements during the process of creating the web application, these can be easily incorporated into the HTML of the application with some simple coding.

To summarize the development phase: for the most part, BulgyoLoc was developed using mainly GIS software as well as HTML and CSS programming languages.

Future Development

The goal is to progressively improve BulgyoLoc, making it a more complete and transversal resource, without compromising its ease of use or the legitimacy of its data. Due to the large size of the project, this is a medium-long term goal, as the achievement of reliable and first-rate information already takes time and transferring it to the web application requires even greater effort. However, although these are not immediate additions, they are worth commenting on, as the project has been developed within a framework designed to be modified and expanded over time.

One of the upcoming tasks in the further development of this first version of BulgyoLoc is the migration of the web application to an app for mobile devices. Although it is unlikely that this would become the preferred method of access during the research process, it is true that more and more mobile devices are being used while carrying out research, since they allow the researcher, among other things, to view more items at the same time, to work with two or more applications at the same time, and so on. Therefore, following the principle of simple and direct access on which BulgyoLoc is based, it is necessary to offer a research experience as multifaceted as possible.

Along these lines of seeking the biggest possible impact, it would also be interesting to translate the data and localize the web application into other languages, making it easier to access information that, as previously mentioned, is usually found mainly in Korean. However, this is a complex task that requires not only time and effort, but also the collaboration of translation experts, so it does not seem that this update will take place in the near future.

In relation to content rather than form, the spirit of BulgyoLoc is based on providing relevant information and facilitating access to it, so the content that is currently shown in the web application will not be the only information that will be part of the project. It is not possible to state categorically what exact information will be included in BulgyoLoc, since this will depend on the needs that users show or express, but it is possible to talk about elements that will enrich the project in general. Some of these future changes will be the inclusion of images in the information tab and the expansion of the data offered for each temple, as well as the metadata, with the focus on information that is easily interrelated, generating as a result a kind of semantic web.

Finally, another objective for the future, which, although not expected to be immediate, is one of the main goals, is collaboration with other projects. The inclusion of references to three digital humanities websites in the information tab of each temple was mentioned earlier precisely because cooperation between similar projects expands the scope of knowledge present in each one and, in addition, increases their impact as well. While these are the developments and updates that are expected in the medium-near future, the academic community specialized in digital humanities is moving forward in leaps and bounds, at a frenetic pace, so it really is impossible to know what other possibilities for expansion and update will arise in the future. In any case, regardless of how it is executed, the ultimate goal is the expansion of BulgyoLoc's content, impact and usefulness.

Final Remarks

As a conclusion to this chapter, which serves as a presentation of BulgyoLoc, it seems coherent first to highlight some of the results that the project helps us achieve. These are key as a representation of the main function of the project, since they are immediate conclusions, that is, that they can be reached through direct navigation of the web application, without the need for parallel research work.

First of all, in terms of spatial distribution, the unequal presence of Buddhist temples in the current territory of North and South Korea is striking.[14] To understand this, it is necessary to look at three aspects of the development of Buddhism in the territory that currently makes up North Korea: (a) for historical reasons, the construction of temples was mainly concentrated on the territory that currently corresponds to South Korea, although there is also an important Buddhist architectural tradition in North Korea; (b) during Japanese colonization, a very high number of Buddhist temples were destroyed; (c) the political system established in North Korea after the Korean War imposed the Juche doctrine (주체) as the state religion,[15] which impedes the creation of temples and the reconstruction of those destroyed, unless it is for the benefit of historical and cultural heritage.[16] While these are conclusions that are not directly linked to digital humanities, it is interesting that all this information can be quickly obtained through accessing the project, which allows for greater dynamism during research activities.

In addition, the web application allows users to visualize spatial distribution in relation to the chronology of the temples. An even distribution of temples in relation to their era of foundation can be observed at a general level, although, when observed thoroughly, particularities that correspond to different historical contexts can be discovered, such as, for example, the presence of numerous temples built during the Goryeo era in the North Korean city of Kaesong which was the capital of the kingdom during the era. Furthermore, the view by eras that can be selected in the map legend in the app allows users to see the eras with the highest and lowest temple construction rate. Thus, in the eras in which Buddhism was introduced and consolidated — the Three Kingdoms and South and North Kingdoms eras — a huge number of temples were built, however, the pace of construction slightly lowered during the era in which Buddhism become the official religion of the whole of

---

[14] Donald Baker, "Is North Korea a Religious Country? Juche and the Definition of Religion," Paper presented at the Institute for the Study of Religion, Sogang University, Seoul, June 18, 2013.
[15] James H. Grayson, *Korea — A Religious History* (London: Taylor and Francis, 2013).
[16] Bernard Senécal, "Buddhists in the Two Koreas: North-South Interactions," *Journal of Korean Religions* 4, no. 2 (2013): 9–50.

Korean territory — the Goryeo era — and was greatly reduced during the Joseon era, in which Buddhism was repressed. From this time on, the construction of temples was minimal until the twentieth century.

However, as has been indicated throughout this chapter, BulgyoLoc intends to provide more than just cartographic representation with the dataset created for its representation being one of the key elements of the project. As mentioned above, this information is not only used for its representation and visualization, but also to establish all kinds of connections that, in turn, can be useful for research.

The layout of the data in a spreadsheet or a CSV file allows for simple creation of graphs for the representation of these connections. The following graphs (Figs. 4–7) made with the Open-Access tools RAWGraphs, CytoScape and Neo4j can be taken as an example:[17]

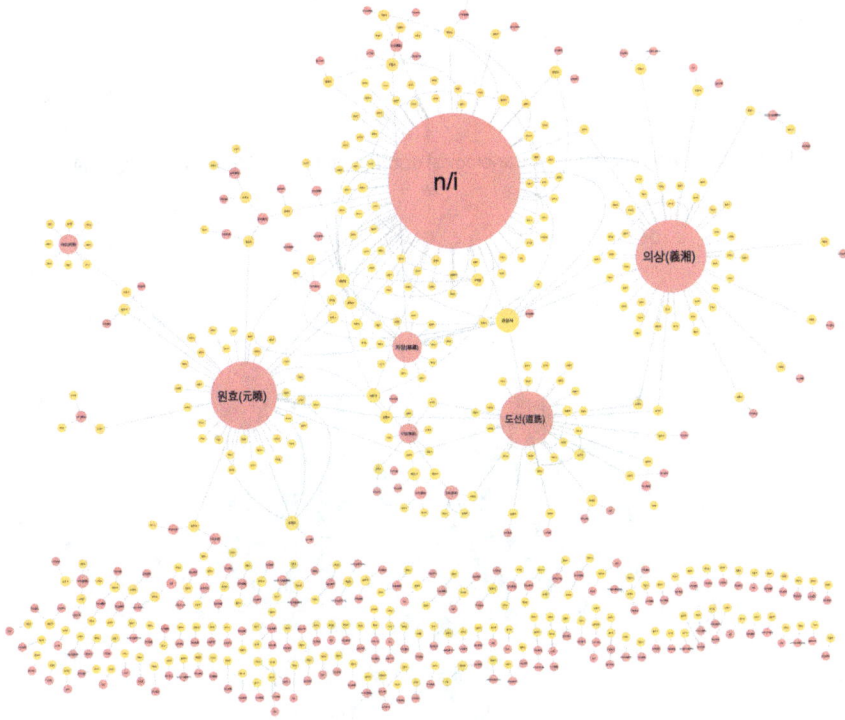

Fig. 4: Network graph showing the connection between temples and founders. (BulgyoLoc).

---

17 Graphs created for illustrational purposes only. Complete and bigger graphs are included in the download page of the BulgyoLoc application website. See: RAWGraphs, https://rawgraphs.io/; CytoScape, https://cytoscape.org/; Neo4j, https://neo4j.com.

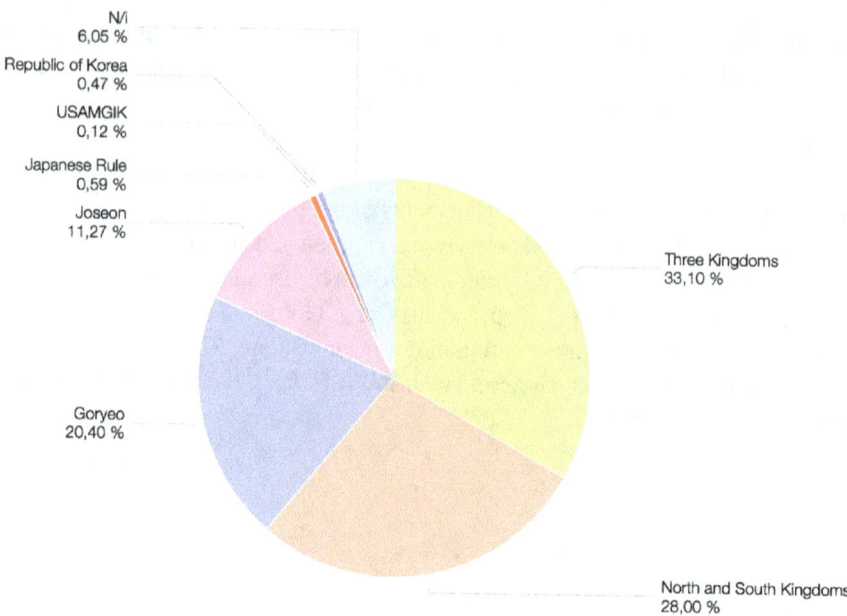

Fig. 5: Pie chart showing percentage chronological distribution by era of foundation. (BulgyoLoc).

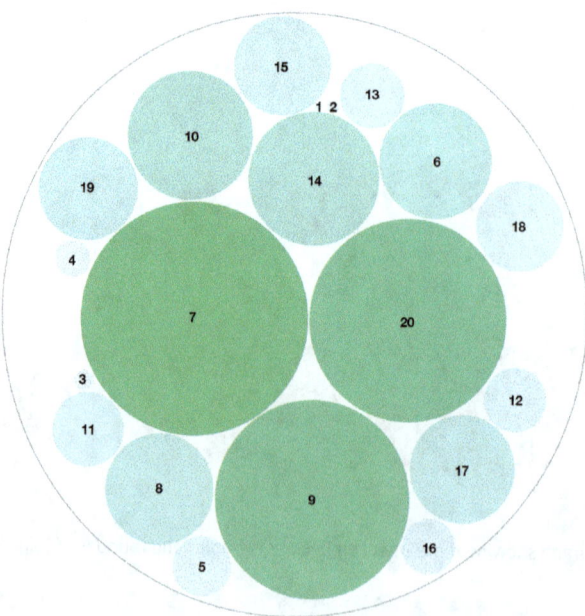

Fig. 6: Circular packing graph showing the distribution of the foundation of temples throughout the centuries. (BulgyoLoc).

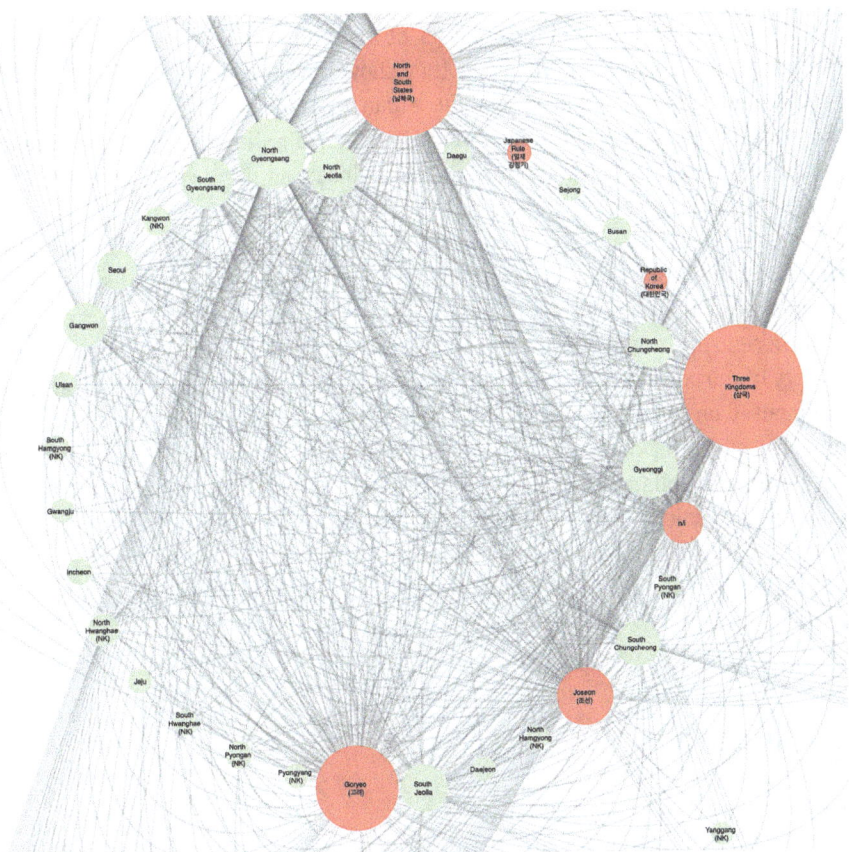

Fig. 7: Fragment of a complex network graph showing the foundation of temples distributed according to province. (BulgyoLoc).

As can be seen, the data contained in BulgyoLoc serve for different types of visualization that lead to the varied conclusions and subsequent developments. Thus, Figure 4 clearly shows the multiplicity of temple founders of which we have evidence, among which Uisang, Doseon and Wonhyo stand out, although it is also clearly identified that, for most temples, the founder is not known. Figure 5 on the other hand, shows through a traditional pie chart, what percentage of the total number of temples built in Korean territory were founded in each era. Figure 6 represents data related to the foundation of temples, only this time the distribution is based on the number of temples founded in each century. Finally, Figure 7 is one more network graph, but this time with a number of connections three times greater than in Figure 4, since it represents the construction of temples distributed by era of foundation and province.

While this is not a complex analyses of these topics, the visualization broadly represent the utility of BulgyoLoc, as they show how researchers who are knowledgeable in the field can make use of these data to complete their projects or presentation, and at the same time, how junior researchers or scholars who are beginning to take an interest in the study of Korean Buddhism can use them to get started on related research topics.

As a final conclusion, after having discussed several issues regarding both the content of the project and its development, it should be noted that BulgyoLoc represents only one type of digital humanities project, simple to use and create, but that there are many other projects developed in different ways aimed at a wide variety of purposes and users. This project, as indicated throughout the chapter, is not focused on complex analysis of detailed data, but aims to provide a broad view and ease of use for both research and dissemination. Thus, we can only hope that the number of collaborators that are part of BulgyoLoc will increase in the future and that the project will be useful for any individual interested in the topic, regardless of their degree of specialization, since these are, ultimately, the cornerstones of any project within the field of digital humanities and the primary focus that is kept in mind during its development.

Bibliography

ArcGIS, https://www.arcgis.com/index.html.
Baker, Donald. "Is North Korea a Religious Country? Juche and the Definition of Religion." Paper presented at the Institute for the Study of Religion, Sogang University, Seoul, June 18, 2013.
Bingenheimer, Marcus. "Digitization of Buddhism (Digital Humanities and Buddhist Studies)." In *Oxford Bibliographies Online* in *Buddhism*, 2020, https://www.oxfordbibliographies.com/view/document/obo-9780195393521/obo-9780195393521-0265.xml.
BulgyoLoc, http://www.bulgyoloc.com/.
CytoScape, https://cytoscape.org/.
Encyclopedia of Korean Culture, https://encykorea.aks.ac.kr.
Encyves Wiki, http://dh.aks.ac.kr/Encyves.
Grayson, James H. *Korea — A Religious History.* London: Taylor and Francis, 2013.
Hwang, Ingyu. "Bukanjiyeong goguryeowa balhaeui bulgyo sachal — goguryeowa balhaeui sachal balgul bogwon" [Buddhist temples in Goguryeo and Balhae, North Korea — excavation and restoration of temples in Goguryeo and Balhae]. *Bulgyoyeon-gu* 32 (2019): 139–170.
Jogye Order of Korean Buddhism, http://www.buddhism.or.kr/jongdan/main/index.php.
Kim, Sung-woo. *Buddhist Architecture of Korea.* Elizabeth, NJ: Hollym, 2007.
Nagasaki, Kiyonori, Toru Tomabechi, and Masahiro Shimoda. "Towards a digital research environment for Buddhist studies." *Literary and Linguistic Computing* 28, no. 2 (2013): 296–300.
Neo4j, https://neo4j.com.
OpenStreetMap, https://www.openstreetmap.org/.

Preservation of Traditional Temples. Evaluation of Maintenance Projects and Mid- to Long-term Development Plans, https://mcst.go.kr/kor/s_policy/dept/deptView.jsp?pSeq=157&pDatacD=0406000000&pType=.
QGIS, https://www.qgis.org/en/site/.
RAWGraphs, https://rawgraphs.io/.
Senécal, Bernard. "Buddhists in the Two Koreas: North-South Interactions." *Journal of Korean Religions* 4, no. 2 (2013): 9–50.
Sillok Wiki, http://dh.aks.ac.kr/sillokwiki.
Status of Traditional Temples [based on 972 Locations, 2021.1.31.], https://www.mcst.go.kr/kor/s_policy/dept/deptView.jsp?pCurrentPage=1&pType=03&pTab=01&pSeq=1450&pDataCD=0417000000.
Stausberg, Michael, and Steven Engler. "Introduction: Research methods in the study of religion's." In *The Routledge Handbook of Research Methods in the Study of Religion*, edited by Michael Stausberg and Steven Engler, 3–20. London: Routledge, 2011.
Stausberg, Michael, and Mark Gardiner. "Definition." In *The Oxford Handbook of the Study of Religion*, edited by Michael Stausberg, and Steven Engler, 9–32. Oxford: Oxford Academic, 2017.
Veidlinger, Daniel, ed. *Digital Humanities and Buddhism: An Introduction*. Berlin: De Gruyter, 2019.

Elizabeth Lee
Rock-Carved Buddhist Images on Mt. P'algong: An Exploration of the Utility of GIS Analysis in Art Historical Research

Over the past several decades, a marked spatial turn in art historical scholarship has resulted in the development of a stream of discourse that articulates the layered reciprocity between material culture, visual experience, and complex spatial environments.[1] In the study of religions too, attention paid to the phenomenology of sacred spaces has yielded new insights into the dialectical relationship between belief and ritual practice. Research in the rich subfields of Buddhist and Daoist mountains, for example, has identified unique ways in which religion shaped and was shaped by the mountains which its practitioners inhabited.[2] More recently, scholars have explored the utility of digital tools in conducting historical analysis on the spatial conditions of religious and artistic subjects. In the realm of East Asian Buddhism, digitized hagiographies and lineage records of monks have been skillfully employed in conjunction with Geographic Information Systems (GIS) to challenge long standing assumptions about sectarian affiliations.[3] Large scale digital humanities initiatives at museums such as The Frick Collection's Digital Art History Lab (DAHL) have been producing innovative resources for art historical research using GIS technologies.[4] However, despite the clear understanding that religion, visual culture, and space are intimately entwined, surprisingly few scholars have

---

1 A special issue of *Historical Geography* (vol. 45, 2017) guest edited by Susan Elizabeth Gagliardi and Joanna Gardner-Huggett offers a wide range of examples of art historians creating maps and engaging with mapping practices to further their analyses.
2 An engaging discussion of the Chinese sacred mountain Nanyue by James Robson provides a good look into how the spatial parameters of a geological feature shapes the way religious agents of two different religious traditions interacted with each other. See: James Robson, *Power of Place: The Religious Landscape of the Southern Sacred Peak (Nanyue) in Medieval China* (Cambridge, MA: Harvard University Asia Center, 2009).
3 The pioneering work by Jason Protass reassesses the *Lamp Records* (*denglu*) of Chan Buddhism by drawing upon GIS and network visualizations. See: Jason Protass, "Toward a Spatial History of Chan: Lineages, Networks, and the *Lamp Records*," *Review of Religion and Chinese Society* 3 (2016): 164–188.
4 The Digital Art History Lab at the Frick Collection, in conjunction with the Center for Advanced Research of Spatial Information at Hunter College, CUNY have created an interactive online tool that uses GIS software to map the movement of the Frick Art Reference Library's photographic campaigns across the country during 1922–1967. Images and metadata are linked to a dynamic map that feature artwork in private and obscure collections, many of which have been lost or

https://doi.org/10.1515/9783110747607-003

leveraged the interpretive potential of GIS to explore the environmental factors that have influenced the creation of religious objects and images in medieval Asia.

This chapter proposes methods for answering art historical questions about religious visual culture with GIS assisted analysis through an investigation of the geospatial circumstances of several medieval stone sculptures of Buddhist deities on Mount P'algong in South Korea. These images, called *maaebul* in Korean (磨崖佛 in *hanja*), are relief carvings of Buddhas and bodhisattvas on monoliths, cliff faces, and rocky outcroppings that are by design embedded into the environment. Though ubiquitous on the Korean peninsula, they are not well understood in part because the textual sources that reference them are few and far between.[5] Limited by traditional methodologies that are highly dependent on such textual references, the handful of art historical studies that have been conducted on rock-carved Buddhist images thus remain wedded to stylistic analysis and cataloguing.[6]

To augment the paucity of premodern documents, I adopt the location and geospatial context of these statues as significant primary source data to help expand our understanding of the production and function of *maaebul* during the late Unified Silla-early Koryŏ period (roughly from the late ninth to eleventh centuries CE). Far from being the first study of rock-carved images to incorporate spatial information, my research builds upon key observations made by scholars working primarily with historical texts and 2D maps. Early work by cultural historian Park Sung-sang, for example, suggests that the construction of late Unified Silla period *maaebul* was sponsored by local strongmen who were eager to demonstrate their authority.[7] Park identified that many of these *maaebul* were placed next to or near national roads, which suggests their public prominence. His analysis, however, hovers on the macro scale of the entire kingdom, forgoing engagement with local features of the landscape or detailed investigations of particular images or sites. Conditioned

---

remain inaccessible to the public. See: The Frick Collection Library, https://www.frick.org/research/photoarchive/history.

5 In addition to the dearth of primary source documents, the study of Buddhist art in South Korea has long privileged text-based analysis. By this I mean there is a wide-spread preoccupation with iconographic identifications and searching for doctrinal correlates to specific types of imagery.

6 Well known scholars have published descriptive catalogues of rock-carved images. See: Myŏng-dae Mun, *Maaebul* [Rock-carved Buddhas] (Seoul: Taewŏnsa, 1991); Songeun Choe, *Sŏkpul, maaebul* [Stone Buddhas, Rock-carved Buddhas] (Seoul: Yegyŏng, 2004). Other books that deal with *maaebul* are for general audiences such as T'ae-ho Yi and Kyŏng-hwa Yi, *Han'gug-ŭi ma'aebul* [Rock-carved Buddhas of Korea] (Seoul: Tarŭn sesang, 2002). Often textbooks on Korean sculpture will have a chapter dedicated to *maaebul* listing the most famous sculptures. For an example, see note 9 below.

7 Sung-sang Park, "9 segi maaebulssangŭi punp'ojŏk t'ŭksŏnge taehan koch'al," [A study on the locations of rock-carved Buddha images of the ninth century] *Munhwa Sahak* 21 (2004): 537–551.

by the flattened maps he was referencing the topography of the peninsula was not an element he could readily explore.

In this chapter, two case studies highlight how the enhanced visualization and computational suite of GIS tools can be used to employ three-dimensional topographic data to better contextualize our understanding of religious images within their spatial parameters and enrich traditional forms of art historical analysis. Both examples are found along the slopes of Mt. P'algong in the southeastern corner of the Korean peninsula, just north of present-day Taegu city. They are commonly identified as the rock-carved images of the hermitages that attend to them. In the first example, the temple is no longer active and so the carving is called the *maaebul* of the Samsŏng hermitage site (Samsŏngamji *maaebul*). The second example features two images carved on adjacent sides of a pyramidal boulder currently under the stewardship of Yŏmbul hermitage (Yŏmburam). Though they are part of the religious development of the mountain, these sculptures have received little scholarly attention.[8] Therefore, to situate these images within the context of Korean Buddhist art history, this chapter provides a short introduction to the political and religious significance of Mt. P'algong during the medieval period and interprets the stylistic features of the sculptures and then presents the GIS-assisted findings.

Before delving into the history of the mountain, a brief overview of the technical procedures and the decisions made throughout the computational process will clarify the necessity of such digital analysis and the meaning of the results. I began the project by documenting the latitude and longitude of the images, their elevation, and the cardinal direction that they are facing. Identifying their spatial context by plotting this information into a three-dimensional model of the mountain was the first step in confronting the ambiguous nature of the remaining textual sources. Then I used two types of GIS analysis to address the question of how these *maaebul* were interacting with the landscape and with the people moving through the mountain. The first method, called Least Cost Path (LCP) analysis, proposes the most efficient way to get from one point to another in a three-dimensional space. The second, called Viewshed analysis, identifies which units of geographic space

---

8 The study of rock-carved images in South Korea is not as well developed as the study of Buddhist sculpture made of wood, bronze, clay, or other smaller stone statuary. There are many reasons for this, but chief among them is the fact that art historians, especially in Korea, place high emphasis on textual documents as their primary data source. Due to the fact that these images are rarely mentioned in contemporaneous documents, they have received little attention. When art historians mention *maaebul*, it is usually those carvings with dated inscriptions, and they are used to stylistically corroborate the dating of other sculpture. For an example of this approach see Songeun Choe, *Koryŏsidae pulgyojogak yŏn'gu* [Research on Koryŏ Buddhist sculpture] (Seoul: Iljogak, 2013), 87–89.

can be seen by an observer from a specific position in the landscape. Though these techniques are more commonly used by environmental scientists to track, for example, the migration patterns of wild animals through a specific region, when applied to the geographic parameters of Mt. P'algong, these analyses begin to explain why certain images were placed where they are.[9] Incorporated into this art historical study, such digital analysis can help us understand how the visibility of certain rock-carved sculptures allowed medieval patrons to integrate a rugged, mountainous environment into the Buddhist fold. The conclusion of this chapter stresses the potentialities of GIS and how art historians can work critically with them. There I posit that incorporating digital tools into the study of art historical subjects creates both a technical route for productive experimentation and a theoretical framework within which we can explore old evidence in new ways.

Mt. P'algong: A Medieval Center of Political and Religious Significance

Mt. P'algong, more accurately described as a small mountain range, covers a total area of over 120,000 square kilometers with its summit, Piro-bong (meaning Vairocana peak), rising 1,192 meters above sea level. Positioned between the capital of the Unified Silla dynasty and the Naktong River transportation vector, the mountain played a significant role in military battles and political schemes and was an especially active Buddhist locale during the Unified Silla — Koryŏ dynastic transition. Unsurprisingly, Mt. P'algong is also the site of several conspicuous rock-carved images of the Buddha, stone statues of the Buddha, and the only true Buddhist cave grotto in South Korea.[10] From as early as the Three Kingdoms period (traditionally dated from the first century BCE to 660 CE), we know that mountains were incorporated into ritual systems of animistic belief on the peninsula. In the seventh century, Silla royalty and aristocrats used the logic of the five sacred marchmounts (*oak*) to identify locations for the performance of national ritual services to benefit

---

[9] For an example from mammalian biology, see: Maren Huck et al., "Analyses of Least Cost Paths for Determining Effects of Habitat Types on Landscape Permeability: Wolves in Poland," *Acta Theriologica* 56, no. 1 (January 2011): 91–101.
[10] The most famous cave grotto in South Korea is undoubtedly Sŏkkuram on Mt Toham near the old Silla capital, Kyŏngju. Technically, however, Sŏkkuram is not a true cave as it is actually a domed room constructed with stone blocks that was then buried under piled earth.

and prolong the state.¹¹ Through this process Mt. P'algong was selected as one of these five sacred mountains and its main summit became the "Central Peak" (*chungak*) in that system.¹²

According to the twelfth century text *History of the Three Kingdoms*, in 689 King Sinmun (r. 681–692), expressed the desire to move the capital of the kingdom from the old Silla capital of Kyŏngju to Talgubŏl (modern day Taegu).¹³ Despite the fact that his wish was never carried out, this record shows that the area south of Mt. P'algong was economically and symbolically important enough to be considered an appropriate site for the Unified Silla court. Travelers making their way by land from almost any other part of the country to the Silla capital would have had to pass through the Taegu area and would have stopped there to spend the night before completing the remaining roughly fifty-kilometer journey to their final destination. As the most-used thoroughfare between Kyŏngju and the Nakdong river, which allowed for north-south travel as well as travel to the western parts of the peninsula, Mt. P'algong was heavily trafficked by commercial, military, and religious enterprises during the Unified Silla period and thereafter.

Over time the number of visitors to, and patronage of, the mountain continued to flourish as Mt. P'algong was already home to several significant temples and hermitages by the tenth century. On the northwestern side of the mountain, lies the Kunwi cave which houses an elegant stone Amitabha triad thought to date to the early eighth century. The sophistication of the carving and iconographic features of these sculptures suggests that this cave temple, one of only two from the medieval period, constituted a substantial investment and was a highly visible place of worship and patronage.¹⁴ Moreover, according to the eminent Silla literatus Ch'oe Ch'iwŏn (857–d. after 908), one of the ten notable monasteries associated with the Hwaŏm (C. Huayan) tradition at that time was Mirisa 美利寺 on Mt. P'algong.¹⁵ In his text he identifies these temples with their establishment on a specific sacred

---

11 Ki-min Han, *Koryŏ sawon ui kujo wa kinung* [The Organization and Functions of Monasteries during the Koryo Period] (Seoul: Minjoksa, 1998), 367.
12 Richard D. McBride believes that the Central Peak mentioned in this text is Mt. P'algong, whereas others believe it is Mt. Tansŏk (Stone-cutting Mountain 斷石山). For a review of this issue see: Richard D. McBride, *Domesticating the Dharma: Buddhist Cults and the Hwaŏm Synthesis in Silla Korea* (Honolulu: University of Hawai'i Press, 2008), 155 n. 46.
13 *Sinmun 9-yŏn, Samguk sagi* [History of the Three Kingdoms] 8 (Seoul: Ŭryu Munhwasa, 1983).
14 Given the difficulty of carving such a cave into this cliff and the quality of the stone statues, it is difficult to conceive of this site as existing without an accompanying temple. Unfortunately, there are no records of such a temple near the cave from the Three Kingdoms or Unified Silla period.
15 *Tang Taech'ŏnboksa kosaju pŏn'gyŏng Taedŏk Pŏpchang hwasang chŏn 1* [Biography of the Eminent Tang Upadhyaya Fazang of Dajianfu Monastery], Taishō 2054, 50.285a29-b2 (Tokyo: Daizōkyōkai, 1924–1935).

mountain signaling the strong correlation between religious and political locales during the late Unified Silla period. This overlap of the five sacred marchmount and monastic systems illustrates the symbiotic relationship between the Buddhist and political realms.[16]

Throughout the Unified Silla and Koryŏ (918–1392) periods the royal court leveraged the symbolic power of Buddhist ritual and patronage to buttress their right to rule. An important example found on the southern slopes of Mt P'algong is the three-storied stone pagoda at Piro hermitage 毘盧庵, a subsidiary temple of Tonghwasa 桐華寺.[17] Dedicated in 863, the pagoda and the materials enshrined inside were offered by King Kyŏngmun (r. 861–875) as prayers for the peaceful repose of King Minae (r. 838–839) who, in the struggles for power in the Unified Silla court, was killed when he was only 23 years old.[18] Significantly, Minae was the last ruler of the In'gyŏm lineage, the line from whom Kyŏngmun's predecessors took the throne. Enlisting the help of the monk Simji (d.u.) who was a relative of Minae, the court's offering may have been made to placate uprisings from would-be claimants to the throne.[19] During the subsequent Koryŏ dynasty, the nearby monastery Puinsa 夫人寺 (also written 符仁寺) was the repository of the printing blocks of the First Koryŏ Tripitaka commissioned by King Hyŏnjong (r. 1009–1031) but tragically destroyed during the Mongol invasions that started in 1231. Scholars have interpreted the impetus for this massive undertaking as the Khitan incursions from the northern border in 1010 and the production of the Tripitaka as a spiritual technology used to protect the kingdom.[20] The continued royal patronage of Buddhist temples along the southeastern slope of Mt. P'algong indicates that the

---

[16] McBride has also suggested that this points to the particular promulgation of the Hwaŏm school during the latter half of the Unified Silla period. See: Richard D. McBride, *Domesticating the Dharma: Buddhist Cults and the Hwaŏm Synthesis in Silla Korea* (Honolulu, HI: University of Hawai'i Press, 2008), 130–131.

[17] The foundation legend of Tonghwasa relates that the monk Kŭktal 極達 (d.u.) founded the temple in the fifteenth year of Silla King Soji (493) and called it Yugasa. Based on the fact that Kŭktal was known to be in Tang at that time, this claim was probably constructed to extend the age of the temple. Furthermore, because the name Yuga 瑜伽 indicates Yogacara belief, the name belies its later attribution as it is highly unlikely that the Yogacara sect was active in Korea almost at the same time as its genesis in China.

[18] These objects were stolen in 1966, after the restoration of the pagoda in 1960, but were donated to the Dongguk University Museum in 1968 by the holder.

[19] Jeong-hwan Jin, "Tonghwasa sŏkt'abe taehan koch'al," [A study on the stone pagoda at Tonghwa temple] *Misul sahakchi* 4 (2007): 68–69.

[20] Vermeersch posits a more nuanced reading that incorporates the contested manner in which Hyŏnjong came to the throne. Sem Vermeersch, "Royal Ancestor Worship and Buddhist Politics: The Hyŏnhwa-Sa Stele and the Origins of the First Koryŏ Tripitaka," *Journal of Korean Studies* 18, no. 1 (2013): 115–146.

area functioned as a spiritual center not only of the mountain but also of the state during the late Unified Silla to early Koryŏ periods.

Interactions between Rock-Carved Images and the Landscape

From the historical sources, it is clear that Mt. P'algong was an important facet of the political and religious landscape of medieval Korea. Yet in terms of the lived experience of the mountain, the ways in which people traversed, interacted, or creatively manipulated the mountain and its environment, the received texts are unfortunately silent. For example, travel literature composed by scholar-officials of the subsequent Chosŏn period provides rich evidence of what people thought about specific locales and how they moved through the country.[21] However, such accounts from the early Koryŏ period are exceedingly rare. Thus, text-based methods of analysis have produced limited descriptions of the human activity on Mt. P'algong, and even thinner explanations of the numerous artworks that dot its environment. I propose that an investigation of *maaebul* in conjunction with their spatial contexts can be productively used to clarify some of the ambiguities that textual methods have had difficulty addressing. In doing so, we can come closer to an understanding of how these sculptures were experienced as part of the mountain.

By virtue of being immovable, carved onto the surface of living rock or on the side of rocky cliffs, *maaebul* evince a relationship with the landscape that remains fairly constant from the moment of their creation. Despite the exploitation of the peninsula's timber resources and the changing patterns of travel and transportation over time, the remote locations of many of these rock-carved images precluded significant degradations of the landscapes around them. The stone statues and rock-carved images on Mt. P'algong all appear to have been created between the late seventh to early twelfth centuries. Through stylistic analysis, most of them have been attributed to the ninth and tenth centuries — around the decline of the Silla royal house and the rise of the Koryŏ state. Given the numinous power that was afforded to images of the Buddha during this period, it follows that the

---

[21] For a thorough investigation into the ways in which Chosŏn period scholar-literati described their peregrinations in travel literature see: Maya Kerstin Hyun Stiller, "Kumgangsan: Regional Practice and Religious Pluralism in Pre-Modern Korea," Doctoral thesis (University of California Los Angeles, 2013).

spiritually potent mountain was purposefully demarcated with *maaebul* according to a cultural logic that can only obliquely be grasped in textual records.[22]

Though a discussion of this spatial logic is outside the scope of this chapter, the specificity of *maaebul* placement in relation to geological features of the landscape can be seen in the two rock carvings flanking Mt. P'algong's main peak, Pirobong. Both placed along or close to the ridge that affords apical access, these two images are less than half a kilometer away from the sacred summit. In fact, the Buddha on the east side faces Pirobong and can be seen looking towards it from the vantage point of the mountain top (Fig. 1). The other *maaebul* is a short distance to the west, situated along a path that connects up to the ridge. As a set, the three manifest spiritual power in the form of an orographic triad with the pinnacle of Mt. P'algong serving as the central locus of worship echoing Pirobong's role as the "Central Peak" of the Five Marchmount system. The granite composition of the ancillary Buddhas, crafted from the same rocky substrate as the main icon, presents an additional case to see these features of the landscape as ontologically related.

Fig. 1: East Peak *maaebul* seen from Piro Peak. (Photo by the author).

Placed at meaningful locations, these artworks are important clues into how the medieval environment was perceived, traversed, and modified.[23] In the Pirobong

---

22 Images of the Buddha were thought to be efficacious at preventing calamity but were also considered auspicious signs.
23 In another text I discuss how the physical features of the mountain lent themselves to be used by medieval Buddhists in specific ways, namely as appropriate sites for images of the Buddha and

example, the two *maaebul's* relationships to the summit is obvious even on a printed map. However, not all rock-carved images on Mt. P'algong have such clear geological points of reference. In the following sections, I examine the Samsŏngamji *maaebul* and the Yŏmburam *maaebul* along with their mountainous context using both traditional visual analysis and digital methods to construct a more complete picture of how medieval travelers may have interacted with these sculptures and why they are located in what are today remote parts of the mountain.

Cost-Distance Analysis: *Samsŏngamji Maaebul*

The Samsŏngamji (Samŏng hermitage site) *maaebul* is currently not easy to find, nor is it near any geologically significant sites like a mountain peak or a freshwater spring. The Samsŏng hermitage is not attested to in any Koryŏ period sources; but, given that this *maaebul* is about 1.5 kilometers uphill from Puinsa, this small outpost was most likely related to the larger temple. The Samsŏngamji sculpture (Fig. 2) is carved on the east side of a 3.6 m tall, 2.2 m wide granite boulder that unfortunately, has not been well preserved. It has cracked completely to the right of the image so that the Buddha is now leaning significantly to the left. The image itself also suffers a large fissure that runs from the top of the boulder down and across the Buddha's left shoulder and arm. Furthermore, severe weathering has exacerbated the illegibility of the lower half of the Buddha's legs. Based on what remains, it appears that the legs were not carved as carefully as the rest of the figure, or that a pedestal had been made for this image, though this is difficult to say with certainty. Currently, the upper three-fourths of a bas-relief carving of a standing Medicine Buddha can be identified by the medicine bowl in his left hand. Furthermore, his right hand grasps the hem of his robe, a gesture that finds precedents in images of this particular Buddha starting from the late seventh century.[24]

Notably, the robes and style of the *maaebul* present in a later fashion. Geometric and stiff U-shaped folds repeat down the front of the Buddha's body while the loose collar exposes his chest. The figure's narrow body contrasts with his puffy face, and his swollen chin and cheeks seem to be pushing his mouth and nose together. The tightly pursed lips, wide nose, and small, squinting eyes give a distinctly disinterested impression, which is reminiscent of a gilt bronze image discovered on

---

his attendants. Elizabeth Lee, "Landscape of Buddhas: Rock-carved Buddhist Images on the Korean Peninsula from the 9th to 12th centuries CE," Doctoral thesis (New York University, 2022).

24 Such an example was found in a pagoda in Kuhwangdong dated to 692 CE. This object is now in the collection of the National Museum of Korea, accession number: Bon 14753.

Fig. 2: Rock-carved standing Buddha at Samsŏng hermitage site. Unified Silla-Koryŏ, ca. late ninth to early tenth century. Height: 2.36 meters. Mt. P'algong, Tong-gu, Taegu. Taegu Tangible Cultural Property No. 21. (Photo by the author).

Mt. Sŏnsan in Kumi county, just north of Mt. P'algong.[25] The two images also share similar depictions of their U-shaped collars, smooth chests, and short necks that are dominated by the three rings that identify them as enlightened beings. However, the Samsŏngamji *maaebul* was clearly crafted by less skilled hands. Though some of the same visual idioms were employed, they are more fluid and subtle on the gilt bronze statuette. The handling of the rock also lacks the delicacy and ease that other stone sculptures of the eighth and early ninth century display. The facial and sartorial features of the carving and the stiffness of the figure align with what is seen in sculptures of the late ninth and early tenth centuries making that the most probable date of its creation.

This type of stylistic analysis is necessary in cases like the Samsŏngamji *maaebul* where there is little by way of textual evidence. It can help in dating the sculpture and providing a sense of the visual episteme from which it was created, but it does not help us understand why it is where it is or how the image functioned in its outdoor context. One way to tackle the lack of written sources is to combine digital tools with this analog mode of research. This hybrid approach allows us to take advantage of the available data and posit answers to art historical questions such as function and reception. Thus, to understand why this rock-carved Buddha was

---

[25] This object, National Treasure 182, is also in the collection of the National Museum of Korea, accession number: Su 3297.

placed in this location, I turned to GIS software to incorporate the surrounding environmental data into an analysis of the ways in which the environment influenced how and where actors moved through the landscape.

Using a Digital Elevation Model (DEM) as the base layer in QGIS, I extracted a cost raster layer of the differences in elevation. Consider the DEM as a topographic grid that contains an elevation value of every square. The cost raster layer is a layer of points that contains the value difference between each square and the eight squares that surround it, representing the eight directions available to an individual with one move from that square (north, south, east, west, northeast, southeast, southwest, and northwest). This difference in value is the cost-distance measure which tallies up the difference in elevation and distance. For example, if you want to go east but the elevation of the square to your east is +5 and the elevation value of the square to your southeast is only +2, the least expensive path would involve moving southeast first. After extracting the cost raster layer, I ran a Least Cost Path plug-in that calculated all the possible paths one could take to travel from a source point to a destination point. This algorithm then generates the least expensive path in terms of elevation that one could take, delineating on a map the most probable route that would have been taken to get from point A to point B. These types of time consuming and complex calculations would be nearly impossible for an individual to do and can realistically only be generated with computer assistance.

With the Least Cost Path plug-in running a cost-distance analysis, I generated the most gradual but time efficient paths one could take to travel between the various temples and geological features of Mt. P'algong. One of the longest routes was from Kunwi cave on the northwestern side of the mountain to Puinsa. Predictably, it crosses over the mountain ridge at its lowest point between West peak and P'agye peak (Fig. 3). However, it continues on to run right past the *maaebul* at the Samsŏng hermitage site indicating that this image was accessible from the proposed travel route. The least cost path descended the mountain in a way that would have very easily taken travelers from the northwest part of the country to Puinsa. From there it would have been a roughly 4 km trek along fairly flat terrain to Tonghwasa.

Before conducting the GIS analysis, the Samsŏngamji *maaebul's* location was difficult to understand because it did not align with the patterns of placement that had characterized other images on the mountain. It was not particularly close to a mountain peak, or on a large cliff, and it was placed behind a major temple instead of in front of it — the type of positioning seen at neighboring Tonghwasa.[26] Yet by incorporating into the analysis the possibility that the *maaebul* was placed along a

---

26 In fact, there is a *maaebul* half a kilometer south of Puinsa that has been attributed to the Koryŏ period, though stylistically it appears much later to me.

Fig. 3: Least Cost Path from Kunwi cave to Puinsa and Tonghwasa (yellow line). (Photo by the author).

route that connected the northwestern and southeastern edges of the mountain, we can infer that it functioned as a kind of signpost for travelers moving between the northwestern part of the country and the Kyŏngju basin. This interpretation correlates with the historical sources that indicate the southern slopes of Mt. P'algong were home to large and politically significant temples and the fact that people moved through Mt P'algong to access the Silla capital in the southeast corner of the peninsula. Travelers could have taken a more circuitous route around the western side of the mountain, but considering its wide breadth and manageable elevation, going around it might not have been an efficient choice. Because temples during the Silla and Koryŏ periods often served as waystations for government officials and places of rest for itinerant monks, the mountain route may have been preferable given the number of temples that are nestled along the mountain's slopes. In addition to the bustling religious activity on Mt. P'algong, commercial and artisanal enterprises also operated on the southwestern side as well. In the area currently called Yŏngsu-dong 龍水洞 a tile kiln site presumably supplied the temples around it — specifically Puinsa and Tonghwasa.[27] Even today this area is nicknamed "Pile Valley"

---

[27] Yong-jin Yun, *Taegu Yongsu-dong Wayoji chosa pogosŏ* [Excavation report of Yongsu-dong Kiln Site, Taegu] (Taegu: Taegu Chikhalsi, 1986).

chaengigol because of the heaps of tile shards found there.²⁸ The presence of a kiln here further underscores the amount of human traffic that must have enlivened the southern slopes of Mt. P'algong.

Despite the Samsŏngamji *maaebul's* modest scale and rustic aesthetic, the image would have inspired devotion and comfort to weary travelers still ensconced within the mountain's rugged terrain. Pilgrims would have welcomed the healing ministrations of the Medicine Buddha, especially towards the end of their journey to Puinsa. Particularly during the tumultuous tenth century, images of the Medicine Buddha and the salvific bodhisattva Avalokitesvara were popular objects of veneration. Given the dangers of traveling through the mountains of Korea, which at that time were filled with tigers and thieves, the presence of either of these two deities embedded into the landscape would have been reassuring on both a spiritual and logistical level. In the context of Mt. P'algong, the Samsŏngamji *maaebul* functioned as a guide through a this-worldly mountain passage as well as the imagined spatial soteriology of pilgrimage.²⁹

Viewshed Analysis: *Yŏmburam* Rock-Carved Buddha and Bodhisattva

Such dual-natured functions also characterize the *maaebul* carved on adjacent sides of an enormous pyramidal boulder at the rear of Yŏmburam 念佛庵 "Chanting Buddha's name hermitage."³⁰ Embedded into a valley (Fig. 4), with the north and east sides partially covered by earth and foliage, the rock's west-facing side features a shallowly incised image of a Buddha seated in meditation on a lotus pedestal. Filling most of the available smooth surface, the Buddha itself is about 4 meters tall and 3.3 meters wide (Fig. 4a). Due to its westerly direction, this image is commonly thought to represent Amitābha Buddha because he is considered to reside in

---

28 Ki-min Han, *Koryŏ sawon ui kujo wa kinung* [The Organization and Functions of Monasteries during the Koryo Period] (Seoul: Minjoksa, 1998), 207.
29 I borrow the term "spatial soteriology" from: Heather Blair, *Real and Imagined: The Peak of Gold in Heian Japan* (Cambridge, MA: Harvard University Asia Center, 2015), 152–158.
30 The term *yŏmbul* 念佛 refers to a variety of meditative practices but today is commonly associated with the recitation of the name of the Buddha. In Korea, a popular Buddhist chant is "Namu Amit'a Pul Kwansaeŭm Posal" which offers homage to Amitabha (Amit'a) and Avalokitsevara (Kwansaeŭm), probably the two deities presented on this boulder. The name of this hermitage therefore likely derives from to these two carved figures.

the western pure land.³¹ The south side features an unconventional depiction of a bodhisattva; most likely Maitreya or Avalokitesvara given that it is holding the stem of a plant in its right hand — an iconographic feature of both deities. This figure is around 4.5 meters tall and carved on a more irregular and uneven surface than the Buddha (Fig. 4b). Despite the scale of these carvings and their placement on a significant mountain, they are not well understood. With the help of GIS, however, we can see that the two images at Yŏmburam mark the landscape of Mt. P'algong, much like the Samsŏngamji *maaebul*, but that they perform their signaling functions in a slightly different way.

Fig. 4: Rock-carved seated buddha and bodhisattva at Yŏmburam. Koryŏ, ca. late tenth to eleventh century. Height of boulder: 6 meters. Tonghwasa, Taegu. Taegu Tangible Cultural Property No. 14. (Photo by the author).

To understand how these carvings interacted with the landscape, I first looked to the trails leading to and around the hermitage. A difficult two-kilometer ascent from Tonghwasa leads to Yŏmburam today, though it is unclear if this was the same path used to access the hermitage in the past. Further complicating an easy

---

31 Described in Mahāyāna sūtras, sukhāvatī is the name of the pure lands of the Buddha Amitabha and is often referred to as "the western pure land." For a description of the Yŏmburam image as Amitabha, see: Yŏng-ho Chŏng, "P'algongsan Yŏmburam" [Yŏmbul hermitage, Mt. P'algong], *Kogomisul* 2, no. 2 (1961): 71–73.

Fig. 4a: Rock-carved seated buddha at Yŏmburam. (Photo by the author).

conclusion is the fact that this site sits squarely between the two Least Cost Paths rendered by QGIS between Tonghwasa and Piro peak on the west, and Tonghwasa and Yŏmbul peak on the east. Three Chosŏn period hermitages lie on the eastern LCP, suggesting that at least parts of this route were in use during the subsequent dynasty.[32] Because it is nestled into a valley, accessing the hermitage from either path requires a steep and winding descent. This raises the question: why build a hermitage with such large rock-carved sculptures in a location so difficult to reach?

Part of the answer can be found in the geological characteristics of the living rock on which the two Buddhist deities are carved. The exposed portion of the boulder is about 6.4 meters tall and over 6 meters wide. Its large and relatively smooth surfaces offered an ideal opportunity for the creation of *maaebul*. I have described the dialectical nature of the lapidary process that occurs between humans and the

---

[32] These three hermitages are Budoam, Yangjinam, and Naewŏnam.

Fig. 4b: Rock-carved seated bodhisattva (Avalokitsevara) at Yŏmburam. (Photo by the author).

landscape elsewhere.[33] Here, I will briefly note that the visual features of many of Mt. P'algong's Buddhist images are determined by the environment as well as the stylistic episteme of the time. For the boulder at Yŏmburam, its pyramidal shape and large size provided a unique way for artisans and their patrons to incorporate the presence of Buddhist deities into peregrinations of the mountain. More specifically, the two images, by virtue of being carved on different sides of the boulder, operate on and are visible from different facets of the landscape.

---

33 Elizabeth Lee, "Landscape of Buddhas: Rock-carved Buddhist Images on the Korean Peninsula from the 9th to 12th centuries CE," Doctoral thesis (New York University, 2022).

This observation leads to another component of the answer which is brought into view by incorporating GIS tools into the analysis. Before explaining Yŏmburam's location and function, elaborating on the computational process will clarify how GIS addresses the spatial relationships between the monolith and the paths that were taken to get to and go beyond this site. After running the cost-distance analysis to determine the LCP between various sites to and around Yŏmburam and discovering that none of these paths align with the hermitage's location, I ran a viewshed analysis plug-in in QGIS to specify the boulder's range of visibility. Viewshed analysis produces a 2D rendering of which parts of a 3D landscape can be seen from a specified location at a given height (Fig. 5). Knowing what is visible from a certain location and from where a site is visible, is useful when interpreting the visual impact a site or artwork has on the surrounding landscape. Using the elevation values contained in the DEM, a viewshed analysis run on a single viewer location yields a binary raster layer that correlates to the DEM indicating whether or not a square of the landscape is visible or not from that location.

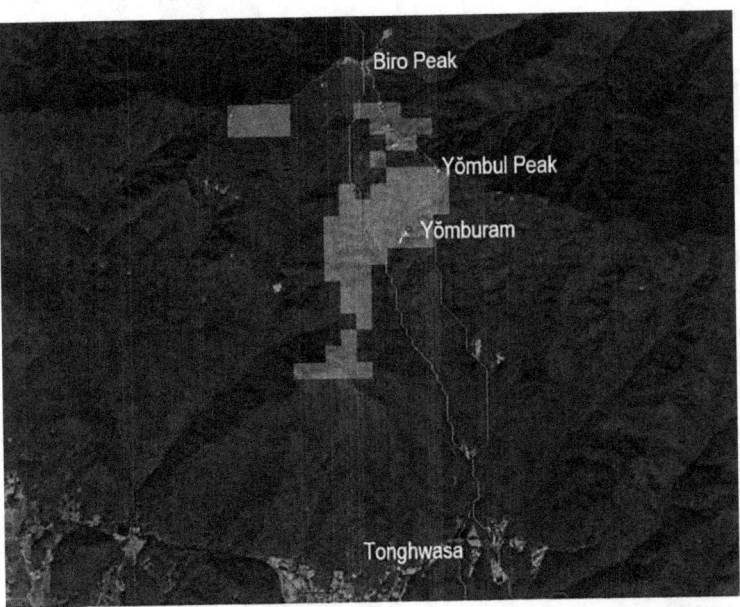

Fig. 5: Viewshed analysis of Yŏmburam and Least Cost Paths from Tonghwasa to Biro Peak and Yŏmbul Peak. (Photo by the author).

Using a model of Mt. P'algong constructed in QGIS, I ran a viewshed analysis on the location of the Yŏmburam boulder to determine what the deities could see and in turn, from where they were visible. In Figure 5, the areas that are lighter in color are the places that are visible from the exact location of the boulder at a height of 4 meters (roughly around the heads of both deities). I discovered that the *maaebul* are each visible from various points along the two paths that lead up to Piro peak and Yŏmbul Peak, less than 1 km to the east of East Peak. More specifically, from locations to the south along the LCP from Tonghwasa to Piro peak, one can see the seated Buddha rock carving. Additionally, from spots along the LCP from Tonghwasa to Yŏmbul peak to the west, travelers can see the bodhisattva image. Given the large scale and exposed nature of these images, the *maaebul* may have performed their utilitarian function as travel markers from a distance. Unlike the Samsŏngamji *maaebul*, which is easily accessed from the road, these two images may have served as long-range signposts for the two paths that led to the various peaks of Mt P'algong.

This use of such a large natural feature helps explain not only the scale and outdoor presentation of these sacred images, but also the location of the two deities. Reassuring travelers as they moved through the mountain, the *maaebul's* position and purpose were important to maintain. Later historiographic sources attest to Yŏmburam's significance by associating the hermitage with eminent monks of the Koryŏ period. The Tonghwa temple record stele records that Yŏmburam was established by the Sŏn master Yŏngjo 靈照 禪師 in 928, though we know that this is highly improbable given that other historical sources place Yŏngjo in Hangzhou at that time.[34] A more contemporaneous source, the stele for National preceptor Wŏnjin 圓眞 (1172–1221) at Pogyŏng temple, relates that the high ranking monk resided and then passed away at Yŏmburam in 1221.[35] Additionally, the stele for National preceptor Chinul 知訥 (1158–1210) recounts that during his stay at nearby Kŏjo temple between 1185 and 1198, he restored Yŏmburam.[36] Based on these two epigraphic texts, this hermitage was active during the twelfth century and was most likely established during the tenth or early eleventh century.

Stylistic analysis of the carvings, particularly of the bodhisattva image, also supports a late tenth century attribution. A dated stone carving of a seated Avalokitesvara excavated from Koryŏng, Kaepodong, 45 miles southwest of Yŏmburam shares

---

[34] Another source, Chosŏn sach'al saryo 朝鮮寺刹史料 [The historical sources of Chŏson temples] notes that the hermitage was established in 1621 by the monk Yuch'an 惟贊 (d.u.).
[35] Pogyŏngsa Wŏnjin'guksa pi 寶鏡寺圓眞國師碑 [Stele Inscription of National Preceptor Wŏnjin, 1224], Han'guksa Teit'ŏbeisŭ, https://db.history.go.kr/KOREA/item/gskoDetail.do?levelId= gsko_001_0300.
[36] "Stele Inscription of Pojo Chinul" in *Anthology of Stele Inscriptions of Eminent Korean Buddhist Monks*, vol. 12, *Collected Works of Korean Buddhism*, ed. John Jorgensen, trans. Patrick R Uhlmann (Seoul: The Jogye Order of Korean Buddhism, 2012), 368–369.

stylistic and iconographic features with the Yŏmburam bodhisattva. The Kaepodong image is a humble, shallow engraving on a small stone stele (Fig. 6), but because of the inscription on the back with a dedication date of 985, it is an invaluable artifact. This seated image is only 128 cm tall and 78 cm wide but clearly draws on the same iconographic model as the bodhisattva at Yŏmburam. The crown of both figures has the same wide, splayed open shape. The wavy, almost trembling patterns of the robes are unmistakably congruent. Their left hands hold the bottom of a thin, tall stem with several leaves and flowers. Though the flowers of the Yŏmburam image bloom over the bodhisattva's right shoulder, the overall effect is made similar by the thin reed-like stem of the flower traversing the undulating pattern of the robes. The

Fig. 6: Stone seated Avalokitesvara bodhisattva at Kaepodong, Koryŏng. Koryŏ, 985 CE. Height: 128 centimeters. Koryŏng-gun, North Kyŏngsang Province. Tangible Cultural Heritage of North Kyŏngsang Province No. 118. (Photo by the author).

bodhisattvas' left shoulders are covered by a fluttering outer garment that cascades down over their arms and legs. The Kaepodong image displays this in stubby incised lines whereas the Yŏmburam image's robes are carved away and ripple across the rock at points. The Kaepodong bodhisattva's feet are depicted as small ovular shapes floating amidst the ripples of his robes with a prominent line running down the center that points to an idea of iconographic consistency rather than an attempt at realism. The Yŏmburam Avalokitesvara also has this vertical line running down the exposed sole of his left foot.[37] These parallels suggest that the Yŏmburam images were created around the same late 10th century date as the Kaepodong carving.

With the dating and religious value of Yŏmburam and its *maaebul* corroborated, we can now contextualize the location and visual characteristics of the rock carvings within its historical setting. Though the scale of the incised Buddha and bodhisattva as well as the textual sources point to the importance of the hermitage, its position in between the two LCP presented a functional ambiguity. As reviewed above, the area around the southeastern side of the mountain was politically and historically significant during the Silla and early Koryŏ periods. Even after the dynastic transition, the former capital of the Silla in the southeast was politically and economically important; the area of Mt. P'algong was very likely one of the chief thoroughfares for commuting between Kyŏngju and the rest of the kingdom. Therefore, specifying the most expedient and least strenuous routes through the mountain and between its sacred sites would have been beneficial for both the state and the sangha. Marking these routes with symbols of salvation and assurance, either along the roads or visible from them, were techniques that Silla and early Koryŏ peoples used to integrate the topographical features of the local landscape into the iconographic program of the mountain as a whole. Not only were the patrons of these images able to create regional icons on Mt. P'algong, but in so doing, they were also able to reveal the ubiquity of the Buddhist realm. The Yŏmburam boulder's position in between the two probable paths, its large and relatively smooth surfaces, and their southern and western directionality provided the opportunity to create a type of spiritual marker that leveraged the visibility of a natural feature in space.

---

37 Interestingly, the flowering lotus on which the Kaepodong image is seated is depicted in a manner more akin to that of the Buddha at Yŏmburam. The seat is a simple lotus, with the petals pointing up. More specifically, only a few petals at the center are decorated and the rest are bare.

Conclusion: From Cost Distance and Viewshed to Phenomenological Experience

As the preceding pages illustrate, the computational tools in GIS software can provide added spatial context to religious images and sites whose stories are only partially known. In the case of the *maaebul* on Mt. P'algong in medieval Korea, the cost distance and viewshed analyses support the patterns of placement that previous scholars had proposed but could not substantiate due to the lack of contemporaneous maps and the paucity of extant travel literature outlining the location of roads. The identification of Least Cost Paths that align with the location of *maaebul* within the landscape reinforces the view that rock-carved images were placed at strategic locations along or visible from roads that connected religious, political, and economic centers. Through quantitative methods we can surmise that these artworks demarcated the peninsular terrain and provided geographic points of reference for travelers moving through the mountains.

Although GIS software helped to structure the available evidence and clearly expose spatial connections between sites of worship, it is important to reflect on the limitations of digital methods in humanities research. The maps and models that augment my assessment of Silla and Koryŏ period *maaebul* are ultimately speculative representations, not mimetic recreations of the medieval landscape. Digital models are only as complete as the datasets they reference; and for medieval Korea much is still unknown. For example, an important factor in determining visibility in viewshed analysis is vegetation coverage. However, it is, as of now, undeterminable how dense the foliage on Mt. P'algong was during the centuries discussed. To address this variable, I set the height of the viewshed analysis for Yŏmburam at 4 meters, which is the height of the faces of the rock-carved Buddha and bodhisattva. As desirable as it might be to add more layers to the model, no amount of data will be able to describe a historical circumstance with complete fidelity. And yet the scientific authority of high-tech scans and satellite imagery lends an empirical veneer that obscures a key issue in GIS art history: the fact remains that the spatial descriptions of historical data is fuzzy at best and practitioners must be wary of the potential inaccuracy of digital models just as much as they question primary source documents, secondary sources, and modern scholarship.

Still, by acknowledging the limitations of GIS technologies, art historians and humanists can work critically with them to broaden the field of available evidence and explore historical contexts at different scales. Combining analog modes of research with digital methods is a powerful way to address a physical object's complex and varied relationship to space and its reception at a certain moment in time. Least Cost Paths are capable of modeling large, infrastructural systems like travel itineraries. Viewshed projections can help us visualize on a more immediate scale, the influence and experienced presence of the Buddhist realm on a locale or even a road. Consequently, these tools together allowed me to connect the macro-level concept of networks of movement to the phenomenological experience of peregrination and pilgrimage vis-à-vis an investigation of *maaebul*. Learning to work with and against what is known is an important part of conducting humanistic research with digital tools. The ambiguity that characterizes the incomplete historical accounts, particularly in the way that an artwork such as *maaebul* was encountered within nature, can thus be resolved in part by scholars working with machine readable data and human intelligible data. By modeling a way to critically engage with medieval Buddhist visual culture and explore the potentialities and limits of digital visualizations and analysis, I hope this foray will inspire more productive experimentation in the field of digital Buddhist art history.

Bibliography

Blair, Heather. *Real and Imagined: The Peak of Gold in Heian Japan*. Cambridge, MA: Harvard University Asia Center, 2015.

Choe, Songeun. *Sŏkpul, maaebul* [Stone Buddhas, Rock-carved Buddhas]. Seoul: Yegyŏng, 2004.

Choe, Songeun. *Koryŏsidae pulgyojogak yŏn'gu* [Research on Koryŏ Buddhist sculpture]. Seoul: Iljogak, 2013.

Chŏng, Yŏng-ho 鄭永鎬, "P'algongsan Yŏmburam" 八公山 念佛庵 [Yŏmbul hermitage, Mt. P'algong]. *Kogomisul* 考古美術 2.2 (1961), 71–73.

Gagliardi, Susan Elizabeth, and Joanna Gardner-Huggett, eds. *Historical Geography* 45 (2017).

Han, Ki-min. *Koryŏ sawon ui kujo wa kinung* [The Organization and Functions of Monasteries during the Koryo Period]. Seoul: Minjoksa, 1998.

Han, Ki-min. *Koryŏ sawon ui kujo wa kinung* [The Organization and Functions of Monasteries during the Koryo Period]. Seoul: Minjoksa, 1998.

Huck, Maren, et al. "Analyses of Least Cost Paths for Determining Effects of Habitat Types on Landscape Permeability: Wolves in Poland." *Acta Theriologica* 56, no. 1 (January 2011): 91–101.

Jin, Jeong-hwan. "Tonghwasa sŏkt'abe taehan koch'al" [A study on the stone pagoda at Tonghwa temple]. *Misul sahakchi* 4 (2007): 68–69.

Jorgensen, John, ed. *Anthology of Stele Inscriptions of Eminent Korean Buddhist Monks*. trans. Patrick R Uhlmann. Vol. 12, Collected Works of Korean Buddhism. Seoul, Korea: The Jogye Order of Korean Buddhism, 2012.

Lee, Elizabeth. "Landscape of Buddhas: Rock-carved Buddhist Images on the Korean Peninsula from the 9th to 12th centuries CE." Doctoral thesis, New York University, 2022.

McBride, Richard D. *Domesticating the Dharma: Buddhist Cults and the Hwaŏm Synthesis in Silla Korea*. Honolulu, HI: University of Hawai'i Press, 2008.

Mun, Myŏng-dae. *Maaebul* [Rock-carved Buddhas]. Seoul: Taewŏnsa, 1991.

Park, Sung-sang. "9 segi maaebulssangŭi punp'ojŏk t'ŭksŏnge taehan koch'al" [A study on the locations of rock-carved Buddha images of the ninth century]. *Munhwa Sahak* 21 (2004): 537–551.

Pogyŏngsa Wŏnjin'guksa pi 寶鏡寺圓眞國師碑 [寶鏡寺圓眞國師碑 [Stele Inscription of National Preceptor Wŏnjin, 1224], Han'guksa Teit'ŏbeisŭ, https://db.history.go.kr/KOREA/item/gskoDetail.do?levelId=gsko_001_0300.

Protass, Jason. "Toward a Spatial History of Chan: Lineages, Networks, and the *Lamp Records*." *Review of Religion and Chinese Society* 3 (2016): 164–188.

Robson, James. *Power of Place: The Religious Landscape of the Southern Sacred Peak (Nanyue) in Medieval China*. Cambridge, MA: Harvard University Asia Center, 2009.

Kim Pu-sik, *Samguk sagi* [History of the Three Kingdoms]. Seoul: Ŭryu Munhwasa, 1983.

Stiller, Maya Kerstin Hyun. "Kumgangsan: Regional Practice and Religious Pluralism in Pre-Modern Korea." Doctoral thesis, University of California Los Angeles, 2013.

Takakusu Junjirō and Watanabe Kaikyoku, eds. *Taishō shinshū daizōkyō*. Tokyo: Daizōkyōkai, 1924–1935.

The Frick Collection Library, https://www.frick.org/research/photoarchive/history.

Vermeersch, Sem. "Royal Ancestor Worship and Buddhist Politics: The Hyŏnhwa-Sa Stele and the Origins of the First Koryŏ Tripitaka." *Journal of Korean Studies* 18, no. 1 (2013): 115–146.

Yi, T'ae-ho, and Kyŏng-hwa Yi, *Han'gug-ŭi ma'aebul* [Rock-carved Buddhas of Korea]. Seoul: Tarŭn sesang, 2002.

Yun, Yong-jin. *Taegu Yongsu-dong Wayoji chosa pogosŏ* [Excavation report of Yongsu-dong Kiln Site, Taegu]. Taegu: Taegu Chikhalsi, 1986.

Manuscripts

Dick van der Meij and Jan van der Putten
DREAMSEA Digital Repository of Endangered and Affected Manuscripts in Southeast Asia. A Multiple Religious and Cultural Digitization Experience

Introduction

Southeast Asia comprises a diverse and vast area that is populated by around 650 million people. It has an astonishing number of different religions, cultures, languages, scripts, architecture and histories. The religions in the area include Hinduism, Buddhism, Islam, Protestantism, Roman Catholicism, and curiously, Confucianism[1] and local and translocal offshoot of these religions next to local convictions and faiths that do not belong to the internationally recognized world religions. Manuscripts on religion in the region contain a wide variety of texts ranging from the core text of these religions such as the Qur'an, the Bible, Rāmāyana, Mahābhārata, the Vedas, Jātakas and many others. Other manuscripts contain exegeses and elaborations of these foundational texts, theological treatises, Sufism, and fragments of such texts with their interpretations, religious practices and rituals. The manuscript cultures also abound in religiously inspired prose and poetic texts ranging from one to thousands of pages and include texts on history, medicine, witchcraft, black and white magic, divination and astrology, architecture, correspondence and many more. There is no strict divide between secular and religious manuscripts, or texts for that matter, in Southeast Asia, as many secular texts draw on religious backgrounds while religious manuscripts may contain everyday household topics including recipes for cooking, medicines and sex education. It is not uncommon to compare Southeast Asia to a laboratory, where processes of technological innovation, cultural change, ethnic variation and political volatility are close to the surface and may show themselves in sudden surges. At the same time remnants of older cultural, political and religious forms are also clearly visible, as the existence of many manuscript collections in local homes and small educational institutions shows.

Many manuscripts in the area are at present being digitized by local and translocal programs and the resulting images and metadata are put on the internet in a wide variety of websites and digital databases. Programs concerned with digitizing Southeast Asian manuscripts include DREAMSEA, the topic of this chapter, the

---

1 To see Confucianism as religion is questionable and seems to be limited to Indonesia.

https://doi.org/10.1515/9783110747607-004

Endangered Archives Program of the British Library, and programs of the national and regional offices of the Ministry of Religious Affairs in Indonesia and several others in island and mainland Southeast Asia. Below we will explore some of the challenges we met, and their solutions based on our own experience with the DREAMSEA digitization program.[2]

DREAMSEA

The Digital Repository of Endangered and Affected Manuscripts in Southeast Asia (DREAMSEA) is a cooperation between Hamburg University in Germany and the Center for the Study of Islam and Society of the State Islamic University Syarif Hidayatullah in Jakarta, Indonesia. The program started in December 2017 and will end in December 2022, while an extension due to the COVID-19 Pandemic has added more years to its lifespan. The program is funded by Arcadia, a Charitable Fund established by Lisbet Rausing and Peter Baldwin based in London. Its website displays the objectives of the foundation: "Arcadia supports work to preserve endangered cultural heritage, protect endangered ecosystems, and promotes access to knowledge. Our aim is to defend the complexity of human culture and the natural world, so that coming generations can build a vibrant, resilient and green future."[3] The Endangered Archives Program mentioned above is also funded by Arcadia. DREAMSEA is a project and it is unclear how much longer it will continue. However, the danger Van Lit identified for project-based digitization programs[4] is no problem here because the maintenance of the digital environment is assured since the DREAMSEA database is hosted by Hill Museum and Manuscript Library (HMML) in Minnesota.[5]

DREAMSEA's aim is to digitize as many privately-owned manuscript collections as possible that are in danger of becoming lost for a variety of reasons that will be explained below. The program has been devised to ensure that the religious and cultural variety found in manuscript cultures in the region of Southeast Asia will be

---

[2] For an earlier introduction to the DREAMSEA programme see: Dick van der Meij and Jan van der Putten, "Preserving manuscripts for future generations. The digital repository of endangered and affected manuscripts in Southeast Asia (DREAMSEA)," *IIAS Newsletter* 88 (2021): 44–45.
[3] Arcadia, https://www.arcadiafund.org.uk/.
[4] See: L.W.C. van Lit, *Among Digitized Manuscripts. Philology, Codicology, Paleography in a Digital World.* (Leiden: Brill, 2020), 54.
[5] For more about HMML amazing work visit: Hill Museum and Manuscript Library, https://hmml.org/.

preserved through digitization by presenting the images and their accompanying metadata in open-access online databases to be used by anyone interested in them.[6]

So far 44 missions have been made in total, 40 of which in Indonesia and the remaining 4 were carried out in Laos and Thailand. These missions have yielded a grand total of 7353 digitized manuscripts.

To express the program's appreciation for the care and love the manuscript owners have in preserving their manuscripts, social media and a website have been added to the program to build a community of people who share interest in manuscripts and their contents. In this way, DREAMSEA endeavors to enhance interest in Southeast Asian manuscripts, not only in the area itself but also in the world at large. We ensure that the manuscripts stay where they are with their owners and give advice on better preservation techniques and practices which, in Indonesia, we do in cooperation with the professional staff of the Indonesian National Library.

Manuscripts and Threats to Their Continued Existence in Their Original Surroundings

Many manuscripts in Southeast Asia are owned by private individuals, religious schools, temples and monasteries, while others are preserved in libraries and museums. There are multiple threats to manuscripts and manuscript traditions in Southeast Asia both privately and publicly owned. The first is the physical threat of mismanaging existing manuscripts, but perhaps an even bigger threat is the dwindling attention to and appreciation for manuscripts as text containers. As physical objects they are now often seen as objects to get rid of — and indeed many have been thrown away or burned in the past[7] — or as artifacts that can be traded or displayed in showcases but play no longer any other role in modern society at present and probably also not in the future. We should not forget that the manuscript collections are privately owned and the owners are free to do with their manuscripts as they please. This means that a collection today may not be the same collection tomorrow. Manuscripts may have been added or manuscripts may have been removed.[8]

---

6 See: DREAMSEA Repository, https://www.hmmlcloud.org/dreamsea/ and DREAMSEA, https://dreamsea.co/.
7 For threats to manuscripts in Indonesia, see: Dick van der Meij, *Indonesian Manuscripts from the Islands of Java, Madura, Bali and Lombok* (Leiden: Brill, 2017), 144–147.
8 See also below about the collection of Mr. Lulut Santosa in Malang, East Java.

Fig. 1: Seriously damaged manuscript from Kuningan, Indonesia (2018). (DREAMSEA).

Existing manuscripts in Southeast Asia are often in danger of irreplaceable damage caused by accidental or intentional mistreatment, neglect, moist tropical climatic circumstances, insects and other pests, natural disasters and social and political upheavals (see Figs. 1, 2 and 3). Often manuscripts are not handled properly because they are owned by people who simply have no idea how to treat them better as nobody in their immediate surroundings can advise them or because nobody is aware that manuscript collections even exist. Most people also have other things on their minds like making a living and seeing their children through school and their manuscripts are not the focus of their daily attention. Because of these circumstances, it is safe to say that many manuscripts are now already in precarious condition and undoubtedly will further deteriorate in the near future, so that their contents will become lost forever.

In many parts of Southeast Asia, manuscripts are considered heirlooms handed down from generation to generation and never read or even looked at. We should not forget that in the field, manuscript are not necessarily seen as highly valued objects to be preserved in national libraries or other, specialized repositories. We should also remember that in many places, texts people need can simply be bought in bookshops and nowadays downloaded from the internet. In some rare places in Southeast Asia, such as Bali, manuscripts remain objects of daily use, are still being produced today and used in religious ceremonies and educational

Fig. 2: Storage conditions of manuscripts in a temple in Nam, Thailand (2018). (Dick van der Meij).

institutions.[9] However, because digitization missions have been visiting manuscript owners, some people have started to consider their private and other collections in a different light and some collectors now view their manuscripts as objects worth of attention and as cultural and religious heirlooms to be proud of, and possibly to be used for financial gain when need arises. Whether this is only a temporary phenomenon and attention will fade over time remains to be seen.

It stands to reason that in the twenty-first century, many consider manuscripts as relics of a more or less ancient past and they are considered to have been surpassed by modern, technologically advanced modes of reproduction through the

---

9 This is, for instance, the case in Bali where many rituals require the presence of handwritten manuscripts. Writing palm leaf manuscripts has recently been given a serious boost by the present Governor of Bali who has a keen interest in the continuation of manuscript writing practices.

Fig. 3: Storage conditions of manuscripts in Bau-bau, Indonesia (2018). (DREAMSEA).

printing press and computer printing, and texts in digital versions. Moreover, former types of expression have now become rare and not infrequently, texts have become totally incomprehensible to the general public. This is because much of the vocabulary in these texts has been forgotten, and no reliable dictionaries exist for many languages and no knowledgeable scholars exist anymore. This is because literary styles and codes have changed and the local scripts used in manuscripts have been abolished for political, economic, or practical reasons and replaced by Latin[10] or Arabic script.[11]

As few people are still able to read the scripts used in the manuscripts, the interest in and attention for manuscripts has dwindled seriously and modern media such as cellular telephones and laptops have seen the departure from reading manuscripts (and printed materials, for that matter) on a global scale, including in Southeast Asia. People who still copy the occasional manuscript in the region

---

10 Because Javanese script takes up a lot of space, it was already largely replaced by Latin script during colonial times. The knowledge of the local scripts was also not helped by programs that made Roman transcriptions of manuscripts causing scholars to resort to them rather than the manuscripts in their original scripts.

11 In Muslim Java, Javanese script is no longer used for texts in Sundanese, Javanese and Madurese and in the past it was replaced by a form of Arabic script — called *pegon* — adapted to the requirements of the Javanese language. Malay was written in a similar script called *jawi* and in South Sulawesi the adapted Arabic scripts is called *serang*. It was rumoured in Java that a fatwa had been issued prohibiting the production and reading of materials in Javanese script.

Fig. 4: *Mocoan*-reading session in Banyuwangi at the Eastern tip of Java (2019). (DREAMSEA).

are few and far between and despite governmental and private efforts to preserve and even revive the craft, there is a great chance that the art of copying texts or producing artful manuscripts in calligraphic scripts will soon be lost or reserved to a very limited number of people in Southeast Asia. Not only the skill to write the scripts is dwindling, the often complex and long processes to prepare organic traditional writing supports, such as palm leaf (usually called *lontar* in Indonesia)[12] or tree bark paper, are becoming rare or are taken up by professional book and paper conservators who may use this material to repair and preserve older items in collections. In certain areas of Southeast Asia such as in Thailand and Java heritage programs may aid such activities of trying to reinvent the tradition of the production of tree bark books or local papermaking methods. At present, in Bali, school children have to learn to write Balinese script on palm leave materials and new businesses have sprung up to cater for this market and their owners prepare the palm leaves themselves or do so in cooperation with others (see Fig. 5). In Denpasar, the regional capital of Bali, *lontar* leaves, the knives (*pangrupak*) to inscribe them and the black soot (*kemiri hitam*) to blacken the inscribed letters can be bought in bookshops.

---

12 For an extensive description of *lontar* manuscripts see: Van der Meij, *Indonesian Manuscripts*, 152–242.

Fig. 5: I Nyoman Oka. The poster behind him mentions the lontar products he sells (2022). The poster mentions the products he sells: Palm leaves for writing, writing knives, wooden boards, black candle nuts, decorated palm leaf manuscripts, A3 posters. (Dick van der Meij).

For a number of reasons, in most if not all nations in Southeast Asia the reading and interpretation of handwritten texts is nowadays only being done by a handful of people as they have turned into subjects for which no or little employment exists (see Fig. 4). Institutions of higher learning have trouble finding students to study older texts written in older languages and scripts and the students they do have often choose this subject to be able to study at the university at all even though it is not the main subject of their choice. Once they finished their studies they seldom, if ever, return to the manuscripts they studied before.[13]

---

[13] It may be useful to mention that literary texts from manuscript used to be known as "sastra skripsi" or thesis literature.

Finding Manuscript Collections

In Indonesia DREAMSEA cooperates with MANASSA (Masyarakat Pernaskahan Nusantara/Indonesian Association of Manuscript Scholars), which comprises a wide network all over the country with much knowledge about small local manuscript collections that may be digitized. The cooperation between the DREAMSEA Program and MANASSA has proved indispensable in tracking private collections all over the country. As similar networks do not exist on the mainland, tracing manuscript collections poses a larger challenge and DREAMSEA depends on private networks of scholars in the field of manuscript studies. Looking for manuscripts outside MANASSA's network is in Indonesia also not easy, but in some cases the owners come to us quite unexpectedly. This was the case when DREAMSEA's liaison officer and academic advisor Dick van der Meij was in Malang, East Java where he gave a lecture one day. He was approached by Mr. Lulut Edi Santosa, a keen manuscript collector, who showed him and the audience some of his manuscripts. Contacts were made and the collection was assessed, after which one of the field teams digitized this interesting collection of 60 mostly Javanese manuscripts and archival documents.

The DREAMSEA team tries to find manuscript collection in many different places in the country to preserve manuscript contents of as many different cultures as possible. This may mean that collections are skipped in favor of other collections. However, in future program extensions the program may return to places already visited and digitize manuscripts that have not been digitized so far. Also, collections that have already been digitized may need to be visited again because since the first digitizing mission manuscripts were added to the collection. This is for instance the case of the collection of Mr. Lulut Edi Santosa.[14]

DREAMSEA Procedures

Once a manuscript collection has been found, an assessment is made to see if the collection is fit to be digitized. When this is the case, a formal agreement is made with the owner to ensure that the owner knows exactly what is going to be done and to seek his formal permission. It has not happened that permission was refused which means that the identifying teams use the proper approach to help the owners make up their minds. After this bureaucratic hurdle has been taken, a team is sent off into the field to digitize the collection. We take the blanket digitization approach which

---

14 DREAMSEA collection DS 0031.

means that each and every manuscript in a collection is digitized irrespective of quality, completeness and readability. The images we take show one page per image and they are not cut, so that the entire pages are visible. This is very important especially in view of the many Islamic manuscripts with marginal glosses.

Once the pictures and metadata are in Jakarta they are checked by the Data Manager and his staff and the metadata are translated into English. The images and data are sent to Hamburg for finalization and then dispatched to HMML to be uploaded on the DREAMSEA database.

Challenges

Because of the large variety of languages and scripts and the many different writing supports used for the production of manuscripts in the region, in many cases the technical digitizing process posed a challenge. This means that DREAMSEA is highly dependent on local people and experts to ensure that the manuscripts are digitized properly and no pages are skipped because people cannot read the numerals used in the pagination or pages are done twice because the script is unknown. The materials used as writing support range from imported European paper, with or without watermarks, which we predominantly find in insular Southeast Asia where the manuscripts are often in a book form bound in a middle eastern binding or as modern customized notebooks. The most frequently encountered manuscripts in Indonesia have the format of the Western book. Some manuscript cultures in Indonesia use the beaten inner tree bark (*tapa*) of mulberry or other trees as writing support for manuscripts or to strengthen the bindings of written books. In Java this material is named *dluwang* but it is also known from other parts of Southeast Asia, such as Thailand where texts were written on Saa paper.[15] The material is normally somewhat sturdier than European paper. Most common in Thailand are leporello manuscripts in which the tree bark writing support is folded in a concertina or harmonica way, while different parts are glued together to extend the manuscript's length. This book format is also found among the Batak in North Sumatra, where they are called *pustaha* and reserved to contain notes on divination, medicine and various types of magic.[16] The Batak also used other organic materials to carry other

---

[15] For an exhaustive description of *dluwang* paper and its manufacture see: René Teygeler, *Dluwang; Cultural-Historical Aspects and Material Characteristics* (Leiden: Leiden University Faculty of Languages and Cultures of Southeast Asia and Oceania, Projects Department, 1995).
[16] On *pustaha* see: René Teygeler, "Pustaha; A study into the production process of the Batak book, Manuscripts of Indonesia," *Bijdragen tot de Taal-, Land- en Volkenkunde* 149 (1993): 593–611; Jan

types of texts such as laments, divination calendars and threatening letters on prepared bamboo sticks and tiles, while spells and divination tables were inscribed on buffalo bones, particularly the shoulder blades. Other manuscript cultures in Sumatra quite frequently used prepared animal skins, bones and other materials to record their messages. The most common and variable other material used as writing support are palm leaves that we find throughout the mainland and in parts of maritime Southeast Asia where Indianized cultural productions have been preserved, such as in Java, Bali, Madura, Lombok and some other parts such as South Sulawesi. It doesn't come as a big surprise that these different materials pose their own challenges in capturing the details of the writing on the manuscript, which are needed so that the digital images can indeed function as true representative surrogates of the original manuscripts. It is extremely important that the metadata and the images are of a very high quality, so that the images do not blur when enlarged.

It may be clear that in the digitizing business the norm is set by the format of Western-produced books, for which many techniques and instruments have been developed and adjusted to capture everything. In the West the digitizing is done in libraries with state-of-the-art equipment and comfortable tables, chairs and the perfect lighting. But how about conditions in the field? How do we capture a meters long paper manuscript that is brittle and partly darkened by water stains? What if some parts of the manuscript still allows for digitization whereas other parts are so badly damaged that the digitizing itself means its final destruction. As a short reminder of what DREAMSEA is doing, we want to make clear that we normally digitize on location, in the house of the collection owner. Although the circumstances are not always optimal, to put it mildly, we prefer to keep the manuscripts to be digitized at the premises of their owners to avoid misunderstandings and to allow the owners to be present during the digitizing process. This is often not an ideal situation and setting up the camera stand and the camera lights pose problems that are solved on the spot. This means that the digitizing process is often even done on the floor as a proper table and chairs are unavailable (see Fig. 6). In certain missions, e.g. for certain repositories in Laos, we had the chance to take the manuscripts out of their location and bring them to the office of our local partners where conditions for the digitization are more favorable.

---

van der Putten and Roberta Zollo, *Ausstellungskatalog "Die Macht der Schrift: Die Manuskriptkultur der Toba-Batak aus Nord-Sumatra" / Exhibition Catalogue "The Power of Writing: The Manuscript Culture of the Toba Batak from North Sumatra,"* Manuscript Cultures 14 (Hamburg: Centre for the Study of Manuscript Cultures, 2020).

Fig. 6: Digitizing on the floor in Palembang, South Sumatra, Indonesia (2018). (DREAMSEA).

It is clear that digitization conditions at the modest homes of the collection holders differ dramatically from those in libraries and other official repositories, especially in the West, where the equipment is often technologically far more advanced and manuscripts are taken to the equipment rather than the other way around. Below, we will give a few descriptions of digitizing missions undertaken by our teams.

Metadata

Special forms were created to standardize the metadata to be made for each manuscript. The information gathered pertains to the collection itself and its owner and guardian history, manuscript numbers and metadata pertaining to measurements, numbers of written and blank pages, colophons and so on. It appeared that simply filling in forms is not something everyone can do and checking the metadata proved a very time-consuming and elaborate task. It also transpired that not everybody was equally convinced of the importance of good metadata even after having been trained about the use and importance of metadata, how to make them and how to fill out the forms.

Before discussing the metadata further, it may be good to put Indonesian manuscript studies in their proper scholarly context. Behrend (in a review of Van der

Meij 2017) summarizes expertly what the state of the art in Indonesian manuscript studies is:

> When compared to other academic disciplines focused on manuscript traditions, those associated with the Indonesian archipelago have a poorly developed set of scholarly tools. The plethora of reference works available to researchers in Classical Studies, to take an example, includes libraries of concordances, lexicons, historical and dialectical dictionaries, geographical, technical and personal onomastica, vast catalogues of scholia, searchable lexical corpora, mythological dictionaries, encyclopaedias of various sorts, thousands of critically edited texts [...] The list goes on. By comparison, Javanese, the most highly developed philological field for Indonesia, has not a single published concordance [...]

Indeed. We also do not have any of the other reference works. When faced with manuscripts in the field that are heavily damaged, incomplete, untitled and fragmentary, we cannot draw on the materials Behrend mentions because we simply do not have them.

Another challenge the DREAMSEA Program is facing in the production of the metadata of the manuscripts is that no person in Southeast Asia is able to understand all the languages and read all the scripts used in the manuscripts or would be knowledgeable about their contents. We should not forget that many manuscripts contain multiple texts in multiple scripts and in multiple languages so that a proper assessments of their contents is a difficult job. Moreover, as usual, many manuscripts have no titles, are seriously damaged and incomplete and lack the start and/or end of the text and some manuscripts only consist of a few pages. We should also not forget that some texts are known under multiple titles and this is not always known by the person who compiles the metadata. This makes identifying the texts very hard and sometimes virtually impossible. When the manuscripts have no title, titles are assigned and written between square brackets. This leaves the problem of the interpretation as to what the contents of the manuscript is and what the title might be to the expert. Manuscripts that are written partly in Arabic, partly in a local language in its adapted form of Arabic script with additional pages, for instance in Javanese, are often encountered. Proper descriptions of these manuscripts are also not easy as a decision has to be made about how much detail to include. In these cases it is even hard to make a choice whether the text direction is from left to right or from right to left as both occur in the same manuscript.

A very good example of the challenges manuscripts pose appeared from the mission one of the digitizing teams did in Northern Thailand where many manuscripts were written in the old Tham Lan Na script that is different from modern Thai. Much of the time the team spent in the field was used to transcribe colophons from one into the other script so that they could be typed to make them recognizable and understandable to a more general public. The academic advisor in the team was the senior scholar Chaichuen Khamdaengyodtai who is well versed in the Than Lan Na script. Giving a proper summary of the contents of a manuscript in an unfamiliar script and language can lead to serious mistakes that need to be corrected with the help of local or international experts. Therefore, it is important that the work is done as accurate as possible, but as we use a relatively large number of different people as members of the digitizing teams, the next challenge of maintaining consistency in the metadata between teams, manuscript cultures, languages and nations within the Program is extremely difficult to overcome and very time-consuming. A big challenge in the metadata was also posed by large collections of hundreds of manuscripts made in Laos. The texts in these manuscripts were often the same but the summaries in the metadata were not and they had to be standardized one by one. Similar problems occurred with texts with an Islamic content that were digitized in different areas in Indonesia. Each team had its own way of summarizing contents and streamlining these will prove a serious challenge in the future, when the cataloguing process of the digitized manuscripts will start.

Training

At the start of the DREAMSEA Program in 2018, techniques of digital photography in the field together with the recording of basic metadata and anticipation and solution to mishaps that may occur on location were explained by Walid Mourad, the director of field operations of the Hill Museum & Manuscript Library, based in Beirut. During a two-day workshop this highly experienced photographer conducted an intensive workshop and training for a select company of members of the Indonesian MANASSA Association and several members of digitizing teams who were to work on the mainland. The results of this workshop and the training sessions were recorded and turned into a manual in Indonesian and English to be used in subsequent training sessions and workshops. After further development and testing these manuals in smaller sessions in Indonesia, the Department of Southeast Asian Studies at the University of Hamburg took care of their translation into Thai, so that they could be used as reference material in training workshops in Thailand and Laos as well. This plan materialized in May 2018, when members of the DREAMSEA field station in Jakarta and Hamburg participated in a workshop at the Nan Buddhist College, Mahachulalongkornrajavidyalaya University in Thailand. The two-day workshop there made it possible to reconnect with some people who had also participated in the earlier workshop in Jakarta and to expand the number of members of future digitizing teams. The result of these efforts based on Mr. Walid Mourad's initial training was the establishment of several digitizing teams whose members are more or less familiar with the local manuscript culture they are going to digitize, who know how to digitize the manuscripts under not always very fortunate circumstances and who are able to record sets of metadata that enable further identification of the manuscripts, such as the colophon with data about the copying and the date and scribe, and other important data.

Due to training sessions and the experience of teams in both the islands and on the mainland, we can safely state that the quality of the images is high and that the texts can be easily read by viewers. Of course, elongated bamboo poles and sticks and other non-flat materials pose much bigger challenges in digitizing them, but the people in the field are creative in the ways to deal with such cases. So far we have not had to deal with this problem, though.

Still because of the quality of the digital cameras and the technical knowledge required for making digital images of these manuscripts is relatively simple for standard-sized paper and paper-related materials, the missions encounter relatively few problems that they cannot solve while they are in the field.

Field Trips

The field team members themselves bring along a full camera set with extra lenses, a copy stand, lightning and other equipment such as cleaning brushes and many others from the center in Jakarta or from one of the centers on the mainland. Sometimes, technical equipment had to be sent separately, as in the case of a mission in Palembang in Sumatra (Indonesia), where the copy stand could not be used and an extra tripod was needed. These technical issues often do not pose big problems and they do not prevent the production of clear images. Other problems that the teams encounter are socio-cultural in nature, such as visits of other people than the owners, last minute rituals to be performed before collections can be digitized and other time-consuming realities encountered during activities in the field where everybody is curious as to what is happening. The teams need to come well prepared because missions cannot be repeated and everything has to be done properly in one go.

From the first mission onwards DREAMSEA digitizing field teams are composed of five members, each with her or his specific tasks. Here again we need to stress the importance of the members of the Indonesian Association of Manuscript Scholars (MANASSA) who have been crucial in the operation of the DREAMSEA Program. MANASSA members make the first contacts with the manuscript owners and they usually come from the same ethnic and linguistic background as these owners and this familiarity makes things run very smoothly indeed.[17] Each team was led by a team leader whose tasks it was to coordinate and take responsibility for the whole mission and make sure that the digital images were sent to Jakarta through various ways to minimize the possibility that hard disks get lost during the shipping process. Next is the photographer who is familiar with standard operation protocol of the DREAMSEA Program and responsible for taking the images during the field operation and for the quality of the images. The third member is an academic expert — who is mostly a MANASSA member in Indonesia — who is familiar with the manuscript culture, the script, and the rituals surrounding the opening and reading of the manuscripts, and other particular reading practices of the manuscript culture. This person is responsible for identifying the texts in the manuscripts, checks if the texts in the manuscripts are complete, reads the colophons containing data about the age and copying process of the text and other relevant data that can be obtained on the spot. This academic expert is responsible for the recording of most of the metadata that need to be clear so that the text in its surrogate form can be identified and catalogued in the right way in Jakarta or in Hamburg. Quite often this expert is also the person who knew about the collection and its owner and made the first contact to negotiate permission to digitize. The members four and five are assistant academic advisors, local assistants, a local helper who assists in the process of carrying out the operation, and other people who help out.

The standard operation procedure followed by the team that goes to the field to carry out a mission is to collect the sets of materials that are kept at the PPIM office in Jakarta and in a private residence we use in Lamphun in Northern Thailand. These sets consist among others of two camera sets together with its lenses, brushes and other instruments to clean the manuscript surfaces, a copy stand, color checkers, foam to support the manuscripts for the digitization, and gadgets and paper to support the process. Upon arrival at the location where the manuscript collection is situated, after team members have renewed their acquaintance, if necessary, the other team members are introduced and the collection is inspected. Quite often there is quite some variance in the size and nature of the objects and we need to decide what the best digitization order is. Once a preliminary decision has been made, a table is set up (when available) and the camera and lighting equipment put in place. Team members start to clean the manuscripts and see if the writing is clear or not and if problems may be expected during the digitization process. Palm leaf

---

17 Almost all Indonesians speak the Indonesian national language, Bahasa Indonesia. However, speakers from the same ethnic background continue to use their own specific language, often in combination with Bahasa Indonesia, which feels more intimate and makes contacts much easier.

manuscripts with the writing symbols carved into the leaves may need some extra help to ensure that the writing is clearly visible in the digital images. First the leaves are cleaned with 90% alcohol and when legibility is found lacking, the leaves are blackened with the soot of burned candlestick nuts to make the incised script much easier to read. After cleaning the manuscript, the recording of the metadata starts by taking measures, checking pages and page numbers and making notes about or transcribing the colophon. Then the digitization of the first manuscript can start: a DREAMSEA number is given and shown on the photographs for easy recognition, lighting is checked and the photographer also checks the resolution and the result on the computer screen. One helper turns the pages or unfolds the leaves, while other members of the team prepare the other manuscripts and can also interview the collection owner or search for other data. Each team will keep a mission diary where notes are made about the collection, time of arrival, difficulties encountered, and other data, while there is also a documentary film maker to record visuals about the place and the mission, which after editing are put on the DREAMSEA website and also distributed through the DREAMSEA YouTube Channel.

To give an impression about a digitizing mission what follows are some samples taken from the diary of the mission to Indramayu in Java, Indonesia in September 2018.

Day 1: We arrived at the location in the district of Indramayu at 7 p.m. and we were welcomed by Ki Tarka, our local agent and we immediately went to Sanggar Aksara Jawa Kidang Pananjung where he is based. There we talked about how we would proceed with the digitization with the local people who showed us the manuscripts and who also held a performance of *wayang potel*, a shadow-play performance with an Islamic message delivered by a senior speaker accompanied by a gamelan orchestra and lady singers.[18]

Day 2: Over breakfast we had a briefing about how we would proceed with the concrete technical details. We went to the place where we would photograph the manuscripts which was in the Bandar Cimanuk Museum, where we made the setup in accordance with the DREAMSEA standards. Members of the team started to select the items to be digitized grouped by their owners. We first did the collection of Nang Sadewo and one owned by Archi Sadewa. His collection consists of 8 manuscripts. We cleaned the manuscripts from the dust and gave them DREAMSEA numbers (DS0017-00001 etc).[19] After the photographers started the digitization, other members of the team interviewed the owner, Pak Nang Sadewo, and another person who knows more about the origins of the manuscripts, named Pak Yayan. The latter told us that Pak Nang Sadewo inherited the manuscripts from Shaikh Abdul Manan. Several manuscripts that were mentioned in the initial report could not be digitized. We also bought

---

[18] Performances may be found on YouTube after searching for wayang potel or wayang potel channel.
[19] See: "DS 0017 0001," DREAMSEA Repository, https://www.hmmlcloud.org/dreamsea/detail.php?msid=1627.

an electric fan to cool the room in the museum. (On the Third day they digitized one collection, while visiting two other locations where collections were kept).

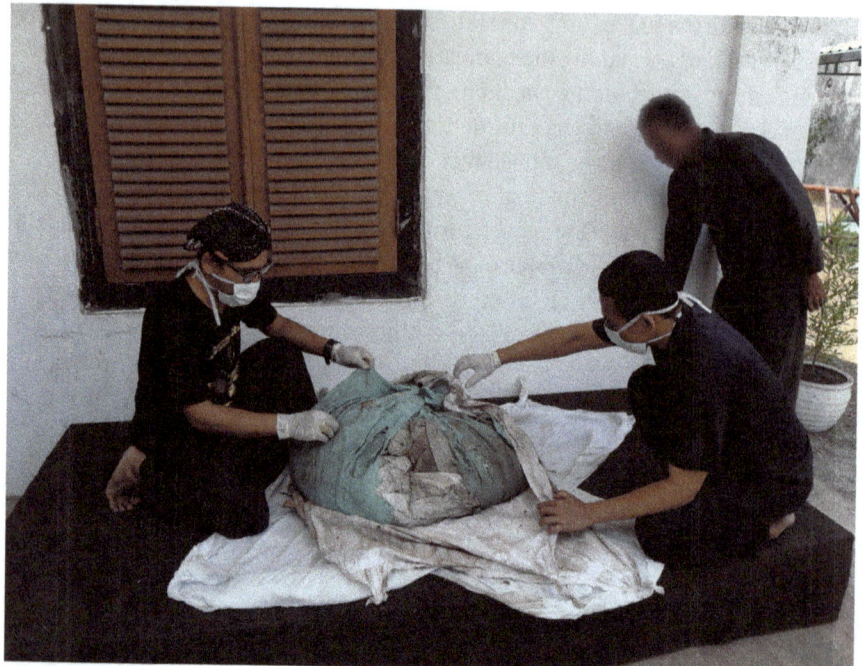

Fig. 7: Storage conditions of mostly palm leaf manuscripts in Indramayu, Indonesia (2018). (DREAMSEA).

Day 4: We continued digitizing paper manuscripts and started with palm leaf manuscripts as well. In total we digitized 750 pages today which means we now have a total of 3,050 pages. The digitizing today was very time-consuming because of the poor state of the manuscripts and we needed to be very careful so as not to damage them any further. A large number of loose and damaged palm leaves was wrapped in white cloth and the whole, called "buk" was considered sacred by the inhabitants of the village (see Fig. 7). After opening we saw that these contained quite some data about the historical background of the area. A big problem was that the leaves could not be ordered systematically and were quite damaged, but we decided to digitize them anyway as we found them. As the mission was scheduled to already have been finished, we contacted the DREAMSEA office in Jakarta and negotiated an extension so that the manuscript could be digitized. As a result of this we received an invitation from the village head of the village Legok — Lohbener which gave us an opportunity to promote the DREAMSEA Program in the region. During this visit and talking about the digitizing program, two additional owners of manuscript collections approached us with the request to digitize their collections as well. We assessed these collections and left them for a future mission.

Digital Scholarship

DREAMSEA adds to the wealth of manuscripts already preserved in public and private collections all over the world. Not every public collection of Southeast Asian manuscripts has been digitized so far. Some have, such as the collection of Indonesian manuscripts in the Staatsbibliothek zu Berlin and parts of the collections in the British Library and Leiden University Libraries or in the Indonesian National Library. The Centre for the Study of Manuscript Cultures at the University of Hamburg, involved in the operation of the DREAMSEA Program, has also been digitizing and collecting manuscripts, mostly in digital form, but these are part of research projects that are not openly accessible to outsiders.

DREAMSEA is also not the only program concerned with digitizing Indonesian collections. Many other programs exist at the national and sub-national levels and no comprehensive list of these programs and their websites exists at the moment. In order to enhance interest in manuscripts, a list is at present being prepared and will be uploaded on the DREAMSEA website where visitors will also be invited to add to the list to make sure it is as complete as possible.

Digital scholarship offers new and interesting opportunities for the kind of studies that were virtually impossible in the past. Because of the huge numbers of manuscript images readily available on-line, manuscripts from all over the world can be compared easily and new avenues of study are being explored. For instance, it is now possible to trace and track ways manuscript cultures travelled from one place to the next by comparing many manuscripts from different places. Now we can easily see that manuscripts with an Islamic content from Sub-Sahara Africa[20] can be compared with similar manuscripts from Aceh in North Sumatra and other places in Indonesia, which follow a very similar layout and conventions that are used also in other parts of the Muslim world. We see the same phenomenon: the main text is in Arabic and either around the text or between the lines we see glosses that contain translations and/or commentaries on the main text. Invariably, the main text in Arabic is in Arabic script and the text in the local vernacular is written in a form of Arabic script adapted to the requirements of the local vernaculars. We can now see that the way these texts were produced and used in education and moved, probably from Mecca, to different places in the world in the same or similar ways. The same holds for ways these texts are adorned with illuminations and rubrications that may point to cultural contacts between people never imagined before. In other words, the provincial ways of looking at manuscripts and

---

[20] See the Ajami project of the Center for the Study of Manuscript Cultures at: Ajami Lab, https://www.csmc.uni-hamburg.de/research/current-projects/ajami-lab.html.

texts needs to change into a global way of interpreting what is out there. Because of the new insights we may gain from these comparisons, we need to redefine our notions of manuscript numbers, manuscript texts and manuscripts contents that may shatter our views on popularity and or the impact these texts may have (had) in the Muslim world and in other manuscript cultures as well e.g., in a Sanskrit cosmopolis.

Another development that is pushed partly by the digitization of the manuscripts is the focus on manuscripts as objects and interesting text carriers, rather than only on the text they contain. To see manuscripts as objects that had or have cultural roles is one of the main principles behind the research projects that are conducted at the Centre for the Study of Manuscript Cultures at the University of Hamburg. On the one hand, we are digitizing manuscripts of many cultures and put them together to try to make relevant comparisons between the principles behind them, while on the other hand we also are expanding research to include the natural sciences, for instance, to discover the DNA of palm leaf materials to assess where the trees grew whose leaves were cut and prepared to be used as writing supports and the exact preparation processes involved in writing palm leaf manuscripts.

The Database

Last but not least we come to the database itself which is hosted at Hill Museum and Manuscript Library (HMML) in Minnesota in the US. As part of the cooperation HMML has provided DREAMSEA with a cloud to store and present the digital images and the metadata. This data may be accessed through the HMML website or at www.dreamsea.co.

The digitized images cannot be downloaded. The images have been provided with a watermark which sometimes may hinder the proper reading of the text.

As of now, not all the images that have been taken or the metadata of the manuscripts have been uploaded to the database. We are still working on this as the program is still in progress.

Following the criteria mentioned by Van Lit in his book *Among Digitized Manuscripts*,[21] we can concisely assess the quality of the DREAMSEA output as follows:

---

21 L.W.C. van Lit, *Among Digitized Manuscripts*, 64–68.

1. Size. The sizes of the collections digitized by DREAMSEA differ enormously from just some to many hundreds. Each collection is digitized in a blanket way so that all manuscripts are digitized and none are skipped.
2. Online. The images and the metadata are all free available through the portals of DREAMSEA (https://dreamsea.co/) and by clicking repository which will redirect the user to the DREAMSEA cloud at HMML: https://www.hmmlcloud.org/dreamsea/index.php.
3. Downloadable. Unfortunately, the images of the manuscripts in the *DREAMSEA* database cannot be downloaded.
4. Portal: https://dreamsea.co
5. Viewer. The images can be viewed in total and can be enlarged and otherwise manipulated. Screenshots can be made before and after manipulating the images. The images are very clear and easy to read. Getting used to the database and the ways the images can be manipulated may take some time as it is not always clear what should be done to get from one screen to the previous or next ones. A guidebook on how to use the database will be made and put on the DREAMSEA website for easy reference.
6. Page numbers. Page numbers are clearly indicated by the added verso and recto indications to the image numbers.
7. Resolution. The resolution of the images is very high. The picture's dimensions are JPEG 3:2 (L) 6240 x 4160/RAW: (RAW) 6240 x 4160. The sizes are 26.2 Mega Pixels while the photos in the database are 6–9 MB.
8. Color balance. We use a QP card 101 V4 to ensure that the colors are good and can be calibrated.
9. Lighting. Because the lighting in situ is unreliable, we bring light stands and lamps to ensure that the lighting is the same regardless of where the images are made.
10. Cut. No part of the pages or other materials are cut. We ensure that the entire manuscript support is visible on the images.

Conclusion

So far, most of the 44 digitizing missions DREAMSEA has executed were in Indonesia, while on the mainland we have been in Thailand (Chiang Mai and Lamphun) and Laos (Luang Prabang). That most collections were digitized in Indonesia is primarily due to the fact that Indonesia is by far the largest country in Southeast Asia and houses most of the different ethnic groups in the region all with their own languages and cultures. In Indonesia field missions were made to West Java (Kuningan), East

Java (Malang, Gresik and Banyuwangi), Bali, Lombok, Sulawesi (Makassar, Buton), Sumatra (Padang, Palembang) etc. This means that many places have not yet been visited and are scheduled to take place before the program ends. This also applies to mainland Southeast Asia where many regions have yet to be explored by DREAMSEA teams to search and digitize private collections that are under threat of being destroyed or get lost. With this in mind and because of operations that were seriously hindered because of the COVID-19 Pandemic during the years 2020 and 2021, we have managed to extend the initial 5 years of funding with Arcadia by two years.

As is the case with other programs, the previous two years of the COVID-19 Pandemic have seriously hampered the flow of this initiative because travel and social contacts were limited if not impossible because of the COVID regulations and restrictions. This situation has given even more weight and relevance to the continuation of programs such as DREAMSEA and making the data available to everybody through the internet that is easily accessible from our safe homes. We are convinced that this is the way forward in the preservation of text carriers and their study which are under threat of dwindling attention from students, but ironically hold huge potential for their study in the age of digital humanities.

Bibliography

Ajami Lab, https://www.csmc.uni-hamburg.de/research/current-projects/ajami-lab.html.
Arcadia, https://www.arcadiafund.org.uk/.
Behrend, Timothy E. "Th. C. van der Meij, Indonesian Manuscripts from the Islands of Java, Madura, Bali and Lombok (Handbook of Oriental Studies, Section 3 Southeast Asia, Vol. 24), 2017." *Bulletin de l'Ecole française d'Extrême-Orient*. Vol. 104 (2018): 409–411.
DREAMSEA, https://dreamsea.co/.
DREAMSEA Repository, https://www.hmmlcloud.org/dreamsea/.
"DS 0017 0001," DREAMSEA Repository, https://www.hmmlcloud.org/dreamsea/detail.php?msid=1627.
Hill Museum and Manuscript Library, https://hmml.org/.
Lit, L.W.C. van. *Among Digitized Manuscripts. Philology, Codicology, Paleography in a Digital World*. Leiden: Brill, 2020.
Meij, Dick van der. *Indonesian Manuscripts from the Islands of Java, Madura, Bali and Lombok*. HdO III vol. 24. Leiden: Brill, 2017.
Meij, Dick van der, and Jan van der Putten. "Preserving manuscripts for future generations. The digital repository of endangered and affected manuscripts in Southeast Asia (DREAMSEA)." *IIAS Newsletter* 88 (2021): 44–45.
Putten, Jan van der, and Roberta Zollo. Ausstellungskatalog *"Die Macht der Schrift: Die Manuskriptkultur der Toba-Batak aus Nord-Sumatra"* / Exhibition Catalogue *"The Power of Writing: The Manuscript Culture of the Toba Batak from North Sumatra"*. Manuscript Cultures 14. Hamburg: Centre for the Study of Manuscript Cultures, 2020.

Teygeler, René. "Pustaha; A study into the production process of the Batak book, Manuscripts of Indonesia." *Bijdragen tot de Taal-, Land- en Volkenkunde* 149 (1993): 593–611.

Teygeler, René. *Dluwang; Cultural-Historical Aspects and Material Characteristics*. Leiden: Leiden University Faculty of Languages and Cultures of Southeast Asia and Oceania, Projects Department, 1995.

L.W.C. van Lit
Getting Ready for the CV Revolution

Introduction

Images are for us who have human vision, a composition of objects. For computers, they are merely a raster, a table, full of color values. Computer vision is technology that allows computers to detect cohesion between pixels, coming closer to our ability to detect objects by sight. It is this technology specifically that I suspect will make a deep impact across the Humanities in the years to come. I will give four directions from which I see a move in the direction of computer vision coming. They are, in a way, the same story told from a different perspective. Together they show that truly a revolution is building up. I shall first describe the rise of computer vision from the technological side. Then we look at it from a data perspective. We continue with methods and how they have been readying us for using computer vision. We finish with the manpower required, and what role DH will play in this.

The Tech-Drums Call: Arise

When I was at DH2019, the leading international conference on digital humanities, I had an interesting conversation with a German colleague. She said that this was the *least* technical conference she had ever been to. This surprised me, as for me it was the *most* technical conference I had been to.[1] Looking onto the conference with fresh eyes, it did strike me as odd that the technology sector was missing. No generous sponsorships by big tech firms, no recruiters, no goodies. Instead, what we got was Gale coming at us with products like their *Eighteenth Century Collections Online*. Nothing wrong with that per se, but it was evidence of the *sitz im leben* of digital humanities. I would describe this *sitz* as one of essentially adaptors of technology. Early adaptors. But adaptors, nonetheless. We are in the business of sharpening the available technology, making it into specialized tools that do jobs just for us. For example, the TEI encoding standard is a way to digitally represent text in a scholarly fashion and was (and is) created by academic stake holders. But it is built upon XML which simply comes from the tech industry. Indeed, a survey by Barbot et al. on tools and technologies commonly used in digital humanities makes

---

[1] Not counting the several conferences, I attended as a Flash developer over a decade ago, or that one time when I went to Microsoft TechEd.

https://doi.org/10.1515/9783110747607-005

this patently clear: Of the fifty most popular tools and technologies, only six could be said to be developed from within the humanities.[2] These are Stylo by Maciej Eder, CollateX by the Interedition research group, TXM (Textométrie) by Matthieu Decorde and his group, Voyant Tools by Stéfan Sinclair and Geoffrey Rockwell and their group, Juxta by the NINES research group, and Palladio, by the Humanities + Design research group. Only three of them are in the top twenty. Considering these six tools, it should be clear that none of them are as fundamental as an OCR engine or a database format. They are either specialized analytical instruments or graphical user interfaces.

Further, all these tools are developed with text in mind.[3] Of course, text is the main raw material we work with in the humanities. But a very great part of our texts are only available in images. The digital surrogate of manuscripts and archival materials, and even many printed publications from the last two centuries, are scans and photos. Up until now, the digital humanities have not been ready to adequately use them. From a technological point of view, this is because the tech industry has not given us the necessary prerequisites to do so. Sure, there has been image manipulation and analysis for a very long time, but the technology was not developed enough to leverage it with relatively little cost in exchange for meaningful benefits. This is, to be sure, the right way of proceeding. Going against the tide of technology makes very little sense. There is an analogy from weather forecasting: in the earliest stages of modeling forecasts, it would take more time to calculate than it would to actually reach that point in time. For example, to forecast the weather in ten minutes would require a computation that would take longer than ten minutes. This translates to us, in the (digital) humanities, as a warning not to embark on projects that will be caught up by technology. This has mostly to do with the exchange of manual labor for automation.

So, when will we be ready? Whereas we rely on our eyes to assess a photo and immediately see objects emerge out of the shapes and colors; an image is for a computer nothing more than a roster, a table, with in each cell a combination of values (between 0 and 255) for red, green and blue. Each of these combinations is

---

2 Laure Barbot, Frank Fischer, Yoann Moranville, and Ivan Pzdniakov, "Which DH Tools are Actually Used in Research?" *weltliteratur.net*, December 6, 2019, https://weltliteratur.net/dh-tools-used-in-research/.

3 Palladio is an outlier, which actually fits better with seven other tools in this top fifty list that have been adopted by digital humanities but were created by the people and institutions from the GLAM world (Omeka, Neatline, Zotero, HathiTrust, EEBO-TCP, MEI, and KWIC). Three other tools should be mentioned here as well: Mallet, NLTK, and AntConc; these natural language processing tools come from computer science departments. The 34 other items of the top fifty list have no relationship with academia, let alone the humanities.

converted on our monitor to a pixel with a certain color. If we stand away far enough we do not notice the roster anymore, as pixels with similar colors will merge into shapes; but a computer will only "see" an image as a matrix of triplets.

The answer to bridge this gap has only recently matured enough to be used proficiently and effectively, and this is due to the rise of new machine learning technology. Its implementations are increasingly simple to use, and tutorials for it are coming online as we speak. Riding on the coattail of ML is a resurgence of so-called computer vision; libraries that try to give computers some of the discerning faculties that our human vision has, when presented with an image. This, then, is exactly the kind of technology we need, to handle digital photos. From lower-level languages like C, and more bloated ones like Java, these technologies now pour into higher-level languages that offer a greater agility like Python and JavaScript. It is the perfect opportunity for us in the humanities to customize them, with relative ease, into specialized analytical instruments or graphical user interfaces.

Of course, computer vision technology is not new to the humanities. But what I am talking about as the CV Revolution is that this technology is accessible enough to be used by individuals who did not major in computer science, using open source software on consumer hardware. It will be easy enough to be used directly by students and scholars as part of their toolbox.

For example, before, automated layout analysis had to be outsourced to colleagues in CS departments or to engineers, requiring large grants, a lot of waiting for development to finish, resulting in closed source software, sometimes vanished and irretrievable, with no way of checking whether the developed algorithms actually make sense.[4] Now we can be in control of the entire process, writing our own layout analysis tools. Not only does this allow us to develop in open source, with a greater chance of reusability across disciplines, it gives due credit to scholarly practices of reproducibility and falsification. Moreover, instead of going in one step from no layout analysis to full layout analysis, we get to see all the in-between stages which often times are valuable too. This makes the process akin to surgery, in which we dissect the digitized manuscript carefully, step by step, with freedom to go whichever direction we want at every stage.

I have had myself success with this, in the ecosystem of the programming language Python.[5] Some of my more frequently used libraries include PyPDF2

---

[4] Examples are Arianna Ciula, "Digital palaeography: using the digital representation of medieval script to support palaeographic analysis," *Digital Medievalist* 1 (2005). DOI: http://doi.org/10.16995/dm.4. and Hannah Busch and Swati Chandna, "ECodicology: The Computer and the Mediaeval Library," in *Kodikologie Und Paläographie Im Digitalen Zeitalter* 4, ed. Hannah Busch, Frank Fischer, and Peter Sahle (Norderstedt: BoD, 2017), 3–23.
[5] I develop within PyCharm and Jupyter Notebooks.

for generic PDF manipulation, PIL for generic image manipulation, OpenCV for computer vision, Tesseract for optical character recognition, NumPy and Pandas as companion analysis tools, TensorFlow and Keras for ML tasks, and Matplotlib and Seaborn for statistics visualization. If you are a student or scholar, now is a great time to spend an evening per week, or so, reading up, familiarizing yourself, eventually becoming proficient with these technologies. Librarians, too, can play an important role in this regard. It will be helpful in several regards if they connect their collections to somewhat-polished, user-friendly functionalities, such as RetroReveal, VGG, or any of the virtual research environments. Firstly, this helps us digital humanists do our tasks more proficiently. It will also help the dialogue between scholars and librarians for when researchers want to do more advanced things with the digital assets of a library. Lastly, it will introduce and normalize such use of technology to our peers throughout the humanities, paving the way for an ever-wider revolution.

The Data We Have Is the Data We Need

Technological innovations rarely cause a revolution in the sense of an overnight overhaul, as their innovative potential is usually realized in a two-stepped process. First they simply iterate on an existing need, method, or infrastructure. They improve it. But then it is realized that the way they have done so is conducive to optimization or development in an entirely unforeseen way, leading to spectacular growth. Usually, certain conditions need to be met in order for people to see, or realize, this growth potential. For example, other pieces of technology first need to be developed. Nevertheless, when those conditions are met, the process of understanding the technology in this new way requires a paradigm shift that comes only at great cost and very gradually. Often, traces of the earlier application remain. For example, cars were nothing but horse carriages without a horse. Over a hundred years, cars developed into something entirely different, and yet we still speak of horsepower. When keyboards were first made, they looked like typewriters, and we still use their QWERTY layout and speak of the return, reminiscent of the carriage return.

So, it is no wonder that when books and manuscripts were digitized, they looked like physical books and manuscripts. What I mean is that we have for the most part considered them to be such. They were digitized per artifact, per collection, all photos of the artifact held together. And as end users we encounter them as photos that we look at. These photos usually show page spreads like an opened manuscript, placed in a linear, sequential order, with buttons for browsing left-right as though flipping pages. The idea suggested here is that physical books come as a unit — all pages are physically attached to each other — and so it must be in for the digital surrogate. This suggests further that they are primarily for reading, preferably page after page. Indeed, often only those parts of an artifact with text will be photographed and put in sequential order. Further, the items are only visible on the library website as though visiting special collections or through commercial parties such as Google or ProQuest.

Then there is the curious case that digitized books and manuscripts are almost always exclusively made visible and findable by relying on existing catalogs that have themselves been digitized. This funnels users through the existing use case of using a catalog to find a reference to an artifact, then retrieving that reference to look at the (digital surrogate of the) artifact itself.

It may sound like this is obvious and that there is nothing wrong with it. Of course, you might say, we encounter digitized manuscripts as photos that we look at. My point is that all of this means that the digitized manuscripts are set up, and therefore used, as you would use physical books. The improvement is accessibility.[6] It is indeed great to see how fast I can pull up a certain manuscript and start analyzing it, right from my workspace at home and this has silently become a daily reality for many scholars.[7]

But the bigger that pile of digitized books becomes, the more pertinent the question becomes: now what? The amount of digitization has become so large that, as we continue to digitize more, we now can and should think of the next step. This starts by emphasizing not the "books" in digitized books, but "digitized," in other words, in other words, it is data. And data is not just something a human being can read and analyze, but something a computer can handle too. Letting a computer take a whack at it has, in fact, always been the greatest advantage of pouring stuff in the form of digital data, so it is the obvious next step for us to do with all those digitized books. In other words, there is a two-stepped process here: first we optimized access to physical books and manuscripts by creating digital surrogates, turning material manuscripts into digitized manuscripts. But with that optimization process well on its way and in fact in certain areas near completion, an entirely new optimization path lies before us. Instead of considering digitized manuscripts as *manuscripts*, we can also consider them as *digitized*.

As an emphasis on *manuscripts* meant that we wanted to see digitized manuscripts ourselves, the obvious implication is that an emphasis on *digitized* means

---

[6] A deeper dive into the pros and cons of digitization can be found in: L.W.C. van Lit, *Among Digitized Manuscripts: Philology, Codicology, Paleography in a Digital World* (Leiden: Brill, 2020).
[7] Silently because, when it is time to write the bibliography, only the actual artifact is cited as though the digital surrogate provides a neutral window onto the object.

a shift to letting computers "see" them. What could this "seeing" mean? As we use our human vision to see a manuscript, so we can rely on computer vision to see it digitized. To make that second step, then, and truly revolutionize the field of manuscripts studies, we need to tap into the growth potential that computer vision gives us.

Importantly, this argument goes both ways. What does computer vision need? Digital photos. Which we have. In fact, we have them in great quantity, for some collections or for some topics nearly completely. I think that this means that it is not only possible to actualize the growth potential that computer vision allows, but it is *time* to move forward.

We are at the cusp of this. Photos we have in stupidly large numbers. Computer vision technology is ready to be deployed. There are a few more conditions that need to be met in order for the floodgates to be opened and this CV revolution to be unshackled. They fall largely in the domain of the GLAM world. Galleries, libraries, museums will need to disclose their photos not only through a user interface on a website, but consider giving programmatic access, perhaps only to parts.[8] For example, set up an API and give researchers a private key that limits their use to a fair amount. It would be wonderful if such access would extend to the catalog as well, as the information that can be learned from them will be a great leverage to target those specific images that are of interest to a researcher.

Moreover, all parts of the artifact need to be photographed; the cover, the spine, fly leaves, etc. They may not be useful for reading the text, but will be great sources for collecting meta data.

Very importantly, digital watermarks should not be added to photos. They make looking at the photos difficult for human vision, but can completely upset computer vision.

That is not to say that institutions should not leave a trace on these images. Indeed, automatically adding holding information will be crucial since we will no longer be looking at all photos of just one artifact, but may pull in a large amount of photos of different artifacts, even different institutions, possibly in an automated, headless way.[9] Information on the origin of the photo will be crucial in order to determine later on from where it came. Such information could be placed in a

---

[8] The HathiTrust has some of this already in place. See: "HathiTrust Data API," HathiTrust, https://www.hathitrust.org/data_api.

[9] Headless refers here to processes initiated by human beings but executed without direct visual feedback on our monitor. See for example the photos I collected which according to the catalog of the Staatsbibliothek zu Berlin contains seals: L.W.C. van Lit, "Seals from the Staatsbibliothek zu Berlin and their automated detection," Zenodo, February 25, 2020, http://zenodo.org/record/3687296. DOI: https://doi.org/10.5281/zenodo.3687296.

tiny bar at the bottom of the image, so that the providence is baked in. I do not mean the providence of the manuscript production, but I mean your own place, your own library, the manuscript shelf number and the folio number. This would be a direct and easy way for users to keep track of what they are looking at. This is at the moment rarely done,[10] because we did not consider that a photo could be taken out of its sequential context away from the user interface on a website. Such information could also be in the file name, which would be convenient at point of download, but has a high chance of being changed in order to be normalized with other images so that you can iterate over them easier. Such information could also be in the file metadata, and it should be, but it has some chance of being changed too.

In short, then, if we get programmatic access, we have photos of all parts of the artifact, there are no digital watermarks on them, and there is providence information included, there is no doubt that the CV revolution will take off. For students and scholars, in this regard, there is one very important task. Namely, to keep nagging about what you exactly want. To not let your research be curtailed by what libraries offer currently, I mean the simple user interface, but to offer serious project descriptions even if they require API access. The data we need for computer vision, we already have it. Now it is time to restructure that data so that we can optimally make use of it.

Method Precedes Real Possibility

Academic work cannot be done in a vacuum. We situate our work among other works so as to add to the scholarly discussion. We do this based on methodology that gives us direction and a reasoned assurance that what we are doing makes sense. This means that the next, new idea has to land on fertile grounds or else it will wither. Too avant-garde does not bode well for scholars. For example, many ideas of the literary theorists of the middle of the twentieth century have only gained traction rather than lost. Their criticism seemed to be a dissatisfaction with several ways peculiar to the print world. Many of these points of dissatisfaction were solved with the rise of the digital world and its entirely different approach, its different epistemology.[11] At the time, their criticism may have sounded alright

---

10 To the exception of Bibliotheque national de France, which implements this quite nicely on Gallica, be it without folio number.
11 Cf. George P. Landow, *Hypertext 3.0: Critical Theory and New Media in an Era of Globalization*, 3rd edition, (Baltimore, MD: The Johns Hopkins University Press, 2006).

but with no real solution in sight, and yet here we are able to fully account for their criticism and work with it not only in an abstract, theoretical way, but on a practical level. It meant that once digital media, hypertext, the internet became real things, we had a fairly good way of knowing what to do with it, since the theory, the methodology, had already been developed.

Here is one example, from Barthes:[12]

> The goal of literary work is to make the reader no longer a consumer but a producer of the text. Our literature is characterized by the pitiless divorce which the literary institution maintains between the producer of the text and its user, between its owner and its consumer, between its author and its reader. This reader is thereby plunged into a kind of idleness [...] reading is nothing more than a referendum.

For manuscripts, the reader is the producer. For print publications, the medium, that is, publishers who bring about a text, is the producer. For digital documents, it is the author who is the producer. This means that the purpose is different in each case. The purpose of manuscripts is to be read. The purpose of print publications is to be transmitted. And the purpose of a digital document is to be written. This makes the act of reading quite different in each world. To exaggerate the differences, we can say that manuscripts are read charitably, engaged, and focused. Print publications are read docile and acceptant. And digital documents are read egotistical, only for a specific personal purpose. Often times digital documents are entered not from the beginning of the text or the beginning of a chapter, but at the very instance where a keyword search has brought them. And even though the digital document is presented as a fixed product, it can at any moment be changed by the reader, turning themselves into a writer, changing the document into a different fixed state.

There is another group of theorists or critics, closer to our times, for whom the same dynamic holds up. I am referring to the phenomena of New Philology and Distant Reading. In the nineties, they sounded alright but without a practical implementation conceivable. And so, they were accepted as perhaps interesting points of reflection, but made little actual impact.

New Philology was proposed in the nineties, spearheaded by Stephen Nichols. He started from the observation that among Medievalists (and, we might add, other premodern historians) "the medieval artifact [had become] the edited text." This led to an attitude in which "Surplus variations in the manuscript tradition cease to have critical interest because they simply reflect scribal errors," and nothing else. In comes Nichols, who says we have "seriously neglected the important supplements that were part and parcel of medieval text production: visual images and

---

[12] Roland Barthes, *S/Z*, trans. R. Miller (Oxford: Blackwell Publishing, 1990), 4.

annotation of various forms (rubrics, 'captions,' glosses, and interpolations)."[13] We may hear echoes of the work of Roland Barthes and Gerard Genette etcetera in this, but nonetheless it was a new and refreshing point made in manuscripts studies across the humanities. That being said, not a terrible amount has been done with it. Those who have pursued it, and I have seen very fruitful applications of it, are only few and they had to do it at the cost of a great amount of labor.

Meanwhile I would argue that the general trend has been a radicalization of the edited text as the perfect artifact. In the making of large digital text corpora, printed editions are used as a basis and the critical apparatus is invariably stripped away, leaving an even more radically pure and narrow version of the text as the representative of the medieval original. We are, then, creating more distance between us and Nichol's critique, instead of drawing closer to a resolution.

If you really want to know what a text says, this is unacceptable. I will give one striking example. Ibn Taymiyya is one of the great Muslim intellectuals of all times. He is also a favorite of terrorists, who pick and choose from his large corpus in a way that suits their needs but does no justice to the man himself. Take his so-called Mardin fatwa. I hope you will forgive me that I will skip over most of the details here and simply point out that in the earliest printed version this fatwa came to conclude that "non-Muslims are to be killed as they deserve." It was repeated in every print edition, was quoted by terrorists frequently, perhaps not as one of their strongest arguments but certainly with the idea that this giant of Islam would be supportive of their actions, and so it also entered the digital text corpora, such as *al-Maktaba al-Shamela* and the scholarly project OpenITI.[14] But recently it was pointed out that manuscript evidence shows that the conclusion should be "non-Muslims should be treated as they deserve" and in the context of the entire fatwa that means the exact opposite as the previous meaning; they should be treated with respect, not be killed.[15] This should show well enough that a print or digital text cannot be trusted by itself, if it is actually a manifestation of a historical, premodern text that is not native to the print or born-digital world.

The solution is, I suspect, a return to the actual evidence, exactly because this becomes easier and easier with more and more libraries digitizing their holdings. From digital text corpora we will increasingly step over the printed publications

---

13 Stephen G. Nichols, "Introduction: Philology in a Manuscript Culture," *Speculum* 65, no. 1 (1990): 7.
14 Al-Maktaba al-Shamela, http://shamela.ws and Maksim Romanov and Masoumeh Seydi, "OpenITI: A Machine-Readable Corpus of Islamicate Texts," Zenodo, May 20, 2019, https://zenodo.org/record/3082464.
15 Yahya Michot, "Ibn Taymiyya's 'New Mardin Fatwa.' Is Genetically Modified Islam (GMI) Carcinogenic?" *The Muslim World* 101, no. 2 (2011): 145.

and go back to the manuscripts on which ancient texts rely. But I want to be more ambitious here and say that it should not stop there. This is a great success in itself but it does not satisfy what Nichols was actually after, namely, an appreciation of manuscript culture that goes beyond the correct reading of the text. With a return to investigating manuscripts in light of suspect digital texts, the challenge that Nichols presents becomes only more apparent and pertinent.

Before we come to a solution, let us first consider the other thing I mentioned, Distant Reading. As I understand it, this came from Literary Theory and was coined by Franco Moretti. He construed the term as an opposite to close reading. He observed that we only focus on the classics that make up the canon, while, as anybody who has done archival work will know, the vast majority of literature ever produced is not part of the canon. So, are we not losing something significant out of our analysis if we toss aside 99% of available sources?

Here is the key passage from Franco Moretti's *Distant Reading*:

> One last thing that became clear [...] was the enormous difference between the archive of the Great Unread, and the world of the canon. You enter the archive, and the usual coordinates disappear; all you can see are swarms of hybrids and oddities.[16]

What he says here is that our usual methods fail to work when we approach a large, virtually untouched body of literature. We cannot do close reading because we will get nowhere with it. But this does not mean that this body of literature disqualifies for scholarly investigation, it means that we need to come at it with a different method. To remedy this sense of unbalance Moretti advocates that we should do Distant Reading on it. The idea is to find trends and string together different pieces of literature hopping in rapid succession from one work to another.

As he himself shows, this works best if we have the entire corpus as digital texts, because then we can let a computer do all sorts of analyses. The difficulty is that this not something we always have, especially for corpora that were not considered to be part of the canon. Even if we settle on using OCR for printed materials, and even if that OCR quality does not need to be good at all,[17] the objection still stands since the vast, vast majority of our archives are manuscripts. So, the Distant Reading approach has mostly been a dream. Some even think it has failed, being nothing more than a special kind of close reading, with little extra saying power.

If New Philology is interested in anything but deciding what the exact text of manuscripts should be, and Distant Reading is interested in anything but small-scale

---

16 Frank Moretti, *Distant Reading* (London: Verso, 2013), 180.
17 See for example: David A. Smith, Ryan Cordell, and Abby Mullen, "Computational Methods for Uncovering Reprinted Texts in Antebellum Newspapers," *American Literary History* 27, no. 3 (Fall 2015).

readings of what the exact text of an archival object is, then I think they haven't failed, they simply were ahead of their time. What both need is automated analysis of large sets of manuscripts, and for that two conditions need to be met: 1) they both need large quantities of manuscripts in digital format, i.e. digital photos — and this is something we now have through large scale digitization projects, and 2) we need software that can analyze that kind of data in a way that is meaningful to us, much like the software to analyze a corpus in plain text. What do we call software that does that? Computer Vision. And CV is now within hand's reach. Or rather, if you wonder what computer vision truly can do for the humanities, then look no further: The methodology was already there, this is only the practical realization of it.

Forget Everything You Know about Digital Humanities

The term digital humanities may be fairly recent, but its history goes back much further. From the very beginning, a pesky problem crept into the very fabric of DH. Namely, it sought and seeks to use the latest technology to research problems in the humanities so as to be at the cutting edge of tech and in this sense attempt to push the field of DH further. This is understandable, but it means that as DH has pushed further and further, a gap with let us say "classic" humanities appeared and this gap has turned into a *chasm*. This could lead to DH becoming, perhaps already being, incomprehensible by peers and colleagues in our fields, which will ultimately lead to a rejection by the majority who is not tech-savvy. It is not easy to make quantitative arguments that are well understood and well received in our fields and if a piece of technology is mystifying, it remains a black box and its results are not reproducible or falsifiable. These are, I think, serious objections to the use of cutting-edge technology because they make it fundamentally unscientific, and not suitable for scholarly use.

I actually think we are close to a breaking point and I mean it in the good sense. Instead of perceiving it as a chasm between "classical" humanities and digital humanities, it seems that these two are becoming merely extreme ends of a spectrum, with the middle part filling up. We can identify some archetypes to populate this spectrum. At one far end you have people who never have and never will use computational and digital methods, and these I call "ostriches." Talking about this will only make them push back harder. They can be found especially in more senior positions. After all, some of them wrote their dissertation by hand simply because there was no computer or typewriter powerful enough to do the complicated signs and layout that they needed. At the other far end we have what I call "believers": these are people who self-avowedly are in digital humanities. They are so experienced with technology, that their whole thinking has shifted a bit more towards the hard sciences and the tech industry. For example, they (perhaps you?) would not think twice to say "data" when they mean "texts," and would start setting up a Slack channel the moment a group project is conceived. These are estranging things to most people in the humanities who have never heard (or used) that before. Quite advanced on the spectrum but to the left of the believer is what I call the "spider": usually a professor who attracts a grant and builds a team around him- or herself. They would not write code themselves or even know all the technical ins and outs of it, but understand the general idea. Within such a team you could find believers, but because the spider brings them into a web of other researchers, the aim of the joint project is not specifically towards pushing the capabilities of technology, but applying them towards answering research questions that will be readily understood by peers. A smaller version of this team can also be identified on the spectrum: "the blind and the lame." Here we have a faculty member working on a much smaller scale with one or two developers, sometimes students, sometimes members of a DH Lab. The professor cannot take the technical steps, while the developer has no idea where to go: together they try to figure things out. Usually, the results are lacking because not enough resources were at their disposal and because something gets lost in translation between a humanities research question and a technological aim.

The most noteworthy archetype is an even smaller version of this joining of skills, namely in one person, a "centaur," whose head is firmly humanistic but whose feet are digital. This is an ever-larger group of people in "classical" Humanities who are using moderate amounts of technology in a considered manner to boost their research. This means that they will not use any and all technologies typically used within digital humanities. For example, you cannot do "a bit" of natural language procession, you either do it or you do not. It requires a large amount of preparatory time and serious investment in understanding how to use the technology. Done poorly, as is often the case for the blind and the lame, this can end up with research results that do not mean that much because either the statistics are inconclusive, the analysis is not flexible enough, or the dataset too small.

Instead, I would propose that three conditions needs to be met in order for this growing group of centaurs to pick up technology. They need something that is 1) readily available, 2) easy to use, and 3) will gain them results that closely align with their traditional training. What may come to mind is point and click software with graphical user interfaces and it this indeed a good step to get out of Microsoft Word and Excel and make creative use of, for example Evernote and Zotero, and from there move on to research environments such as Transkribus or Gephi. For such applications we are already seeing a much larger group of users than before. We are inching closer to bring non-GUI technology into the mix, and I think computer vision on manuscripts and rare books is a good candidate for this. The technology and the resources required are there, enabling us with relative ease to unleash this technology on meaningful resources, satisfying condition one. There is, admittedly, a learning curve here, because using computer vision requires proficiency with writing and running scripts by yourself, which is a considerable (psychological) leap compared to using software with a GUI. But there is a plethora of learning resources available, increasingly specifically for the humanities, and, importantly, there are high payoffs to be expected already early on. You can actually do "a little" of computer vision. This satisfies condition two. Lastly, computer vision will find a natural fit with "classical" humanities research, given that we already have the proper methodologies such as New Philology or Distant Reading. It need not dominate one's research agenda but may be just one piece in a larger project. This satisfies condition three and makes computer vision one of the most attractive things to do at the lower to intermediate level of the DH spectrum. It can greatly benefit the workflow, analysis, and end products of regular humanities research.

For this to happen at scale will take a few more years. For one, it would need to be more widely acknowledged that DH is not beyond a chasm but is a spectrum. Secondly, that not just some but basically everyone is on this spectrum. This will allow us to consider simple implementations of technology as part and parcel of our research and studies. Right now, it is still exceptional and outstanding to use digital methods in humanities research. In a few years, it will be less exceptional, more normal. In a decade from now, not knowing how to deploy digital methods will be a drawback.

Conclusion

Computer vision is no stranger to digital humanities, having been applied in a variety of ways. Indeed, its immense potential has been pointed out already, notably by Arnold and Tilton's *distant viewing* theoretical framework.[18] My point goes much further than that. Distant viewing is excellent, but it is only one, relatively limited, way of applying computer vision. Once we see that the traditional methods and questions of humanities research in most fields, especially ones occupied with premodern history, benefit from its application, we can see computer vision for

---

[18] Taylor Arnold and Lauren Tilton, "Distant viewing: analyzing large visual corpora," *Digital Scholarship in the Humanities* 36, no. 2 (2021). DOI: https://doi.org/10.1093/digitalsh/fqz013.

the multi-tool that it is. Once we stop using digitized manuscripts as manuscripts and start using them as digitized, as data, a whole new set of possibilities opens up. CV is the key to unlock this. This is not a dream but a fast-approaching reality. The development of technology has made CV easy to use. The data CV requires, digital images, is in ample supply. The methodological way of applying it was already thought-out decades ago with New Philology and Distant Reading. The number of people prepared and excited to take it up is growing rapidly. It seems, then, that we ought to ready ourselves for the impending CV revolution.

Bibliography

Arnold, Taylor, and Lauren Tilton. "Distant viewing: analyzing large visual corpora." *Digital Scholarship in the Humanities* 36, no. 2 (2021): 1–14. DOI: https://doi.org/10.1093/digitalsh/fqz013.

Barbot, Laure, Frank Fischer, Yoann Moranville, and Ivan Pzdniakov. "Which DH Tools are Actually Used in Research?" *weltliteratur.net*. December 6, 2019, https://weltliteratur.net/dh-tools-used-in-research/.

Barthes, Roland. *S/Z*, translated by R. Miller. Oxford: Blackwell Publishing, 1990.

Busch, Hannah and Swati Chandna. "ECodicology: The Computer and the Mediaeval Library." In *Kodikologie Und Paläographie Im Digitalen Zeitalter* 4, edited by Hannah Busch, Frank Fischer, and Peter Sahle, 3–23. Norderstedt: BoD, 2017.

Ciula, Arianna, 2005. "Digital palaeography: using the digital representation of medieval script to support palaeographic analysis." *Digital Medievalist* 1 (2005). DOI: http://doi.org/10.16995/dm.4

Landow, George P. *Hypertext 3.0: Critical Theory and New Media in an Era of Globalization*. 3rd edition. Baltimore, MD: The Johns Hopkins University Press, 2006.

Lit, L.W.C. van. *Among Digitized Manuscripts: Philology, Codicology, Paleography in a Digital World*. Leiden, Brill: 2020.

Lit, L.W.C. van. "Seals from the Staatsbibliothek zu Berlin and their automated detection," Zenodo. February 25, 2020, http://zenodo.org/record/3687296. DOI: https://doi.org/10.5281/zenodo.3687296.

Michot, Yahya. "Ibn Taymiyya's 'New Mardin Fatwa.' Is Genetically Modified Islam (GMI) Carcinogenic?" *The Muslim World* 101, no. 2 (2011): 130–181.

Moretti, Frank. *Distant Reading*. London: Verso, 2013.

Nichols, Stephen G. "Introduction: Philology in a Manuscript Culture." *Speculum* 65, no. 1 (1990): 1–10.

Romanov, Maxim. and Masoumeh Seydi. "OpenITI: A Machine-Readable Corpus of Islamicate Texts," Zenodo. May 20, 2019, https://zenodo.org/record/3082464.

Smith, David A., Ryan Cordell, and Abby Mullen. "Computational Methods for Uncovering Reprinted Texts in Antebellum Newspapers." *American Literary History* 27, no 3 (Fall 2015): E1–E15.

Jonathan Miles Robker
The (Hyper)Text of the Hebrew Bible / Old Testament: Digital and Online Environments — Their Impact on Considerations on the Text, Its Reconstruction, and Its History

Introduction

It is generally safe to say that most people regard the Bible as a kind of literary monolith, irrespective of what they think of its relevance for them personally. The Bible is the big, fat book with very thin pages and tiny print that many people have on their bookshelves and never read. Considerations of where it came from probably rarely enter the minds of most. I don't mean specifically how it got onto their bookshelves, but rather how the contents, the text itself came about, how it developed. In the minds of most, the Bible probably just *is*. Nonetheless, anyone who takes the Bible seriously, whether religiously or academically, should strive to understand the diachrony of the biblical text(s).[1] To understand what any biblical text means requires understanding what it meant when and to whom. Yet, the processes behind the development of that single-volume Bible on the bookshelf are not always clearly understood due to the complexity of its diachrony. This complexity appears on both a macro-level (the structure of a whole manuscript) and a micro-level (distinct variants in individual words) and just about everywhere in between (larger transpositions within a composition, lengthy additions or subtractions consisting of several words, phrases, or even paragraphs).

To garner the nuances of the Bible's textual diachrony necessitates access to the text in its various forms, going even behind the critical editions to the manuscript

---

[1] The comments and observations presented here reflect on the Bible generally, but could be refined further for any composition of biblical or parabiblical literature. The development of the Torah — or any individual "book" within it for that matter — shares some general similarities to basically every other biblical book, though the specifics might vary quite widely. Some books or portions of books underwent more editing over longer periods than others. New Testament works were generally edited over a shorter period of time than many works in the Hebrew Bible. Books like Kings exist in dramatically distinct versions in different languages. And different versions of the whole Bible vary even in their ordering of books. One thinks of the contents and ordering of Tanakh versus the various Septuagint manuscripts in respect to the "prophets" or even more idiosyncratic variants like the Peshitta's placing Job immediately after the Torah.

https://doi.org/10.1515/9783110747607-006

evidence itself. Such an objective presents an overwhelmingly inhuman task considering the number of ancient scrolls and especially codices of each version of each book of the Hebrew Bible.[2] And to this end digital artifacts (for lack of a better term), approaches, and tools offer an unprecedented opportunity to unveil the evidence behind the editions for anyone interested in the Bible as religious, cultural, and historical literature both in and of itself and in the environments in which it was composed and transmitted. That sounds like digitization offers promising — perhaps even perfected — opportunities to appreciate the biblical text. Yes, the promise is there, but that potential remains (largely) untapped, as will become apparent. First, this chapter will reflect on general issues in respect to biblical studies within the discipline of the digital humanities. Then, after a brief overview of general trends in the complicated diachrony of the Bible, this chapter will consider both of those aspects: what digital materials, methods, and tools are available, and what do we still require? More importantly, it will reflect on what is needed to get the discipline of Hebrew Bible where we need it to be regarding digitization. Ultimately, this chapter will commend some steps that many established scholars in the academy might find radical, but the transformation that these steps could provide could indeed radically redefine the discipline's paradigms. Essentially, the current and developing state of the digitization of biblical manuscripts and critical editions could enable the extraction and processing of all known biblical manuscript and collation evidence. This could in turn lead to a renaissance or reformation in text-critical and text-historical evaluations of the Hebrew Bible. The results of these new methods could even methodologically advance more theoretical approaches to biblical diachrony behind the attested manuscript evidence.

What Does the Bible Have in Common with Asian Religions?

Surely, some finding this piece in a collected volume on digital studies and Asian religions will ask themselves why the editors included a chapter on the Bible. Isn't the Bible quintessentially "Western"? Many see "The West" (polemically) as the propagators of "Judeo-Christian Values" or "Ideologies." That should certainly place

---

2 For the sake of brevity, I refer throughout this chapter to the "Hebrew Bible," but within that moniker should also be understood the various ancient translations of this collection, including the materials that are no longer known (in their entirety) in either Hebrew or Aramaic, i.e., works transmitted in the Septuagint and/or other ancient translations commonly known under the rubrics "Deuterocanonical" or "Apocryphal."

the Bible within the western tradition. And to some degree, one could rightly follow this argumentation. However, the relationship is actually reversed. The Bible is not some product of western religion, but an Asian product that widely impacted religion and culture in what came to be known as "the West." The Bible originated in areas that stand in the geographical context that we call Asia, in fact much more proximate to what the term "Asia" originally described than most of the regions and religions mentioned in this volume. Particularly regarding the Hebrew Bible, one would hardly consider Palestine or Mesopotamia as anything other than Asian. Mesopotamian, Syro-Palestinian, and Persian religions — all of which fundamentally impacted the Bible — are decidedly not European nor Western. The same observations remain true even for the New Testament in a general sense (Paul was from what is known today as Turkey; Jesus was a Palestinian Jew; likely none of the New Testament authors were from Europe). Sure, the New Testament was composed in Greek, but it is an international Greek found in southwest Asia. Not in Greece. But that does not present the primary impetus for this inclusion.

Many of the same issues that trouble the study of Asian religion in digital environments also hinder biblical studies. The Bible was not originally written in Latin script. Hebrew and Aramaic, in contrast to Latin, are written from right to left. Hebrew manuscripts in the most important tradition (the so-called Masoretic Text) contain superlinear, sublinear, and interlinear vocalization and accents, as well as paratextual notes and commentary about unusual orthographic or syntactic phenomena. While these helped secure the transmission of the text in Antiquity and through the subsequent centuries, they present hurdles for text recognition and the publication of digital editions contemporarily. Editors must consider what elements to include as "the text" and whether to present options to exclude certain elements like cantillation. In terms of morphological tagging, some distinct Hebrew forms share a common morphology, meaning that editors must decide to disambiguate or include multiple potential conjugations. Even the biblical texts in Greek, the translations of the Hebrew Bible known under the rubric Septuagint and in the New Testament, do not resolve such problems. Even though it reads from left to right, Greek script is obviously not Latin. The Greek manuscript tradition often contains abbreviations (*nomina sacra*), ligatures, and some rare cases of ancient Hebrew lettering that increase the complexity of processes like OCR/HTR. Since various forms of these abbreviations and ligatures exist among manuscripts from different periods and regions, it remains difficult to create a broad (to say nothing of universal) dataset for text recognition among Greek biblical manuscripts. Greek Majuscules do not leave blank space between words. These issues should sound familiar to anyone working with Asian religious texts.

Traditional Understanding of the Bible's Diachrony

The diachrony of the Hebrew Bible presents a difficult issue that is likely unfamiliar for many readers of this volume. For the uninitiated, a brief introduction is probably helpful.

From a historical standpoint, no one can really say when the Bible was written. We can postulate much about how the Bible came about, but no one actually knows. Traditionally, the historical-critical method in biblical studies has divided the history of any biblical writing (a book or larger composition) into two general phases: composition and transmission. Thus, two historical-critical methods address the Bible's diachrony: Textual Criticism (transmission) and Redaction History (composition). Each of these covers a postulated period in the development of the Bible's text, but only one of them — particularly in traditional understandings of the historical-critical methodologies — stands on empirical evidence.

The fundamental idea is that any biblical text was composed at some date and edited over time until it came to a fixed literary endpoint — the finalized text — at a specific moment in history. The methodology of redaction history, utilizing the results of literary-critical analysis, serves to reconstruct the compositional phases of the development of any biblical text from the moment the first letter of the text was written until it reached it final state.[3] After the date of the text's final completion, so the theory goes, we find manuscripts of the biblical text in various versions and translations, none of which (to my knowledge) is precisely identical with any other. Regarding the distinctions in these manuscripts, versions, and translations is the purview of textual criticism, i.e., the process of removing intentional and unintentional changes that occurred over the course of handwritten transmission to arrive back at the theorized ultimate version of any text.[4] In this traditional understanding then, each of these phases of biblical diachrony shares a fixed endpoint with the other. The method of redaction history traces the development of text *before* this endpoint, whereas textual criticism traces changes in the text *since* this endpoint. Graphically, one could consider it like this (Fig. 1):

---

[3] Cf., e.g., Uwe Becker, *Exegese des Alten Testaments*, 4th ed. (Tübingen: Mohr Siebeck, 2015), 81–103 and essentially the whole of Walter Dietrich, et al., *Die Entstehung des Alten Testaments* (Stuttgart: Kohlhammer, 2014) for examples of diachronic models of this process.

[4] Cf., e.g., Becker, *Exegese*, 16–41 for an overview of the methodology. For detailed analyses of the issues and witnesses involved in textual criticism, especially those mentioned here, cf. Alexander Achilles Fischer, *Der Text des Alten Testaments. Neubearbeitung der Einführung in die Biblia Hebraica von Ernst Würthwein* (Stuttgart: Deutsche Bibelgesellschaft, 2009) and Emanuel Tov, *Textual Criticism of the Hebrew Bible*, 3rd ed. (Minneapolis, MN: Fortress, 2012). The issue of textual criticism becomes essentially moot after the invention of the printing press, which created — for the first time — perfectly identical textual witnesses.

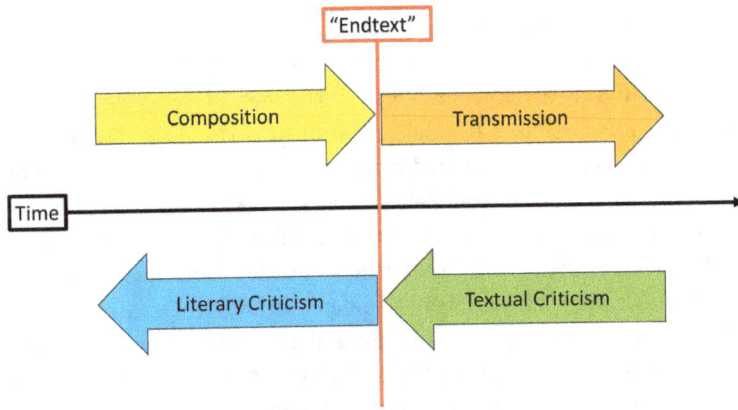

Fig. 1: A Traditional Understanding of Textual Diachrony in the Historical-Critical Method. (Graphic by the author).

As hopefully should be apparent from this brief overview, only textual criticism stands on empirical evidence attested in the actual artifacts of manuscripts, many of which have been collected and collated into critical editions. Redaction-historical reconstructions stand on postulates that may or may not conform to the demonstrable diachronic phenomena identified in the process of textual criticism. To this point we can return (in the conclusion).

More recent studies, focusing particularly on the manuscript and versional evidence (i.e., ancient translations and recensions), have demonstrated that this process was more complex than traditional methodologies suppose.[5] It remains difficult — perhaps impossible — to state with any kind of certainty when a biblical book's composition concluded. Only relatively sparse data from that fundamental period has been preserved, and substantial evidence comes from ancient translations of the Hebrew/Aramaic text. The earliest evidence illuminating the process of the finalization of texts comes from the translation of the Hebrew/Aramaic text into Greek (commonly known as "the Septuagint") beginning in the third century BCE.[6]

---

[5] For such methodological discussions and specific examples and counter-examples, cf., e.g., the volumes Juha Pakkala, Romeny Bas ter Haar, and Reinhard Müller, eds., *Evidence of Editing* (Atlanta, GA: Society of Biblical Literature, 2014); Raymond F. Person Jr. and Robert Rezetko, eds., *Empirical Models Challenging Biblical Criticism*, AIL 25 (Atlanta, GA: Society of Biblical Literature, 2016); and Reinhard Müller and Juha Pakkala, eds., *Insights Into Editing in the Hebrew Bible and the Ancient Near East. What Does Documented Evidence Tell Us About the Transmission of Authoritative Texts?*, CBET 84 (Leuven: Peeters, 2017).

[6] The Septuagint, particularly as used in common scholarly parlance, also should not be regarded as a monolith. It has its own remarkable editorial history, attested through several known recensions. For an introduction to these issues, cf. Natalio Fernández Marcos, *The Septuagint in Context*.

The absolute end of the process of textual finalization of the Hebrew Bible could be any time before the Vulgate in the fourth or early fifth century CE, since the Latin text it preserves and that text's presumable *Vorlage* generally matches what we would consider the final version of the Hebrew/Aramaic texts.[7] Thus, the process of finalization can only really be delimited from the beginnings of the Septuagint in the third century BCE until the completion of the Vulgate, some seven *centuries* later. We have manuscripts in Hebrew (such as the findings from Qumran and elsewhere in the Judean Desert) and Greek (such as Codex Vaticanus) that stem from that period. The evidence from this period demonstrates the transmission of parallel versions of the text in this era and not a single finalized version of the text. That plurality of versions means that the periods traditionally studied through text-critical (transmission) and redaction-historical (composition) methodologies were not conterminate at a single, fixed point. Rather, they actually overlapped for a longer period. That is, the commonly shared period between textual composition and transmission is not a single point, but a spectrum. We could consider drawing it graphically thus (Fig. 2):

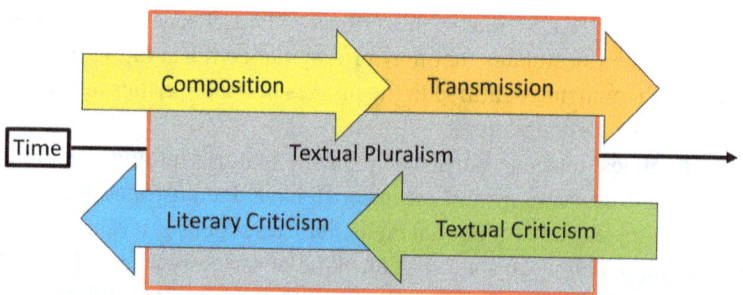

Fig. 2: A More Evidence-Based Understanding of Biblical Diachrony. (Graphic by the author).

Such observations have led us to recognize that — empirically speaking — the transmission of any biblical text was polyvalent. The manuscripts and versions demonstrate this. An example from my own research on the book of Kings could help appreciate what this looks like. Admittedly, Kings presents a single and particularly difficult case. It nonetheless hardly represents an outlier and suggests

---

Introduction to the Greek Version of the Bible, trans. Wilfred G. E. Watson (Atlanta, GA: Society of Biblical Literature, 2000). For methodological considerations of the use of the Septuagint in the diachronic study of the Hebrew Bible, cf. Emanuel Tov, *The Text-Critical Use of the Septuagint in Biblical Research,* 3rd ed. (Winona Lake, IN: Eisenbrauns, 2015).

7 Including the larger group of texts commonly identified as "Deuterocanonical" or "Apocryphal"; cf. Tov, *Textual Criticism,* 153.

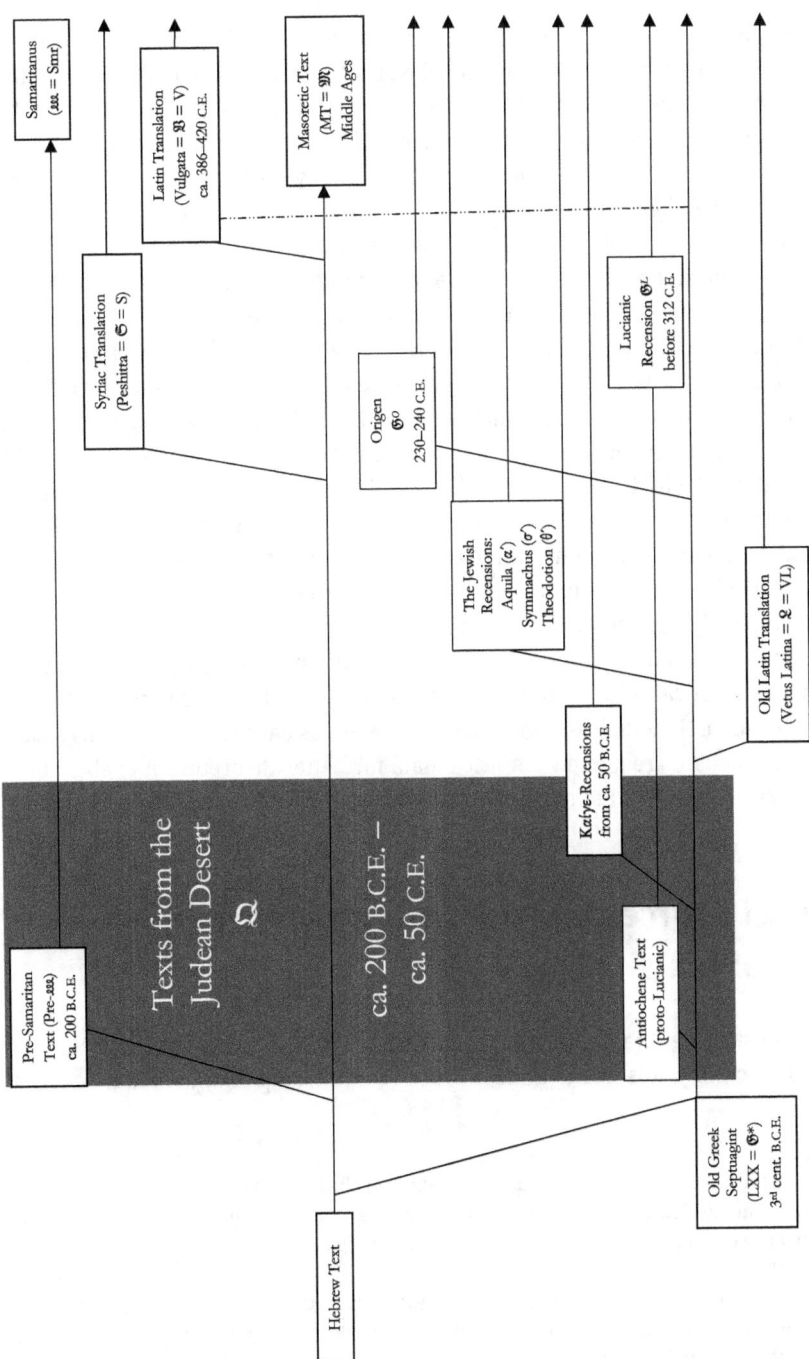

Fig. 3: General Text-History of the Book of Kings (Not to Scale). (Graphic by the author).

similar phenomena occurred in other biblical literature.⁸ Based on the known evidence, the text history of Kings, i.e., the attested transmission of the text of the biblical book of Kings may have looked something like this: Extrapolating from the evidence for the book of Kings and including other major textual traditions that do not contain Kings (e.g., Smr), biblical textual history must have generally looked something like Figure 3, To speak nothing of the diachronic processes that might have preceded the attested evidence passed down from Antiquity. And it should be noted that this image focuses only on larger strands of biblical tradition, not individual manuscripts. That brings us to the key point in all of this.

The best conception of the biblical text, any biblical text is not a monolith. Perhaps a more fitting image for biblical textual traditions would be a rope or a cord: a single broad structure, composed of many individual strands. Any strand's precise location in the chord at any moment depends on where you cut the cross-section. All of this is to say that biblical diachrony is complicated, with many manuscripts in several languages that cover multiple recensions and manifold variants, more than the human mind can comprehend. Adding to this, the relevant empirical evidence has only sometimes been collected and collated, often long ago or incompletely. Another added issue: this data — even when it has been precisely recorded — is not always widely available.⁹ Traditionally, help has been available in analogue critical editions. But some nascent work has begun to improve this in a digital fashion. Nonetheless, digital tools and methods have the potential to replace the analogue and create new empirical data for better theoretical models, should we desire to do so. But I am getting ahead of myself.

Digital Sources and Resources for Accessing Biblical Texts

After considering the substantial problems we face in reconstructing biblical textual diachrony, it is worth taking a look at some examples of the kinds of digital

---

8 Cf., e.g., the discussion and reconstruction in Julio Trebolle and Pablo Torijano, "From the Greek Recensions to the Hebrew Editions: A Sample from 1 Kgs 2:1–10," in *Insights Into Editing in the Hebrew Bible and the Ancient Near East*, ed. Reinhard Müller and Juha Pakkala (Leuven: Peeters, 2017), 267–293.

9 Here, I am thinking of undertakings like the *Septuaginta-Unternehmen* in Göttingen. Over the course of its lifespan, this project collated all of the known Septuagint manuscripts instead of transcribing them. Though that organization and its successors have all of this data, they do not make it generally available to scholars without question.

materials — both sources and resources — that are available. A number of projects, institutions, and even individuals have made the text of the Bible or of specific versions of the Bible available online. Some of these projects have focused on specific manuscripts or collections. Others have tried to make the Bible more generally available in a digital environment. Some focus on ancient language versions of the text and critical editions, whereas as other focus on modern translations. For scholars all of these projects are simultaneously beneficial and disadvantageous, though in idiosyncratic ways. Allow me to elaborate on some specific examples, starting with presentations of specific manuscripts before discussing critical versions of the biblical text.

Digital Sources: Online Photographic Facsimiles

What primary sources are available online for biblical studies? Published photographic facsimiles of many manuscripts — some of them fundamental to the diachronic study of the Bible — are available online. The list presented here is certainly not exhaustive, nor does it strive to be. Yet, it does feature some of the most important biblical manuscripts for the field of Hebrew Bible. The examples described here demonstrate the great opportunity of finding such materials online, but also embody some of the limits of these editions. I will handle the Hebrew texts first before turning to some Greek manuscripts. I have focused on manuscripts from these languages, since they are within my particular expertise, are generally recognized as important for biblical diachrony, and are provided online in photographic facsimiles. Within the bounds of Hebrew and Greek, the manuscripts are covered in chronological order, though it should be noted that the Hebrew manuscripts described in this section are centuries younger than the Greek manuscripts described here.

Hebrew Manuscripts

The Aleppo Codex

The Aleppo Codex is one of the most important Hebrew manuscripts of the Masoretic textual tradition, stemming from the tenth century CE.[10] It was a complete manuscript of the Hebrew Bible, but many folios have gone missing, including most of the Torah. Nonetheless, the quality of the manuscript on the whole and the fact

---

10 For a brief overview of this manuscript, cf. Fischer, *Text des Alten Testaments*, 52–53 and the introduction to the facsimile edition cited below.

that it was the oldest known complete biblical manuscript make it important. An analogue photographic facsimile of the manuscript has been published.[11] Currently it is being critically edited in the diplomatic edition of the Hebrew University Bible, though not much of it has been published to date.[12] (That should not be taken as criticism; it is a huge project and remarkably detailed.) The lack of a complete published typographical facsimile or diplomatic edition makes access to the manuscript all the more important.

In terms of online accessibility, the current state is apparently temporary and the future is unclear. For years the manuscript had its own website featuring a photographic facsimile of every folio of the manuscript.[13] This site additionally featured information about the manuscript's background and relevance, in addition to a user interface (UI) that allowed viewers to access specific folios based on the range of verses featured on the page. However, as this site was based on the no-longer-supported Flash technology, it is now defunct (at least at the time of this writing). In a personal communication from the site's administrators, I was told that another site is in development, though it had not been published by the time that support for Flash ended (December 31, 2020), nor to date.[14] The photographic facsimiles are still available online on the photographer's private site.[15]

With the transfer to this new site, several things changed. No background information is currently available. Nor is there is a UI for accessing specific folios or texts; rather, users have to scroll or page through each folio to find what they need. The folios are not tagged with information about the verses that appear on them. That makes finding a specific text particularly time-consuming. More importantly, the photographic facsimiles exist essentially in a vacuum with no available typographical facsimile that could be searched for specific terms or phrases. That was even an issue in the now defunct legacy website, but remains an issue to this day. The image files also now all contain a watermark that was not present on the older website. However, the image resolution is very good, making clear observations in crisp detail through the zoom function on the site possible. Since — as far as

---

11 Moshe H. Goshen-Gottstein, ed., *The Aleppo Codex. Provided with Masoretic Notes and Pointed by Aaron Ben Asher. The Codex Considered Authoritative by Maimonides. Part One: Plates* (Jerusalem: Magnes Press, 1976).
12 Only the volumes for Isaiah, Jeremiah, and Ezekiel have appeared by the time of this publication. As far as I see, their internet presence has more or less completely vanished, making finding information about the continuing development of this project quite difficult.
13 It was available under the URL http://aleppocodex.org/. Currently, this URL redirects to the photographer's site. See below.
14 22 June 2023.
15 Cf. "Aleppo WM," Touching History: Digitization Projects by Ardon Bar-Hama https://barhama.com/ajaxzoom/viewer/viewer.php?zoomDir=/pic/AleppoWM/&example=viewer5.

I know — the Hebrew University Bible project editions are unavailable in a digital version, digital access to the Aleppo Codex — while extant — is quite rudimentary and presents no advantages over the printed photographic facsimile edition.

Codex Leningradensis

The other primary Hebrew codex used as the basis for diplomatic critical editions such as the *Biblia Hebraica* series is Codex Firkovich B 19 A of the State Library in St. Petersburg, commonly known as Codex Leningradensis.[16] This august codex indeed presents the oldest known still complete biblical manuscript in Hebrew and Aramaic, dating to roughly 1008 CE. Like the related Aleppo Codex, an analogue photographic facsimile edition is available.[17] Unlike the Aleppo Codex, this manuscript has not had its own internet site, nor has the library that houses it made it available as a photographic facsimile online. Rather, should one seek a digital photographic facsimile — to my knowledge — the only fully online version can be found at archive.org.[18] While that is certainly usable, it hardly reflects well on the discipline that such is the only freely available digital access to photographs of essentially the most important Hebrew biblical manuscript in the world.

Nonetheless, at least access to the manuscript's text is more readily available. A number of online resources provide access to typographical facsimiles of this manuscript's main text (see below). While that is good for anyone wishing to access the biblical text of the manuscript, these opportunities do not provide access to the paratextual elements such as the *Masorot*. So, while one can access the manuscript's primary text, all of the other elements that make this codex stand out are lacking in an online environment. Regarding the primary text in its context within the manuscript, including its visualization and paratextual elements, requires jumping back and forth between resources. That hardly presents an ideal circumstance.

Greek Manuscripts

The most relevant Greek manuscripts present a spectrum of accessibility, from the most rudimentary and somewhat flawed to a fully digitized version of a manuscript, which still presents some usability issues. I will cover some of these manuscripts

---

[16] For a brief overview of this manuscript and its importance, cf. Fischer, *Text des Alten Testaments*, 53–54 and the introduction to the facsimile edition cited below.
[17] David Noel Freedman, ed., *The Leningrad Codex. A Facsimile Edition* (Grand Rapids, MI; Leiden: William B. Eerdmans Publishing Company; Brill Academic Publishers, 1998).
[18] Cf. The Leningrad Codex, https://archive.org/details/Leningrad_Codex.

in the following, again without making any claims toward something like creating an exhaustive list.[19]

Codex Vaticanus

The oldest known complete Bible manuscript — in this case, with both the Septuagint and New Testament — is Codex Vaticanus (Vat.gr.1209, commonly identified as B). While the age of the completeness of this manuscript must be relativized (a substantial portion of Genesis has been lost and replaced with a copy from an unidentified manuscript), it still presents the most substantial biblical manuscript known to date. The Vatican State Library houses this manuscript and has, thankfully, made a high-resolution digital photographic facsimile of the whole manuscript freely available online.[20] While that is certainly welcome, the presentation has some significant drawbacks. For unclear — perhaps even inconceivable — reasons, the Vatican Library embedded a huge watermark on every folio. More substantially, the site's UI does not commend easy access to individual chapters or verses, though it does provide hyperlinks to move between books by accessing the menu in the site's upper left corner.[21] Beyond the level of moving between books, no easy interface is available. The Vatican library has also collected a solid bibliography of resources about the manuscript and linked it to the manuscript's site. Looking at high-resolution individual folios, it is possible to zoom and even download individual pages as .jpg images, though not at the highest available quality.

The text cannot be searched or copied; i.e., the photographic facsimiles have not been coded for users to really access the contents or to perform lexical or concordance searches. The problem is exacerbated since a typographical facsimile of Vaticanus is not freely available in a digital version.[22] The most important aspects about the usability of Vaticanus in this digitized form are its availability online, the trustworthiness of the site that houses it, the ability to zoom and download images,

---

[19] For the briefest overview of these manuscripts, cf. Tov, *Textual Criticism*, 133. For somewhat more information (and an overview of a few more majuskels, cf. Fischer, *Text des Alten Testaments*, 142–146.
[20] Cf. "Manuscript — Vat.gr.1209," DigiVatLib, https://digi.vatlib.it/view/MSS_Vat.gr.1209.
[21] It is worth noting that Codex Vaticanus is an exception in the ability to even jump easily between books. Other important manuscripts housed in the Vatican Library (and thankfully online) do not even receive this treatment. Cf. Codex Basiliano-Vaticanus (N), Vat.gr.2106, available at: "Manuscript — Vat.gr.2106," DigiVatLib, https://digi.vatlib.it/view/MSS_Vat.gr.2106.
[22] Since the critical editions of the Septuagint present eclectic texts, there is no "pure" typographical facsimile of most manuscripts, particularly those referenced here.

as well as the bibliography of resources for further research on the manuscript itself. All of these are laudable.

Codex Sinaiticus

Working digitally with Codex Sinaiticus, another of the most important more or less complete Greek Bibles, affords much greater usability. This manuscript once contained the entire biblical text, but it has not aged as well as the other Greek manuscripts mentioned here. Substantial portions of text are currently missing. An international collaboration has fully digitalized the extant text and made it freely available online, without watermarks.[23] Since this manuscript was divided up into pieces and is housed in several locations, the digital version of this manuscript presents a significant advancement in working with the manuscript itself: Only online can one see the whole manuscript in one place.

The site that publishes the manuscript is reliable and the sources behind it are trustworthy and renowned. The manuscript's official website provides information about the manuscript and the research project in several languages. The site's presentation of this manuscript includes both digital and typographical facsimiles of the manuscript's text. The combination of these two elements places it in a league of its own when contrasted with the other manuscripts presented here. It is possible to access the manuscript's contents regarding the biblical text sought, and not merely the folio or biblical book. The typographical facsimile can be copied and manipulated in other programs. Clicking on a word in the typographical facsimile highlights it in the photographic facsimile and vice versa, easing both the reading of the manuscript and providing an opportunity to quickly check reconstructions and unsure or idiosyncratic readings. All of these options make this site much more usable than the others discussed here.

Nonetheless, the online presentation of Sinaiticus does have some drawbacks. It is not possible to download image files for specific pages using the UI. Nor is it possible to download the typographical facsimile as an .xml or .txt file or similar. The UI is buggy and sluggish at times, and the images often load poorly. I have often had issues getting the zoom function to work. The highlighting of the elements in the photographic facsimile often remains quite imprecise when compared to the typographical facsimile; i.e., sometimes clicking a word only highlights a portion of the word or an area near the sought-after word. The UI again lacks any method to perform lexical or concordance searches in spite of having a full typographical facsimile of the manuscript. That means interested parties must seek concordance

---

23 Cf. Codex Sinaiticus, https://codexsinaiticus.org/en/.

and lexical information elsewhere. So, while the presentation of Sinaiticus is the best among online biblical manuscripts, there is still much to be desired and plenty of room for improvement.

Codex Alexandrinus

In all due brevity, the digital presentation of Codex Alexandrinus, the third old and important complete Bible manuscript containing both the Old and New Testaments, presents some similar benefits and issues to the online version of Vaticanus. Yet it also has some other issues of its own. The British Library houses this important manuscript and also has made a partial photographic facsimile available online.[24] Thus, it has the same accessibility and trustworthiness benefits of Vaticanus and Sinaiticus. The British Library also provides information on the volume at the top of the page. Additionally, it lacks any unsightly watermark, making its presentation in that regard more authentic and, therefore, better than Vaticanus. However, only one volume — covering most of the New Testament — of the manuscript's four has been made available online, making it entirely irrelevant for anyone working in Hebrew Bible. So, in sum, only roughly twenty-five percent of the text has been made available online and even that has no hyperlinks to aid in finding what one seeks beyond links to the individual folios. The same issues of searchability and lack of a coded text, as in the preceding examples excepting Sinaiticus, also applies in this one. In total, that makes this manuscript less than ideally usable for anyone looking to work with it digitally.

General Comments on Digital Facsimiles of Manuscripts Available Online

With that brief survey of some of the exemplary manuscript facsimiles available as digital images online, an evaluation of the available materials seems advisable. First, the benefits of having access to high-quality digital photographic facsimiles of important biblical manuscripts cannot be overstated. The ease of access these facsimiles provide makes this the best time ever to work with biblical manuscripts. And the situation continues to improve as ever more manuscripts are digitized. However, many desires remain unfulfilled.[25]

---

24 Cf. "Royal MS 1 D VIII," British Library, http://www.bl.uk/manuscripts/Viewer.aspx?ref=royal_ms_1_d_viii_fs001r.
25 Since I am primarily interested in the diachrony of the text, I focus on issues impacting that and not otherwise interesting — but irrelevant for biblical diachrony — codicological issues that could

Of the most important manuscripts covered here, only one provides access to both photographic and typographical facsimiles — Codex Sinaiticus. That should be the standard, not the exception. Equally useful would be the opportunity to download the data — photographic and typographical — for manipulation in other applications. Since these are ancient documents, it seems unlikely that copyright or similar issues should impede that desideratum. The user interfaces should be updated such that texts are better identifiable and can be more easily accessed.[26] The addition of typographical facsimiles should enable the cataloguing of the text such that lexical, concordance, or semantic searches should be possible, though that would admittedly require substantially more work in the case of lexical support. However, more and more such linguistic resources are becoming available. The sources of the information should also be verified. Particularly noteworthy in this regard are the most important Hebrew Manuscripts, neither of which currently has an adequate online host for a manuscript of such repute. These manuscripts' issues in their online presence are exemplary, but other, more extensive manuscript collections online demonstrate the same or similar issues.[27]

Digital Resources

German Bible Society

In addition to modern German (and other language) translations, the German Bible Society publishes a variety of scholarly Bible editions, such as the standard diplomatic critical edition of the Hebrew Bible, the *Biblia Hebraica Stuttgartensia*,[28] the *Biblia Hebraica Quinta* (its successor),[29] the revised *Handausgabe* of Rahlfs's edition

---

also be much better presented digitally online. For one such project to digitally develop models of manuscripts' physical aspects, cf. VisColl, https://github.com/KislakCenter/VisColl.

26 This is apparently a common issue in other fields as well; cf. Matthew James Driscoll and Elena Pierazzo, "Introduction: Old Wine in New Bottles?" in *Digital Scholarly Editing. Theories and Practices*, ed. Matthew James Driscoll and Elena Pierazzo (Cambridge: Open Book Publishers, 2016), 5.

27 Other noteworthy collections of biblical manuscripts — again, not exhaustive — are the Leon Levy Dead Sea Scrolls Digital Library, https://www.deadseascrolls.org.il/home; the Friedberg Genizah Project of the Friedberg Jewish Manuscript Society, https://fgp.genizah.org/FgpFrames.aspx?mode=home, and the Polonsky Foundation Digitization Project, http://bav.bodleian.ox.ac.uk/, to name just a few.

28 Rudolph Kittel, ed., *Biblia Hebraica Stuttgartensia. Fünfte, Verbesserte Auflage* (Stuttgart: Deutsche Bibelgesellschaft, 1997).

29 For an overview of this continuing project, cf. Biblia Hebraica Quinta, https://www.bibelwissenschaft.de/bibelgesellschaft-und-bibelwissenschaft/editionsprojekte/biblia-hebraica-quinta-bhq/.

of the Septuagint,[30] and the critical edition of the Vulgate.[31] All of these editions are available in beautiful and practical print editions, with the primary text either eclectically reconstructed by the editors or as a diplomatic version of a particular witness, depending on the case. Conveniently, the primary biblical texts of these critical editions in their original languages are available online and permit looking up any verse in the Bible via dropdown menus.[32]

Two big positive aspects present themselves here: accessibility to the primary text and reliability of the quality of the information. Neither of these can be doubted. On the other hand, a number of shortcomings remain: there is no way to search other than by verse; there is no easy method to export the text — other than copy and paste — for editing or accessing it offline; the data is not open source; there is no way to display synopses; and the apparatuses for the critical editions are not available online. In total, while access to these trustworthy resources from the German Bible Society is great, much room for improvement regarding usability and access to important tools remains outstanding. The main positives are access and reliability of the data.

Parabible

Parabible presents another web application, has reliable sources for the versions of text that it uses,[33] and resolves some of the issues present in the resources from the German Bible Society. The data is open source. The site is generally intuitive and user-friendly, with more options in the user interface than that of the German Bible Society. You can perform basic searches for terms according to lexemes, delivering some important information from the concordance. It is possible to create synopses, at least of the critically edited Septuagint and the Hebrew texts, though

---

[30] Alfred Rahlfs and Robert Hanhart, eds., *Septuaginta. Id est Vetus Testamentum graece iuxta LXX interpretes. Editio altera quam recognovit et emendavit. Duo volumina in uno* (Stuttgart: Deutsche Bibelgesellschaft, 2006).
[31] Robert Weber and Roger Gryson, eds. *Biblia Sacra. Iuxta Vulgatam versionem. Editionem quintam emendatam retractatam* (Stuttgart: Deutsche Bibelgesellschaft, 2007).
[32] Cf. "About the Online-Bibles," Deutsch Bibelgesellschaft, https://www.academic-bible.com/en/online-bibles/about-the-online-bibles/ with links to the appropriate versions.
[33] Cf. "Genesis 1," Parabible, https://parabible.com/Genesis/1. It is worth noting that Parabible presents essentially the coding initiative of an individual without an explicit university or library affiliation. That being said, the background data stems from reliable sources, linked at the bottom of the page.

the Septuagint version used as a basis is the unrevised 1935 edition.[34] However, the text-critical issue remains in this case in that Parabible does not present any apparatuses (and I assume that it does not even have the rights or permission to do so). This makes its scholarly usability fairly low.

STEP Bible

Another online application is Scripture Tools for Every Person Bible, abbreviated STEP Bible, from Tyndale House, Cambridge.[35] The user interface is intuitive and has search functionality. The STEP Bible makes more versions available, particularly a variety of modern translations, and is generally open source. It has the added advantage that a version of it can be downloaded for offline operation. Like Parabible, it includes solid lexical and grammatical aids. However, the ancient versions do not always stem from the most recent editions,[36] nor are those editions always clearly identified in the app.[37] That makes it less trustworthy as a source for text-critical exercises than it otherwise might be. It also does not include an apparatus for the versions. While it can be a helpful tool, using it demands discipline in double checking that the sources stem from accurate and reputable editions in addition to the issues already identified in the other sites.

SHEBANQ

At the other end of the spectrum in terms of usability is the powerful and remarkable site SHEBANQ.[38] This project produced the Hebrew textual data — based on the German Bible Society's printed BHS — behind both Parabible and STEP Bible. While this application permits detailed work with the Hebrew text of the Bible

---

34 Alfred Rahlfs, ed., *Septuaginta. Id est Vetus Testamentum graece iuxta LXX interpretes. Duo volumina in uno* (Stuttgart: Deutsche Bibelgesellschaft, 1979 [1935]).
35 Cf. STEP Bible, https://eu.stepbible.org/.
36 For example, as with Parabible, the critical edition of the Septuagint on offer is not the revised Rahlfs/Hanhart (2006) edition, but the significantly older Rahlfs (1935).
37 The transcription of the Aleppo Codex provides another crucial example. This version of the Hebrew Bible is indisputably one of the most important witnesses of the Masoretic Text. However, the Codex is no longer complete and has some extensive lacunae, including essentially the whole of the Torah / Pentateuch. Nonetheless, the STEP Bible presents a version of the text that even includes the missing elements and going through the sources they presented for this edition online did not clarify the issue.
38 Cf. SHEBANQ, https://shebanq.ancient-data.org/.

in a diplomatic edition, the hurdle of understanding basic query formatting will probably keep many experts in the field of biblical studies from using it. At the same time, this site does not (currently) provide access to other versions of the text, presenting the Hebrew text alone. That in itself is quite limiting, but the same issue of the lacking apparatus appears here as well.

Preliminary Conclusions about Biblical Resources Online Generally

The preceding has considered a cross-section of some generally available online tools for scholarly biblical inquiry. They each have advantages, but all currently have more disadvantages in respect to their potential for research in biblical diachrony. While trustworthy sources are available online for specific critical editions, they only feature the main text with no access to the apparatuses. Online tools that permit contrasting distinct versions are also limited either in the spectrum of the versions available or the reliability of the source text offered. Therefore, in order to deal with biblical texts, only limited tools that each cover only limited aspects of the academic exercise currently exist in freely available environs. If one is only interested in the specific main text of a biblical version, tools are available, but access to the data behind that reconstruction, particularly in the case of eclectic editions like that of the Septuagint, are radically limited and therefore incomplete. Anyone interested in the specifics of a text must, then, turn to other resources, particularly facsimiles of particular manuscripts or other larger research projects that compile the data.

Free online access to the critically edited text presents an enormous opportunity for scholars and students. After all, third-party software for researching in these editions runs the spectrum in pricing from expensive to financially ruinous. However, as good and trustworthy as these freely available versions are, they lack the critical apparatuses. So, while the primary text of the edition is readily available and able to be copied and manipulated with other software (an available option to export text as xml or even txt or similar would also be beneficial), as well as citable in the online edition, there is no opportunity to really deal with text-critical matters while relying on the online versions alone.

Additionally limiting are the lack of real search capabilities beyond looking up a text via folio or chapter and verse. The paucity of search options dramatically reduces the usability for anything beyond looking up texts already known to pertain to the research task at hand. It remains impossible to do any detailed lexical or concordance research with the tools provided on these sites, limiting things like linguistic studies. Similarly, doing any text-critical work requires jumping back and forth between windows or creating your own synopses. Neither of those options is particularly conducive to effective text-critical work, particularly when better print resources are available.

Scrolls or Scrolling? Advantages and Disadvantages of Accessing Biblical Texts Digitally

I am of the opinion that we are currently moving toward a new era in transmitting and understanding the Bible's text. The transmission of the biblical text has undergone some significant paradigm shifts over the millennia, from the scroll to the codex to the printed volume. Now we find ourselves moving back toward the scroll, albeit with a distinctly new understanding of that term. The preceding will hopefully have provided some cursory insights on freely available digital materials for the study of the Hebrew Bible. Having examined some exemplary materials available online, it is worth reflecting on the advantages and disadvantages, on the objectives fulfilled and those that remain outstanding. We can consider these aspects both in turn and in conversation with one another.

Let's consider the positive aspects first. Access to photographic facsimiles of individual manuscripts certainly presents a positive development for scholars and students, as well as for anyone interested in such amazing cultural artifacts. Unfettered access to these digital objects — theoretically available to everyone in the world — represents an important step in the democratization of scholarship, making research on the text and its representation available to a wider audience and thus to ever greater numbers of discerning eyes than was previously possible.

The same is true of the typographical facsimiles of particular manuscripts or editorial editions, whether eclectic (Rahlfs' *Handausgabe* of the Septuagint) or diplomatic (the *Biblia Hebraica* Series). By making the text of these manuscripts and editorial projects freely available online, students and scholars now have better access to the material. An aspect of this that should not be overlooked is financial, since these critical editions can carry heavy price tags that can make them unavailable to students generally or scholars and students at under-financed institutions. The usability presents another important aspect. By having the texts in an already digitized format, manipulation with other software becomes easier and the possibility of errors in transcription recedes.

Each of these aspects fulfills a general need in the discipline: ease of access, greater usability and visibility, reduction of potential errors. Those needs are foundational. That leads naturally to the unfulfilled needs and desires for the discipline. So, what is missing from the picture described above?

First, the expansion of the breadth of the available resources presents a natural first step. A large number of photographic facsimiles are available and more are continually being made so. That is good, but quicker expansion would be better. The same is true for typographical facsimiles, both of individual manuscripts as well as critical editions. The logical answer to this issue is for the responsible libraries or housing or publishing institution to make access to the data more available. Achieving this end would require substantial work and, potentially, substantial financing,[39] but those are matters to which we can return.

More importantly, the dissociation of the typographical data from the photographic facsimiles should be remedied. Having the photographs is great. Having the text is great. Having them in one place is ideal. "Digital scholarly editions can help dissolve the distinction [. . .]"[40] Substantially more work is necessary in this regard.

Regarding critical editions, two aspects would greatly benefit the discipline. The first would be greater access to the data in the apparatuses. These treasure troves of data represent essentially centuries of collation work by scholars too numerous to name. It is frankly wasteful and contrary to academic ideals to keep this work hidden from wider audiences of scholars, students, and interested lay-persons. Making the data in the apparatuses available online would represent an important first step, but another step would help even more: reconstructing typographical facsimiles of each individual manuscript.[41] While the data divorced from its idiosyncratic context in a particular manuscript can be helpful, understanding an individual reading within that context provides even greater understanding and essentially more textual metadata, i.e., data about the reading impacting the reading and impacted by the variant but beyond the variant itself. That information could be critical for fulfilling the greatest promise for the diachronic study of biblical texts.

From this wishlist, three clear desires crystalize. First, the breadth of the available information should be increased, i.e., more manuscripts and editions should be made available as photographic facsimiles. Second, the depth of the information should be furthered, i.e., more typographical facsimiles as both machine- and

---

[39] Cf. Phlipp Roelli, "Petrus Alfonsi, or: On the Mutual Benefit of Traditional and Computerised Stemmatology," in *Analysis of Ancient and Medieval Texts and Manuscripts: Digital Approaches*, ed. Tara Andrews and Caroline Macé (Turnhout: Brepols, 2014), 62.
[40] Mats Dahlström, "Copies and Facsimiles," *International Journal of Digital Humanities* 1 (2019): 197.
[41] Cf. the projects described in Gregory Crane, "The Open Philology Project and Humboldt Chair of Digital Humanities at Leipzig," April 4, 2013, http://sites.tufts.edu/perseusupdates/2013/04/04/the-open-philology-project-and-humboldt-chair-of-digital-humanities-at-leipzig/.

human-readable text are necessary (such as xml or txt).⁴² This greater depth should include the primary text of any manuscript or edition, as well as both material from apparatuses and paratextual elements such as marginalia. Finally, the combination of both of these varieties of data would provide the most fruitful structure for engaging with the material. Together, these aspects represent a huge amount of work. So, how do we get there, and what should we do with the information thus gleaned?

Perspectives: Transforming an Auspicious Present into a Grand Future

Optimism is the name of the game moving forward. There has never been a better time to advance the nascent work in digitizing biblical texts. Here I would like to discuss two primary ideas: how to get the data and what to do with it.

Gathering the Data

Two c-words could be key to gathering the data: cooperation and crowd-sourcing. Each of these is likely necessary in order to achieve the objective of the largest number of digitized biblical texts. Scholars, students, and interested people should be involved in both of them.

Scholars should collaborate with libraries and manuscript-housing institutions to develop a working order for the digitization of manuscripts and arrange funds for the photographing, data-storage, and online publication with generally open access. Likely this will call for the financial support of third-party supporters and private benefactors. However, since the publishing of manuscripts in this way represents a combination of technology and humanities research, the number of providers could potentially be doubled and interest piqued in each area of research. Such publications have a clear objective, present an obvious desideratum, and deal with some of the most influential texts — not just in the humanities' history, but in humanity's history.

---

42 Some preliminary steps have been made in this regard, though not always with the clearest intentions or organizational responsibility. Cf., e.g., Tanach, http://tanach.us/Tanach.xml and Kata Biblon, https://en.katabiblon.com/us/index.php?text=LXX&book=Gn&ch=1 with the sources cited there.

At the same time, scholars and housing institutions should communicate openly about what they are doing and encourage similar work and cooperation with other scholars and institutions. Of fundamental importance here is not overlooking libraries, institutions, and scholars that may be in regions without larger programs to finance such research and publication. In such cases, work should be undertaken to finance and support the necessary infrastructure where the manuscripts are located without digitally pilfering the cultural good from where it stands or while overlooking the work of regional scholars and institutions in researching and publishing the manuscripts.

Collaboration will also be required to develop standards for the quality of published photographic and typographical facsimiles. Some steps have been undertaken in this regard, but wider knowledge of initiatives like TEI among biblical scholars would certainly speed up the process. For example, there is currently no project at TEI-C dedicated to developing coding standards for biblical texts or literature.[43]

Involving students in this process could also serve to advance this process more quickly. On the one hand, students could help with matters like identifying and photographing the relevant manuscripts. But, more importantly, students in language courses and methodology seminars could be activated to transcribe the manuscripts and create typographical facsimiles. The training required for that is limited, and language instructors could be involved in the process of confirming transcriptions. Functionally, that would represent a form of crowd-sourcing to more rapidly achieve results in producing typographical facsimiles. Since the numbers of students in theological and religious studies programs taking Hebrew and/or Greek is comparatively large, this method could dramatically increase the speed of text transcription and encoding. So simply bringing the task into the classroom could represent a significant step in resolving the issue of such an undertaking's size and scope.

A similar process could be undertaken with critical editions, with students and scholars working together to reconstruct typographical facsimiles of individual manuscripts from text-critical apparatuses in legacy editions. Undertakings like the *Septuaginta Unternehmen Göttingen*, for example, did not produce transcriptions of individual manuscripts, producing collations in notebooks with lines for each term instead. Thus, such typographical reproductions of specific manuscripts do not yet exist, except in special circumstances. Typographical facsimiles produced in this fashion could then be checked against photographic facsimiles (or the original,

---

43 Cf. Text Encoding Initiative, https://tei-c.org/Activities/Projects/.

where possible) for accuracy. They could then even serve as input data to advance the process of automatic text recognition (see the immediately following).

It is conceivable and desirable to develop and foster projects focused on increasing the automation of this process.[44] Collaboration with scholars and students in information sciences, particularly in the fields of computer vision and OCR/HTR could provide methods for increased automation. To this end, the crowd-sourced transcriptions could serve as the ground-truth for the development of even codex-specific algorithms for OCR/HTR.[45] Freely available programs, such as OCR4All can theoretically be used in precisely this way.[46] Further, by including ever more transcriptions of individual pieces of a manuscript would permit refining the iterative process for the recognition of the text, leading to ever-faster results. That could then lead to ever greater automation and increased speed and accuracy in the transcription of manuscripts.

Together, all of these practices would serve to bring together typographical and photographical facsimiles as codable digitized artifacts. They would create a huge volume of data, theoretically covering the whole of the known biblical textual tradition and even perhaps portions lost since their incorporation in older critical editions. That would be a huge victory for anyone interested in the diachrony of the biblical text or the transmission of texts in general. But the question remains unanswered, what exactly should be done with all of this data.

Using the Data

From my perspective, even having the data is important. The data itself is invaluable and priceless. Yet that is really only the first step. The data cannot be regarded as an end without means or an end unto itself. So what should be done with the data won from these processes?

The first aspect has been addressed briefly above. Initially, data can serve for the quicker and better automated creation of more data. Photographic facsimiles

---

[44] Cf. L.W.C van Lit, *Among Digitized Manuscripts* (Leiden: Brill, 2020), 113, who described such an automated process as "The crown jewel of digital manuscript studies."
[45] We have undertaken precisely such a project, creating an interactive web platform for the development and refining of text-recognition in Codex Vaticanus. This platform included a leaderboard in order to encourage a competitive spirit to more rapidly transcribe the manuscript using digitally supported manual input. Within a few weeks we had identified and rechecked tens of thousands of letters relying on volunteer and student support. We were able to use these data to create a ground-truth with a reliability of 99% for automated letter recognition.
[46] Cf. OCR4all, https://www.ocr4all.org/.

can lead to the creation of typographical facsimiles, which can serve as the basis for quicker and better digitization of more photographic facsimiles in a virtuous circle. But that is still mostly only winning more data.

Another aspect of such digital work with manuscripts that has deservingly received much attention is paleography.[47] Such approaches should be applied to biblical manuscripts more broadly than has commonly been the case. Such paleographical approaches can support text-critical undertakings by using the data and its visualization to identify potential errors in transcription.[48] Computer-supported text-critical work could also endeavor to reconstruct more precisely and with greater probability any text that has degraded over time.[49] That is, we could secure better data or better secure the textual data in this fashion.

As the amount of data increases and becomes more certain, the evaluations of data can become more pronounced, more thorough, and more accurate. Having a more explicit and nuanced data profile of the variants in as many versions and manuscripts as possible will enable a more well-defined reconstruction of the biblical diachrony as traditionally studied with the method of textual criticism.

---

47 Cf., e.g., Mark Aussems and Axel Brink, "Digital Palaeography," in *Kodikologie & Paläographie im digitalen Zeitalter / Codicology & Palaeography in the Digital Age*, ed. Malte Rehbein and Bernhard Assmann (Norderstedt: Books on Demand, 2009), 293–308; Ainoa Castro Correa, "Palaeography, Computer-Assisted Palaeography and Digital Palaeography: Digital Tools Applied to the Study of Visigothic Script," in *Analysis of Ancient and Medieval Texts and Manuscripts: Digital Approaches*, ed. Tara Andrews and Caroline Macé (Turnhout: Brepols, 2014), 247–272; Arianna Ciula, "The Palaeographical Method Under the Light of a Digital Approach," in *Kodikologie & Paläographie im digitalen Zeitalter / Codicology & Palaeography in the Digital Age*, ed. Malte Rehbein and Bernhard Assmann (Norderstedt: Books on Demand, 2009), 219–235; Wernfried Hofmeister, Andrea Hofmeister-Winter, and Georg Thallinger, "Forschung am Rande des paläographischen Zweifels: Die EDV-basierte Erfassung individueller Schriftzüge im Projekt DAmalS," in *Kodikologie & Paläographie im digitalen Zeitalter / Codicology & Palaeography in the Digital Age*, ed. Malte Rehbein and Bernhard Assmann (Norderstedt: Books on Demand, 2009), 261–292; Mark Stansbury, "The Computer and the Classification of Script," in *Kodikologie & Paläographie im digitalen Zeitalter / Codicology & Palaeography in the Digital Age*, ed. Malte Rehbein and Bernhard Assmann (Norderstedt: Books on Demand, 2009), 237–349; Peter A. Stokes, "Computer-Aided Palaeography, Present and Future," in *Kodikologie & Paläographie im digitalen Zeitalter / Codicology & Palaeography in the Digital Age*, ed. Malte Rehbein and Bernhard Assmann (Norderstedt: Books on Demand, 2009), 309–338; and Lior Wolf, et al., "Automatic Palaeographic Exploration of Genizah Manuscripts," in *Kodikologie und Paläographie im Digitalen Zeitalter 2*, ed. Malte Rehbein and Bernhard Assmann (Norderstedt: Books on Demand, 2010), 151–179.

48 Cf. one such visualization (of digits) in Laurens van der Maaten and Geoffrey Hinton, "Visualizing Data Using t-SNE," *Journal of Machine Learning Research* 9 (2008): 2579–2605.

49 Cf. Markus Diem, et al., "Recognizing Degraded Handwritten Characters," in *Kodikologie und Paläographie im Digitalen Zeitalter 2*, ed. Malte Rehbein and Bernhard Assmann (Norderstedt: Books on Demand, 2010), 295–306.

A wider dataset would enable the reconstruction of more accurate stemmata for the development of specific readings and, in turn, books or larger compositions.[50] This digital data could feed into digitally assisted processes of evaluation like the Coherence-Based Genealogical Method of the *Institut für Neutestamentliche Textforschung*. This process is applied to the manuscript tradition of the New Testament in order to reconstruct the oldest attainable New Testament text. It in turn serves as the basis for the publication of the *Editio Critica Maior* of the individual books of the New Testament.[51] In this way, documented evidence could be more accurately understood for a better picture of how the biblical texts in Greek and Hebrew were transmitted through history and how the various manuscripts relate to one another based on common variants.

This refined review of the empirical data could then serve the reconstruction and evaluation of more theoretical models of biblical diachrony no longer attested in the manuscripts and traditions. Moving beyond "merely" text-critical questions, it would become possible to evaluate the empirical data and work out any implications for redaction-historical models of biblical diachrony.[52] On the one hand, this could initially take up models of biblical diachrony proposed over the past few centuries and evaluate their plausibility. In other words, does the empirical data permit or reject certain theoretical models or even types of models for the diachronic development of biblical literature? For the first time, this could be based on broader sets of empirical data. At the same time, more nuance in understanding factually attested diachronic phenomena could lead to the development and refining of (digital) methods to better incorporate empirical data into theoretical modelling. Access to more data would likely demand developing better evaluative and reconstructive methods. That would, in turn, probably lead to new models, based now on more well-founded data from broader datasets.

Taken together, two aspects should, in conclusion, be emphasized here. First, there has never been a more auspicious time to advance this work beyond what has already been done. Both the breadth and depth of the undertaking could be rapidly expanded in a way thus far inconceivable. In order to afford that, a culture of cooperation and openness remains fundamental. Working together, with all of our cards on the table, would provide the quickest means to progress this work. Secondly,

---

[50] Cf. Tuomas Heikkilä, "The Possibilities and Challenges of Computer-Assisted Stemmatology," in *Analysis of Ancient and Medieval Texts and Manuscripts: Digital Approaches*, ed. Tara Andrews and Caroline Macé (Turnhout: Brepols, 2014), 19–42 and Roelli, "Petrus Alfonsi."
[51] Cf. Gerd Mink, "The Coherence-Based Genealogical Method: What is It About?" https://www.uni-muenster.de/INTF/Genealogical_method.html.
[52] This kind of work on the Hebrew Bible is essentially entirely in its infancy; cf., e.g., Idan Dershowitz, et al., "Computerized Source Criticism of Biblical Texts," *JBL* 134, no. 2 (2015): 253–271.

winning this data could potentially open a new era in our understanding of the Bible's diachrony, the likes of which was never previously possible. The availability of the largest possible dataset would enable the best conceivable possible models and the most empirically sound reconstructions of diachronic processes behind the Bible's composition. Never before has such an understanding really been so tantalizingly close to being within our reach.

Bibliography

"About the Online-Bibles," Deutsch Bibelgesellschaft, https://www.academic-bible.com/en/online-bibles/about-the-online-bibles/.
Aleppo Codex, http://aleppocodex.org/.
"Aleppo WM," Touching History: Digitization Projects by Ardon Bar-Hama, https://barhama.com/ajaxzoom/viewer/viewer.php?zoomDir=/pic/AleppoWM/&example=viewer5.
Aussems, Mark, and Axel Brink. "Digital Palaeography." In *Kodikologie & Paläographie im digitalen Zeitalter / Codicology & Palaeography in the Digital Age*, edited by Malte Rehbein and Bernhard Assmann, 293–308. Norderstedt: Books on Demand, 2009.
Becker, Uwe. *Exegese des Alten Testaments*. 4. Auflage. Tübingen: Mohr Siebeck, 2015.
Biblia Hebraica Quinta, https://www.bibelwissenschaft.de/bibelgesellschaft-und-bibelwissenschaft/editionsprojekte/biblia-hebraica-quinta-bhq/.
Castro Correa, Ainoa. "Palaeography, Computer-Assisted Palaeography and Digital Palaeography: Digital Tools Applied to the Study of Visigothic Script." In *Analysis of Ancient and Medieval Texts and Manuscripts: Digital Approaches*, edited by Tara Andrews and Caroline Macé, 247–272. Turnhout: Brepols, 2014.
Ciula, Arianna. "The Palaeographical Method Under the Light of a Digital Approach." In *Kodikologie & Paläographie im digitalen Zeitalter / Codicology & Palaeography in the Digital Age*, edited by Malte Rehbein and Bernhard Assmann, 219–235. Norderstedt: Books on Demand, 2009.
Codex Sinaiticus, https://codexsinaiticus.org/en/.
Crane, Gregory. "The Open Philology Project and Humboldt Chair of Digital Humanities at Leipzig," April 4, 2013, http://sites.tufts.edu/perseusupdates/2013/04/04/the-open-philology-project-and-humboldt-chair-of-digital-humanities-at-leipzig.
Dahlström, Mats. "Copies and Facsimiles." *International Journal of Digital Humanities* 1 (2019): 195–208.
Dershowitz, Idan, Navot Akiva, Moshe Koppel, and Nachum Dershowitz. "Computerized Source Criticism of Biblical Texts." *JBL* 134, no. 2 (2015): 253–271.
Diem, Markus, Robert Sablatnig, Melanie Gau, and Heinz Miklas. "Recognizing Degraded Handwritten Characters." In *Kodikologie und Paläographie im Digitalen Zeitalter 2*, edited by Malte Rehbein and Bernhard Assmann, 295–306. Norderstedt: Books on Demand, 2010.
Dietrich, Walter, Hans-Peter Mathys, Thomas Römer, and Rudolf Smend, eds. *Die Entstehung des Alten Testaments*. Stuttgart: Kohlhammer, 2014.
Driscoll, Matthew James, and Elena Pierazzo. "Introduction: Old Wine in New Bottles?" In *Digital Scholarly Editing. Theories and Practices*, edited by Matthew James Driscoll and Elena Pierazzo, 1–15. Cambridge: Open Book Publishers, 2016.

Fernández Marcos, Natalio. *The Septuagint in Context. Introduction to the Greek Version of the Bible*, translated by Wilfred G. E. Watson. Atlanta, GA: Society of Biblical Literature, 2000.
Fischer, Alexander Achilles. *Der Text des Alten Testaments. Neubearbeitung der Einführung in die Biblia Hebraica von Ernst Würthwein*. Stuttgart: Deutsche Bibelgesellschaft, 2009.
Freedman, David Noel, ed. *The Leningrad Codex. A Facsimile Edition*. Grand Rapids, MI; Leiden: William B. Eerdmans Publishing Company; Brill Academic Publishers, 1998.
"Genesis 1," Parabible, https://parabible.com/Genesis/1.
Goshen-Gottstein, Moshe H., ed. *The Aleppo Codex. Provided with Masoretic Notes and Pointed by Aaron Ben Asher. The Codex Considered Authoritative by Maimonides. Part One: Plates*. Jerusalem: Magnes Press, 1976.
Heikkilä, Tuomas. "The Possibilities and Challenges of Computer-Assisted Stemmatology." In *Analysis of Ancient and Medieval Texts and Manuscripts: Digital Approaches*, edited by Tara Andrews and Caroline Macé, 19–42. Turnhout: Brepols, 2014.
Hofmeister, Wernfried, Andrea Hofmeister-Winter, and Georg Thallinger. "Forschung am Rande des paläographischen Zweifels: Die EDV-basierte Erfassung individueller Schriftzüge im Projekt DAmalS." In *Kodikologie & Paläographie im digitalen Zeitalter / Codicology & Palaeography in the Digital Age*, edited by Malte Rehbein and Bernhard Assmann, 261–292. Norderstedt: Books on Demand, 2009.
Kata Biblon, https://en.katabiblon.com/us/index.php?text=LXX&book=Gn&ch=1.
Kittel, Rudolph, ed. *Biblia Hebraica Stuttgartensia. Fünfte, Verbesserte Auflage*. Stuttgart: Deutsche Bibelgesellschaft, 1997.
Leon Levy Dead Sea Scrolls Digital Library, https://www.deadseascrolls.org.il/home.
Lit, L.W.C. van. *Among Digitized Manuscripts: Philology, Codicology, Paleography in a Digital World*. Leiden: Brill, 2020.
Maaten, Laurens van der, and Geoffrey Hinton. "Visualizing Data Using t-SNE." *Journal of Machine Learning Research* 9 (2008): 2579–2605.
"Manuscript — Vat.gr.1209," DigiVatLib, https://digi.vatlib.it/view/MSS_Vat.gr.1209.
"Manuscript — Vat.gr.2106," DigiVatLib, https://digi.vatlib.it/view/MSS_Vat.gr.2106.
Mink, Gerd. "The Coherence-Based Genealogical Method: What is It About?" https://www.uni-muenster.de/INTF/Genealogical_method.html.
Müller, Reinhard, and Juha Pakkala, eds. *Insights into Editing in the Hebrew Bible and the Ancient Near East. What Does Documented Evidence Tell Us about the Transmission of Authoritative Texts?* CBET 84. Leuven: Peeters, 2017.
OCR4all, https://www.ocr4all.org/.
Pakkala, Juha, Romeny Bas ter Haar, and Reinhard Müller, eds. *Evidence of Editing*. Atlanta, GA: Society of Biblical Literature, 2014.
Person, Raymond F. Jr., and Robert Rezetko, eds. *Empirical Models Challenging Biblical Criticism*. AIL 25. Atlanta, GA: Society of Biblical Literature, 2016.
Rahlfs, Alfred, ed. *Septuaginta. Id est Vetus Testamentum graece iuxta LXX interpretes. Duo volumina in uno*. 1935. Repr. Stuttgart: Deutsche Bibelgesellschaft, 1979.
Rahlfs, Alfred, and Robert Hanhart, eds. *Septuaginta. Id est Vetus Testamentum graece iuxta LXX interpretes. Editio altera quam recognovit et emendavit. Duo volumina in uno*. Stuttgart: Deutsche Bibelgesellschaft, 2006.
Roelli, Phlipp. "Petrus Alfonsi, or: On the Mutual Benefit of Traditional and Computerised Stemmatology." In *Analysis of Ancient and Medieval Texts and Manuscripts: Digital Approaches*, edited by Tara Andrews and Caroline Macé, 43–68. Turnhout: Brepols, 2014.

"Royal Ms 1 D VIII," British Library, http://www.bl.uk/manuscripts/Viewer.aspx?ref=royal_ms_1_d_viii_fs001r.
SHEBANQ, https://shebanq.ancient-data.org/.
Stansbury, Mark. "The Computer and the Classification of Script." In *Kodikologie & Paläographie im digitalen Zeitalter / Codicology & Palaeography in the Digital Age*, edited by Malte Rehbein and Bernhard Assmann, 237–349. Norderstedt: Books on Demand, 2009.
STEP Bible, https://eu.stepbible.org/.
Stokes, Peter A. "Computer-Aided Palaeography, Present and Future." In *Kodikologie & Paläographie im digitalen Zeitalter / Codicology & Palaeography in the Digital Age*, edited by Malte Rehbein and Bernhard Assmann, 309–338. Norderstedt: Books on Demand, 2009.
Tanach, http://tanach.us/Tanach.xml.
Text Encoding Initiative, https://tei-c.org/Activities/Projects/.
The Friedberg Genizah Project of the Friedberg Jewish Manuscript Society, https://fgp.genizah.org/FgpFrames.aspx?mode=home.
The Leningrad Codex, https://archive.org/details/Leningrad_Codex.
The Polonsky Foundation Digitization Project, http://bav.bodleian.ox.ac.uk/.
Tov, Emanuel. *The Text-Critical Use of the Septuagint in Biblical Research*. 3rd ed. Winona Lake, IN: Eisenbrauns, 2015.
Tov, Emanuel. *Textual Criticism of the Hebrew Bible*. 3rd ed. Minneapolis, MN: Fortress, 2012.
Trebolle, Julio, and Pablo Torijano. "From the Greek Recensions to the Hebrew Editions: A Sample from 1 Kgs 2:1–10." In *Insights into Editing in the Hebrew Bible and the Ancient Near East*, edited by Reinhard Müller and Juha Pakkala, 267–293. Leuven: Peeters, 2017.
VisColl, https://github.com/KislakCenter/VisColl.
Weber, Robert, and Roger Gryson, eds. *Biblia Sacra. Iuxta Vulgatam versionem. Editionem quintam emendatam retractatam*. Stuttgart: Deutsche Bibelgesellschaft, 2007.
Wolf, Lior, Nachum Derschowitz, Liza Potikha, Tanya German, Roni Shweka, and Yaacov Choueka. "Automatic Palaeographic Exploration of Genizah Manuscripts." In *Kodikologie und Paläographie im Digitalen Zeitalter 2*, edited by Malte Rehbein and Bernhard Assmann, 151–179. Norderstedt: Books on Demand, 2010.

Adrian Plau
Digital Orientalism? Philology, Digital Methodologies, and Reflections on the Study of Primary Sources to North Indian Religions

In this chapter, I will not present neat findings, but rather attempt to hit the pause button in the middle of a research project to reflect more deeply around what exactly it is that I am doing. Working on a critical edition of Nainsukh's *Vaidyamanotsava*,[1] a late sixteenth-century medical treatise from North India, I apply TEI encoding to structure my information on manuscripts available to me, use visual representations of their variations to guide my collation, and mapping tools to illustrate their geographical histories. However, the apparent clarity and neatness of these outputs constantly threaten to mask the problematic undertones of the project, as well as the colonial legacies of my field, my research, and my own absurdly privileged positionality as a straight white male researcher in a Western institution. If left unacknowledged, the application of imperialist methodologies into the digital humanities gives rise to what I call *digital Orientalism* — more on which soon — which is simply racist, imperialist Orientalism all over again.

Of course, digital Orientalism is not a new term. It is frequently used in a variety of discussions and interventions on Orientalist practices and material in digital spaces.[2] However, when I speak of digital Orientalism in the following, I have in mind a sense of the phrase that also involves the practice of Orientalism using digital tools. In other words, not only the appearance of Orientalist material in digital media but the ways in which the inherent biases of the tools underpinning these media, such as digital humanities tools, precondition Orientalist output even before the media is presented to an audience. Of course, these biases spring from Orientalist minds, and that is why this chapter deals with self-reflection more than it does with digital humanities tools in themselves.

---

1 In the name of accessibility, I have opted not to use diacritics in transliterations from Devanagari. The exceptions are when these are used as part of the titles of items in the bibliography or when I want to bring out variations in quotations.
2 See, for instance, Mahsa Alimardani and Mona Elswah, "Digital Orientalism: #SaveSheikhJarrah and Arabic Content Moderation," *POMEPS Studies 43: Digital Activism and Authoritarian Adaptation in the Middle East* 7 (2021).

I do not propose clear solutions here but simply want to document some of my thoughts. If anything, I propose that the accessibility and reusability of the data is key and that the increased availability of the material itself to other, more capable and relevant scholars than myself should not be seen as an optional aspect of the work but as a crucial, essential output in itself. However, having passed through my hands, the material, now digital, is not without my conceptual fingerprints. The solution to this conundrum partly lies beyond the scope of what I can do as an individual researcher but, as I argue, this state of affairs should not restrain me from foregrounding the problematic aspects of my work.

Vaidyamanotsava — Elements of a Study

Vaidyamanotsava (*A Celebration of Physicians*) is a late sixteenth-century medical treatise by Nainsukh, a Jain layman based in the Punjab region. Given its early date, it has been suggested as possibly the very first treatise of its kind in an early North Indian vernacular and so holds great interest as a source for the history of medicine in South Asia.[3] Wellcome Collection holds eleven manuscripts containing the text, four of which are complete and covering a date range from 1688 to the nineteenth century. Beyond an excellent study by Joshi and Kulkari based on a single manuscript in the holdings of the Bhandarkar Oriental Research Institute,[4] the *Vaidyamanotsava* has received little attention from research. This is regrettable, as the text's range of topics, covering pulse diagnosis to gynecology, coupled with a variety of unique recipes that cumulatively provide a unique snapshot of early modern medical practice.

As a textual source composed by a self-confessed Jain on matters that are not necessarily religious, the *Vaidyamanotsava* and its reception holds interest to the study of South Asian religions as an example of a site — the practice of medicine

---

[3] While the vernacular language of the Vaidyamanotsava may be described as an early format of Hindi, and the categorical terminology of shelfmark numbering (i.e., "MS Hindi") suggests the same, it is prudent to note the pitfalls involved in retrospectively applying modern-day monikers such as "Hindi" to historical languages with porous borders. As is typical of other texts from the time, Nainsukh himself refers to the fluid vernacular simply as "bhasha" ("tongue; language"), a catch-all for any vernacular as opposed to Sanskrit, Prakrit, and Persian. For a study of related issues of language borders in a vernacular Jain text from the same period, see: Adrian Plau, "Jain Narrative Literature in Brajbhāṣā: Discussions from an Understudied Field," *Religions* 10, no. 4 (2019): 262. DOI: https://doi.org/10.3390/rel10040262.

[4] Supriya C. Kulkari and Mohan R. Joshi, "Study of Manuscript Vaidyamanotsava," *Journal of Sanskrit Samhita Siddhanta* 3, no. 1 (2017): 19–25.

— where religious identities and practices adjoined other cultural and socio-historical currents. On this note, it is striking to note a variation that appear across some the *Vaidyamanotsava* manuscripts. In the earlier ones, such as MS Indic Gamma 325[5] (dated 1688 AD) and MS Hindi 460[6] (dated 1723 AD), Nainsukh refers to himself as *"shravak kul hi nivasa"* — *"a member of the lay Jain community."* However, some later manuscripts, such as MS Hindi 114[7] (undated, but based on paper and layout most likely eighteenth or nineteenth century), change the phrase to *"ja ke dharma nivas"* — simply *"a virtuous man."* The variation subtly replaces Nainsukh's Jain identity with something vaguer, possibly inviting audiences to understand the text's composer as conforming to a then more distinctly emerging Hindu identity.[8]

It is, however, equally striking to note that this is the only alteration needed to remove the composition's Jain imprint. Most other variations in the Wellcome manuscripts appear at first sight to be inessential, interchangeable phrasings of individual lines, or the inclusion or exclusion of recipes. This is not too surprising, and we know from other early modern Jain sources that it was not uncommon for laymen to be familiar with and, at times, partake in a variety of religious practices. The *Ardhakathanaka*, the seventeenth-century autobiography of the Jain merchant Banarsidas, famously presents Banarsidas reciting Islamicate romances to a mixed, popular audience, dipping in and out of different Jain traditions, and at times experimenting with devotion addressed to Hindu deities.[9]

Tracing the variations across manuscripts beyond what appears to be the case after a quick comparison entails a more rigorous study. It seems clear that establishing a critical edition of the *Vaidyamanotsava* based on the available manuscripts would be a beneficial starting point for further studies of medical history

---

5 Nainsukh, "Vaidyamanotsava," MS Indic Gamma 325 (Wellcome Collection, 1668).
6 Nainsukh, "Vaidyamanotsava," MS Hindi 460 (Wellcome Collection, 1723).
7 Nainsukh, "Vaidyamanotsava," MS Hindi 114 (Wellcome Collection, n.d.). A full transcript of which is available at: Health, Medicine and Treatment in early modern North India: Early Hindi medicine manuscripts in the Wellcome Collection, https://adrianplau.github.io/mss/MSHindi114.html.
8 Friedlander notes another similar variation in other *Vaidyamanotsava* manuscripts. See: Peter G. Friedlander, *A Descriptive Catalogue of the Hindi Manuscripts in the Library of the Wellcome Institute for the History of Medicine* (London: The Wellcome Institute for the History of Medicine, 1996), 34. For further, introductory reading on the formation of Hindu identities in early modern South Asia, see: Adrian Plau, "Early Modern Hinduism," in *Oxford History of Hinduism: Modern Hinduism*, ed. Torkel Brekke (Oxford: Oxford University Press, 2019), 17–35.
9 An accessible translation of the *Ardhakathanaka* is Banārsīdās, *Ardhakathanak: A Half Story*, trans. Rohini Chowdhury (New Delhi: Penguin Books, 2009). A classic study is Banārsīdās, *Half a Tale: A Study in the Interrelationship between Autobiography and History (The Ardhakathanaka)*, ed. Mukund Lath (New Delhi: Rupa, 2005).

and religious identity within professional practices in early modern North India. This is exactly what I have set out to do, using a variety of digital humanities tools.

I use TEI to structure the manuscripts' cataloguing metadata, working from a template based on the msDesc schema developed by the Bodleian Library and Cambridge University Library and that mandates sufficient information for the files to be compliant with the minimum viable description framework set out in the Collections Trust's Spectrum standard for inventory.[10] To aid my collation of the manuscripts into an edited text with a critical apparatus, I transcribe the manuscripts directly into the <body> element of the TEI files and use different software services to provide visual outputs and analysis of variations across the manuscripts. Finally, I output any available information from the <history> elements in my TEI files, along with the same from files on comparable medical manuscripts at Wellcome Collection, and enter the resulting data into mapping tools to create timelines and visualizations that enable me to identify the trends and currents of medical manuscripts in which the *Vaidyamanotsava* circulated.

This is all quite straightforward, and I have done exactly the same in earlier manuscript collation projects. But, to invoke the precise language of MasterChef Australia, this approach comes with several conceptual pressure points and I cannot ignore them.

Variations

First of all, when I input my TEI transcriptions in software such as Juxta,[11] I am presented with an appealing and beautiful overview of the variations between the manuscripts. I can click to choose which manuscript I want to see as the root text, against which all others are compared, and I am immediately presented with the Devanagari text, expertly rendered and with a myriad of colored shades overlaying some of the words. The greater the number of variations, the deeper the color. I can click on a shaded word, and a box appears to present me with a list of the variations across the manuscripts. This is all phenomenally satisfying and, not the least, extraordinarily helpful in terms of both the time spent and accuracy I might have achieve.

---

10 For more on the msDesc schema, see: "TEI P5 Customization and Encoding Guidelines for Manuscript Description," https://msdesc.github.io/consolidated-tei-schema/msdesc.html. For the Collections Trust Spectrum standard for inventory, see: "Inventory — the Spectrum Standard — Collections Trust," https://collectionstrust.org.uk/resource/inventory-the-spectrum-standard/.
11 Juxta (https://www.juxtasoftware.org/) is no longer supported by its developer, Performant Solutions.

But as I work my way through the lines of the manuscripts, the neatness of the digital presentation turns out to constantly trouble my reading of the text. The possibilities for identifying patterns across the variations are bewildering but they also seem to suggest that I should be looking for something that the manuscripts actually do not contain. Often a click on a deeply shaded word, frequently a common marker such as the Brajbhasha equivalent to modern Hindi's *ko*, presents me with an enormous number of variations, such as *kau/kauṃ/ko/koṃ/kuṃ/kū/kūṃ* and so on. They all mean the same and their variations are all, most of the time, completely meaningless in themselves. They reflect a vernacular language without a formal grammar and a text probably transmitted orally as much as through writing.

Viewed in this light, the variations are not an obstacle on the path to an original text, but rather essential parts of the text's fabric. This is the argument Cerquiglini developed on the basis of his work on early vernacular French manuscripts.[12] When the language(s) were fluid and with porous borders to other languages, similar to the compositions that circulated in and across those languages, variations, in Cerquiglini's phrase, are not to be endlessly categorized and sanitized, but to be praised. In the context of early modern North India, Bangha has elegantly argued that the individual manuscript can be understood as a unique performance, complete in and of itself.[13]

The collating software, just as the expectations I bring to it along with my TEI files, is underpinned by an assumption that the practice of collation is predicated on the philology of ancient languages. Within the discipline currently known as South Asia Studies, this all connects with a deeper historical current surrounding the place, privilege, and role of the Sanskrit language. I will pick up on this thread and its implications for my argument in a moment, but we must first turn to another of my pressure points: The map!

Mapping

On the other end of the project, I wish to create a map and a timeline to lay out the spatial history of the manuscripts in a visually appealing way. The project initially grew out of a work of scoping Wellcome Collection's medical manuscripts

---

12 Bernard Cerquiglini, *In Praise of the Variant: A Critical History of Philology* (Baltimore, MD: Johns Hopkins University Press, 1999).
13 Imre Bangha, "Dynamics of Textual Transmission in Premodern India: The Kavitavali of Tulsidas," *Comparative Studies of South Asia, Africa and the Middle East* 24, no. 2 (2004): 33–44. For more on Cerquiglini's argument applied to the study of early modern North Indian vernaculars and manuscript traditions, see: Plau, "Jain Narrative Literature."

in early modern vernaculars. Working from the cataloguing metadata supplied by Friedlander's pioneering work,[14] I identified 19 manuscripts for which, based on their colophons, we have both a time and a place of their copying. Using the brilliant tool TimeMapper,[15] an open source project from the Open Knowledge Foundation Labs, I can simply enter the data in a spreadsheet and find it converted into an appealing timeline with each manuscript also pinpointed on a map of India.

It is pleasingly familiar to see the manuscripts laid out on the map over an area that roughly corresponds with where the vernacular Brajbhasha of the medical manuscripts circulated in the period as a whole, forming a triangle between sites in Punjab, Rajasthan, and around Agra. Just as pleasingly, the lone Hindi manuscript copied in Tamil Nadu in the south stands out more clearly as unique in the collection. All in all, the map and timeline comfortably confirm with most of my expectations of how and where early modern North Indian vernacular manuscripts circulated.

And yet the visual appeal of the data as laid out on the map again serves to obscure my analysis and obfuscate the more complicated histories that the manuscripts might tell. Since the manuscripts without date or place information within their colophons necessarily are left out, the visualization obviously gives an impression of better oversight than I actually have. For the remaining nearly 180 manuscripts, I might have nothing but (more or less informed) guesses about their origins. While the map looks impressive, the really impressive thing here is the gap in our knowledge. Leaving this not insignificant problem aside for a moment, another issue is more problematic still: How did the manuscripts come to Wellcome Collection in the first place?

While this is a question with urgent ethical implications, I want to first consider the practical challenges it entails for my research. The manuscripts were, like most of Wellcome Collection's South Asian manuscript, purchased over a period of several decades, mostly in the first half of the twentieth century. Henry Wellcome employed full-time purchasing agents who travelled the world, including the colonized regions, purchasing manuscripts and other items from a variety of vendors and sites. Alongside this global activity, Wellcome purchased consistently, broadly, and lavishly from London auction houses. Throughout this period, an enormous amount of material flowed into Wellcome's storage sites at a rate far exceeding the London library team's ability to accession and catalogue. Many items, even whole collections, remain uncatalogued to this day.

---

14 Peter G. Friedlander, *A Descriptive Catalogue of the Hindi Manuscripts in the Library of the Wellcome Institute for the History of Medicine* (London: The Wellcome Institute for the History of Medicine, 1996).
15 See: TimeMapper, https://timemapper.okfnlabs.org/.

Studying the early modern North Indian medical manuscripts, including those of Nainsukh's *Vaidyamanotsava*, also entails researching these provenance histories. However, the map I have made seems to erase even the thought of provenance and acquisition histories, replacing it instead with an ahistorical neatness that might occlude rather than clarify. Where they, for instance, purchased in another site from where they were copied? How did they make it to that site? What manuscripts were not purchased at all? Would the lone Hindi manuscript in Tamil Nadu always stand out so uniquely? And does my map not really tell me anything about early modern circulation of manuscripts in North India, but rather of the purchasing practices of twentieth-century institutions in the UK?

All this is not to say that there is anything wrong with the tools themselves. I am definitely not saying that the issue will be resolved simply by having better tools. What I am saying is that these are issues that arise outside of the tools, prior to their use, and that the tools cannot be used to resolve them unless the researcher speaks of them. In the present case, that means turning to consider the Sanskrit-oriented underpinnings of my field and the wider histories that accompany both them and me.

Philology, Colonialism, and Orientalism

Western philological study of South Asian literary traditions has tended to overwhelmingly focus on material in Sanskrit. Indeed, William Jones's famous identification of Sanskrit as a close relative to Greek and Latin and so, to Jones's mind, a subject worthy of study, was a defining moment for the later rise of philology as *science* in the nineteenth century and, as Said has made clear, as a cultural power tool for imperialism.[16] The relative lack of studies on North India's vernacular traditions follows this tendency as a shadow, along with the often-repeated assumption that vernacular material essentially is Sanskrit translated and made accessible to wider audiences. There is little to no allowance for inventiveness, originality, or genuine cultural influence outside of Sanskrit.[17]

---

16 Edward W. Said, *Orientalism* (New York: Pantheon Books, 1978).
17 For further reading on the innovative aspects of early modern North Indian literary culture, see, for instance, Kenneth E. Bryant, *Poems to the Child-God: Structures and Strategies in the Poetry of Sūrdās* (Berkeley, CA: University of California Press, 1978); Francesca Orsini, "How to Do Multilingual Literary History? Lessons from Fifteenth- and Sixteenth-Century North India," *Indian Economic & Social History Review* 49, no. 2 (2012): 225–246; John Stratton Hawley, *A Storm of Songs: India and the Idea of the Bhakti Movement* (Cambridge, MA: Harvard University Press, 2015).

The narrative arc of a golden age followed by medieval decline is a core tenet of imperialism, in that it serves to provide an apparent rationale for colonization. Philology as the recovery of ancient splendor is a cornerstone of what was habitually presented as a humanist, rather than a capitalist, pursuit. The ideology is clearly on view in a lecture given by Captain Peter Johnston-Saint to the Indian Section of the Royal Society of Arts in 1929. Speaking on the theme "An Outline of the History of Medicine in India," Johnston-Saint gave a textbook example of the golden-age-to-medieval-lapse narrative. On the one hand, he lavished enormous praise on the ancient composers of medical treatises in Sanskrit, such as Sushruta and Charaka, even describing ancient India as the birthplace of medicine. On the other hand, Johnston-Saint was fiercely critical of the state of medicine in India at the time of colonization, stating, in a typical euphemism, that "the European introduction" found Indian medical science at "perhaps the lowest point in the curve in all its long history."[18] The cause of the decline? Johnston-Saint blames emergent restrictions on purity and, in an Islamophobic turn all too familiar to modern-day readers, "Moslem conquerors."[19]

Within this scheme, European colonialism invokes the familiar narrative of white saviors restoring ancient culture to the conquered. The scheme also mandates that the late medieval to early modern period must be inconsequential and stagnant. But, as Pollock points out,[20] the history of the changes colonization brought to South Asia cannot be written without knowing what was there to change immediately prior to colonization. Still, the inheritance of the "golden age" schema casts a shadow over studies of South Asian history, both within South Asia itself and beyond, as early modern sources are forced into a narrative dictated by colonialist knowledge production. Sources like Nainsukh's *Vaidyamanotsava* show that early modern South Asian medicine, like other aspects of early modern South Asian society and culture, was far more dynamic and diverse than the schema would have it. Still, many of the conceptual tools of the field, as well as the narratives surrounding it, remain informed by the expectations so clearly voiced by Johnston-Saint.

As for the linkage between intellectual narratives and colonial power, Johnston-Saint was not primarily a scholar but a Wellcome employee with varied roles, including periods as a purchasing agent. In the years following his 1929 lecture, he travelled through Palestine and Syria (in 1930, 1933, 1934, 1935) as well as India,

---

[18] Peter Johnston-Saint, "An Outline of the History of Medicine in India," *Journal of the Royal Society of Arts* 77 (1929): 846.
[19] Ibid., 868.
[20] Sheldon I. Pollock (ed.), *Forms of Knowledge in Early Modern Asia: Explorations in the Intellectual History of India and Tibet, 1500–1800* (Durham, NC: Duke University Press, 2011).

Sri Lanka, Egypt (1933, 1934), purchasing items in great quantities for what is today Wellcome Collection. His travels were partly made possible by his earlier career. Having joined the British Indian Army in 1907, Johnston-Saint spent the following seven years in India, rising to the rank of Cantonment Magistrate of Sitapur in 1914, and proceeded to spend most of WW1 in France as part of the Indian Cavalry.[21] Johnston-Saint embodies the marriage of military, intellectual, and institutional power.

It goes without saying in all this that Johnston-Saint is able to make his sweeping claims and go on his tours on the basis of his being a white man at the heart of the British Empire. His objectivity is predicated on assuming the universality of his privileged experience and its relevance to capital-t Truth. On a related note, Adluri and Bagchee have shown how nineteenth-century German Indology, often held aloft as a gold standard of philology in the study of South Asia, was riddled with racist assumptions and claims to genuinely objective insight about ancient Sanskrit literature.[22] This Eurocentric exceptionalist claim to privileged understanding is of course also racist. As Adluri recounts,[23] people from South Asia were, and still are, excluded from discussing South Asian literature in Western universities on bases such that only Europeans can fully understand it in an "objective" sense. While philology and related digital humanities technologies may have developed in progressive ways over the last centuries and decades, Adluri's all-too-common experiences of racism in contemporary academia highlight that social justice does not naturally follow from methodological innovation.

Returning to my research project, it is clear to me that some of my tools suggest that the early modern vernacular material should behave as Sanskrit because they believe that that would be a worthier thing to study. And taken at face value, they also present my data in ways that suggest a high degree of certainty and disinterested objectivity. I enter the data, and the digital humanities tools present an output that seems overwhelming in its apparent ability to provide broad and pathbreaking analysis. But looking closer I sometimes trace the outlines of problems that trouble the world in general: twenty-first century technology powered by

---

21 The details on Johnston-Saint's military career come from his own CV, submitted to Wellcome in 1919, see :"CV of Percy Johnston-Saint." WA/HMM/ST/Lat/A.115:Box 501. Wellcome Collection, 1919. Details on his purchasing tours are available through his diaries and reports, see: "Johnston-Saint Reports." WA/HMM/RP/Jst. Wellcome Collection, 1925.
22 Vishwa Adluri and Joydeep Bagchee, "German Indology and Hinduism," in *Handbook of Hinduism in Europe*, eds. Knut Axel Jacobsen and Ferdinando Sardella (Leiden: Brill, 2020), 90–122.
23 Adam-Jason Aronstein, "Against Occidentalism: A Conversation with Alice Crary and Vishwa Adluri on 'The Nay Science'," August 7, 2017, http://socialresearchmatters.org/against-occidentalism-a-conversation-with-alice-crary-and-vishwa-adluri-on-the-nay-science-2/.

nineteenth-century thinking. Beneath my code, my graphs, and my visualizations lie the ghosts of a self-avowed science that has a political and existential need to be *certain*.

Where Theory Is Most Rife

I have just referred to Adluri in the case of German Indology, but I am also inspired by Flood's critique of phenomenology in the study of religion.[24] There, Flood argues, the historical emphasis on exacting methodology distracts from the equally historical lack of willingness to engage with theory. The philosophical roots of this tendency, Flood finds, are in the influence from Husserl's idea of the transcendental subject. Through the methodological bracketing of phenomenology, in which a temporary suspension of judgments enables a genuinely pure vision, the transcendental subject is supposed to attain a state of total separation from other subjects, turning these into observable *phenomena*. As such, they appear to the transcendental subject as objects of study to be categorized, compared, and analyzed from a perspective that is neutral, devoid of value judgments.

Countering this conceptual structure by drawing on Bakhtin, Flood points to the inescapability of intersubjectivity. The interrelations of the researcher, the objects of study, the context of contemporary research cultures, the social, economic, and political pressures of academia, and the historical legacies that shape our lives; these are just a few of the elements that spring to mind. Acting as if these interrelations do not exist or, even worse, as if they can simply be disregarded in the name of perfected science, leads to their imprint leaving even deeper marks on the research itself. All this is even before the obvious interrelations of race, class, and privilege are taken into account. As Flood famously puts it, where *"theory is disavowed in the interests of objectivity, there theory is most rife."*[25] The same can be said about politicizing research: a stance not acknowledging the social and political context of the research being undertaken is the most political.

If used indiscriminately, and without critical reflection, digital humanities tools may serve to further decontextualize both the researcher and their activity in the name of neutrality, mimicking Husserl's detached and pure spirit that hovers above the muddy waters of the world. It is still the case that most researchers who are given access to digital humanities and get the opportunity to build careers in

---

[24] Gavin D. Flood, *Beyond Phenomenology: Rethinking the Study of Religion* (London and New York: Cassell, 1999). I am grateful to Anne Stensvold for introducing me to Flood's volume.
[25] Flood, *Beyond Phenomenology*, 17.

research are straight white men based in Western academic institutions that are in turn *literally* built on the exploitation of the rest of the world. Digital humanities can revolutionize the humanities, but the revolution is not meaningful if it is not also a revolution of access and a dismantling of historically accumulated influence, power, and wealth.

All this is not to say that there has not been a wealth of crucial and progressive developments in the fields of philology, South Asia Studies, and indeed the humanities as a whole over the last decades. Indeed, my own research work in this very chapter draws on developments such as these (I have already mentioned Bangha, Cerquiglini, and Pollock). Digital humanities, too, are rich in theoretical and methodological innovations that overturn problematic issues in earlier fields. However, just as novel ideas in classical philology cannot be applied wholesale to South Asia Studies without considering the particular historical power dynamics of that field, the digital humanities cannot turn its focus and apply its tools to primary source material from the majority world without reflecting on the specific historical and contemporary patterns of privilege, exclusion, and access involved.

This, then, is what I mean by digital Orientalism: the belief, conscious or not, that digital methodologies absolve researchers from their situatedness, allowing the practices and assumptions of academic Orientalism and racism to not only be carried over wholesale into digital spaces but actively wielding the tools of digital humanities to assert their power anew.[26] I am, of course, not thinking here of any generalized act of decontextualization on the part of a researcher or author, but of the kind that shrouds or negates a position of power derived from the particular historical trajectory of Western imperialism.

Vaidyamanotsava — Resuming the Study

With these thoughts in mind, I return to the *Vaidyamanotsava* manuscripts and my research project. How may I proceed in ways that are not only mindful of these reflections, but attempt to go one step further and try to act on them?

---

26 It should be noted that "digital Orientalism" is not the same as "digital colonialism," though the two are connected in both obvious and subtle ways. While the latter speaks to the ways digital methodologies may, for instance, be forcefully applied to exert ownership or authority over other people's material, digitized or born-digital, "digital Orientalism" concerns how racist othering, conscious or otherwise, becomes entrenched by using digital tools without reflecting on structures of privilege, power, and exclusion that are, at times, historical in origin but continue to shape personal and professional lives in the here and now.

A beginning might be to ask whether, and to what extent, my work does anything to increase the accessibility of the manuscripts themselves. As I mentioned earlier, my TEI files contain cataloguing information that is compliant with minimum viable description standards, mostly based on Friedlander's catalogue. Sadly, the standard for many collections of South Asian manuscripts held by Western institutions seems to still be to store the metadata in print catalogues that may or may not be made available in PDF or other digital formats. And while these catalogues contain expertly collected information, they are as a rule produced by academic researchers. This is evident in the terminology used, the amount of knowledge presumed on the part of the user, and in the use of Western academic standards and norms that, to many users, are more challenging to navigate than the manuscripts themselves.[27]

What I can do, however, is to share my files with the institution that holds the manuscripts, as well as making them freely available for anyone to read and use for their purposes, whatever they may be. In my case, even as I am now working within Wellcome Collection as a cataloguer, this also means acknowledging my shortcomings. I might be able to read and make sense of early modern North Indian manuscripts, but professional, trained librarians and archivists are far better than me in crafting consistent, accessible, and discoverable cataloguing metadata from whatever information I might possess. Similarly, I do not trust myself to create a database that will be comprehensible and useful to people outside of my field.

Similarly, I intend to publish the collated, critical edition of the *Vaidyamanotsava*, but I will also publish every single file with their individual transcripts. I think the shift here is mainly conceptual. I want to think of the research I make from these materials not as the endpoint, but as the appendix. I cannot take myself out of the equation, but I can do my best to enable others to do better, richer work than I am capable of. That also means ensuring that researchers in South Asia can, at the very least, access my transcriptions of the manuscripts that historical philology and its colonialist practices have claimed.

I am not saying that my TEI files are accurate representations of the manuscripts. They are not, and my position weighs heavily on them, as do all of my assumptions and the privilege of confidence that I, as a straight white man, default to. I obviously don't think a handful of TEI files can undo structural inequality. But I do think that engaging in digital humanities work, writing about it, and publishing

---

27 Mass digitization might not be a universal solution to the issue. Digitizing manuscripts is a costly and time-consuming process, frequently relying on an equally expensive process of conservation even to get started, and it in turn relies on a minimum of cataloguing work for the online images to make sense and be discoverable at all. See also the chapters by Van Lit and Van der Meij and Van der Putten in this volume for studies on the various aspects of digitization.

edited volumes about it, without mentioning structural inequality at all, is sure to entrench it further.

Which brings me to a second path forwards. The flexibility that digital humanities allow in describing and working with primary source material can bring enormous possibilities for going beyond conceptual assumptions. TEI, for instance, allows for a far more extensible register of descriptors and hierarchies in the description of primary source material than most forms of cataloguing software. Another obvious boon is the ability to input a variety of scripts. Being able to indicate in a consistent and structured way that there is a range of similar, but not identical, vernacular languages at play in the same manuscript renders that manuscript in turn more discoverable. Linking formats of the same title allows for bypassing the Sanskrit-based IAST transcription standard and render vernacular titles in formats that make more sense to language users.

These are just a few top-of-my-head examples, but the overall theme here is that the digital humanities should not aim to be too neat but rather for fuzziness. In my work with the *Vaidyamanotsava*, I was initially drawn to using digital tools not only for efficiency but in order to impose a sense of clarity and neatness on the otherwise overwhelming complexity and newness of the material before me. But that is exactly what I should not be doing. As I have argued throughout, the imposition of digital neatness is not free of implicit assumptions. If anything, what I should highlight is the moment when the enormous number of inessential variations for a single word across the manuscripts causes a bug and the software crashes. The vernacular variants, praise be to them, resisted what I was trying to do, and I am left with my messy desktop. And this is also part of what I hope digital humanities can do: show the places where systems break down, because that is where the new knowledge is.

Concluding Reflections

Digital Orientalism manifests as the appearance of Orientalist material in digital media and as the use of digital tools and methodologies to graft Orientalist thinking and assumptions onto primary source material from the majority world. Using several such tools while working on manuscripts of Nainsukh's *Vaidyamanotsava*, I am at every point likely to commit digital Orientalism unless I make a conscious effort to interrogate my thinking, my methodologies, and my positionality as a straight white male at a well-funded institution that holds thousands of majority-world items. Within the confines of my particular research project, I can do my best to free the primary source material — the manuscripts — from myself and my research by taking care to make it more accessible and discoverable than it was when I approached it. This is the primary outcome of my work, and I see it as, amongst other things, an enabling step for the restitution of items to the communities to whom they matter the most. I do welcome and support restitution as a slight beginning of Western institutions' acknowledgment of their participation in colonialist exploitation and actual dismantling of their hold on material to which they have no moral claim.[28]

A parting thought: it is now an emerging practice to speak of digital humanities when applied to the study of the majority world as "digital Orientalism," partly in an attempt to recover the Orientalist-word from the connotations with which I have spoken of it here. I think one can go one step further and acknowledge that thinking of "digital humanities" as referring only to the use of digital humanities in the study of the West, broadly understood, is an exclusionist narrowing — itself deeply Orientalist — and that it should be resisted. If you work on France, say so. If anything, this narrow use of the phrase could be replaced by "digital Westernist." As for "digital Orientalism"? I suggest a further stretch: "Digital globalism" and "digital globalist."

Bibliography

Adluri, Vishwa, and Joydeep Bagchee. "German Indology and Hinduism." In *Handbook of Hinduism in Europe*, edited by Knut Axel Jacobsen and Ferdinando Sardella, 90–122. Leiden: Brill, 2020.

Alimardani, Mahsa, and Mona Elswah. "Digital Orientalism: #SaveSheikhJarrah and Arabic Content Moderation." *POMEPS Studies 43: Digital Activism and Authoritarian Adaptation in the Middle East* 7 (2021).

Aronstein, Adam-Jason. "Against Occidentalism: A Conversation with Alice Crary and Vishwa Adluri on 'The Nay Science'," August 7, 2017, http://socialresearchmatters.org/against-occidentalism-a-conversation-with-alice-crary-and-vishwa-adluri-on-the-nay-science-2/.

Banārsīdās. *Half a Tale: A Study in the Interrelationship between Autobiography and History (The Ardhakathanaka)*, edited by Mukund Lath. New Delhi: Rupa, 2005.

Banārsīdās. *Ardhakathanak: A Half Story*, translated by Rohini Chowdhury. New Delhi: Penguin Books, 2009.

Bangha, Imre. "Dynamics of Textual Transmission in Premodern India: The Kavitavali of Tulsidas." *Comparative Studies of South Asia, Africa and the Middle East* 24, no. 2 (2004): 33–44.

Bryant, Kenneth E. *Poems to the Child-God: Structures and Strategies in the Poetry of Sūrdās*. Berkeley, CA: University of California Press, 1978.

---

[28] Thanks to a Headley Fellowship awarded by the Art Fund, which also supported the study underpinning this chapter, I have had the privilege to explore the possible restitution of Wellcome Collection's Jain manuscripts.

Cerquiglini, Bernard. *In Praise of the Variant: A Critical History of Philology*. Baltimore, MD: Johns Hopkins University Press, 1999.
"CV of Percy Johnston-Saint." WA/HMM/ST/Lat/A.115:Box 501. Wellcome Collection, 1919.
Flood, Gavin D. *Beyond Phenomenology: Rethinking the Study of Religion*. London and New York: Cassell, 1999.
Friedlander, Peter G. *A Descriptive Catalogue of the Hindi Manuscripts in the Library of the Wellcome Institute for the History of Medicine*. London: The Wellcome Institute for the History of Medicine, 1996.
Hawley, John Stratton. *A Storm of Songs: India and the Idea of the Bhakti Movement*. Cambridge, MA: Harvard University Press, 2015.
Health, Medicine and Treatment in early modern North India: Early Hindi medicine manuscripts in the Wellcome Collection, https://adrianplau.github.io/mss/MSHindi114.html.
"Inventory — the Spectrum Standard — Collections Trust," https://collectionstrust.org.uk/resource/inventory-the-spectrum-standard/.
Johnston-Saint, Peter. "An Outline of the History of Medicine in India." *Journal of the Royal Society of Arts* 77 (1929): 843–870.
"Johnston-Saint Reports." WA/HMM/RP/Jst. Wellcome Collection, 1925.
Kulkari, Supriya C., and Mohan R. Joshi. "Study of Manuscript Vaidyamanotsava." *Journal of Sanskrit Samhita Siddhanta* 3.1 (2017): 19–25.
Nainsukh. "Vaidyamanotsava." MS Indic Gamma 325. Wellcome Collection, 1668.
Nainsukh. "Vaidyamanotsava." MS Hindi 460. Wellcome Collection, 1723.
Nainsukh. "Vaidyamanotsava." MS Hindi 114. Wellcome Collection, n.d.
Orsini, Francesca. "How to Do Multilingual Literary History? Lessons from Fifteenth- and Sixteenth-Century North India." *Indian Economic & Social History Review* 49, no. 2 (2012): 225–246.
Plau, Adrian. "Early Modern Hinduism." In *Oxford History of Hinduism: Modern Hinduism*, ed. Torkel Brekke, 17–35. Oxford: Oxford University Press, 2019.
Plau, Adrian. "Jain Narrative Literature in Brajbhāṣā: Discussions from an Understudied Field." *Religions* 10.4 (2019): 262. DOI: https://doi.org/10.3390/rel10040262.
Pollock, Sheldon I., ed. *Forms of Knowledge in Early Modern Asia: Explorations in the Intellectual History of India and Tibet, 1500–1800*. Durham, NC: Duke University Press, 2011.
Said, Edward W. *Orientalism*. New York: Pantheon Books, 1978.
"TEI P5 Customization and Encoding Guidelines for Manuscript Description," https://msdesc.github.io/consolidated-tei-schema/msdesc.html.

Texts

Peter Flügel
The Jaina Prosopography Database: A New Tool for the Humanities

On March 27, 2021, at the 22nd Annual Jaina Studies Workshop at SOAS the new searchable Jaina-Prosopography Database (JPD) was launched, which is freely available online.[1] The database is an outcome of the Centre of Jaina Studies (CoJS) research project *Jaina-Prosopography — Jaina Monastic Lineages, Networks and Patronage*, funded by Leverhulme Trust Grant 2016-454. It is a new sociological tool for the exploration of documented relationships between members of the Jaina mendicant lineages and their supporters, focusing on the nexus of monastic recruitment, geographical circulation of monks and nuns, their careers, literary production, and patronage of mendicant inspired religious ventures.[2] The database enables the investigation of relationships between named individuals, places, events, and works via advanced search and browse functionalities, descriptive statistics, network diagrams, spatial mapping and other visualization techniques.[3] Presently it holds cross-referenced historical data pertaining to more than 21,000 individuals whose attributes and relations were coded with the help of 37 categorical variables and more than 2,500 sub-variables to capture the entire range of associated biodata, social relationships, positions, roles, events and objects recorded in published sources, and over 500 place coordinates, and related bibliographical details on more than 7,000 manuscripts, inscriptions, and published works. The data can be downloaded and used by anyone under Creative Commons Attribution-NonCommercial-ShareAlike 4.0 International License.

---

1 Jaina Prosopography Database, https://jaina-prosopography.org.
2 For a brief description of the database see the webpage itself, Julie Hanlon, "The Jaina Prosopography Project and Database," *Jaina Studies: Newsletter of the Centre of Jaina Studies* 16 (2021): 11–13, and Peter Flügel, "Collaborations in Jaina Prosopography," *Annals of the Bhandarkar Oriental Research Institute* (in press).
3 Peter Flügel, "Jaina-Prosopography I: Sociology of Jaina-Names," in *Jaina Studies. Select Papers Presented in the 'Jaina Studies' Section at the 16th World Sanskrit Conference*, eds. Nalini Balbir and Peter Flügel (Delhi: Rashtriya Sanskrit Sansthan & D.K. Publishers, 2018), 187–267; Peter Flügel, "Jaina-Prosopography II: 'Patronage' in Jaina Epigraphic and Manuscript Catalogues," in *Gift of Knowledge: Patterns of Patronage in Jainism*, eds. Christine Chojnacki and Basile Leclère (Bangalore: National Institute of Prakrit Research Shravanabelagola, 2018), 1–46.

Note: I am grateful to Shailesh Shinde, Priyanka Shah, Kamini Gogri and Jinesh Sheth for providing information and photographs from their own JPD related research, illustrating the craft of the researchers of the Jaina Prosopography Teams and the range of outcomes.

Despite careful production of our books, sometimes mistakes happen. We apologize that in the original version of the chapter by Peter Flügel "The Jaina Prosopography Database: A New Tool for the Humanities", the Devanagari script was displayed incorrectly.
https://doi.org/10.1515/9783110747607-008

A Prosopographical Database

The idea of a prosopographical database with a sociological focus emerged organically from a previous CoJS project on *Johannes Klatt's Jaina-Onomasticon*.[4] The initial aim of the Jaina-Prosopography project was to cross-reference the complex bio-bibliographic data of more than 5,055 historical Jaina individuals that were collated between 1880 and 1892 by Johannes Klatt in his *Jaina-Onomasticon*, and make them available in form of a database with the capacity to incorporate potentially all available historical information on the Jaina tradition. The main case study resulting from the JPD project to date is the prosopographical examination of bio-bibliographical data in Klatt's work which was accomplished by K. Krümpelmann. Statistical analysis of the resulting dataset by P. Flügel and K. Krümpelmann with technical support of Harish Krishnappa led to a substantial book publication of twenty-five prosopographical indexes with an introductory essay, the *Index to Johannes Klatt's Jaina-Onomasticon*.[5]

Key in the process of database construction was the development of a sophisticated data model capable of integrating variant historical information scattered through the vast body of relevant published biographical texts, chronicles, colophons and inscriptions to enable the visualization and analysis of historical networks through data linkage on a large scale. The heart of the database is an extensive, largely inductively generated taxonomy for the coding of information related to named individuals. The expandable and amendable taxonomy was created by the editors P. Flügel and K. Krümpelmann, who between 2017 and 2020 produced the prototype of the Jaina-Prosopography Database together with software engineers of the Digital Humanities Institute at Sheffield University.[6]

---

[4] Funded by Leverhulme Trust Research Grant RPG-2012-620. See: Peter Flügel, "Life and Work of Johannes Klatt," in *Jaina-Onomasticon*, eds. Peter Flügel and Kornelius Krümpelmann (Wiesbaden: Harrassowitz, 2016), 9–164, on the indirect influence of T. Mommsen's project *Prosopographia Imperii Romani* (PIR) on Klatt (p. 113). Reviews: W. Bollée, *Orientalistische Literaturzeitung* 112 (2017) 434; L. De Boer, *Bulletin of the School of Oriental and African Studies* 81 (2018) 2; A. Natu, *Annals of the Bhandarkar Oriental Research Institute* 96 (2019) 108-111; P. Dundas, *Journal of the American Oriental Society* 140, 2 (2020) 526–527; C. Emmrich, "Unfinished Business and Reinventing the New," *Indo-Iranian Journal* 65 (2022) 249–266.

[5] Peter Flügel and Kornelius Krümpelmann, *Index to Johannes Klatt's Jaina-Onomasticon*, Jaina Studies 2 (Wiesbaden: Harrassowitz & Royal Asiatic Society of Great Britain and Ireland, 2024), published with support of the Leverhulme Trust (Project No. 2016–454) and the ERC-Project *Beyond Boundaries: Religion, Region, Language and the State* (Project No. 609823).

[6] The software was developed by Katherine Rogers, Ryan Bloor, Matthew Groves, and Michael Pidd.

The taxonomy features a double register, linking generic terms, required for statistical analysis, with synonymous diplomatically recorded variant terms. Most of the generic terms are Sanskrit and Hindi words selected from the sources by the editors or artificially created in view of their utility for standardization. The binominal structure provides the taxonomy with a standardized framework and with flexibility for the progressive fine-tuning of the system of analytic categories in the light of new evidence, as does the option for individual researchers to create new sub-categories with variants.[7] Effectively the binominal register distinguishes between form and content of a named entity. The resultant capacity of the taxonomy to accommodate historical linguistic detail at a granular level enhances its utility for a multitude of research questions.

A second key feature of the database is that all entries are source-referenced at general and granular levels.[8]

In the process of data analysis the data model was tested, refined and data quality assessed in view of its value for statistical analysis. Experience showed that compilations of primary source data proved to be easier to work with than aggregated meta-data of varying depth and reliability. This practical finding points to the future necessity of producing meta-data in such a way that they can be unambiguously used for context-sensitive secondary analyses of different kinds. To date most indexes, catalogues, onomastica and data repositories were created without taking the potential of meta-data analyses into account.

The "Role" and "Relationship" indexes in the *Index to Johannes Klatt's Jaina-Onomasticon* demonstrate that although Klatt's work records many relations of spiritual, political and material "patronage" — three types of patronage that are

---

[7] It should be noted that the need for a double register for taxonomic units was not premeditated but emerged in the process of coding data. The significance of the design choice became only apparent post factum and was then further elaborated. Binominal registers were initially introduced to provide fields for "variant names" related to "generic names" and for variant "Hindi" (Indic) synonyms of generic categories in "English" designating types of roles and relationships, which were envisioned from the outset.

[8] All linguistic and technical aspects of the database were extensively discussed before and during the project with staff of DHIS and advisers. Official advisers of the project were: Burkhard Quessel (British Library), J.C. Wright (SOAS), Renate Söhnen-Thieme (SOAS), Karin Preisendanz (University of Vienna), and Yigal Bronner (Hebrew University of Jerusalem). Special advisers were: John Bradley (Kings College London), Katherine Keats-Rohan (University of Oxford), Gabriel Bodard (London School of Advanced Study), Dominik Wujastyk (University of Alberta), Kalpana Sheth (Ahmedabad), Nagaraj Kulkarni (Compegence, Bangalore), Harish Krishnappa (Compegence, Bangalore), Himal Trikha (University of Vienna), Michael Willis (Royal Asiatic Society), Charles Li (Bibliothèque nationale de France), Ācārya Ajayasāgara (Koba), Seema Gala (Vapi, Gujarat), Matthäus Heil (Akademie der Wissenschaften, Berlin), and Andrew Ollett (University of Chicago). Special thanks are due to the staff of the Research Office of SOAS, especially Alex Lewis.

rarely distinguished —, only a limited number of the named relationships can be unambiguously coded and statistically investigated, not to speak of inferred patronage links. To some extent this is due to the conceptual vagueness of current models of "patron-client" relationships which take little notice of contextual linguistic and social complexities. But the main difficulty remains the varying quality of primary source data, the recording of which continues to be the focus of historical research on "patronage" relations.[9]

Particularly difficult is the determination of the contextual meaning of "teacher-disciple" relationships. Not even in the primary sources the three principal, sometimes combined, positions and roles of designated Jaina *gurus* are clearly discernible: temporary or perpetual academic teacher (*śikṣā-guru*, etc.), legal preceptor of an initiate (*paramparā-guru*, *dīkṣā-guru*,[10] etc.), and legal leader of the order (*guru*, *dharma-guru*, etc.), not to mention their representations (*sthāpanā-guru*). The specific role of an individual described as "teacher" can generally only be inferred through cross-referencing. It is rarely specified.

To enable analysts to distinguish preceptor-disciple lineages (*gurvāvalī*) and lines of succession (*paṭṭāvalī*),[11] the complementary monastic roles "teacher of_" and "disciple of_" have been classified as types of "monastic relationship" and the complementary roles "predecessor of_" and "successor of_" as "role" types. The somewhat artificial categorization highlights an important difference between the two sets of complementary role types commonly objectified as legal "relationships," depicted as directed graphs or simple lines connecting two points in the network visualizations database, which can be further extended to sequences by connecting three or more points with a continuing line (*āvalī*), representing, for instance, historical links across generations (*paramparā*). In contrast to *guru-śiṣya* relationships which allocate differential role expectations to pairs of living individuals, like father and son or mother and daughter, relationships between predecessors and successors are generally not associated with role expectations affecting pairs of living individuals. They are legal statuses retrospectively attributed to diachronically linked occupants of the position of group leader (*paṭṭadhara* etc.). Diachronic "relationships" of succession or "roles" of predecessor and successor recorded in lineage constructs contrast with a set of synchronic "roles" associated with the "monastic positions" of "head of the order" (*ācārya*, etc.) and "dedicated successor" (*yuvācārya*, etc.), following the model relationship of king (*rāja*) and crown prince (*yuvarāja*).

---

9 See: Flügel, "Jaina-Prosopography II".
10 Distinguished from the role of the mendicant that performs the initiation ceremony (*dīkṣā-dātā*).
11 The terms *gurvāvalī* and *paṭṭāvalī* refer both to lineages and to the lists recording them.

It is clear from this brief exposition of the types of questions faced in the process of database construction at the backend that the term "role" is presently used in two different ways in the data model for lack of alternatives.

Problems of modelling and coding types of named relationships and roles with the help of generic categories such as patron and client, teacher and disciple or predecessor and successor cannot always be resolved. If this is the case it has been recorded in the database field "notes."

Compared to information embedded in meta-catalogues, and colophons, Jaina image inscriptions seem to provide relatively unambiguous data which can easily be classified and statistically analyzed. Yet even in the narrowly circumscribed textual formats employed for recording consecration ceremonies it is often not entirely clear who is who, who exactly paid for what, who offered immaterial forms of political or spiritual support, and where the event took place.[12] The exhaustive statistical investigation of questions such as these is only possible when individual cases are disambiguated through cross-referencing and taxonomic categories are progressively refined in view of both the data and aspects of theoretical generalization.

The conundrums faced in the process of coding in a consistent manner the "roles" of "patron" and "client,"[13] "teacher" and "disciple" and hyphenated "relationships" such as "patron-client," "teacher-disciple" and "predecessor-successor" illustrate that (re-)categorization of historical data for statistical analysis does not necessarily lead to undue simplification but to a fuller exploration of its inherent complexity.[14]

Adding Datasets

To expand the scope of the project beyond the first phase dedicated to the creation of the conceptual and technological infrastructure at the hand of Klatt's meta-data, and explore ways in which the new taxonomy of the database can account for variants in the entire corpus of published information pertaining to Jaina history, a number of supplementary datasets were created to be investigated through case studies in the near future. Simon Winant of the University of Ghent joined SOAS

---

[12] The place of residence of patrons is usually mentioned in image inscriptions, not the place of consecration.
[13] Operationalized in different contexts with different sets of categories such as donor (*dātā*) and receiver (*grāhaka*) or intended receiver (*lābhārthī*).
[14] Cf. Klaus Bruhn, "The Analysis of Jina Images," *Berliner Indologische Studien* 2 (1986): 133–174 (p. 158).

as an intern in 2017 and prepared a dataset on the Jaina inscriptions published in the *Epigraphia Indica* post 1892 (the period not covered by Klatt).[15] At SOAS, P. Flügel, Samani Pratibha Pragya[16] and Alice Rogovoy generated prosopographical data on the aniconic Jaina traditions based on three different sources: Muni Navaratnamala's (1992–1999) *Śāsanasamudra*, a multi-volume anthology on the Terāpanth mendicants, a dataset on Sthānakavāsī and Loṅkāgaccha mendicants collated by P. Flügel,[17] and colophon data from manuscripts on the Loṅkā and Sthānakavāsī traditions prepared by P. Flügel and Kalpana Sheth in Ahmedabad.[18] Work on these datasets is still continuing. A further researcher related to Jain Vishva Bharati London, Samani Punya Pragya, joined the team at SOAS working on the excellent historical data of the Śvetāmbara Terāpanth that were compiled on suggestion of its visionary leader Ācārya Tulasī (1914–1997).

New Analysis to Enrich the Database

In a third phase the scope of the project was further extended, following the signing of two project related MoUs between SOAS and the Bhandarkar Oriental Research Institute (BORI) in Pune on April 19, 2019[19] and the Department of Prakrit and Pali of Gujarat University (GU) in Ahmedabad on September 27, 2019.[20] S.S. Bahulkar and Amruta Natu of BORI and Dinanath Sharma of Gujarat University facilitated the agreements, which have enhanced the visibility of the project and allowed partner institutions to independently raise funds for specific research projects related to the Jaina-Prosopography Database. The institutional collaborations proved to be extremely productive and can serve as models for similar collaborations.

---

15 See: Simon Winant, "Redemption or Death. Jainism's Transformation of the Hindu Villain Kīcaka in Jaina Mahābhāratas," Doctoral thesis (University of Ghent, forthcoming).
16 See: Samani Pratibha Pragya, "Prekṣā Meditation: History and Methods," Doctoral thesis (SOAS, University of London, 2017).
17 The dataset elaborates on Sumana Muni, *Pañjāba Śramaṇa Saṃgha Gaurava Ācārya Śrī Amarasiṃha Jī Mahārāja: Jīvana Carita aura Paramparā Paricaya* (Madrasa: Bhagavāna Mahāvīra Svādhyāya Pīṭha, 1970); Sāgaramala Jaina and Vijaya Kumāra, *Sthānakavāsī Jaina Paramparā kā Itihāsa* (Vārāṇasī: Pārśvanātha Vidyāpīṭha, 2003).
18 Literary Heritage of the Aniconic Jaina Tradition (British Academy and Leverhulme Trust, Project SG15213), https://digital.soas.ac.uk/cojsa.
19 The Bhandarkar Oriental Research Institute, https://www.bori.ac.in/.
20 Gujarat University, Department of Prakrit and Pali, https://www.gujaratuniversity.org.in/web/WebDPrakrit.asp.

At present, the main focus of the research group at BORI, supervised by Amruta Natu, is the prosopographical analysis of H.R. Kapadia's five volume catalogue of the Śvetāmbara Jaina manuscripts at the Bhandarkar Oriental Research Institute.[21] The project at BORI is independently financed through the support of the Sanmati Teerth Sanstha, which initially agreed to sponsor one full-time researcher from 2020, and of the Shri Firodia Trust which after the public launch of the database in 2021 added its support and funded one further full-time researcher at Pune, and five part time postgraduate and post-doctoral researchers in Ahmedabad.

The research group at Ahmedabad comprises of five postgraduate students of Dinanath Sharma who after receiving training in prosopographical methodology volunteered for an entire year working on the prosopographical analysis of the Digambara and Śvetāmbara Jaina inscriptions in Ahmedabad collected by P.C. Parikh and B.K. Shelat.[22] They have now joined the team at BORI focusing on the analysis of the data collated in M.D. Deśāī's and J. Koṭhārī's monumental catalogue of Jaina manuscripts composed in Gujarati, which explicitly builds on Klatt's published articles.[23]

Three further postgraduate volunteers, two from Mumbai[24] and one from Vapi in Gujarat,[25] are presently working on the data on Jaina *sādhvī*s that were compiled by Sādhvī Vijayaśrī "Āryā"[26] to increase the proportion of females represented in the database, and Jinesh Sheth, a volunteer PhD candidate from Mumbai University, analyzed place names and the meta-data of selected Jaina manuscripts published online by the Cambridge University Library.[27]

---

21 Hiralal Rasikdas Kapadia, *Descriptive Catalogue of the Government Collection of Manuscripts Deposited at the Bhandarkar Oriental Research Institute. Volume XVII–XIX: Jaina Literature and Philosophy*, (Poona: BORI, 1935–1977).
22 Praveenchandra Parikh and Bharati Shelat, *Jain Image Inscriptions of Ahmedabad* (Ahmedabad: B.J. Institute of Learning of Research, 1997).
23 Mohanalāla Dalīcanda Deśāī, ed., *Jaina Gūrjara Kavio*, Bhāga 1-4 (Mumbaī: Jaina Śvetāmbara Conference Office, 1926–1944). Second revised edition: Jayanta Koṭhārī, ed., *Jaina Gūrjara Kavio*, Bhāga 1-10 (Mumbaī: Mahāvīra Jaina Vidyālaya, 1986–1997). See: Vol. 9, pp. 7ff. Deśāī linked his pioneering work explicitly to J. Klatt's publications on Jaina *paṭṭāvalis*.
24 Kamini Gogri of Mumbai completed her PhD in 2006 at the University of Mumbai on "Jain Reform Movements." Varsha Shah of Mumbai completed her PhD in 2023 at the University of Mumbai.
25 Seema Gala of Vapi recently joined the Jaina-Prosopography Research Group. She completed in 2019 a PhD at the Open International University for Complementary Medicines with a thesis on the A(ñ)calagaccha, "Biography of Jain Acharya Achal Gacchadhipati Param Pujya Shri Gun Sagar Suri Ji Maharaj Saheb." She is working on data pertaining to the *sādhvī*s of the Añcalagaccha published by Sādhvī "Āryā" Vijayāśrī (see note 24).
26 Sādhvī "Āryā" Vijayāśrī, *Jaina Dharma kī Śramaṇiyoṃ kā Bṛhad Itihāsa*, Bhāga I-II (Dillī: Bhāratīya Vidyā Pratiṣṭhāna, 2007).
27 Cambridge Digital Library, https://cudl.lib.cam.ac.uk/.

The CoJS continues to widen the network of cooperating research institutions and researchers, provides training, and coordinates the work of the research teams. It also helps soliciting sponsorship. The aim is to find funding for all volunteers who have completed their training in prosopographical methodology and are committed to full-time or part-time work on the database, and to further expand the number of researchers to make sure a substantial amount of the published data can be analyzed and entered into the database in the next years. An evident desideratum was the expansion of work on Digambara sources, which was championed by the late Nirmal Sethi, president of the All India Digamber Jain Heritage Preservation Organisation. After his demise the Jivdaya Foundation of V. Jain in Dallas sponsored two independent fulltime postgraduate researchers from 2022.[28]

New Insights

Prosopographical study of selected datasets[29] is not only contributing to the cross-referencing of data and quantitative analysis via the JPD. It also produces new insights in circumscribed fields of study. Herein lies one of the main contributions of this new approach. The following examples of selected findings of researchers in Ahmedabad, Pune, and Mumbai demonstrate how re-analysis of published data leads not only to a refinement of the historical record but also to entirely new insights. They offer a glimpse into the meticulous philological and prosopographical analyses that are required for the development of the contents of the database, through cross-checking and cross-referencing of new data and adjustment of the taxonomy of the JPD progressively refining the quality of the data, and generate a deeper understanding of the evidence, a process that remains largely invisible to the user of the database.

The team of scholars educated at the Department of Prakrit and Pali, School of Languages, Gujarat University in Ahmedabad comprised of five prosopographers in 2020–2021: Purvi Mahendra,[30] Jolly Sandesara,[31] Akshita Sanghvi,[32] Kinjal

---

28 Mansi Dhariwal and Charul Jain.
29 Cf. Klaus Bruhn, "Sectional Studies in Jainology," in *Middle Indo-Aryan and Jaina Studies (World Sanskrit Conference Leiden)*, ed. Colette Caillat (Leiden: E. J. Brill, 1991), 36–59.
30 See: Purvi Darshan Mahendra, "Political and Educational Policy in Maurya Period Based on Prakrit Texts English Language," Doctoral thesis (Gujarat University, 2019).
31 See: Jolly Sandasara, *Literary Criticism of Kuvalaymālā* (Varanasi: Parshwanath Vidyapeeth, 2019).
32 See: A. Sanghvi, "Kanakāmara Muni's (1065 CE) Apabhraṃśa Text Karakaṃḍa Cariu with a Gujarati Translation of Lilāvatī Kahā," MA Thesis (Gujarat University, 2021).

Shah,[33] and Priyanka Shah.[34] The team members initially worked on the prosopographical analysis of 893 Sanskrit Jain image inscriptions in Ahmedabad that were published by P.C. Parikh and B.K. Shelat in 1997 together with a brief introduction and indexes on types of icons, names of mendicants, householders, *gacchas*, *gotras*, castes and places. In the course of prosopographical investigations the reading of the inscriptions could be improved, family relations clarified, dates double checked, abbreviations deciphered, and many cross-references with data compiled by Klatt and Kapadia established. Most of the inscriptions dating from Vi.Saṃ. 1235 to Vi.Saṃ. 1628 are engraved on the back of small movable metal statues. The majority are composed in the same format as in the following example (Fig. 1). The unambiguous text cat. No. 326, records the consecration of a small Vimalanātha bronze statue preserved in the Nemīnātha Mandira in Manasukhabhāī Seṭh's Poḷ in Dośīvāḍa Poḷ in Ahmedabad (new translation):

> saṃvat 1512 varṣe māgha-sudi 5 some Śrīmāla-jñātīya-pitṛSomasī-mātṛMāī-śreyase suta Velā Doīā Varasiṃha etai[ḥ] śrīVimalanātha-biṃbaṃ kāritaṃ śrīPūrṇimā-pakṣe śrīSādhuratnasūriṇām upadeśena pratiṣṭhitaṃ vidhinā Kaṭakastaṃbha-grāme vāstavya

> For the bliss of their father Somasī and mother Māī of the Śrīmāla caste [their] sons Velā, Doīā and Varasiṃha, residents of the village of Kaṭakastaṃbha, had the image of Śrī Vimalanātha made. It was consecrated [by an unknown monk] on instruction of Śrī Sādhuratna-sūri of the Śrī Pūrṇimā-pakṣa in the saṃvat year 1512, on the 5th of the bright half of [the month of] Māgha, a Monday [= January 12, 1456].

Prosopographical coding of the information required *śreyas* (bliss, welfare) in this and other inscriptions to be defined as an "object" "given," in this case to the parents of the donors, in a similar way as the implied payment made by the commissioning donors to the unnamed artist.[35] In contrast to the unidentifiable artist,[36] the consecrating monk was recorded as "unknown," since he is indirectly identified through his relationship to Sādhuratna, which may lead to the future discovery of his identity through cross-referencing. It is generally unclear where the consecration of mobile bronze statues took place, because usually only the place of residence of the main sponsor is mentioned (mendicants have no fixed abode). Cross-referencing with

---

33 See: K. Shah, "Literary Criticism of Rudradasa's Candaleha," Doctoral thesis (Gujarat University, forthcoming).
34 See: P. Shah, "A Critical Study of Prakrit Sarvasawam by Markandeya," Doctoral thesis (Gujarat University, 2018). Her work has won three awards.
35 Cf. John E. Cort, "Doing for Others: Merit Transfer and Karma Mobility in Jainism," in *Jainism and Early Buddhism. Essays in Honor of Padmanabh S. Jaini*, ed. Olle Qvarnström (Fremont, CA: Asian Humanities Press, 2003), 129–150.
36 See editorial note no. 25 at: "Editorial Notes," Jaina Prosopography Database, https://jaina-prosopography.org/about/editorial.

Fig. 1: Vimalanāthabimba, Nemīnātha Mandira, Ahmedabad. (Priyanka Shah, January 27, 2021).

other inscriptions established that Sādhuratna-sūri's successor was Sādhusundara-sūri, who may turn out to be the unidentified consecrating monk. How the studied portable bronze statues ended up in the different temples of Ahmedabad will in most cases never be known. The main prosopographical value of inscriptions are the hard facts they offer which can help identify individual historical agents, in particular Jaina monks, through cross-referencing with other data. The prosopographical analysis of the published dataset on (Digambara and Śvetāmbara) image inscriptions in Ahmedabad can serve as the basis for case studies using descriptive statistics and mapping, which in future may be linked to similar datasets.[37] Many modern bronzes

---

[37] On inscriptions of individual Jaina bronzes see for instance: Johannes Klatt, "Note on an Inscribed Statue of Pârśvanâtha," in "The Samachari-Satakam of Samayasundara and pattavalis of the Anchala-Gachchha and other Gachchhas (Revised with additions by Ernst Leumann)," *The Indian Antiquary* 23 (1894): 183, n. 9. (Photos of the statue in: Peter Flügel, "Life and Work of

are fakes, produced for the international art market.³⁸ But the reliability of the older publications of Jaina image inscriptions is not affected by this recent development.

Until the end of 2021, the team at BORI comprised of project leader Amruta Natu, Assistant Curator,³⁹ and Shailesh Shinde,⁴⁰ Research Assistant, working on the above mentioned volumes of the Kapadia catalogue. For one year Krushna Mali joined this team as well. The catalogue offers much information left out by Klatt, who covered the majority of the sources already in his *magnum opus*. Kapadia also offered a rudimentary outline of unutilized prosopographical categories.⁴¹ The following six examples are indicative of Shailesh Shinde's findings, which are now cross-linked with other data through the JPD and supplement and refine both Klatt's and Kapadia's earlier works.⁴²

a. The use of yellow pigment for erasing colophon renders some passage difficult to read and hence were left undeciphered by Kapadia. For instance, in Vol. 17.1 Cat. no. 415, Page no. 372, the colophon of a manuscript of the *Piṇḍaviśuddhisubodhā* is recorded as follows with spaces for unreadable passages: श्रीखरतरगच्छे श्रीपत्तने श्रीकीर्ति[...] श्रीकल्याणचंद्रोपाध्याय[...]॥

At closer inspection of the referred folio (52b) of the ms. no. 1206/1887–1891 (Fig. 2) it was found that it was written in Pattana (Pāṭaṇa) for Upādhyāya Kalyāṇacandra by Ācārya Kīrtiratna of the Kharataragaccha: श्रीखरतरगच्छे श्रीपत्तने श्रीकीर्तिरत्नाचार्यैः शिष्य श्रीकल्याणचंद्रोपाध्यजी पठनार्थं लिखितो ग्रन्थः॥

Johannes Klatt," in *Jaina-Onomasticon*, eds. Peter Flügel and Kornelius Krümpelmann (Wiesbaden: Harrassowitz, 2016), 105; Ācārya Buddhisāgarasūri, *Jaina Dhātupratimā Lekha-Saṃgraha*, vol. 1-2 (Bombay: Adhyātma Jñāna Prasāraka Maṇḍala, 1918–1924); Muni Kāntisāgara, ed., *Jaina Dhātu-Pratimālekha Saṃgraha*, Bhāga 1 (Sūrata: Mantrī, Jinadattasūri Jñānabhaṇḍāra, 1950); Umakant Premanand Shah, "Bronze Hoard from Vasantagadh," *Lalita Kalā* 1, no. 2 (1955/1956): 55–65; Umakant Premanand Shah, *Akota Bronzes* (Bombay: Department of Archaeology, Government of Bombay, 1959); Lakṣmaṇabhāī Hīrālāla Bhojaka, *Pāṭaṇa-Jaina-Dhātu-Pratimā-Lekha-Saṃgraha* (Delhi: Motilal Banarsidass, 2002); John E. Cort, "A Digambar Icon of 24 Jinas at the Ackland Art Museum," *Jaina Studies: CoJS Newsletter* 7 (2012), 30–33; J. Clifford Wright, "The Ackland Art Museum's Image of Śāntinātha," *Jaina Studies: CoJS Newsletter* 8 (2013): 29–30; J. Clifford Wright, "Two Inscribed Digambara Bronzes," *Jaina Studies: CoJS Newsletter* 9 (2014): 34–35.
38 See: Peter Flügel, Patrick Krüger and Priyanka Shah, "Six Jaina Bronzes," in *Pure Soul: The Jaina Spiritual Traditions*, ed. Peter Flügel, Heleen De Jonckheere, and Renate Söhnen-Thieme (London: Centre of Jaina Studies, SOAS, 2023), 96–103.
39 See: Amruta Natu, *Georg Bühler's Contribution to Indology*, Opera Minora No. 12 (Piscataway, NJ: Gorgias Press, Harvard Oriental Series, 2020).
40 PhD candidate at Deccan College Post-Graduate and Research Institute, Pune, on the topic "Historical Study of Jaina Manuscripts Extracts."
41 See the analysis in: Flügel, "Jaina-Prosopography II."
42 See also: Shailesh Shinde and Krushna Mali, "Jaina Prosopography: Key Findings from the Bhandarkar Oriental Research Institute Manuscripts," *Jaina Studies: Newsletter of the Centre of Jaina Studies* 18 (2023): 17–22.

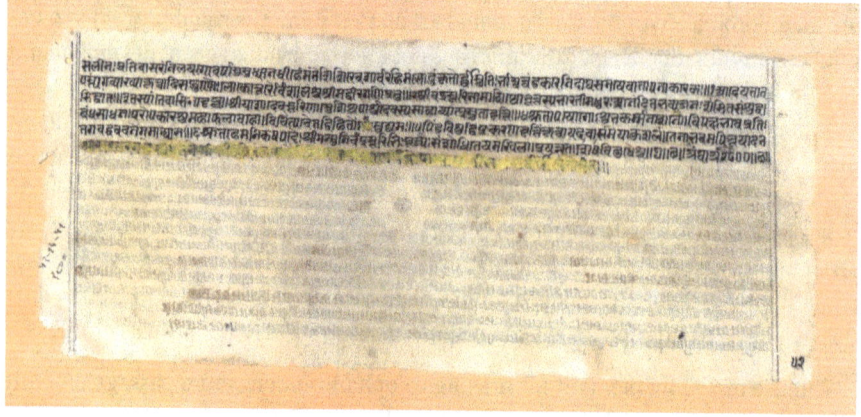

Fig. 2: *Piṇḍaviśuddhisubodhā*, p. 52. (Shailesh Shinde, Pune, January 22, 2021).

b. The use of yellow pigment for erasing a manuscript owner's name prompted Kapadia not to include the last part of last line of the *Bhagavatīsūtraparyāya*, manuscript Vol. 17.1, Cat. no. 53, Page no. 51. It is recorded as इति सूत्रकृतांगपर्यायाः समाप्ताः॥छ॥

Yet the last folio (41b) of ms. no. 736/1875–1876 shows that this manuscript once belonged to Dhīrddhisundarī: इतिसूत्रकृतांगपर्यायाःसमाप्ताः॥छ॥ धीऋद्धिसुंदरीइप रतिदं। धा

c. Names in colophons left unidentified by Kapadia include the following example. His extract from the colophon of *Samavāyāṅgasūtra* manuscript Vol. 17.1, Cat. no. 78, Page no. 73, includes the line no. 23: ॥श्रीमेरा(?)गच्छेशश्रीसौसामा(?)सुंदरसूरिलिषापितं।सं. श्रीमंडलिके॥ At closer inspection of the colophon of ms. no. 215/1873–74, folio 38b, line no. 2 allows to interpret the name of the writer as Saubhāgyasundarasūri rather than as Sausāmāsundarasūri: ॥श्रीमेरा(?)गच्छेशश्रीसौ भाग्यसुंदरसूरिलिखापितं। सं. श्रीमंडलिके॥

d. Identifying uncertain names of proper places proved to be possible by revisiting the original manuscript. In Kapadia's catalogue the non-existing place name पीरसरा is mentioned with reference to the colophon of a *Sthānāṅgasūtraṭabā* Vol. 17.1, Cat. no. 63, Page no. 61, line no. 10. But the ms. no. 259/1871–1872, folio 273a, line no. 12 shows that "pa" must be read as "ṣa," yielding the name खीरसरा (in Kutch, Gujarat) (Fig. 3).

e. A number of new findings can be reported with regard to the manuscript of the *Kalpasūtravṛtti* (Cat. no. 546) of Udayasāgara, pupil of Dharmaśekhara, for both of whom Klatt did not provide a date.

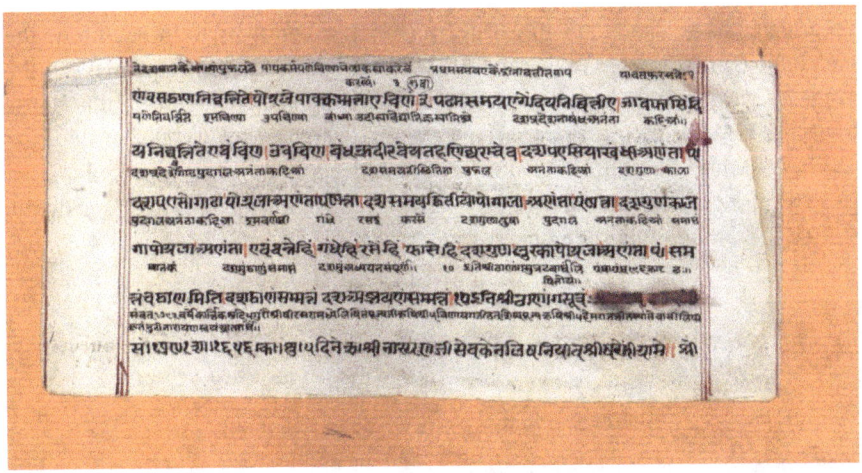

Fig. 3: *Sthānāṅgasūtraṭabā*, p. 51. (Shailesh Shinde, Pune, January 22, 2021).

i. According to Kapadia the manuscript was written in Vi.Saṃ. 1155. But the exact date is Vi.Saṃ. 1552 Jyeṣṭha Pūrṇimā Somavāra (June 15, 1495), as the colophon phrase shows:
संवत्सरे शशिनि चंद्रशरेषुपूर्णे
ज्येष्ठे च मासि सकले शि(श)शिनि प्रभाते।
पूणी(र्णी)कृता च लिखिता च सवृत्तिरेषा
सत्साधुभिश्च जयताक्तिल वाच्यमाना॥

ii. Kapadia does not mention the place of composition. But in the *namaskāra* phrase the author is saluting Vardhamāna of Vardhamānapura. Hence it is possible that the place of composition of the text was Vardhamānapura:
भक्त्यानतासुरसुरेश्वरमौलिमौलिमन्दारमाल्यचयचर्चितपादपीठम्।
श्रीवर्धमानपुरनायकवर्धमानतीर्थङ्करंमनसिकृत्यकृतप्रसादम्॥

iii. The last part of the manuscript recording details of the donation of the ms. was deleted using white ink. This part was not recorded by Kapadia. Some letters are however readable (Fig. 4):
संवत् १६३३ वरषे कारतग सुदि १० गुरु। श्रीअहृणपुरपतने प्रागवाडलघुश्रेष्ठ गोवाल तत्पुत्र श्रेष्ठ वक्क्तइ भार्या धर्मधूर्या श्राविका वइजलदे निजन्यायोपार्जितवित्तेन श्रीमत् […] लेखवाचने […] श्रीविविधिपक्षमुक्षाभिधा—भट्टारकश्रीश्रीश्रीश्रीजयकीर्तिसूरिक्रम […]काचार्यश्रीश्रीश्रीऋषिवर्द्धनसूरि […] ५ जिनप्रभगणि। त.विनेय वा.श्री ५ चारित्रलाभगणि। तत्शिष्य श्रीमदंचलगच्छमु ख्याचारित्राह्मनेकगुणै— वा.श्री ५ गजलाभगणि […]

The following information could be gathered from this deleted portion recording the donation of the manuscript copied by a scribe whose name is unreadable in

Vi.Saṃ. 1633 Kārttika Śuklā 10 Guruvāra (= November 1, 1576) in Pāṭaṇa by the merchant Govāla's[43] son Vakka and his wife the Jaina *śrāvikā* Vaijaladevī of the Prāgvāṭa caste to the Añcalagaccha (Vidhipakṣa) monk Gajalābha-gaṇin, whose lineage is given as follows in a list that combines a *paṭṭāvali* and a *gurvāvali*:

In the line of Bhaṭṭāraka Jayakīrti-sūri and Ṛṣivardhana-sūri[44] was Jinaprabha-gaṇin's disciple Cāritralābha-gaṇin's disciple Gajalābha-gaṇin, who evidently started the Lābhaśākhā sometime before Vi.Saṃ. 1633.[45]

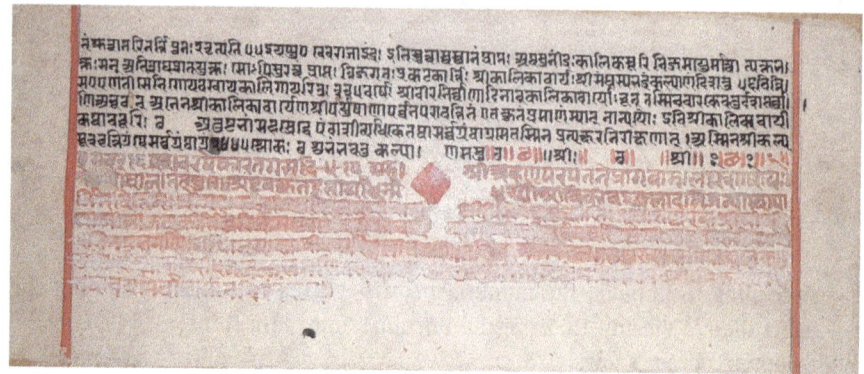

Fig. 4: *Kalpasūtravṛtti* colophon. (Shailesh Shinde, Pune, June 8, 2021).

f. Last but not least, by revisiting the manuscript of Vinayavijay Gaṇi's *Kalpasubodhikā* (Cat. no. 523) Shailesh Shinde solved the inconsistency of the dates presented by Klatt and Kapadia regarding its date of composition. In Kapadia's catalogue the following composition date is given:

रसशशिरसनिधि(१६९६)वर्षे ज्येष्ठे मासे समुज्ज्वले पक्षे।
गुरुपुष्ये यत्नोऽयं सफलो जज्ञे द्वितीयायाम्॥
But some words are misplaced: रसशशिरसनिधि(९६१६)>रसनिधिरसशशि(१६९६)

Evidently, the date is Vi.Saṃ. 1696, Jyeṣṭha Śuklā 2 Guruvāra (June 3, 1639). The date of composition of Vi.Saṃ. 1616 given in Klatt (2016) is implausible, because the *Kalpasubodhikā* comments on the *Kalpakiraṇāvalī* which was composed Vi.Saṃ. 1628 according to Kapadia, Cat. no. 509.

---

43 JPD: ID 11061.
44 Mohanalāla Dalīcanda Desāī, *Jaina Sāhityano Saṃkṣipta Itihāsa* (Saṃpādaka; Sūrat: Ācārya Municandrasūri; Ācārya Oṃkārasūri Jñānamandira, 2009), no. 768 dates him about Vi.Saṃ. 1500.
45 This piece of information is given in: Śivaprasāda, *Añcalagaccha kā itihāsa* (Vārāṇasī: Pārśvanātha Vidyāpīṭha & Jayapura: Prākṛta Bhāratī Akādamī, 2001), 144.

Kamini Gogri and Varsha Shah of Mumbai[46] work on the prosopographical analysis of the bio-bibliographical data of the *sādhvī*s of the Kharataragaccha and A(ñ)calagaccha in the early modern period that were published in Sādhvī Vijayāśrī "Āryā"s doctoral thesis on Jaina nuns, which presently offers the only compilation of recorded names of the nuns of all the main denominations of the Jaina tradition. The data are useful for balancing the male dominated accounts in chronicles, colophons and inscriptions. Gogri noted a number of peculiar features in this segment of data which she cross-referenced:

a. The names of early Kharataragaccha *sādhvī*s tend to end with the suffixes °*śrī*, °*prabhā*, °*lakṣmī*, °*siddhi*, °*vṛddhi* etc. meaning "auspicious," "illuminating," "meritorious," "miraculous" and "expanding," which are rarely found in other Jaina sects.

b. Many nuns inspired males to get initiated, such as the unnamed *sādhvī*s who motivated Somacandra to renounce, the later Jinadatta-sūri (Vi.Saṃ. 1150–1165) of the Kharataragaccha (Vijayāśrī 2007, p. 269, no. 5.1.3).

c. At the time of a *pravartinī-pada-sthāpanā*, and other special occasions, it was customary that a great number of *sādhvī*s were consecrated (e.g. ib., p. 279, no. 5.1.55).

d. The term *kṣullikā*, generally associated with Digambaras, is used in connection with nuns such as Dharmaprabhā and Devaprabhā, who in Vi.Saṃ. 1341 were initiated by Jinaprabodha-sūri (ca. VS 1331–1341) (ib., p. 279, no. 5.1.58).

e. Many nuns seem to have been well educated. Some *sādhvī*s composed literary works, though usually only in regional languages. Mahattarā Guṇasamṛddhi, a *śiṣyā* of Jinacandra, composed in Vi.Saṃ. 1477 Caitra Śuklā 13 = March 27, 1420 at Jaisalamera a work in Jaina Mahārāṣṭrī on Hanumāna's mother, known as *Aṃjaṇāsuṃdarī Cariyaṃ* (503 verses). This seems to be the only work written in Prakrit created by a Jaina *sādhvī* (ib., p. 283, no. 5.1.81). The epithet *mahattarā*, literally designating the "oldest, most respectable, chief, principal" nun, can be interpreted in three ways and coded either as a designation of a monastic position equal to a *pravartinī*, a position of seniority in monastic age equal to a *jyeṣṭha*, or as a combination of these possibilities, recorded in the form of entries under more than one category.

Jinesh Sheth of Mumbai[47] first worked on place names and on the published metadata on Jaina manuscript at the Cambridge University Library. He found, amongst

---

46 Varsha Shah worked at the University of Mumbai and completed her PhD entitled "Paradigm of Consciousness in Sramana Tradition with special reference to Jainism and Yogacara Buddhism" in 2023.

47 PhD Candidate and UGC Junior Research Fellow at the Department of Philosophy, University of Mumbai is presently writing a thesis on "A Critical Study of Anekāntavāda: Investigating some Unexplored Dimensions."

other things, that the Cambridge meta-data of "*Laghukṣetrasamāsavṛtti*" (ID 4841 in the JPD dataset "Work") helped to identify the Kṛṣṇagaccha as a sub-branch of the Tapāgaccha. Through cross-referencing with a paper published in the IJJS, he further identified the place "Phalavardhigrāma" (ID 187 in the JPD dataset "Places") as Phalodi in Rajasthan.[48]

The resulting personal records can be visualized in the JPD in form of multi-variable statistics, maps, and relationship diagrams, such as the following example of the famous Tapāgaccha *ācārya* Hīravijaya-sūri, Vi.Saṃ. 1610–1652, ID 466 (Fig. 5):

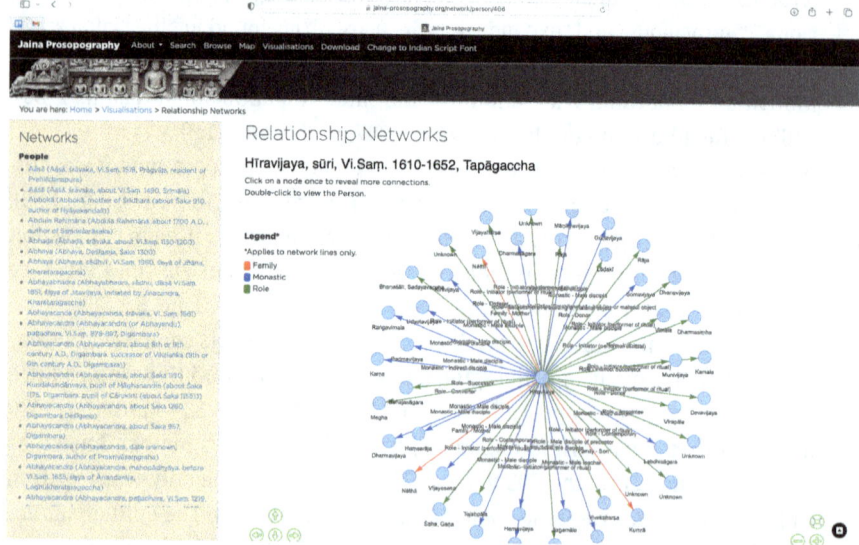

Fig. 5: Visualization of the relationship network of Ācārya Hīravijaya. (Jaina-Prosopography Database).

Ambition and Preliminary Results

From the outset the Jaina-Prosopography Database was conceived as an open ended collaborative venture informed by the vision of producing a new resource capable of supporting a wide range of future research projects. More than twenty researchers have worked on the Jaina-Prosopography Database to date, funded by different sponsors such as the Leverhulme Trust, Sanmati Teerth Sanstha, Shri

---

[48] Basile Leclère, "The Gold of Gods: Stories of Temple Financing from Jain Prabandhas," *International Journal of Jaina Studies (Online)* 16, no. 2 (2020): 11.

Firodia Trust, Jivdaya Foundation, Jain Vishva Bharati London, and private supporters.[49] It is hoped that the mix of contracted full-time and part-time work and volunteering will progressively be balanced towards the former and that through the attraction of more scholars through sponsorships, research grants and institutional research collaborations the Jaina-Prosopography Database can reach a saturation point in the next five to ten years.

The aim of this long-term project is the creation of a set of cross-referenced historical data pertaining to about 100,000 recorded names of historical Jaina personalities. Linking data of the Jaina-Prosopography Database through Google and other search engines with databases of research libraries and museums, such as QALAMOS,[50] and specialist South Asia related databases such as CIC,[51] EIAD,[52] Jain Epigraphy,[53] PANDiT,[54] Siddham,[55] and databases of South Asia focused on TEI projects is already opening new avenues in the fields of Indology, South Asian History and Sociology and provides useful open-access information for the general public. Free downloading and re-use options assure the longevity of the data. With progressive improvement of data-consistency and upgrading of its unique data model and search, browsing, and visualization functionalities the Jaina-Prosopography Database has the potential to become a standard research tool not only for Jaina Studies but for South Asian Studies in general.

Bibliography

Bhojaka, Lakṣmaṇabhāī Hīrālāla. *Pāṭaṇa-Jaina-Dhātu-Pratimā-Lekha-Saṃgraha*. Delhi: Motilal Banarsidass, 2002.
Bruhn, Klaus. "The Analysis of Jina Images." *Berliner Indologische Studien* 2 (1986): 133–174.
Bruhn, Klaus. "Sectional Studies in Jainology." In *Middle Indo-Aryan and Jaina Studies (World Sanskrit Conference Leiden)*, edited by Colette Caillat, 36–59. Leiden: E. J. Brill, 1991.
Buddhisāgarasūri, Ācārya. *Jaina Dhātupratimā Lekha-Saṃgraha*. Vol. 1–2. Bombay: Adhyātma Jñāna Prasāraka Maṇḍala, 1918–1924.
Cambridge Digital Library, https://cudl.lib.cam.ac.uk/.

---

[49] Dilesh Mehta and Bipin Shah are to be thanked for their generous support of the project.
[50] Qalamos, https://www.qalamos.net/content/index.xed.
[51] "Corpus of the Inscriptions of Campā," École Française d'Extrême-Orient, https://www.efeo.fr/base.php?code=794.
[52] Early Inscriptions of Āndhradeśa, http://hisoma.huma-num.fr/exist/apps/EIAD/index2.html.
[53] "Jain Epigraphy," Jain Heritage Centres, https://www.jainheritagecentres.com/jainism/jain-epigraphy/.
[54] PANDiT: Prosopographical Database for Indic Texts, https://www.panditproject.org/.
[55] Siddham: The Asia Inscriptions Database, https://siddham.network/.

"Corpus of the Inscriptions of Campā," École Française d'Extrême-Orient, https://www.efeo.fr/base.php?code=794.
Cort, John E. "Doing for Others: Merit Transfer and Karma Mobility in Jainism." In *Jainism and Early Buddhism. Essays in Honor of Padmanabh S. Jaini*, edited by Olle Qvarnström, 129–150. Fremont: Asian Humanities Press, 2003.
Cort, John E. "A Digambar Icon of 24 Jinas at the Ackland Art Museum." *Jaina Studies: CoJS Newsletter* 7 (2012): 30–33.
Deśāī, Mohanalāla Dalīcanda, ed. *Jaina Gūrjara Kavio*. Bhāga 1–4. Mumbaī: Jaina Śvetāmbara Conference Office, 1926–1944.
Deśāī, Mohanalāla Dalīcanda. *Jaina Sāhityano Saṃkṣipta Itihāsa*. Sampādaka; Sūrat: Ācārya Municandrasūri; Ācārya Omkārasūri Jñānamandira, 2009.
Early Inscriptions of Āndhradeśa, http://hisoma.huma-num.fr/exist/apps/EIAD/index2.html.
"Editorial Notes," Jaina Prosopography Database, https://jaina-prosopography.org/about/editorial.
Flügel, Peter. "Collaborations in Jaina Prosopography." In *Annals of the Bhandarkar Oriental Research Institute* (in press).
Flügel, Peter. "Jaina-Prosopography I: Sociology of Jaina-Names." In *Jaina Studies. Select Papers Presented in the 'Jaina Studies' Section at the 16th World Sanskrit Conference*, edited by Nalini Balbir and Peter Flügel, 187–267. Delhi: Rashtriya Sanskrit Sansthan & D.K. Publishers, 2018.
Flügel, Peter. "Jaina-Prosopography II: 'Patronage' in Jaina Epigraphic and Manuscript Catalogues." In *Gift of Knowledge: Patterns of Patronage in Jainism*, edited by Christine Chojnacki and Basile Leclère, 1–46. Bangalore: National Institute of Prakrit Research Shravanabelagola, 2018.
Flügel, Peter. "Life and Work of Johannes Klatt." In *Jaina-Onomasticon*, edited by Peter Flügel, and Kornelius Krümpelmann, 9–164. Wiesbaden: Harrassowitz, 2016.
Flügel, Peter, Patrick Krüger and Priyanka Shah. "Six Jaina Bronzes." In *Pure Soul: The Jaina Spiritual Traditions*, edited by Peter Flügel, Heleen De Jonckheere, and Renate Söhnen-Thieme, 96–103. London: Centre of Jaina Studies, SOAS, 2023.
Flügel, Peter, and Kornelius Krümpelmann. *Index to Johannes Klatt's Jaina-Onomasticon*. Jaina Studies 2. Wiesbaden: Harrassowitz and Royal Asiatic Society of Great Britain and Ireland, 2024.
Gujarat University, Department of Prakrit and Pali, https://www.gujaratuniversity.org.in/web/WebDPrakrit.asp.
Hanlon, Julie. "The Jaina Prosopography Project and Database." *Jaina Studies: Newsletter of the Centre of Jaina Studies* 16 (2021): 11–13.
"Jain Epigraphy," Jain Heritage Centres, https://www.jainheritagecentres.com/jainism/jain-epigraphy/.
Jaina Prosopography Database, https://jaina-prosopography.org.
Jaina, Sāgaramala, and Vijaya Kumāra. *Sthānakavāsī Jaina Paramparā kā Itihāsa*. Vārāṇasī: Pārśvanātha Vidyāpīṭha, 2003.
Kāntisāgara, Muni, ed. *Jaina Dhātu-Pratimālekha Saṃgraha*. Bhāga 1. Sūrata: Mantrī, Jinadattasūri Jñānabhaṇḍāra, 1950.
Kapadia, Hiralal Rasikdas. *Descriptive Catalogue of the Government Collection of Manuscripts Deposited at the Bhandarkar Oriental Research Institute. Volume XVII–XIX: Jaina Literature and Philosophy*. Poona: BORI, 1935–1977.
Klatt, Johannes. "The Samachari-Satakam of Samayasundara and pattavalis of the Anchala-Gachchha and other Gachchhas (Revised with additions by Ernst Leumann)." *The Indian Antiquary* 23 (1894): 169–183.
Koṭhārī, Jayanta, ed. *Jaina Gūrjara Kavio*. Bhāga 1–10. Mumbaī: Mahāvīra Jaina Vidyālaya, 1986–1997.
Leclère, Basile. "The Gold of Gods: Stories of Temple Financing from Jain Prabandhas." *International Journal of Jaina Studies (Online)* 16, no. 2 (2020): 1–25.

Literary Heritage of the Aniconic Jaina Tradition, https://digital.soas.ac.uk/cojsa.
Mahendra, Purvi Darshan. "Political and Educational Policy in Maurya Period Based on Prakrit Texts English Language." Doctoral thesis, Gujarat University, 2019.
Muni, Sumana. *Pañjāba Śramaṇa Saṃgha Gaurava Ācārya Śrī Amarasiṃha Jī Mahārāja: Jīvana Carita aura Paramparā Paricaya*. Madrasa: Bhagavāna Mahāvīra Svādhyāya Pīṭha, 1970.
Natu, Amruta. *Georg Bühler's Contribution to Indology*. Opera Minora No. 12. Piscataway, NJ: Gorgias Press, Harvard Oriental Series, 2020.
PANDiT: Prosopographical Database for Indic Texts, https://www.panditproject.org/.
Parikh, Praveenchandra, and Bharati Shelat. *Jain Image Inscriptions of Ahmedabad*. Ahmedabad: B.J. Institute of Learning of Research, 1997.
Pragya, Samani Pratibha. "Prekṣā Meditation: History and Methods." Doctoral thesis, SOAS, University of London, 2017.
Qalamos, https://www.qalamos.net/content/index.xed.
Sandasara, Jolly. *Literary Criticism of Kuvalaymālā*. Varanasi: Parshwanath Vidyapeeth, 2019.
Sanghvi, A. "Kanakāmara Muni's (1065 CE) Apabhraṃśa Text Karakaṃḍa Cariu with a Gujarati Translation of Lilāvatī Kahā." MA Thesis. Gujarat University, 2021.
Shah, K. "Literary Criticism of Rudradasa's Candaleha." Doctoral thesis, Gujarat University, forthcoming.
Shah, P. "A Critical Study of Prakrit Sarvasawam by Markandeya." Doctoral thesis, Gujarat University, 2018.
Shah, Umakant Premanand. "Bronze Hoard from Vasantagadh." *Lalita Kalā* 1, 2 (1955/56): 55–65.
Shah, Umakant Premanand. *Akota Bronzes*. Bombay: Department of Archaeology, Government of Bombay, 1959.
Shinde, Shailesh, and Krushna Mali. "Jaina Prosopography: Key Findings from the Bhandarkar Oriental Research Institute Manuscripts." *Jaina Studies: Newsletter of the Centre of Jaina Studies* 18 (2023): 17–22.
Siddham: The Asia Inscriptions Database, https://siddham.network/.
Śivaprasāda, *Añcalagaccha kā itihāsa*. Vārāṇasī: Pārśvanātha Vidyāpīṭha & Jayapura: Prākṛta Bhāratī Akādamī, 2001.
The Bhandarkar Oriental Research Institute, https://www.bori.ac.in/.
Vijayaśrī, Sādhvī "Āryā". *Jaina Dharma kī Śramaṇiyoṃ kā Bṛhad Itihāsa*. Bhāga I-II. Dillī: Bhāratīya Vidyā Pratiṣṭhāna, 2007.
Winant, Simon. "Redemption or Death. Jainism's Transformation of the Hindu Villain Kīcaka in Jaina Mahābhāratas." Doctoral thesis, University of Ghent, forthcoming.
Wright, J. Clifford. "The Ackland Art Museum's Image of Śāntinātha." *Jaina Studies: CoJS Newsletter* 8 (2013): 29–30.
Wright, J. Clifford. "Two Inscribed Digambara Bronzes." *Jaina Studies: CoJS Newsletter* 9 (2014): 34–35.

Mariana Zorkina
Daoist Immortals as a Poetic Image in the Tang Dynasty: A Corpus Study

Introduction

Immortals (*xian* 仙) are an integral part of the traditional Chinese belief system. A belief into a possibility of prolonging life, even escaping death is an ancient one and does not originate from Daoism, but as a religion it has developed the concept — making achieving immortality one of its important goals — and devised the methods of doing so starting in Han 漢 dynasty (202 BCE–220 CE).[1] And, as the popularity of Daoism grew, so did the number of accounts of *xian* in literature: during the same dynasty accounts of supernatural beings started appearing in "tales of the strange" (*zhiguai* 志怪), late Han is also the time when the earliest of the extant poetic accounts of immortals were written.[2]

Several centuries later, during the Tang 唐 dynasty (618–907) several important things happened. First, the dynasty's founder claimed to be related to Laozi 老子, the assumed author of one of the most prominent Daoist texts, *Daodejing* 道德經 in order to legitimize his rule. Subsequently, the prestige of Daoism as state ideology increased greatly and at some periods knowledge of Daoist texts was necessary to pass state examinations and gain a bureaucratic position.[3] Secondly, closer to late Tang the view towards collecting and saving poetic works shifted: poetry started to be seen in terms of being a vocation and "legacy" and as such started to be preserved more carefully. This created a unique situation, where — despite libraries being destroyed and collections lost throughout history — an unprecedented amount of poetic works, including those mentioning Daoist realia were created and preserved.[4] This leaves us ample material, on one hand, to do a quantitative study of the depiction of immortals in poetry of the period and, on the other hand, to reflect on how they were viewed by the literati of the period.

---

1 Zornica Kirkova, *Roaming into the Beyond: Representations of Xian Immortality in Early Medieval Chinese Verse* (Leiden: Brill, 2016), 14.
2 Stephen R. Bokenkamp, "Taoism and Chinese literature," in *Encyclopedia of Taoism*, vol. 1 and 2, ed. Fabrizio Pregadio (London: Routledge, 2008), 176; Kirkova, *Roaming into the beyond*, 3.
3 Charles D. Benn, "Taoism and the civil service examinations," in *Encyclopedia of Taoism*, vol. 1 and 2, ed. Fabrizio Pregadio (London: Routledge, 2008), 165–167.
4 Stephen Owen, *The Late Tang: Chinese Poetry of the Mid-Ninth Century (827–860)* (Cambridge, MA: Harvard University Press, 2009), 9; Stephen Owen, "The manuscript legacy of the Tang the case of literature," *Harvard Journal of Asiatic Studies* 67, no. 2 (2007): 295–326.

https://doi.org/10.1515/9783110747607-009

Using a statistical approach for this topic has an important advantage over traditional ones in the humanities: it allows us to look beyond separate works, authors or anthologies created by humans, and captures the usage of the word *xian* in the available corpus in its entirety. While works of one author are likely to reflect their personal understanding of immortals, and qualitative approaches on their own are prone to cognitive biases more than the quantitative ones, the latter makes it possible to concentrate on common factors instead of variation. In other words, the aim of this chapter is to look at some typicalities related to immortals in Tang poetry; patterns in commonplace descriptions that might have been unknown even to the poets and reveal how they have been perceived.

At the same time there are few established and readily available practices in the computational analysis of Classical Chinese, so I feel compelled to describe and justify each of the steps taken — even the ones that would very likely have been overlooked as belonging to "common practice."

This chapter will adapt a broadly structuralist approach and will explore the word "immortal" in Tang *shi* 詩 poetry from the point of view of two axes of word usage as defined by Ferdinand de Saussure and expanded in application to poetry by Jakobson: "The poetic function projects the principle of equivalence from the axis of selection into the axis of combination."[5]

In other words, we will be looking at the syntagmatic, or horizontal dimension in order to see which words can be used together with *xian*, and at the paradigmatic, or vertical dimension, in order to see what *xian* can be meaningfully substituted with.

Corpus and Text Pre-Processing

The corpus for this study is *Quan Tang shi* 全唐詩 (Complete Tang Poems),[6] a collection of verse commissioned by emperor Kangxi 康熙 (r. 1662–1723) in 1705. It contains more than forty thousand poems and at the time of the creation was supposed to be the most complete corpus of Tang poetry.[7]

---

5 Roman Jakobson, "Closing statement: linguistics and poetics," in *Style in Language*, ed. Thomas A. Sebeck (Cambridge, MA: MT Press, 1960), 350–377. A discussion of the limits of applicability of Jakobson's theory to Tang poetry can be found in: Yu-Kung Kao and Tsu-Lin Mei "Meaning, Metaphor, and Allusion in T'ang Poetry," *Harvard Journal of Asiatic Studies* 38, no. 2 (1978): 281–356.
6 Hereafter QTS.
7 William H. Nienhauser, *The Indiana Companion to Traditional Chinese Literature*, vol. 1 (Taipei: SMC Publishing, 2003), 364 states that the number of poems is 48,900; the corpus used in this study contains 42,864.

Although QTS is often used for quantitative research of phenomena related to language, creative process and culture during the Tang, it is still a collection created in a much later Qing 清 dynasty (1644–1912) — and it was not constructed in a way a "representative corpus" would be made today. This brings a problem of historicity and the biases that might have been introduced by the compilers at later time periods. However, creating a methodologically sound corpus of Tang poetry is a rather impossible task: a large amount of Tang poetry was never preserved and what remains is what Stephen Owen characterized as "a conjunction of historical accident and the period taste in the ninth and tenth centuries."[8] Tang poetry as it existed during the dynasty — especially its earlier period — is lost, and QTS as an "opportunistic corpus" is at this time the fullest collection created in premodern China and, as such, the most suitable for a quantitative analysis.[9]

The text was obtained from ctext[10] and, since the focus of interest were the contents of the poems en masse, everything else, including author information, poem titles and epigraphs were removed. For the next stage, the text was tokenized, i.e., the word boundaries were defined and inserted as spaces into the text. Tokenization for Chinese, especially for the Classical Chinese is a non-trivial matter because of the lack of spaces and punctuation in the script — some inscriptions and educational texts being an exception — as well as the problematic nature of wordhood in the language.

In many cases it is possible to avoid this operation altogether and to do textual analysis on a character-by-character basis (as will be done in section "Patterns" of this chapter). But such methods are means to avoid a problem, not to solve it. Many researchers work with Classical Chinese poetry under the assumption that the words in it overwhelmingly equal characters — and while that may be true, the actual percentage of multi-character words in QTS has to my knowledge not been measured and is, according to my own estimates, not negligible.

---

8 Owen, *The Late Tang*, 1096.
9 For more information on literary collections see: Christopher M. B. Nugent, "Literary collections in Tang dynasty China," *T'oung-Pao* 93, Fasc. 1/3 (2007): 1–52. On compilation projects of the tenth century that shaped the Tang poetry legacy see: Owen, *The Late Tang*. Ideally, the corpus could be extended with separate collections not included in QTS and materials from the manuscripts found in Dunhuang. This, however, would be very labor-intensive and since such works are not numerous, they are unlikely to drastically change the results of statistical analyses.
10 More specifically, the version with minimal markup was used from this repository: "poetry-source," snowtraces, https://github.com/snowtraces/poetry-source. This, in principle, is the same corpus as used in Zorkina (2019) with a few minor changes: some errors in markup and character representations were fixed. See: Mariana Zorkina, "Describing Objects in Tang Dynasty Poetic Language: A Study Based on Word Embeddings," *Journal of Chinese Literature and Culture* 5, no. 2 (2019): 250–275.

Nevertheless, some kind of tokenization is essential for the study of collocations: the algorithms that search for collocations in texts will try to find units that have significant relationships between them (different algorithms defining this significance in a statistically different way). Searching for significant connections on the character level, one is very likely to find combinations of characters that form multi-character words as the top results. When some kind of tokenization is performed, it is possible to look at higher-level results — the multi-word expressions, that were determined lexically and were recognizable at the time of the creation, but still could be easily split up if the author wished to do so. And, to reach this level, some tokenization is required.

For this chapter, a very simple tokenizer was used: it "crawls" through the text line-by-line and tries to match the character combinations to the entries from a provided dictionary, starting from the longest allowed length of a combination and subsequently reducing the length of a searched combination when unsuccessful. The dictionary used for this case was CDICT Mandarin Chinese Dictionary,[11] with a maximum allowed length of 2.[12]

This approach has been proven to be quite successful, even if it tends to make mistakes in some cases because of its simplicity: in a line ABCD, where the correct segmentation would be "AB" + "CD," if the word "ABC" exists in the dictionary, the "greedy" algorithm will do an erroneous segmentation, as it always prefers longer words to shorter ones.[13]

The resulting corpus has 2,120,332 words after the punctuation is removed: 33,022 unique 2-character words (types) that are used 473,957 times (tokens) and 7,241 1-character words that occur 1,646,306 times. This means, that 2-character words constitute more than 22% of the corpus — this is far from being a "negligible amount." This number has to be taken with a grain of salt though: the tokenization process was not perfect, because of its simplicity and the dictionary that could have introduced some anachronistic word boundaries or had expressions such as "white snow" (*baixue* 白雪) as entries.

---

[11] CDICT 國語辭典, downloaded from: zh_TW Dictionaries, http://download.huzheng.org/zh_TW/. This dictionary records 157,686 words of Taiwanese Mandarin and includes Classical Chinese. I am not aware of well-digitized and freely available dictionaries of specifically Classical Chinese — the ones that can be found use modern simplified characters and cannot be used.

[12] The definition of a "word" for this study is thus utilitarian and very limited: "character sequences under a certain length that appear as headwords in a dictionary."

[13] The algorithm can be accessed at: "Tutorials," mzorki, https://github.com/mzorki/tutorials.

Collocations

Method

In a structuralist analysis, words are often described from the point of view of their usage on axes — the horizontal or syntagmatic and vertical or paradigmatic ones. The plane of syntagmatic relationships is the one of combination[14] — which words can be used together? Is there some kind of pattern in this usage?

One of the ways to test the horizontal relationships of a word is to study *collocations* in text, although this is a controversial term that might mean different things in different context and is notoriously hard to define. *Sensu lato* it refers to some word combinations that occur together often enough to pass a certain threshold of significance.[15] This significance can also be measured in a multitude of ways — from occurring more than a certain number of times, to passing a certain threshold in a ranking based on various statistical association measures — the general idea being one of looking for word combinations that have a probability of occurring together that is higher than random.[16]

Although the definition of such collocations is unbiased in a sense that the computer will not favor some word combinations over others, because they seem "more meaningful," it is important to remember that the analysis as a whole is riddled with subjective decisions. The definition of "significant association" is a good example: decisions on which association-measure to use, and which results should be considered significant, are often made on the basis of practical needs (a recurring motive throughout this chapter, as the reader will discover). My argument for using computational approaches is not concerned with finding something that is "true" and opposed to the "fallacies" of the traditional humanities. At the end of the day, studies like this are ultimately just another way of "finding a new perspective" and "reading against the grain," nothing more. The most valuable part of the computational approach is probably twofold: it becomes possible to *consciously* choose some of one's biases and to trace them back. At the same time, it allows one

---

14 Jakobson, "Closing statement," 358.
15 As opposed to defining collocations as phraseological expressions or lexicalized items which raises a plethora of subsequent methodological questions. On different possible definitions see, for example: Anke Lüdeling and Merja Kytö, *Corpus Linguistics: An International Handbook*, vol. 2(Berlin: De Gruyter, 2008), 1212–1248. Another term, co-occurrence, complicates the matter even further: sometimes it is used interchangeably with collocations, sometimes — to distinguish collocations from words that occur together, but not often enough to have a significant relationship. See: Lüdeling and Kytö, *Corpus Linguistics: An International Handbook*, vol. 2, 1215.
16 A very detailed explanation can be read in: Lüdeling and Kytö, *Corpus Linguistics: An International Handbook*, vol. 1, 1212–1248.

to use all the information available in the corpus instead of pre-selecting it. Doing so may lead to a discovery of patterns that were not recognized by the poets themselves and are hard to trace, but are revealing some views about immortals, shared by literati of the time.

As mentioned before, there are several different association measures for collocations and there are multiple considerations to be taken.[17] "Mutual Information" (MI) measures seem to be used the most in corpus linguistics, as they are one of the most theoretically sound approaches. However, they bring several problems: MI measures tend to give a lot of importance to raw frequencies, so they require one to remove a number of words on both extremities of the frequency distribution: those that appear less often than a certain threshold (i.e., lower cut-off) and those that appear so frequently that they do not provide much information (i.e., a stop list; usually these are function words).[18]

Stop lists are extremely useful for computational analysis and, if a certain list is accepted by a community of researchers and used universally, it can simplify the reproducibility of results. But they are also methodologically problematic: in many cases they are created as a combination of a statistical metric and manual addition of words that, in view of a researcher, impede their analyses. This leads to these lists containing words that can be important in many research cases and the decisions behind such inclusions tend to be badly documented. It has been shown that this is the case with stop lists developed for English language[19] and this practice has been carried over to premodern China studies: Edward Slingerland with colleagues used an aggressive list of words that were removed without a justification,[20] and while Colin Allen and colleagues do provide a short explanation, they only name

---

17 Ibid.
18 More information on what most frequent words in QTS are and the possible outcomes of their exclusion can be found in: Zorkina, "Describing Objects," 257. In addition to this, MI metric is very sensitive towards tokenization decisions. Given the imperfect nature of the tokenizers available for Classical Chinese, this is yet another argument against using it.
19 Joel Nothman Qin Hanmin, and Roman Yurchak, "Stop Word Lists in Free Open-source Software Packages," *Proceedings of Workshop for NLP Open Source Software* (2018): 7–12. DOI: http://doi.org/10.18653/v1/W18-2502.
20 Edward Slingerland, Ryan Nichols, Kristoffer Neilbo, and Carson Logan, "The Distant Reading of Religious Texts: A 'Big Data' Approach to Mind-Body Concepts in Early China," *Journal of the American Academy of Religion* 85, no. 4 (2017): 985–1016. He and his co-authors have changed the method to one that allows to avoid using a stop list since then, but this is not justified. See: Ryan Nichols, Edward Slingerland, Kristoffer Laigaard Nielbo, Peter Kirby, and Carson Logan, "Supernatural Agents and Prosociality in Historical China: Micro-Modeling the Cultural Evolution of Gods and Morality in Textual Corpora," *Religion, Brain & Behavior* 11, no. 1 (2021): 46–64.

the methods without justifying the decisions made.[21] For these reasons, uncritically using these two lists for further research is problematic.

Creating a sensible stop list that is reusable for many applications and is justified requires a careful and thoughtful approach and is beyond of the scope of this chapter. As a result, I will follow the example of John Lee and Wong Tak-sum in avoiding creating such a list altogether.[22] However, it is possible to improve the results by choosing a collocation metric that is less influenced by high frequency words and thus makes removing "uninformative words" less pressing. For this chapter the t-score measure will be used: although it is less sound from a theoretical perspective, it has been proven that it returns robust results and under certain circumstances can outperform other association measures.[23]

How collocations should be interpreted is yet another question. While it is agreed that they show some kind of patterns, without a syntactic and semantic tagging it can be hard to discern the exact mechanisms behind the formation of such patterns. If a word is polysemic or, as if often happens in Classical Chinese, can act as different parts of speech, there might be several usage patterns that contributed to formation of one collocation. Below, for the top collocation found in the corpus we find xian + jia 仙 + 家, where jia can be both a noun meaning "home" or a nominal suffix denoting someone who belongs to a school or a profession.[24] Several different patterns may be disguised as one in this way and the different mechanisms that brought these patterns to life may be lurking in the background. Whether related to the evolution of language, to cultural practices in a broad sense that favor some expressions over others in all language registers or to practices that are specific to poetic language, primarily producing formulaic expressions within this genre, the surface realization of the collocation will not show.

In this context it is dangerous to make any sweeping generalizations about the nature of the discovered patterns and the domains to which they belong. However, it is also impossible to deny their significance within the corpus. The bottom line is: what the nature of the corpus and the nature of the tool allow me to talk about are tendencies in language usage, formulas that are consistently used and that stem

---

21 Colin Allen, Hongliang Luo, Jaimie Murdock, Jianghuai Pu, Xiaohong Wang, Yanjie Zhai, and Kun Zhao, "Topic Modeling the Hàn diǎn Ancient Classics," *Journal of Cultural Analytics* 2, no 1 (2017): Appendix 3.
22 John Lee and Wong Tak-sum, "Glimpses of Ancient China from Classical Chinese Poems," *Proceedings of COLING 2012: Posters* (2012): 621–632.
23 For a very detailed analysis of different association measures, their strengths and weaknesses see: Lüdeling and Kytö, *Corpus Linguistics: An International Handbook*, vol. 1, 1212–1248.
24 Although, as we will show below, the statistics used for this chapter is good in excluding functional words, so in this case they did not pose a big problem.

from some kind of common practice in Tang dynasty *shi* poetry. Moreover, as a principle the interpretation of collocations does not provide information about the most widespread patterns, but the most *typical* ones, specifically the most typical for the social group of "immortals."[25]

The collocation search was performed on the QTS corpus with the following parameters: no stop list was used; basic punctuation removed; the window size (the number of words on each side of the source word) considered for collocations was set to five. This means that for each occurrence of *xian*, not only its immediate neighbors were considered, but everything that appeared in the same line and in adjacent lines, if the length of a line was shorter than that of the window. Although a series of metrics were run for comparison, as discussed above, in this particular case using the t-score was most useful. It also made it possible to maintain the low-frequency words in the corpus.[26] Moreover, only the top 50 collocations were taken into consideration. The appendix contains the table containing these collocations with additional information of frequencies of each of the words and the collocation scores.

Interpretation

There are several conclusions that can be derived from the results. First, the collocations can be roughly divided into several groups according to the meanings of the collocates of *xian*. In corpus linguistics this division is often called "semantic preference" — "a lexical set of frequently occurring collocates, which share some semantic feature" as defined by Michael Stubbs.[27] Although the groups below were

---

[25] It should be mentioned, that with the parameters used below ranking by frequencies yielded very similar results to one with a more complex statistic, so in this particular case statements about typicality and prevalency are both possible. Nevertheless, this should not be taken as a given.

[26] The code with more comprehensive results can be accessed at: "qts_immortals," mzorki, https://github.com/mzorki/qts_immortals. To run the collocation search, Python nltk library was used (see Bird et al., 2009). The methods used in this library rely on Manning and Schütze (1999). See: Steven Bird, Ewan Klein, and Edward Loper, *Natural Language Processing with Python* (Sebastopol, CA: O'Reilly, 2009); Christopher D. Manning and Hinrich Schütze, *Foundations of Statistical Natural Language Processing* (Cambridge, MA: MIT Press, 1999), 151–187.

[27] Michael Stubbs, "On inference theories and code theories: Corpus evidence for semantic schemas," *Text & Talk* 21, no. 3 (2001): 449. Yet again, there are multiple ways to arrive at semantic preferences. This chapter follows Stubbs in using collocates derived from a student-t metric. In other studies, such as Partington (1998), a simple search is performed without additional calculations. Alan Partington, *Patterns and Meanings: Using Corpora for English Language Research and Teaching* (Amsterdam: J. Benjamins Pub, 1998), 33–39.

defined based on semantics, it became apparent that each had a prevailing syntactic relationship too. As there seems to be a correlation, the groups will be described from both angles.[28]

The first group of collocates is where *xian* acts as a modifier in a genitive construction. A great number of such collocates are man-made objects:

(1) "palace (of the immortals)" (*xian gong* 仙宮), "boat (of the immortals)" (*xian zhou* 仙舟), "road (of the immortals)" (*xian lu* 仙路), "terrace (of the immortals)" (*xian tai* 仙台),[29] "capital (of the immortals)" (*xian du* 仙都), "pavilion (of the immortals)" (*xian ge* 仙閣), "raft (of the immortals)" (*xian cha* 仙槎), "cart (of the immortals)" (*xian jia* 仙駕),[30] "carriage (of the immortals)" (*xian yu* 仙輿),[31] "temple" or "watchtower (of the immortals)" (*xian guan* 仙觀), and "side door (of the immortals)" (*xian ye* 仙掖).[32]

There are only two collocates denoting material objects that are not man (or immortal)-made: "mountain" (*shan* 山) and "cinnamon tree" (*gui* 桂).[33] So it seems that in such cases *xian* can be used as a marker with a group of objects that might belong to both the realm of humans or the immortals and to distinguish them from each other: in case of "cinnamon tree": using *xian* clarifies, that it is the mythological tree of immortality that grows on the moon. One might have expected a popular image of a fruit that allowed one to escape death — "peach of immortality" — to appear in this group. After all, distinguishing between it and its common counterpart is crucial for a mortal. But this is not the case. The poetic language did not need to answer the question to which realm the natural phenomena may have belonged

---

[28] And, since words that are not immediately next to each other were also accounted for, one should not make a judgement on syntactic relationships judging by the look of the collocations: for that reason, before making any generalizations, it was verified whether the syntactic relationship was true in the majority, if not all, cases.
[29] The character variant 台 surprisingly appears much more often in the corpus than 臺. This seems to reflect an error in digitalization rather than a variant form. Additionally, the latter seems to never occur together with *xian*, so the results should not have been influenced by this mistake.
[30] There is a similar collocate, *yu* 馭, that can mean a "chariot," but more often — "to ride a chariot" or "one driving the chariot." It is used in all of these senses in the corpus.
[31] Since in Classical Chinese same word could function as different parts of speech, multiple interpretations are possible for some of the words, including the three variants of "carriage" in (1). Such instances were manually checked to ensure they are included in the right group. Others that proved hard to assign to a single group, such as *xia* 下 (as a postposition "underneath," or as a verb "descend"), were not included in the analysis.
[32] The last example is a special case, since it denotes two ministries at the Tang court in combination with *xian*.
[33] Unless the word *lu* was not used by some poets meaning "area," not "road."

to — partly because the line between the two were rather blurred, especially when it comes to life on Earth. The plants and locations humans and immortals have access to are often the same, the question is to which extent they can exploit the potential of these things.

But when it comes to something manufactured, the situation changes. Saying that something is connected to the realm of the immortals can be a way to complement its fine qualities: if celestial beings are "realized humans" then, by association, their belongings are the better versions of what ordinary humans possess.[34] But in a wider sense it is also a marker that there is a celestial being present. One could attain *xian*-ship while maintaining their corporeal integrity and appearance. In this case, recognizing some special qualities in the objects belonging to immortals was important for recognizing an immortal amongst people. At the same time, another reason why marking objects was so important might have been achieving a specific poetic effect, stressing how elusive were the beings that were so sought after in poetry: a palace or a boat are there, but the owners are not to be seen, distant and unapproachable.

It is also important to notice that half of the collocates in this group are connected to travels. This is an interesting find that could reflect the transience of *xian* appearances in the mortal world and the inability of humans, who have no access to their dwellings, to witness them other than during the times of transition. Again, one of the popular poetic topics connected to immortals, that can be identified starting from the third century and was popular during the Tang — "roaming into immortality" (*youxian* 遊仙) — often depicted the persona seeking these beings or travelling as one of them,[35] but combined with the results in groups (4) and (5) below, (1) shows a rather paradoxical situation: it is the persona who usually seeks, but the immortals who possess the means to travel.

Unlike (1), the next group mostly contains adjectival attributions, in other words, entities that can be "immortal":

(2) "(immortal) beauty" (*xian e* 仙娥), "(immortal) official" (*xian li* 仙吏), "(immortal) old man" (*xian weng* 仙翁), "(immortal) companion" (*xian lü* 仙侶), "(immortal) bird" (*xian qin* 仙禽), and "immortal maiden," sometimes also meaning "beauty" (*nüxian* 女仙).[36]

---

[34] The people who own these objects are also superior: *xian* can be used to denote a high standing of the owner.

[35] For a comprehensive overview on establishment and functioning of *youxian* poetry in Early Medieval China, see: Kirkova, *Roaming into the beyond*.

[36] Although grammatically there is a different relationship here and *xian* takes the role of the head instead of a modifier, it groups well with others by meaning. "(Immortal) companion" is also

This is a rather interesting combination: putting aside the bird and the official for a while, let us take a look at the societal and gender roles expressed through these collocations.

Several of the "five relationships" (*wulun* 五倫) of Confucianism (i.e., father and son, husband and wife, ruler and subject, elder and younger brother, older and younger friend),[37] are reproduced here, although not to the letter: the male persona[38] can enter some kind of relationship with an "old man": presumably seeing him as a master, and with an "immortal companion" — this term can be used also to generally denote immortals. Lastly, there are "immortal beauties" — those a poet can be romantically involved with.

The disparity between the gender roles is not at all surprising: an "immortal companion" came to mean someone who is a good friend who also possesses high moral qualities, whereas an "immortal maiden" was used to describe alluring women. But then, women enjoyed a very high status in Daoism during Tang and constituted a large portion of clergy, and there were several high-status female immortals in the pantheon — and yet, this is not reflected in the collocations. So, in a way, immortals are used to express one's fantasies of idealized social relationships: with a wise teacher, a soulmate or a female lover. They do not reflect the more ambiguous ones.

On the other hand, it is important to note that not all fictional relationships with the supernatural followed the same pattern: in the case of stories about fox spirits, for example, involvement with both male and female ones generally ended in sexual relationships and these stories were more often than not used to express desires that were breaking the social norms.[39] At the same time, homoerotic themes formed an integral part of both poetry and prose in Classical China.[40] However, while homosexual relationships between humans and other humans or between

---

a grammatically ambiguous example, as it can be translated as a "companion of an immortal" as well, but it fits with the group in both cases.
37 This list was defined by Mencius 孟子 (372–289 BCE) and became one of the classical paradigms of Confucianism since.
38 And the overwhelming majority of poets and poetic personae of the time, especially among works that were saved, were male.
39 See, for example: Rania Huntington, "Foxes and Sex in Late Imperial Chinese Narrative," *Nan Nü* 2, no. 1 (2000): 78–128.
40 See, for example: Mark Stevenson, and Cuncun Wu, *Homoeroticism in Imperial China: A Sourcebook* (New York, NY: Routledge, 2013). A very informative account of sexuality of fox spirits in Chinese literature, although of a later period than Tang, can be found in: Huntington, "Foxes and Sex."

humans and foxes appear in the literature, the same type of relationships between humans and immortals are not reflected by the collocates.[41]

This, in a way, confirms the observations that "the immortals were not entirely alienated from the secular world. Their ideas and behaviors were deeply rooted in this world."[42] If for Daoism immortals are a type of humans who realized their true potential, then the collocates show what kinds of humans were Tang poets willing to see as "perfected" and that are allowed in an ideal world: an older man as a teacher figure, a male companion, or a beautiful woman, whose time was frozen in her prime.

In another group of words, *xian* takes the role of the head in a nominal phrase. These include:

(3) "perfected (immortal)" (*zhen xian* 真仙), "golden (immortal)" (*jin xian* 金仙), "earthbound (immortal)" (*di xian* 地仙), "grotto (immortal)" (*tong xian* 洞仙), "numinous (immortal)" (*ling xian* 靈仙), *Penglai xian* (immortal) 蓬萊仙, "scattered (immortals)" (*san xian* 散仙), "multitude (of immortals)" (*qun xian* 群仙), "nine (immortals)" (*jiu xian* 九仙).

A large number of the collocates refer to the place of an immortal within the hierarchy of immortality: the term "nine immortals," apart from referring to nine concrete beings or a mountain, can also refer to nine classes of immortals described in two Daoist schools that appeared during the Six Dynasties 六朝 (220–589) period: the Shangqing 上清 and Lingbao 靈寶.[43] "Perfected" and "numinous" immortals are a part of this classification. "Earthbound" immortals are yet another rank of "middle-level" *xian*, who did not ascend to Heaven: this type would usually inhabit landmarks also represented in this group — the grotto heavens (*dongtian* 洞天) in the mountains or Blissful Lands (*fudi* 福地) represented by the island of Penglai.[44]

---

[41] This does not mean they do not appear in the poems at all, as such topics are very likely to be described indirectly. But then, unlike prose, homoerotic poetry about supernatural is not well researched in general and very rare for any kinds of beings.

[42] Mu-chou Poo, "The Images of Immortals and Eminent Monks: Religious Mentality in Early Medieval China (4–6 c. A.D.)," *Numen* 42, no. 2 (1995): 180.

[43] Wang Ka 王卡 *Zhongguo dao jiao ji chu zhi shi* 道教基础知识 [Basic knowledge of Chinese Daoism] (Beijing: Zong jiao wen hua chu ban she, 1999), 27–31; Kirkova, *Roaming into the beyond*, 138.

[44] Thomas E. Smith, "Penglai," in *Encyclopedia of Taoism*, vol. 1 and 2, ed. Fabrizio Pregadio (London: Routledge, 2008), 788–790; Kunio Miura, "Xianren," in *Encyclopedia of Taoism*, vol. 1 and 2, ed. Fabrizio Pregadio (London: Routledge, 2008), 1092–1094; Kunio Miura, "Zhenren," in *Encyclopedia of Taoism*, vol. 1 and 2, ed. Fabrizio Pregadio (London: Routledge, 2008), 1266.

It seems, therefore, that the rank of the immortals was an important trait for Tang poets: despite a popular interpretation of immortality in Chinese literature claiming that the discourse about it was a way of fantasizing about ultimate freedom and the anarchic sentiments of early Daoism,[45] not only do immortals comfortably fit into prevailing norms of social relationships in QTS, they also did so as a members of a distinct yet familiar Tang bureaucrat hierarchy that was compatible with the secular one, even if only superficially.

It is unlikely that Tang poets as a whole paid a lot of attention to which exact rank they ascribed to a *xian*, but rather chose one of the commonplace titles that fit the occasion. It is very likely, that on many occasions they were used simply as fillers that would help one adhere to the metric requirements of the genre — the choice of a concrete title would then also depend on the tonal requirements of the verse. Still, the poets could have used a wide variety of one-syllable epithets if their goal was solely to fill an empty slot: they could have concentrated on appearances, on provenance, age or any other attribute. Despite that, the choice was to concentrate on the markers of the social hierarchy, so it may be concluded that it was consistently seen as a trait that is more important than others.

At the same time, another aspect of *xian*-ship, namely their official duties, has almost no reflection in the collocations. While the world of the immortals was generally believed in Daoism to be modelled after the social hierarchy of the human realm (with an emperor, ministries and officials), only a single bureaucratic title, "official" (*li* 吏), from (1) appears in the top 50 collocations.

Based on this, it seems that the sentiment pertaining to the description of immortals in Tang poetry was not to break free from the norms and its inherent hierarchies, but rather to *expand* them. The ultimate goal of this was to gain contact with the supernatural and the possible benefits that come with it, without the dangers of disgracing oneself within the human society and with disregard to the additional responsibilities *xian*-ship might bring.

Finally, there are two groups of verb phrases that can be separated along the role of *xian* that acts either as the subject or the object. In this case this coincides with the roles of an agent or patient. In (4) the persona is the implicit or explicit agent and *xian* the patient:

---

45 Kirkova, *Roaming into the beyond*, 46, 79 and throughout: Aleksandr Storozhuk, *Tri učenija i kul'tura Kitaja: konfucianstvo, buddizm i daosizm v xudožestvennom tvorčestve èpohi Tan* [Three Teachings and the Chinese Culture: Confucianism, Buddhism and Taoism in Tang Creative Works] (St. Petersburg: Izdatel'stvo Karo, 210), 340; T. H. Barret, "Taoism and the state," in *Encyclopedia of Taoism*, vol. 1 and 2, ed. Fabrizio Pregadio (London: Routledge, 2008), 162.

(4) "learn (from immortals)" (*xue xian* 學仙), "obtain (immortality)" (*de xian* 得仙), "seek (immortals)" (*qiu xian* 求仙), "visit (immortals)" (*fang xian* 訪仙), "search (immortals)" (*xun xian* 尋仙), "meet (immortals)" (*hui xian* 會仙).

And in (5) the immortal is the agent:

(5) "(immortals) go" (*xian qu* 仙去), "(immortals) travel"[46] (*xian bi* 仙蹕).

As the collocates show, the most "typical" actions, directed at the immortals are exactly those one would expect: they are consistent with the topos of immortality seeking, even if it was not done in earnest.[47]

On the other hand, the lack of activities typical for immortals is somewhat contradictory: as shown by (1), they are typically depicted in possession of a variety of vehicles, be they waterborne or travelling overland. The poetic persona sees them on carriages and boats, but in the collocates they never seem to possess any agency: even for the verb "to go" in (5), one discovers upon closer inspection that it is often a complement of direction and it is not the immortals who perform the act (as in, for example "goes to seek for immortals" *xun xian qu* 尋仙去). To be sure, the immortals exist in QTS, the traces of them are visible and the objects belonging to them can be distinguished from those belonging to the realm of mortals. And yet, what distinguishes them is their motionless quality. They possess the means to travel but stay passive and detached.

Patterns

Method

Another way of looking into patterns of word usage would be to explore the vertical or "paradigmatic" axis of word usage, which concerns itself with words that can substitute each other in a certain context/place.[48]

Although the paradigmatic relationship is one of contrast — as Barthes has famously described it, these would be clothing items that cannot be worn at the

---

[46] This verb has a complex meaning: it usually refers to the carriage of the emperor; both his travels and the halt of all other traffic in his presence can be described. One can only speculate that the common denominator in case of immortals is that of separation of the persona from them.
[47] Storozhuk, *Tri učenija i kul'tura*, 356–365.
[48] Jakobson, "Closing statement," 358.

same time[49] — and the choice of one word over another is what defines the meaning of an utterance, the words that form paradigmatic relations with each other follow a certain order: they form a group based on some rules. If the grammar of a sentence allows a noun in a certain place, it does not mean that just *any* noun could sensibly be used there. Usage of one item from a semantic group is the type of intertextuality that evokes those other members of the group that could potentially be used in the place but were not. Incidentally, this very notion of semantic relations between words that form such groups lies at the foundation of modern machine-based sense disambiguation and synonym detection algorithms.[50]

Coming back to the images of immortals in Tang poetry, to look into paradigmatic relations of "immortals," could not only show which attributes they had and what kind of situations they were described in, but *what or who they were similar to*. Do they engage in the same activities as mortal people do? Were these some specific kinds of activities or types of people that belong to the same group as poetic immortals or would they be conceptually closer to ghosts or perhaps to natural phenomena? This is the kind of questions one could hope to answer by looking into paradigmatic relations.

To achieve this, one needs to look for textual patterns different from those of collocations. More precisely, one needs to find a way to look for the lines that mention immortals and then cross-reference them with *all* other lines in the corpus, select those which provide the same context and look which entities can substitute immortals there.

There are many ways to approach this problem,[51] but one of the more straightforward ones is using *edit distance*. This metric measures the number of simple edit operations one needs to perform on a sequence of characters in order to transform it into another. For example, to transform the word "cram" into a "car" one would

---

49 Roland Barthes, *The Fashion System*, trans. Matthew Ward and Richard Howard (New York, NY: Hill and Wang, 1983).

50 More specifically, context-based learning is used for creation of neural network-based language models. For more information see: Dan Jurafsky and James H. Martin, *Speech and Language Processing: An Introduction to Natural Language Processing, Computational Linguistics, and Speech Recognition* (2019), 94–122. In the context of Medieval Chinese poetry, see: Zorkina, "Describing Objects."

51 For an overview see: Lüdeling and Kytö, *Corpus Linguistics: An International Handbook*, vol. 1, 1249–1271. Somewhat different approaches have been used for researching intertextuality in early Chinese literature (Sturgeon, 2018) and Classical Chinese poetry (Liu et al., 2019). See: Donald Sturgeon, "Unsupervised identification of text reuse in early Chinese literature," *Digital Scholarship in the Humanities* 33, no. 3 (2018): 670–684; Chao-Lin Liu, Thomas J. Mazanec, and Jeffrey R. Tharsen, "Exploring Chinese Poetry with Digital Assistance: Examples from Linguistic, Literary, and Historical Viewpoints," *Journal of Chinese Literature and Culture* 5, no. 2 (2019): 276–321.

need to perform the following operations: remove the letter "m," replace the letter "a" with "r" or vice versa.⁵² The less steps one has to perform to travel from one character sequence to another, the smaller the edit distance, and the more similar are the compared entities.

The units of comparison can be set differently for this test: one could work with separate words, with sentences or longer documents where each character — including the whitespace — is used, or by splitting the text into words and taking each as a single unit of measurement. This flexibility of application works in one's favor when it comes to Classical Chinese: as discussed before, the definition of word boundaries is problematic, both from a theoretical standpoint of criteria defining wordhood and as an operation that introduces new errors into the corpus — something that should be accounted for very carefully, when it comes to smaller corpora. Unlike collocations, edit distances allow to operate on poetic lines straightforwardly, avoiding the tokenization step altogether.

Finding similar character sequences is the primary goal of edit distances, but to arrive at the point of interest for the particular research question of this chapter, one, and only one, additional step is needed: once all the lines that have similar context to the ones mentioning immortals have been found, one can start comparing the differences in order to see what the immortals can be substituted with.⁵³

For this chapter, all lines that contained the character *xian* 仙 were extracted from the QTS.⁵⁴ Each of them was compared against all other lines in QTS. If the similarity of two lines was higher than 70%, these lines were recorded. Given that

---

52 There is, of course, no universal agreement on what constitutes a "simple operation." In this chapter the Levenstein distance is used, and it only allows deletion, insertion and substitution. Other approaches apply different sets of operations and would yield different distances.
53 One might argue that this approach can be misleading: it only accounts for a small group of words appearing in a very specific pattern. Yet again, if we take the language of Tang poetry as an isolated phenomenon and study its system, through the utterances that are available to us and without embedding this system of signification into a larger framework, the analysis starts to look more comprehensive, albeit incomplete. The scope of relevance of such system is debatable: Kao and Mei (1978) argue to expand Jakobson's definitions, namely by adding the "tradition" to the equation, but this is a very broad term that deserves its own extended discussion. See: Kao and Mei, "Meaning, Metaphor, and Allusion in T'ang Poetry," 374–352.
54 The code can be found at: "qts_immortals," mzorki, https://github.com/mzorki/qts_immortals. It can be referred for a more detailed walkthrough with examples and commentaries. For the analysis, Python library "fuzzywuzzy" was used. The feature of this library is that it recounts edit distances into similarity in percent, which makes it easier to compare the results of a series of edit distance searches — a longer sequence of characters allows for a bigger edit distance to achieve the same degree of similarity than a shorter one.

in QTS lines rarely exceed 7–10 characters,⁵⁵ this cut-off still ensures that the lines are identical except for several changes. With a higher threshold there were not enough results to make meaningful comparisons.

Subsequently, for each of the source lines a group of similar target lines in QTS is recorded; if there are none, the source line is removed from consideration. Generally, if a line A is matched to a line B in the corpus, this means that line B is recorded as matching to line A as well. In such cases the second occurrence was removed from the results in order to avoid duplicates, so that each group of similar lines would only appear once. For the last step, only those cases were considered, when the matching lines in the groups did not contain the word *xian*, i.e. where it was substituted by something else.

As a result, the original 3,475 lines⁵⁶ that contain the word "immortal" in QTS were reduced to 40 groups including the relevant similar lines.⁵⁷

It is important to note two things, before I proceed to interpretation. First, QTS contains a considerable number of duplicate poems that are ascribed to different authors. The same text repeated several times might produce an impression that the pattern is more widespread than it actually is.⁵⁸ Secondly, even if we are to confirm that the sources of similar lines are indeed different works, given the nature of Tang poetry which puts a great emphasis on intertextuality and allusions,⁵⁹ the probability is high that one of them is quoting the other or both of them are quoting a third source that is not in the corpus. While this impacts frequency, this need not be an issue since the independence of utterances is not what is important here. Rather, we are after the choices that were made regarding the substitutions of the word *xian* with something else.

---

55 This is the case, for example, of Du Guangting's 杜光庭 (850–933) poem "Unravelling dao and de" (*Ji daode* 紀道德) where the number of characters in lines of each couplet increase, starting with one and ending when reaching 15. There are only circa 100 such cases in QTS, generally they are single long lines in poems with irregular line lengths.
56 The number of lines is smaller than the number of times *xian* occurs in the text, since the word can appear several times in one line.
57 See Appendix. For more information on process and comparisons of how altering the strictness of the matches influences the results, see the code: "qts_immortals," mzorki, https://github.com/mzorki/qts_immortals.
58 According to my rough estimate, around 5% of content in QTS is duplicate, but removing such a large amount of text requires serious justification and is beyond the scope of this chapter.
59 On functioning of citations and allusions in Tang poetry see, for example: David Lattimore, "Allusion and T'ang poetry," in *Perspectives on the T'ang*, ed. Arthur F. Wright and Denis Crispin Twitchett (Taipei: Rainbow-Bridge Book Co., 1973), 405–439.

Interpretation

Similarly to the case of collocations, the results can be grouped. For the sake of readability some extra context is provided in the examples in addition to the words of interest; within each "conceptual group" phrases that actually substitute each other in QTS are delimited with semicolons.[60]

People and authority:

(6) "immortal person" (*xian ren* 仙人), "person" (*ren* 人), "beauty" (*meiren* 美人); "immortal" (*shenxian* 神仙), "girl" or "prostitute" (*ajiao* 阿嬌).

(7) "(palace of) immortal" (*xiangong* 仙宮), "royal (palace)" (*wanggong* 王宮); "ancient (and old)" (*gulao* 古老), "immortal (and old)" (*xianlao* 仙老); "(power of a) general" (*jiangjun li* 將軍力), "(power of a peach of) immortality" (*xiantao li* 仙桃力); "*langgong* official" (*langgong* 郎官), "immortal" or "*xianlang* official" (*xianlang* 仙郎).

Types of immortals:

(8) *tianzhen* 天真, *zhenxian* 真仙.

Nature:

(9) "(see) immortal" (*jianxian* 見仙), "(see) mountain" (*jianshan* 見山); "mountain (house)" meaning "house of a recluse" (*shanjia* 山家), "(house of) immortal" (*xianjia* 仙家); "(group of) mountains" (*shanqun* 山群), "(group of) immortals" (*xianqun* 仙群); "(road in the) mountain of immortals" (*xianshan lu* 仙山路), "(road in the native) mountains" (*jiashan dao* 家山道), "(road in the Song) mountain" (*Songshan lu* 嵩山路); "(palace of) immortals" (*xiandian* 仙殿), "mountain (palace)" (*shandian* 山殿).

(10) "overlooking a stream" (*linxi* 臨溪), "immortal spring" (*xianyuan* 仙源); "immortal plays" (*xiannong* 仙弄), "Heaven plays" (*tiannong* 天弄); "carriage of an immortal" (*xianjia* 仙駕), "clouds and rain" (*yunyu* 雲雨).

---

[60] I am inclined to overlook some of the results, such as the case of "immortal" being replaced with a "chicken" at one place.

Social norms:

(11) "follower of wine" (*jiutu* 酒徒), "immortal of wine" (*jiuxian* 酒仙), "drunken madman" (*jiukuang* 酒狂).

This reveals several things about the depiction of immortals: first, despite being different from humans, they function within the same paradigm, unlike other types of supernatural beings, be that different types of ghosts, demons and tricksters,[61] which never appear in same paradigmatic groups as the immortals. All the words in (6) often appear in the similar context of being sought after, like in lines "immortals cannot be seen" (*xianren buke jian* 仙人不可見) or "this person cannot be seen" (*ciren buke jian* 此人不可見). Another word that appears in the same context is "beautiful woman" as in the line: "at which place does the beautiful woman exist?" (*meiren hechu zai* 美人何處在). Interestingly enough, more particular types of *xian*, such as "old man" or "companion" from (2) do not appear in similar patterns. Could it be that an old teacher was not as exciting to search for? It is hard to tell, given that there are too few occurrences of such patterns.

The paradigmatic relations revealed in (7) show, that *xian* were seen as figures of authority, as they are used interchangeably with different figures of power such as kings, generals, officials or worthies and heroes from ancient times — as saying that something was ancient was often a way to add credibility to a source. There might be several intertwining reasons for such a pattern to appear. First, as in case with the "palace," things associated with immortals were thought of as something possessing high quality, just like the ones belonging to the rulers. At the same time, Daoism as a religion did offer an idea of the world order that closely copied the imperial one but was a better version of it. As a result, Tang dynasty witnessed some rivalry between the spirit and the human world over authority, which was not just a theoretical debate about the religious hierarchy but had real life consequences

---

61 There is a plethora of terms related to these supernatural beings: for example, "foxes" (*hu* 狐), "spirits" (*yao* 妖), "ghosts" or "demons" (*gui* 鬼) and "souls" (*hun* 魂). Sometimes these also appear in combinations, i.e. "bewitching fox" (*yaohu* 妖狐). For all the supernatural beings in this group results of the analyses were substantially different from the ones for *xian*, in most cases there were very few similar lines and there were no cases of being interchanged with a human. The only exception are souls *hun*, that were interchangeable with humans, but very rarely — Judith T. Zeitlin (1997) has noticed that ghosts did enjoy a somewhat higher status than foxes in literature of Late Imperial China. See: Judith T. Zeitlin, "Embodying the Disembodied: Representations of Ghosts and the Feminine," in *Writing Women in Late Imperial China*, ed. Ellen Widmer and Kang-I Sun Chang (Stanford, CA: Stanford University Press, 1997), 242–264.

for Daoist priests and the officials.⁶² And this power relationship was reflected in poetry as well: Heavenly and Earthly officials competed for authority, both generals and peaches of immortals had power over people, and both mortal and immortal wise men of the ancient times ruled the minds of the poets' contemporaries in QTS.

As for (9), a close connection with mountains was expected, as mountains were thought to be a common dwelling place of immortals, but it is interesting to see that they appear not only in collocations but can in many cases be used interchangeably in the same context. This shows that the association between the two was strong enough for them to enter a relationship of metonymy: despite there being a variety of objects and places, associated with *xian*, no other seem to reach this extent. This can be connected with (3), as immortals that resided in mountains were also believed to be the middle-tier ones constitute a large part of that group.

The examples in (11) are the only traces of immortal behaviors breaking norms found by the analyses. All of them are connected to excessive consumption of wine. In particular, *jiuxian* would often refer to one specific person — the famous Tang poet Li Bai 李白 (701–762). Despite a popular trope that connected immortals and Daoism with wine-drinking,⁶³ judging by the analyses above the immortals themselves did not have a strong connection with alcohol. The ones who do the drinking are mortal men, as wine and the state of intoxication are capable of freeing one from social norms and temporarily bringing them closer to being their "true self;" to being one.⁶⁴ Can it be, that as *xian* themselves have already achieved the higher state of being do not require the liberating effect of wine and do not need to be intoxicated anymore?

There are surely some exclusions. For example, QTS contains poems ascribed to an immortal Lü Dongbin 呂洞賓 who is known to be associated with heavy drinking and whose cult gained popularity during the period of Five Dynasties and Ten Kingdoms (五代十國, 907–960). But while Song 宋 (960–1279) miscellanies *biji* 筆記 telling the tales of his intoxication were so extreme that even led to Lü Dongbin

---

62 Judith M. Boltz, "Not by the Seal of Office Alone: New Weapons in Battles with the Supernatural," in *Religion and Society in T'ang and Sung China*, ed. Patricia Buckley Ebrey and Peter N. Gregory (Honolulu, HI: University of Hawaii Press, 1993), 241–305; Partington, *Patterns and meanings*, 162–163.
63 See, for example: Storozhuk, *Tri učenija i kul'tura Kitaja*, 346–350.
64 On connection of wine-drinking to the idea of liberation in in Tang poetry, see: Storozhuk, *Tri učenija i kul'tura Kitaja*, 346-350; Zong-qi Cai, *How to Read Chinese Poetry in Context: Poetic Culture from Antiquity Through the Tang* (New York, NY: Columbia University Press, 2018): 223-235. For Early Medieval prose, see: Nanxiu Qian, *Spirit and self in medieval China: the Shih-shuo hsin-yü and its legacy* (Honolulu, HI: University of Hawai'i Press, 2001), 136.

ordered to be arrested; in QTS he enjoys a somewhat more dignified representation, although wine and being drunk are mentioned in quite a few of the poems.[65]

The analysis of the paradigmatic axis of usage of *xian* supports some of the results of the analysis of collocations: the world of the supernatural was not unified in Tang poetry and immortals had something unique to offer. First, because of the pervasive "beauty" we can see that female *xian* were as sexualized as ghosts and foxes and Tang poets readily drew parallels between a woman being immortal and desirable. But it happened in a somewhat different way: the latter were seen as seductresses and, as shown above,[66] were unlikely to fall into the same paradigmatic group as humans, while the status of the latter was close to, if not superior to humans. Secondly, immortals as a whole maintained the societal structure and norms, familiar to the poets, but were generally associated with more privileged positions.

The world of ghosts offered a thrill, but immortals were offering a world of glory, that was familiar but better. The freedom related to immortality that is represented in QTS is not an anarchic freedom from norms — yet again, this is one of the reasons why "immortal maiden" was an appropriate epithet to describe a real-life woman without implications of her promiscuity — but rather the freedom to bend the rules in a way like a person in a privileged position and without suffering the consequences. And, judging by the strong connection of *xian* in QTS to the "mid-tier" *xian*, that achieved the status but were not assigned an official position in Heaven, it was the privilege but not the responsibilities or even the power that kindled poets' interest.

Yet again, this does not mean that there are no poems in QTS that depict immortals in a more serious light, reflecting the feeling of loneliness, or self-perfection. What is described here are language patterns connected to one particular word, which show its characteristic and distinct usage.

---

[65] Paul R. Katz, *Images of the Immortal: the Cult of Lü Dongbin at the Palace of Eternal Joy* (Honolulu, HI: University of Hawai'i Press, 1999), 57; Mariana Zorkina, "Perception of Immortals in Popular and Elite Daoism: the Case of Lü Dongbin," *St. Petersburg Annual of Asian and African Studies* 4 (2015): 99–112.

[66] See footnote 61.

Conclusion

Unlike supernatural beings, immortals in QTS are safely anchored within the conceptual field of the human world. They can partake in relations close to those upheld by mortals and are constantly depicted as a part of societal hierarchy, while their status is nevertheless higher than that of humans.

Judging by the results of the analyses, a topos characteristic for poetry about *xian* was the fantasy of extending one's possibilities and quality of life, the privilege to act upon one's wishes, but not the pursuit of anarchic ideals characteristic of early Daoism. As shown by the lack of bureaucratic titles in the results and consistently strong representation of "mid-tier" immortals, poets as a whole did not have the ambition to take a place among the celestial bureaucrats or to use the magical powers.

Another fantasy connected to *xian* was the possibility of a romantic encounter with a celestial beauty. These fantasies do not intersect with those involving ghosts or fox spirits: immortals are described as humans and as an extension of the human world. Unlike ghosts and fox spirits, *xian* belong to the same paradigmatic class as humans and this is something that makes them fundamentally different from other supernatural beings.

Exactly because immortals were conceptually and performatively close to humans, there was a need to specifically mark the manufactured objects belonging to them in order to distinguish them from the ordinary ones and their owners, i.e. from mortals.

Immortals are closely connected to travel: collocations show them being characteristically depicted on boats and carriages, but at the same time they do not possess agency, as most actions are addressed at them, but almost nothing is typically done by them. In Daoism, celestial beings have the power to influence the human world, for example by doing magic or fighting demons. But in poetry, the *xian* are *passive*: even notwithstanding a strong association with travels and often depicted in possession of various vehicles, immortals seem to stand still. They occur rather as patients than agents, beings who are sought after and objects of the gaze of the persona.

Appendix

Table 1. Top 50 results for collocations with *xian* 仙.
Specifications:
- Tokenised with 2-word crawler and CDICT dictionary.
- Removed punctuation (',', '．', '。', ',', ' ').
- Algorithm: ngram='bigram', min_freq=None, window=5, nmax=50, results='long'.
- Measure – student_t.
- See 'collocations_single_word' file.

Tab. 1: Top 50 results for collocations with *xian* 仙.

collocation	f1	f2	t-score
仙 – 家	2012	2763	4.14
仙 – 掌	2012	336	3.74
仙 – 翁	2012	603	3.21
群 – 仙	1225	2012	3.11
仙 – 宮	2012	1521	3.08
仙 – 舟	2012	1141	2.97
靈 – 仙	1192	2012	2.78
仙 – 侶	2012	477	2.7
學 – 仙	1069	2012	2.68
得 – 仙	4393	2012	2.66
求 – 仙	1148	2012	2.56
有 – 仙	8742	2012	2.52
仙 – 桂	2012	746	2.37
仙 – 路	2012	3479	2.36
真 – 仙	1291	2012	2.32
仙 – 去	2012	6191	2.27
仙 – 台	2012	2286	2.25
尋 – 仙	1785	2012	2.23
仙 – 駕	2012	416	2.21
仙 – 娥	2012	145	2.19
望 – 仙	2945	2012	2.13
仙 – 山	2012	9227	2.07
仙 – 都	2012	668	2.06
是 – 仙	4177	2012	2.03
九 – 仙	1164	2012	1.96
仙 – 掖	2012	121	1.95

Tab. 1 (continued)

collocation	f1	f2	t-score
仙 – 馭	2012	172	1.93
有神 – 仙	79	2012	1.9
金 – 仙	3158	2012	1.9
會 – 仙	1066	2012	1.87
仙 – 術	2012	273	1.83
仙 – 槎	2012	142	1.81
洞 – 仙	678	2012	1.81
訪 – 仙	692	2012	1.8
地 – 仙	3112	2012	1.79
仙 – 觀	2012	724	1.79
仙 – 蹤	2012	286	1.75
仙 – 蹕	2012	46	1.64
仙 – 下	2012	4577	1.63
迎 – 仙	945	2012	1.56
散 – 仙	1407	2012	1.53
仙 – 閣	2012	1070	1.51
泛 – 仙	691	2012	1.5
下 – 仙	4577	2012	1.5
仙 – 輿	2012	176	1.49
蓬萊 – 仙	232	2012	1.47
仙 – 禽	2012	646	1.44
仙 – 日月	2012	484	1.43
女 – 仙	864	2012	1.43
仙 – 吏	2012	678	1.43

Table 2. Groups of lines, that match those that contain *xian* at more than 70%. Specifications:

- For each line that contained *xian* 仙, a Levenstein distance with all the other lines in QTS. was calculated. Lines that matched more than 70% were recorded.
- All lines that did not have matches were removed.
- All groups that were duplicating each other (e.g. with a group for line A that matches B and another line that records that line B matches A, the second instance was deleted).
- Only the groups where *xian* was swapped for something else in other lines were saved.

Tab. 2: Groups of lines, that match those that contain *xian* at more than 70%.

1	故人不可見, 故人不可見, 故人不可見, 故人不可見, 仙人不見我, 此人不可見, 古人不可見, 上仙不可見, 故人不可見, 故人不可見, 遊人不可見, 故人不可見, 仙人不可見, 仙舟不可見, 人不見, 神仙不可見
2	歌宛轉, 歌宛轉, 歌宛轉, 歌宛轉, 歌宛轉, 歌宛轉, 仙歌宛轉聽, 仙歌宛轉聽, 歌宛轉, 歌宛轉, 歌宛轉, 歌宛轉
3	不知精爽歸何處, 不知仙駕歸何處, 不知此地歸何處, 不知雲雨歸何處, 不知雲雨歸何處, 不知功歸何處, 不知何處
4	可中得似紅兒貌, 得似紅兒今日貌, 神仙得似紅兒貌, 稍教得似紅兒貌, 若教得似紅兒貌, 若教得似紅兒貌, 阿嬌得似紅兒貌
5	暗從何處來, 問從何處來, 子從何處來, 又從何處來, 三從何處來, 仙從何處來
6	不可得, 神仙不可求, 神仙不可得, 神仙不可學, 神仙不可見
7	壺中別有日月天, 應是壺中別有家, 壺中別有仙家日, 應是壺中別有家
8	卻向人間作酒徒, 且向人間作仙, 罰向人間作酒狂, 謫向人間作酒狂
9	仙雲在何處, 仙雲在何處, 在何處
10	仙人不見我, 仙人不可見, 人不見
11	門前便是家山道, 門前便是嵩山路, 門前便是仙山路
12	先皇曾向此中游, 曾向此中游, 神仙曾向此中游
13	通籍在金閨, 通籍在金閨, 已通仙籍在金閨
14	三千功滿仙升去, 三千功滿好歸去, 三千功滿去升天
15	不知何處是天真, 不知何處偶真仙, 不知何處
16	叢篁發仙弄, 叢篁發天弄
17	仙人何處在, 美人何處在
18	雲歸帝鄉遠, 雲歸仙帝鄉
19	玉醴浮金菊, 玉醴浮仙菊
20	東風吹雪舞山家, 東風吹雪舞仙家
21	仙人樓上鳳凰飛, 樓上鳳凰飛去後
22	仙尉其何如, 其何如
23	五雲抱仙殿, 五雲抱山殿
24	我思仙人乃在碧海之東隅, 乃在碧海之東隅
25	授以仙藥, 授以神藥
26	始知萬族無不有, 始知仙事無不有
27	雞犬逐人靜, 仙犬逐人靜
28	貌棱棱, 仙貌玉棱棱

Tab. 2 (continued)

29	郎官能賦許依投, 仙郎能賦許依投
30	眾香天上梵仙宮, 眾香天上梵王宮
31	仙人居其中, 人乃居其中
32	不知誰是豔陽才, 不知誰是謫仙才
33	曉上青樓十二重, 正上仙樓十二重
34	仙吏不知何處隱, 不知何處
35	神歸碧落, 要伴神仙歸碧落
36	嘗聞古老言, 嘗聞仙老言
37	此去臨溪不是遙, 此去仙源不是遙
38	仿佛列山群, 仿佛列仙群
39	看雲忽見仙, 看雲忽見山
40	當時不得將軍力, 當時不得仙桃力

Bibliography

Allen, Colin, Hongliang Luo, Jaimie Murdock, Jianghuai Pu, Xiaohong Wang, Yanjie Zhai, and Kun Zhao. "Topic Modeling the Hàn diǎn Ancient Classics." *Journal of Cultural Analytics* 2, no 1 (2017): 1–23.

Barret, T. H. "Taoism and the state." In *Encyclopedia of Taoism*, vol. 1 and 2, edited by Fabrizio Pregadio, 162–165. London: Routledge, 2008.

Barthes, Roland. *The Fashion System*. Translated by Matthew Ward and Richard Howard. New York, NY: Hill and Wang, 1983.

Benn, Charles D. "Taoism and the civil service examinations." In *Encyclopedia of Taoism*, vol. 1 and 2, edited by Fabrizio Pregadio, 165–167. London: Routledge, 2008.

Bird, Steven, Ewan Klein, and Edward Loper. *Natural Language Processing with Python*. Sebastopol, CA: O'Reilly, 2009.

Bokenkamp, Stephen R. "Taoism and Chinese literature." In *Encyclopedia of Taoism*, vol. 1 and 2, edited by Fabrizio Pregadio, 176–179. London: Routledge, 2008.

Boltz, Judith M. "Not by the Seal of Office Alone: New Weapons in Battles with the Supernatural." In *Religion and Society in T'ang and Sung China*, edited by Patricia Buckley Ebrey and Peter N. Gregory, 241–305. Honolulu, HI: University of Hawaii Press, 1993.

Cai, Zong-qi. *How to Read Chinese Poetry in Context: Poetic Culture from Antiquity Through the Tang*. New York, NY: Columbia University Press, 2018.

Huntington, Rania. "Foxes and Sex in Late Imperial Chinese Narrative." *Nan Nü* 2, no. 1 (2000): 78–128.

Jakobson, Roman. "Closing statement: linguistics and poetics." In *Style in Language*, edited by Thomas A. Sebeck, 350–377. Cambridge, MA: MT Press, 1960.

Jurafsky, Dan, and James H. Martin. Speech and Language Processing: An Introduction to Natural Language Processing, Computational Linguistics, and Speech Recognition. 2019. https://web.stanford.edu/~jurafsky/slp3/old_oct19/ed3book.pdf.

Kao, Yu-Kung, and Tsu-Lin Mei. "Meaning, Metaphor, and Allusion in T'ang Poetry." *Harvard Journal of Asiatic Studies* 38, no. 2 (1978): 281–356.

Katz, Paul R. *Images of the Immortal: The Cult of Lü Dongbin at the Palace of Eternal Joy*. Honolulu, HI: University of Hawai'i Press, 1999.

Kirkova, Zornica. *Roaming into the Beyond: Representations of Xian Immortality in Early Medieval Chinese Verse*. Leiden: Brill, 2016.

Lattimore, David. "Allusion and T'ang poetry." In *Perspectives on the T'ang*, edited by Arthur F. Wright and Denis Crispin Twitchett, 405–439. Taipei: Rainbow-Bridge Book Co., 1973.

Lee, John, and Wong Tak-sum. "Glimpses of Ancient China from Classical Chinese Poems." *Proceedings of COLING 2012: Posters* (2012): 621–632.

Liu, Chao-Lin, Thomas J. Mazanec, and Jeffrey R. Tharsen. "Exploring Chinese Poetry with Digital Assistance: Examples from Linguistic, Literary, and Historical Viewpoints." *Journal of Chinese Literature and Culture* 5, no. 2 (2019): 276–321.

Lüdeling, Anke, and Merja Kytö. *Corpus Linguistics: An International Handbook*, vol. 2. Berlin: De Gruyter, 2008.

Manning, Christopher D., and Hinrich Schütze. *Foundations of Statistical Natural Language Processing*. Cambridge, MA: MIT Press, 1999.

Miura, Kunio. "Xianren." In *Encyclopedia of Taoism*, vol. 1 and 2, edited by Fabrizio Pregadio, 1092–1094. London: Routledge, 2008.

Miura, Kunio. "Zhenren." In *Encyclopedia of Taoism*, vol. 1 and 2, edited by Fabrizio Pregadio, 1265–1266. London: Routledge, 2008.

Nichols, Ryan, Edward Slingerland, Kristoffer Laigaard Nielbo, Peter Kirby, and Carson Logan. "Supernatural Agents and Prosociality in Historical China: Micro-Modeling the Cultural Evolution of Gods and Morality in Textual Corpora." *Religion, Brain & Behavior* 11, no. 1 (2021): 46–64. DOI: https://doi.org/10.1080/2153599X.2020.1742778.

Nienhauser, William H. *The Indiana Companion to Traditional Chinese Literature*. Taipei: SMC Publishing, 2003.

Nothman, Joel, Qin Hanmin, and Roman Yurchak. "Stop Word Lists in Free Open-source Software Packages." *Proceedings of Workshop for NLP Open Source Software* (2018): 7–12. DOI: http://doi.org/10.18653/v1/W18-2502.

Nugent, Christopher M. B. "Literary collections in Tang dynasty China." *T'oung-Pao* 93, Fasc. 1/3 (2007): 1–52.

Owen, Stephen. "The manuscript legacy of the Tang the case of literature." *Harvard Journal of Asiatic Studies* 67, no. 2 (2007): 295–326.

Owen, Stephen. *The Late Tang: Chinese Poetry of the Mid-Ninth Century (827–860)*. Cambridge, MA: Harvard University Press, 2009.

Partington, Alan. *Patterns and Meanings: Using Corpora for English Language Research and Teaching*. Amsterdam: J. Benjamins Pub., 1998.

"poetry-source," snowtraces, https://github.com/snowtraces/poetry-source.

Poo, Mu-chou. "The Images of Immortals and Eminent Monks: Religious Mentality in Early Medieval China (4–6 c. A.D.)." *Numen* 42, no. 2 (1995): 172–196.

Qian, Nanxiu. *Spirit and Self in Medieval China: the Shih-shuo hsin-yü and Its Legacy*. Honolulu, HI: University of Hawai'i Press, 2001.

"qts_immortals," mzorki, https://github.com/mzorki/qts_immortals.

Slingerland, Edward, Ryan Nichols, Kristoffer Neilbo, and Carson Logan. "The Distant Reading of Religious Texts: A 'Big Data' Approach to Mind-Body Concepts in Early China." *Journal of the American Academy of Religion* 85, no. 4 (2017): 985–1016.

Smith, Thomas E. "Penglai." In *Encyclopedia of Taoism*, vol. 1 and 2, edited by Fabrizio Pregadio, 788–790. London: Routledge, 2008.

Stevenson, Mark, and Cuncun Wu. *Homoeroticism in Imperial China: a sourcebook*. New York: Routledge, 2013.

Storozhuk, Aleksandr. *Tri učenija i kul'tura Kitaja: konfucianstvo, buddizm i daosizm v xudožestvennom tvorčestve èpohi Tan* [Three Teachings and the Chinese Culture: Confucianism, Buddhism and Taoism in Tang Creative Works]. St. Petersburg: Izdatel'stvo Karo, 2010.

Stubbs, Michael. "On inference theories and code theories: Corpus evidence for semantic schemas." *Text & Talk* 21, no. 3 (2001): 437–465.

Sturgeon, Donald. "Unsupervised identification of text reuse in early Chinese literature," *Digital Scholarship in the Humanities* 33, no. 3 (2018): 670–684.

"Tutorials," mzorki, https://github.com/mzorki/tutorials.

Wang, Ka 王卡. *Zhongguo dao jiao ji chu zhi shi* 道教基础知识 [Basic knowledge of Chinese Daoism]. Beijing: Zong jiao wen hua chu ban she, 1999.

Zeitlin, Judith T. "Embodying the Disembodied: Representations of Ghosts and the Feminine." In *Writing Women in Late Imperial China*, edited by Ellen Widmer and Kang-I Sun Chang, 242–264. Stanford, CA: Stanford University Press, 1997.

zh_TW Dictionaries, http://download.huzheng.org/zh_TW/.

Zorkina, Mariana. "Perception of Immortals in Popular and Elite Daoism: the Case of Lü Dongbin." *St. Petersburg Annual of Asian and African Studies* 4 (2015): 99–112.

Zorkina, Mariana. "Describing Objects in Tang Dynasty Poetic Language: A Study Based on Word Embeddings." *Journal of Chinese Literature and Culture* 5, no. 2 (2019): 250–275.

James Harry Morris
Missiology in the Digital Age: Challenges and Opportunities for the Study of Pre-Modern Christianity in Japan

Introduction

The product of interacting European and Japanese contexts, peoples, and histories, texts related to Christianity in Japan provide unique challenges to the digital humanist grounded in their unique vocabulary, use of multiple languages and scripts, and methods of composition and printing. How do we approach texts that feature both Japanese and European languages and scripts? How do we approach texts in which not only the language and script varies, but also the direction of the text? How do we approach texts that feature vocabulary absent from online dictionaries and word banks that many analytical tools rely on? In the pre-computer age, scholars circumvented these issues by focusing on either the East Asian or the European elements of mission history in East Asia confining themselves to documents written in particular languages or to particular topics, or by learning the multiple languages needed to traverse these documents and corpora. The source materials are certainly challenging to human readers due to their linguistic breadth, but does this mean that they are also challenging for computers and digital tools? The digital age provides opportunities to broaden the ways we interact with the textual products of missions to East Asia, and perhaps to bridge the European-Asian divide which exists not only in the study of missiology itself, but also within the digital humanities. Departing from the optimism that demarks many studies on the digital humanities, the focus here is primarily on the challenges and limitations associated with the study of texts relating to Christianity in Japan in the digital age and particularly for ordinary scholars with little training in the digital humanities. The chapter[1] reflects on potential opportunities and resolutions, whilst also describing and analyzing issues related to the paucity of available resources, digitization, and tools that can be implemented in the analysis of texts relating to Christianity in Japan during and prior to the Edo period (1603–1868). In doing so,

---

[1] The research for this paper was partially funded by a DNP Foundation for Cultural Promotion Graphic Culture Research Grant and a Waseda University Grant for Special Research Projects which sponsor my on-going "Kirishitan-ban in the Digital Age: A Study of the Opportunities and Limitations of Applying Digital Methods to Kirishitan-ban" project.

https://doi.org/10.1515/9783110747607-010

the chapter seeks to offer an assessment of the state of the field and to problematize digital approaches to East Asian texts more generally.

Textual Diversity and Challenges Related to Scripts

Early modern Japanese texts are diverse. They existed in immense number in both manuscript and printed form, they were written, printed, engraved and etched on different materials including paper, wood, and stone, in books, booklets, letters, and diaries, and on posters, scrolls (including hanging scrolls), public notice boards and advertisement boards, gravestones and other monuments and obelisks. Amongst printed materials there were numerous written genres including religious texts, calendars, dictionaries, erotica, maps, military stories, poetry, and textbooks,[2] whereas manuscript materials might include letters, diaries, and official records. There were also radically different writing types with classical Japanese (*bungotai* 文語体) traditionally being divided into: *kanbun* 漢文 (Sino-Japanese), *sōrōbun* 候文 (epistolary style), *wabun* 和文 (classical Japanese) and *wakan-konkōbun* 和漢混淆文 (a style combining elements of both Chinese and Japanese writing styles).[3] Texts were written or printed in different scripts that might be broadly categorized as non-cursive, semi-cursive, or cursive and which varied radically based on the handwriting of the scribe and the degree of cursivity. Whilst usually aligned in right-to-left vertical script, text may be aligned horizontally, in a mixture of alignments, or in no sequential order at all.[4] Printed materials could include illustrations with which the printed text may be intertwined. Early modern Japanese writing used what we now consider to be old forms (*kyūjitai* 旧字体)

---

[2] See the overview given in: Laura Moretti, *Pleasure in Profit: Popular Prose in Seventeenth-Century Japan* (New York, NY: Columbia University Press, 2020), 86–93.

[3] Nanette Gottlieb, *Language and Society in Japan* (Cambridge: Cambridge University Press, 2005), 40–42; Nanette Twine, "The Genbunitchi Movement. Its Origin, Development, and Conclusion," *Monumenta Nipponica* 33, no. 3 (1978): 334–336. Traditionally scholars have compartmentalized these writing types based on the social classes of those who predominantly read and wrote them. This has been challenged by scholars such as Elizabeth Oyler who explores the political aspects of the *kanbun-wabun* framework as it pertains to Japan's relationship with the Asian continent and Laura Moretti who challenges the dichotomization of readership that results from classical categorizations and postulates instead the existence of a spectrum of literacies. See: Elizabeth Oyler, *Swords, Oaths, and Prophetic Visions: Authoring Warrior Rule in Medieval Japan* (Honolulu, HI: University of Hawai'i Press, 2006), 9–14; Moretti, *Pleasure in Profit*, 53–64.

[4] See example in: Alex Lamb, Tarin Clanuwat, and Asanobu Kitamoto, "KuroNet: Regularized Residual U-Nets for End-to-End Kuzushiji Character Recognition," *SN Computer Science* 1: 177 (2020): 7.

of *kanji* 漢字 (Chinese characters), variant *kanji* (*itaiji* 異体字), and historical orthography (*rekishiteki kanazukai* 歴史的仮名遣い), and did not consistently use conventions such as *dakuten* 濁点 and *handakuten* 半濁点 (diacritics for voiced consonants) or punctuation. Additionally, the characters carved on the woodblocks used to print texts were copied from handwritten documents meaning that printed materials share the features of manuscripts in terms of the way that the characters are displayed.[5] Whilst the foregoing summary risks overgeneralization, it should be clear that early modern Japanese texts encapsulated great diversity. This diversity is further complicated when we consider texts pertaining to Christianity.

Roman Catholic missionaries were active in Japan between 1549 and 1644. Although Christianity was banned in 1614, the mission was numerically successful and communities continued to exist underground until their (re-)"discovery" in the nineteenth century. In 1590, Visitor of Missions in the Indies, Alessandro Valignano (1539–1606), arrived in Japan on his second visit bringing with him a printing press and a team of trained staff.[6] The press remained active until 1614 when it was taken to Macau where it subsequently (from 1620) continued to print for the mission.[7] The materials printed by the mission are known as *Kirishitan-ban* キリシタン版 (P. *Cristão edição*). Up to 100 different *Kirishitan-ban* titles were printed, but less than 40 survive.[8] In addition to these, were works for the Chinese mission used in Japan, manuscripts, and works imported from Europe. There is also a large body of manuscript and printed works related to the persecution of Christianity. In his bibliography of texts pertaining to Christianity (broadly defined) in Japan printed or composed between 1543 and 1858, Ebisawa Arimichi includes some 3,648 sources,[9] however, the number of manuscript sources are much greater than this with innumerable letters, documents, and notice boards being produced all over Japan throughout the Edo period.

---

[5] Lamb, Clanuwat, and Kitamoto, "KuroNet: Regularized Residual U-Nets for End-to-End Kuzushiji Character Recognition," 2.
[6] Gonoi Takashi 五野井隆史, *Kirishitan no bunka* キリシタンの文化 (Tokyo: Yoshikawa Kōbunkan, 2012), 170–181; Johannes Laures, *Kirishitan Bunko: A Manual of Books and Documents on the Early Christian Mission in Japan*, 3rd edition (Tokyo: Sophia University, 1957), 4–20.
[7] Laures, *Kirishitan Bunko*, 20.
[8] Peter F. Kornicki, *The Book in Japan: A Cultural History from the Beginnings to the Nineteenth Century* (Leiden: Brill, 1998), 126.
[9] Ebisawa Arimichi, ed. *Christianity in Japan: A Bibliography of Japanese and Chinese Sources, Part I (1543–1858)* (Tokyo: Committee on Asian Cultural Studies, International Christian University, 1960), 3–131.

Kirishitan-ban and other texts pertaining to Christianity in early modern Japan[10] share many of the diverse features of other contemporaneous Japanese texts. Nevertheless, they also diverge from contemporaneous texts in several ways. *Kirishitan-ban* could be written in non-Japanese languages, in multiple languages, in Latin script, Japanese scripts, or in a mixture Latin and Japanese scripts. They were generally printed using moveable type rather than woodblock printing.[11] Furthermore, *Kirishitan-ban* displayed contemporaneously novel and sometimes new features (although some of these would later feature in other early modern Japanese texts) including the use of cursive *hiragana* 平仮名, the use of *furigana* 振り仮名 (interlinear gloss offering a pronunciation guide), the use of *handakuten*, the use of two-color print, the use of copper cuts and vignettes, and the use of movable type printing itself.[12] Texts about Christianity created by non-Christians are much more numerous than those created by missionaries and their converts. These texts shared the same features and encapsulated the same diversity as other early modern Japanese texts, but had a different thematic foci and sometimes included specialist terminology. Whilst *Kirishitan-ban* are likely to introduce new challenges for digital or traditional analysis, texts relating to the persecution of Christianity (i.e., texts by non-Christians) can be grouped with and treated in much the same manner as other early modern Japanese texts. Table 1 shows some of the major differences between *Kirishitan-ban* and other contemporaneous Japanese manuscripts and printed texts.

Tab. 1: The characteristics of early modern Japanese texts and *Kirishitan-ban* in comparison.[13]

	Manuscripts	Printed Materials	*Kirishitan-ban*
Language	Japanese	Japanese	Japanese, Latin, Portuguese, Spanish
Scripts	Japanese	Japanese	Japanese, Latin
Creation Method	Handwritten	Woodblock Print	Moveable Type Print
Number	Innumerable	1.7 Million	Less than 40 (Surviving)

---

10 It is important to note that the mission itself traversed three periods of Japanese history — the Muromachi period (1336–1573), the Azuchi-Momoyama period (1573–1603), and the beginning of the Edo period, as well as Japan's transition from medieval (*Chūsei* 中世) to early modern (*Kinsei* 近世). *Kirishitan-ban*, therefore, were also composed during this transitionary period and their composition and language reflects this.
11 A small number of texts were created using woodblock printing techniques, see: Laures, *Kirishitan Bunko*, 26, 78–79.
12 Laures, *Kirishitan Bunko*, 18.
13 The number of Japanese manuscripts and printed materials is based on the estimation in: Lamb, Clanuwat, and Kitamoto, "KuroNet: Regularized Residual U-Nets for End-to-End Kuzushiji Character Recognition," 1.

Although *Kirishitan-ban* were diverse in terms of genre[14] and this influenced diction and grammatical style, it is the diversity of scripts and languages that present the main challenges for those wishing to process or perform computerized textual analysis on these texts. Shinmura Izuru and Hiragi Genichi's comparison of *Kirishitan-ban* illustrates the presence of four languages (excluding of course the presence of loan words within these languages) and two scripts (Japanese and Latin) used in seven different combinations over the 39 texts included in their study. These are outlined in the table below:

Tab. 2: Script and language usage in *Kirishitan-ban*.[15]

Languages	Japanese Script	Latin Script
Japanese	11	11
Latin	0	7
Portuguese	0	0
Spanish	0	0
Japanese and Latin	0	3
Japanese and Portuguese	0	3
Japanese and Spanish	0	1
Japanese, Latin and Portuguese	0	2
Japanese, Latin and Spanish	0	1
Totals:	**11**	**28**

The use of multiple of scripts is, however, far more extensive than Shinmura and Hiragi's comparison suggests. For instance, whilst Shinmura and Hiragi record that *Hidesu no kyō* ひですの経 (P. *Fides no Quio*, 1611) was written in Japanese in Japanese script,[16] it also includes Portuguese and Latin in Latin script not only on the cover and within the front matter, but within the text itself.[17] Within the front matter Portuguese and Latin appear in horizontal script, whereas Latin within

---

[14] Refer to discussions of genre in: Shinmura Izuru 新村出 and Hiragi Genichi 柊源一, eds., *Kirishitan bungakushū* 1 吉利支丹文学集 1 (Tokyo: Hebonsha, 1993), 86–92; Ebisawa Arimichi 海老沢有道, *Kirishitan Nanban bungaku nyūmon* キリシタン南蛮文学入門 (Tokyo: Kyōbunkan, 1991), 91–236.
[15] Adapted from Shinmura and Hiragi, eds. *Kirishitan bungakushū* 1, 86–92. Similar (though more extensive) tables are given in: Fukushima Kunimichi 福島邦道, *Kirishitan shiryō to kokugo kenkyū* キリシタン資料と国語研究 (Tokyo: Kasama Shoin, 1973), 19–82; Kawai Tadanobu 河合忠信 and Muramoto Masato 村本正人, "Kirishitanban no shoshi kaisetsu" きりしたん版の書誌解説 in *Kirishitanban no kenkyū: Tominaga sensei koki kinen* きりしたん版の研究: 富永先生古希記念, ed. Tenri Toshokan 天理図書館 (Tenri: Tenri Daigaku Shuppanbu, 1973), 160–162.
[16] Shinmura and Hiragi, eds. *Kirishitan bungakushū* 1, 90.
[17] Orii Yoshimi 折井善果, Shirai Jun 白井純, and Toyoshima Masauki 豊島正之, eds., *Hidesu no kyō* ひですの経 (Tokyo: Yagi Shoten, 2011), 6–8, 11, 18–20, 24–26, 36, 42–43, 45, 47–48, 50, 71–72, 176.

the text, which usually serves to demark Biblical quotes, is aligned vertically but retains horizontal reading so that the page must be turned 90 degrees to the left in order to read it. This can be seen in other *Kirishitan-ban* texts and is retained in the modern transcription of *Giya do pekadoru* ぎやどぺかどる (P. *Guia do picador*, 1599) pictured below (Fig. 1).

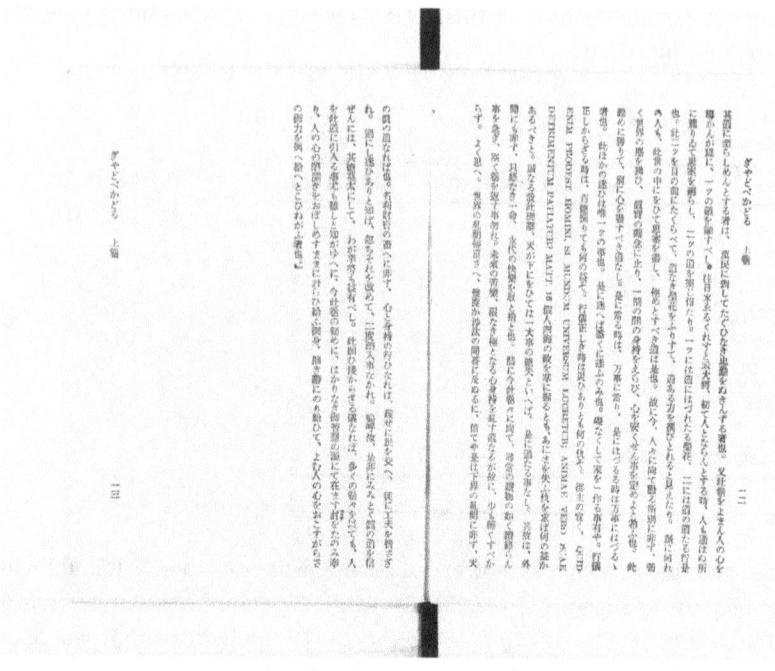

Fig. 1: Latin in *Giya do pekadoru*.[18]
(National Diet Library Digital Collections).

In *Hidesu no kyō*, Japanese appears vertically at all times though there is a variation in font size and an off-center alignment for page numbers on the contents pages.[19] A number of special symbols are also used such as the section symbol § and ligatures. The DS (Deus) and JX (Jesus Christ) ligatures are used widely in *Kirishitan-ban*

---

18 Masamune Atsuo 正宗敦夫, ed. *Giya do pekadoru* ぎや・ど・ぺかどる, *Jōkan* 上巻 (Tokyo: Nihon Koten Zenshū Kankōkai, 1929), 12. Image from: National Diet Library Digital Collections, https://dl.ndl.go.jp/pid/1111597.

19 Orii, Shirai, and Toyoshima, eds., *Hidesu no kyō*, 9–10.

alongside others such as a JS (Jesus), X with a circle above (Christ),[20] and other symbols such as crucifixes.[21] The use of different scripts within *Kirishitan-ban* is, therefore, more complicated than Table 2 suggests. Indeed, Tominaga Makita records that 30 *Kirishitan-ban* texts (of a total of 35 included in the study) contain Latin script, and that 18 of these also included italicized Latin script.[22] The use of Japanese scripts is also more complicated than the singular image that the above table or the use of the term "Japanese script" suggests. Arai Toshi subdivides the use Japanese script based on printing type noting the existence of four texts using a *katakana* 片仮名 print type, three texts using a large *hiragana* print type (*hiragana ōgata katsuji* 平仮名大型活字), and nine texts using a small *hiragana* print type (*hiragana kogata katsuji* 平仮名小型活字), which in addition to the style of characters affects the number and range of characters that one can expect to find.[23] Alongside *kanji* and *kana* 仮名 (Japanese syllabaries i.e. *hiragana* and *katakana*), Latin text, ligatures and special characters, are *furigana*, *kana* with *dakuten* and

---

[20] Charts showing some of the different ligatures can be found in: Florin Popescu, "'Kōgi yōkō' ni okeru goji hongo ni tsuite" 「講義要綱」における合字本語について, *Kyōto Daigaku Kokubungaku Ronso* 京都大学國文學論叢 12 (2004): 3–4, 8.

[21] See usage, for instance, in: Hubert Cieslik H. チースリク, Doi Tadao 土井忠生, and Ōtsuka Mitsunobu 大塚光信, eds., "Dochirina Kirishitan" どちりなきりしたん, in *Kirishitan sho; Haiya sho* キリシタン書; 排耶書, ed. Ebisawa Arimichi 海老沢有道, Hubert Cieslik H.チースリク, Doi Tadao 土井忠生, and Ōtsuka Mitsunobu大塚光信 (Tokyo: Iwanami Shoten, 1970), 14–15. Ligatures may create issues for those wishing to transcribe or interact with *Kirishitan-ban* digitally. They cannot be easily input through a keyboard and it is, therefore, common for scholars and publishers to use placeholders such as the aforenoted DS or JX to render these characters (as I have done here), to replace ligatures with their Japanese readings, to create new fonts to render these ligatures in their transcriptions (though these are not available for public use), or to use images from primary sources. Examples of the use of place holders and the creation of new symbols can be seen in: Orii, Shirai, and Toyoshima, eds., *Hidesu no kyō*, 16; Shinmura and Hiragi, eds. *Kirishitan bungakushū* 1, 174; Orii Yoshimi 折井喜果, ed. *Hidesu no kyō* ひですの経 (Tokyo: Kyōbunkan, 2011), 6. A font that allows ordinary users to input these ligatures has been developed as part of my "Kirishitan-ban in the Digital Age: A Study of the Opportunities and Limitations of Applying Digital Methods to Kirishitan-ban" project funded by the DNP Foundation for Cultural Promotion Graphic Culture Research Grant and Waseda University. Access the font through the GitHub Repository at Kirishitan Ligatures Font, https://github.com/kirishitanbank/KirishitanLigaturesFont.

[22] Tominaga Makita 富永牧太, "Kirishitanban no insatsujutsu" きりしたん版の印刷術 in *Kirishitanban no kenkyū: Tominaga sensei koki kinen* きりしたん版の研究: 富永先生古希記念, ed. Tenri Toshokan 天理図書館 (Tenri: Tenri Daigaku Shuppanbu, 1973), 56–57.

[23] Arai Toshi 新井トシ, "Junsatsushi Varinyānoshi to Kirishitanban no shuppan" 巡察使ヴァリニャーノ師ときりしたん版の出版 in *Kirishitanban no kenkyū: Tominaga sensei koki kinen* きりしたん版の研究: 富永先生古希記念, ed. Tenri Toshokan 天理図書館 (Tenri: Tenri Daigaku Shuppanbu, 1973), 21–30.

handakuten, numbers, joined characters, monograms, cuts and vignettes, and initials.[24] This diversity of language and script affects the task of text segmentation.

Text segmentation (splitting a passage into meaningful sections such as individual words) is one of the most important preparatory steps for analyzing a text with digital tools. For texts written in Latin script, texts can be easily segmented according to the white space that appears between each word. This is more difficult for Japanese where there is no space between words. The issue of segmenting Japanese exists even in the most widely used of digital tools — the word processor. Microsoft Word, for example, counts each character and piece of punctuation as an individual words, whereas Google Docs recognizes the presence of individual characters, but does not identify words. There are a large number of segmentation tools that are designed to (or are able to) segment Japanese into lemmata[25] and some do so fairly well including the online platforms Kuromoji,[26] Web ChaMame,[27] and Voyant Tools,[28] and Python-based tools such as fugashi.[29] However, these tools struggle with historical texts due to the presence of "unknown" words (i.e. words not featured in the dictionaries being used by the segmenting tools),[30] differences in orthography, the use of old and variant characters, and changes to Japanese word usage and grammar over time. The presence of multiple languages and scripts in *Kirishitan-ban* adds another dimension to the task of text segmentation.

---

[24] Arai, "Junsatsushi Varinyānoshi to Kirishitanban no shuppan," 29; Tominaga Makita 富永牧太, "Ōbun moji kō" 欧文文字攷 in *Kirishitanban no kenkyū: Tominaga sensei koki kinen* きりしたん版の研究: 富永先生古希記念, ed. Tenri Toshokan 天理図書館 (Tenri: Tenri Daigaku Shuppanbu, 1973), 123–127.

[25] Japanese is usually segmented according to lemmata rather than words, see discussion in: Paul McCann, "fugashi, a Tool for Tokenizing Japanese in Python," *Proceedings of Second Workshop for NLP Open Source Software (NLP-OSS)* (2020): 46.

[26] Kuromoji, https://www.atilika.org/.

[27] Web ChaMame (Web 茶まめ), https://chamame.ninjal.ac.jp/.

[28] Voyant Tools, https://voyant-tools.org/.

[29] fugashi, https://pypi.org/project/fugashi/.

[30] Tetsuji Nakagawa notes "One of the problems which makes word segmentation more difficult is existence of unknown (out-of-vocabulary) words. Unknown words are defined as words that do not exist in a system's dictionary. The word segmentation system has no knowledge about these unknown words, and determining word boundaries for such words is difficult." Tetsuji Nakagawa, "Chinese and Japanese word segmentation using word-level and character-level information," *COLING '04: Proceedings of the 20th International Conference on Computational Linguistics* (2004): 466. DOI: https://doi.org/10.1587/transinf.E92.D.2298.

I attempted to segment a sentence from *Giya do pekadoru* using *Kuromoji*, *Web ChaMame* and *Voyant Tools*:

御主の宜く、QUID ENIM PRODEST HOMINI, SI MUNDUM UNIVERSUM LUCRETUR; ANIMAE VERO SUAE DETRIMENTUM PATIATUR? MATT. 16 假人四海の政を掌に握るとも、あにまを失ふ仇を求は何の益かあるべきと。[31]

All three platforms were able to segment the Latin text accurately, however, none was completely accurate in its segmentation of Japanese. Including Latin, Voyant Tools identified 47 lemmata (excluding punctuation) whilst Kuromoji and Web ChaMame identified 45 (excluding punctuation and a single white space that the platforms added at the end of the sentence). In reality, however, the sentence consists of 41. The cause of these issues is the presence of both unknown historical and *Kirishitan-ban* specific terms. For instance, each of the tools was unable to correctly segment the Latin loan term, *anima* あにま (soul). Many of the specialized terms that appear in *Kirishitan-ban* are not included in the dictionaries or word banks used by text segmentation tools or within online dictionaries aimed at general usage. I took all (16, excluding derivatives) terms beginning with *a* あ included in the glossary at the end of Ebisawa Arimichi et al., *Kirishitan sho; Haiya sho* キリシタン書; 排耶書,[32] and checked whether these appeared in popular online dictionaries. The results are displayed in Table 3. Jisho[33] which draws on data from a number of sources including JMdict, JMnedict, and KANJIDIC2 features only two of the terms, Kotobank[34] and Weblio[35] which draw on a much greater number of sources and dictionaries including major Japanese dictionaries such as the Shōgakukan's 小学館 Daijisen 大辞泉 include only three of the terms, and the premium subscription-based platform JapanKnowledge[36] which allows users to search over 90 dictionaries and reference works includes five of the terms.

---

31 Masamune, ed. *Giya do pekadoru*, 12.
32 Ebisawa Arimichi 海老沢有道, Hubert Cieslik H. チースリク, Doi Tadao 土井忠生, and Ōtsuka Mitsunobu 大塚光信, eds., "Yōgo ichiranhyō" 洋語一覧表, in *Kirishitan sho; Haiya sho* キリシタン書; 排耶書, ed. Ebisawa Arimichi 海老沢有道, Hubert Cieslik H. チースリク, Doi Tadao 土井忠生, and Ōtsuka Mitsunobu 大塚光信 (Tokyo: Iwanami Shoten, 1970), 1–2.
33 Jisho, https://jisho.org/.
34 Kotobank (*Kotobanku* コトバンク), https://kotobank.jp/.
35 Weblio, https://www.weblio.jp/.
36 JapanKnowledge, https://japanknowledge.com/.

Tab. 3: The presence of specialized terms in online dictionaries.[37]

Terms	Meaning (Language of Origin)	Number of Appearances in Ebisawa et al.	JapanKnowledge	Jisho	Kotobank	Weblio
あうれよら	Aureola (L)	1	0	0	0	0
あぐはべんた	Agua benta (P)	1	0	0	0	0
あじも	Azimo (P)	1	0	0	0	0
あにま	Anima (L, P)	9	1	1	1	1
あねいすてう	Agnus Dei (L)	1	0	0	0	0
あぶらん	Abraham	2	0	0	0	0
あべちと	Apetito (P)	1	0	0	0	0
あべまりや	Ave Maria (L)	4	1	0	1	1
あべらび	Ave Rabbi (L)	1	0	0	0	0
あぽすとろ	Apostolo (P)	10	1	1	1	1
あめん	Amen (L)	3	1	0	0	0
あらばすとろ	Alabastro (P)	1	0	0	0	0
あるか	Arca (L)	1	0	0	0	0
あるたる	Altar (P)	2	1	0	0	0
あるちいご	Artigo (P)	4	0	0	0	0
あんじょ	Anjo (P)	16	0	0	0	0
	Totals:		5	2	3	3

Some terms such as *anjo* あんじょ may be found by writing them in modern orthographic conventions (*gendai kanazukai* 現代仮名遣い) i.e. *anjo* あんじょ, but this is not how the terms appear in the source materials and this therefore adds extra steps to preparing a text for digital analysis or the dictionary resources being used. It is potentially surprising that although the term *anima* appears in all four dictionaries, the term was not recognized by any of the aforenoted text segmentation software. I ran the list of terms through Kuromoji, Web ChaMame and Voyant Tools and found that Kuromoji and Web ChaMame recognized no terms, whilst Voyant Tools, though it is unclear why, segmented three words (*aburan* あぶらん, *abechito* あべちと, and *aberabi* あべらび) correctly. In other words, it appears that the major accessible text segmentation tools are currently unable to segment *Kirishitan-ban* adequately and this likely means that prior to analyzing *Kirishitan-ban* digitally, a scholar will need to build their own dictionaries and word banks or supplement existing ones for use with the tools or code that they choose to use. This implies,

---

[37] Adapted from Ebisawa, Cieslik, Doi, and Ōtsuka, eds. "Yōgo ichiranhyō," 1–2.

however, that the computerized textual analysis of *Kirishitan-ban* is outside of the grasp of casual users.

Although text segmentation tools accurately segmented Latin text, this should not be taken to mean that the use of Latin script in *Kirishitan-ban* (particularly when being used to render Japanese text) provides no challenges. Nowadays, we are likely to use Modified Hepburn romanization (developed in the late nineteenth and early twentieth centuries), *Kunreishiki* romanization (*Kunreishiki rōmaji* 訓令式ローマ字, developed in the 1930s) or *Nihonshiki* romanization (*Nihonshiki rōmaji* 日本式ローマ字, developed in the late nineteenth century, and mostly replaced by *Kunreishiki* in the 1930s) to transliterate Japanese. Whilst these three systems have similarities, *Kirishitan-ban* feature a completely different system of romanization developed by the Jesuits. The sometimes radical differences between Jesuit romanization and modern systems is shown in Table 4.

Tab. 4: Examples of different romanization systems.[38]

Kana	Hepburn	Kunreishiki	Nihonshiki	Kirishitan-ban
あ・ア	a	a	a	a
い・イ	i	i	i	i, j, y
う・ウ	u	u	u	u, v
え・エ	e	e	e	ye
お・オ	o	o	o	uo, vo
あう・アウ	au	au	au	uŏ, vŏ
おう・オウ	ō, ou	ô, ou	ô, ou	uô, vô
か・カ	ka	ka	ka	ca, qa
き・キ	ki	ki	ki	qi, qui
く・ク	ku	ku	ku	cu, qu
け・ケ	ke	ke	ke	qe, que
こ・コ	ko	ko	ko	co
かう・カウ	kau	kau	kau	cŏ
こう・コウ	kō, kou	kô, kou	kô, kou	cô

The issues associated with Latin script extend beyond the use of an alternate romanization system. Although it is possible to use tools such as Voyant Tools to study the relationship between different words written in Latin script, tools designed for use with Japanese are ill equipped for the analysis of texts that include Latin script in addition to Japanese. Many tools designed for use with Japanese language and script do not feature dictionaries that are compatible with

---

38 See discussion in: Ebisawa Arimichi 海老沢有道, *Nanban bunka: Nichiō bunka kōshō* 南蛮文化:日欧文化交渉 (Tokyo: Shibundō, 1958), 76–78.

text written in other languages. In the previous example from *Giya do pekadoru*, Kuromoji and Web ChaMame, which both offer morphological analysis and linguistic information about the terms they segment, were unable to provide definitions for Latin terms and incorrectly identified them as interjections (*kandōshi* 感動詞) or nouns (*meishi* 名詞) depending on the dictionary used. Voyant Tools allows users to create a list of stop words, which would allow a user to exclude anything written in Latin script should they wish. There is also the option to process Japanese and Latin script separately. Nevertheless, both of these options create more work for the user and have no influence on the ability (or lack thereof) of the most accessible text segmentation tools to accurately segment historical texts written in Japanese script. Furthermore, if a user chose to exclude Latin text this would result in the loss of key parts of the text and their exclusion from study and analysis.[39] An additional issue emerges with those texts written in the Japanese language but rendered in Latin script — although many online dictionaries allow users to search for terms by typing Japanese in Latin characters, they do not recognize Jesuit systems of romanization. The solution to this is again to construct new dictionaries or word banks, expand those that already exist, or digitize historical Japanese dictionaries published by the Jesuits. Some historical dictionaries have already been made available and searchable online through Toyoshima Masayuki's project, *Missionary Linguistics*.[40] Users can use the *Missionary Linguistics* website to search for Japanese terms romanized according to Jesuit practices, but the data does not appear to be available to download at present meaning that it cannot be easily integrated into other tools.

In summary, the presence of multiple scripts and languages, and uncommon vocabulary within *Kirishitan-ban* make it difficult to approach these texts when using accessible, entry-level digital tools. Segmenting content written in Latin script is a fairly simple task, but the specialist vocabulary used in *Kirishitan-ban* means that text segmentation software tends to segment Japanese portions of the text erroneously. In addition to this, much of the terminology found in *Kirishitan-ban* (whether in Japanese or Latin script) is not recognized by the different tools and dictionaries that a casual user may want to use. This is particularly problematic when it comes to Japanese language texts written in Latin script since differing romanization practices make terms unsearchable in modern dictionaries. Given all this there is a need to develop new resources, however, for the time being this means that the digital analysis of *Kirishitan-ban* is not accessible to the casual user.

---

39 See related discussion of the issues with using stop lists in Zorkina's chapter in this volume.
40 Missionary Linguistics, https://joao-roiz.jp/.

The next section will explore the current state of and issues associated with the digitization of texts related to Christianity as well as some of the databases that have been created for their study and consumption.

Digitization and Databases

At present there are few places where a scholar can access digitized texts (photographed or transcribed) pertaining to Christianity in early modern Japan. At the time of writing the Laures Kirishitan Bunko Database,[41] linked to the world famous Laures Kirishitan Bunko at Sophia University in Japan, includes 18 fully photographed texts within its Christian artefacts section[42] and two prayer leaves.[43] The majority of its holdings, however, have not been fully digitized. The quality of these digitizations is generally good, and the interface offers ample features for zooming in and out of or rotating the images. Some of the digitized texts include transcriptions and translations into modern Japanese and English within their metadata. In the case of the manuscript sources the user is able to hover over sentences or individual characters within the image in order to highlight it within the adjacent transcription and vice-versa.[44] Nevertheless, with some items such as JL-KOSATSU-1711-KB1 (an anti-*Kirishitan* edict written on a type of notice board called a *kōsatsu* 高札 from 1711) there appear to be discrepancies between the transcription and the text that appears on the photographed artefact.[45] Furthermore, the number of photographs for artefacts is often insufficient. It would be useful, for instance, to have photographs of the rear of the *kōsatsu* and of their metal fittings, as well as data on their dimensions. This would open more avenues for research into the materiality of the pieces. Some entries in the database, although not fully digitized, include

---

[41] Laures Kirishitan Bunko Database (*Rauresu Kirishitan Bunko Dētabēsu* ラウレスキリシタン文庫データベース), https://digital-archives.sophia.ac.jp/laures-kirishitan-bunko/.
[42] "Part VI: Christian Artefacts," Laures Kirishitan Bunko Database, https://digital-archives.sophia.ac.jp/laures-kirishitan-bunko/search?ct=kirishitan_bunko&cat=02_06.
[43] "JL-1591-KB7-7-3a," Laures Kirishitan Bunko Database, https://digital-archives.sophia.ac.jp/laures-kirishitan-bunko/view/kirishitan_bunko/JL-1591-KB7-7-3a.
[44] See this at work with: "JL-JMS-1580-KB2," Laures Kirishitan Bunko Database, https://digital-archives.sophia.ac.jp/laures-kirishitan-bunko/view/kirishitan_bunko/JL-JMS-1580-KB2.
[45] Compare the transcription and images of: "JL-KOSATSU-1711-KB1," Laures Kirishitan Bunko Database, https://digital-archives.sophia.ac.jp/laures-kirishitan-bunko/view/kirishitan_bunko/JL-KOSATSU-1711-KB1.

a few images — the user is able to view two pages from *Giya do pekadoru*[46] and 27 pages from *Manuale ad sacramenta ecclesiae ministranda* (1605),[47] for example. Despite all this, unless the user wants to work with the materials from the Christian artefacts section, Laures Kirishitan Bunko Database, although invaluable for the bibliographical information that it contains (the database features the entirety of Laures seminal bibliographical study *Kirishitan Bunko: A Manual of Books and Documents on the Early Christian Mission in Japan*),[48] is not a particularly useful resource for finding digitized materials to work with.

Google Books, Internet Archive and other major online repositories hold copies of a number of texts associated with the mission printed in Europe such as *Ars grammaticae Iaponicae linguae* (1632),[49] *Dictionarium sive thesauri linguae Japonicae compendium* (1632),[50] *Niffon no cotōbani yô confesion* (1632),[51] and collections of contemporaneous letters. In addition, early histories of the mission printed in Europe such as François Solier's *Histoire Ecclésiastique des Isles et Royaumes du Iapon*[52] are quite accessible. The 359 texts of The Max Besson Library of "Japonica" Collection[53] at the University of Tsukuba have been digitized in monochrome. The collection includes four *Kirishitan-ban*, but with the exception of the aforementioned *Niffon no cotōbani yô confesion* which was written in Japanese in Latin script the collection only contains texts that were printed outside of Japan and written in European languages. The Marega Collection Database[54] run by the Vatican Library and the National Institute for Japanese Language and Linguistics (NINJAL) perhaps

---

[46] "JL-1599-KB22-21-17," Laures Kirishitan Bunko Database, https://digital-archives.sophia.ac.jp/laures-kirishitan-bunko/view/kirishitan_bunko/JL-1599-KB22-21-17.

[47] "JL-1605-KB30-29-24," Laures Kirishitan Bunko Database, https://digital-archives.sophia.ac.jp/laures-kirishitan-bunko/view/kirishitan_bunko/JL-1605-KB30-29-24.

[48] Laures, *Kirishitan Bunko*.

[49] Diego Collado, *Ars Grammaticae Iaponicae Linguae in Gratiam et Adiutorium eorum, qui praedicandi Evangelij causa ad Iaponiae Regnum se voluerint conferre* (Romae: Typis & impensis Sac. Congr. de Propag. Fide, 1632).

[50] Diego Collado, *Dictionarium sive thesauri linguae Iaponicae compendium* (Romae: Typis & impensis Sacr. Congr. de Prop. Fide, 1632).

[51] Diego Collado, *Niffon no cotōbani yô confesion: vo mósu yōdai to màta Confesor yori gòxensà cu mesarùru tàme nò canyônàru giô giô nocòto dànguixà no monpa no Fr. Diego Collado to yu xucqe Roma ni voite còre voxitàte mòno nàri, 1632. Modus confitendi et examinandi Poenitentem Iaponensem, formula suamet lingua Iaponica* (Romae: Typis & impensis Sacr. Congreg. de Propag. Fide, 1632).

[52] François Solier, *Histoire ecclésiastique des isles et royaumes du Iapon*, 2 vols (Paris: Chez Sebastien Cramoisy, 1627–1629).

[53] The Max Besson Library of "Japonica" Collection (*Besson Korekushon* ベッソン・コレクション), http://www.tulips.tsukuba.ac.jp/pub/tree/besson.php.

[54] The Marega Collection Database, https://base1.nijl.ac.jp/~marega/en/.

constitutes the largest collection including 14,643 records pertaining to Christianity in Japan. Most of these (11,938) are manuscriptal population records from the office of the magistrate of religions (*Shūmon bugyō* 宗門奉行) in Usuki Domain (*Usuki-han* 臼杵藩) and therefore relate to the persecution of Christianity.[55] NINJAL has also digitized and transcribed the Amakusa edition of *Heike monogatari, Isoho monogatari, Kinkushū* (1593) in partnership with the British Library (BL).[56] Tenri University Library has digitized its collection of *Kirishitan-ban*, but these can only be accessed on-site.[57] Some texts have also been made available through the National Diet Library Digital Collections,[58] Tokyo's UTokyo Academic Archives Portal,[59] and Waseda's Kotenseki Sōgō Database.[60] As such, even though the principal library for the study of Christianity in pre-modern Japan (Laures Kirishitan Bunko) has not digitized its holdings, a large number of texts mostly relating to the persecution of Christianity (in Japanese) or the mission to Japan as seen from the outside (in European languages) have been digitized and are accessible through other databases and repositories.

Quality varies across each collection. The University of Tokyo's, Waseda University's and the NINJAL's digitizations are all of high quality, although the quality of Tokyo's digitizations tends to fall significantly if the user chooses to use the zoom

---

[55] Similar documents have also been made available through *Danjuro* (*Edo Jidai ni okeru jinkō bunseki shisutemu* 江戸時代における人口分析システム) developed by Kawaguchi Hiroshi. The platform includes the *Shūmon aratamechō bunseki shisutemu*「宗門改帳」分析システム which allows users to search through a large database of transcribed census data relating to population records and systems of religious surveillance that developed following the ban on Christianity. The user can search through the transcribed data or use the analysis tools to automatically select the data they want e.g., on the number of births, the age of marriage, the number of people who changed their names, religious affiliation etc. *Danjuro* is quite unique due to its built-in analytical tools. See: Edo jidai ni okeru jinkō bunseki shisutemu (Danjuro 7.0) 江戸時代における人口分析システム (Danjuro 7.0), http://www.danjuro.jp/.
[56] Images of the Amakusa edition of *Heike monogatari, Isoho monogatari* and *Kinkushū* in the British Library collection (*Daiei Toshokan shozō Amakusaban 'Heike monogatari' 'Isoho monogatari' 'Kinkushū' gazō* 大英図書館所蔵　天草版「平家物語」「伊曽保物語」「金句集」画像), https://dglb01.ninjal.ac.jp/BL_amakusa/en.php.
[57] List of texts held by Tenri University Library that have been designated as important cultural properties, national treasures etc.: "Shiteisho ichiran 指定書一覧," Tenri Toshokan 天理図書館, https://www.tcl.gr.jp/collection/designation-book/.
[58] National Diet Library Digital Collections (*Kokuritsu Kokkai Toshokan Dejitaru Korekushon* 国立国会図書館デジタルコレクション), https://dl.ndl.go.jp/.
[59] UTokyo Academic Archives Portal (*Tōkyō Daigaku Gakujutsu Shisantō Archive Portal* 東京大学学術資産等アーカイブズポータル), https://da.dl.itc.u-tokyo.ac.jp/portal/.
[60] Kotenseki Sōgō Database (*Kotenseki Sōgō Dētabēsu* 古典籍総合データベース), https://www.wul.waseda.ac.jp/kotenseki/.

functions. The Besson Collection's monochrome images are also of an acceptable quality. The NDL's collection contains both color and monochrome images, and although the former tend to be of very high quality, the latter occasionally includes some low quality images that are difficult to read. All of the platforms offer bibliographical information (in some cases i.e., in the Marega Collection Database this is extensive) and allow the user to zoom in or out of a text. NINJAL's, Tsukuba's, and Waseda's platforms offer little beyond this, basic textual navigation functions, and the ability to save or download the images. Of course, in many cases this is all the user needs. Tokyo's platform offers some additional features such as image rotation. The NDL's platform offers the greatest number of functions. It has a robust zoom system although image quality usually decreases from around 50% zoom. The platform offers a number of image manipulation options including options to alter an image's brightness and contrast, which are not available on other platforms and potentially increase workflow when compared to manipulating images post-download. Most platforms offer streamlined textual navigation including the ability to scroll through the texts freely in the case of Tokyo's and Waseda's collections, via clear thumbnails with the NINJAL's and Tsukuba's collections, or by offering a number of methods (thumbnails, digitized table of contents, or drop-down page selection) in the case of the recently improved systems implemented by the NDL. The monochrome materials in Tsukuba's and the NDL's collections occasional contain specks of black or other extratextual materials in the images and some users will likely feel that the monochrome nature of the materials results in the loss of some of the materiality of the text such as the characteristics and colors of the paper, ink, and stamps. The NDL's, Tokyo's and some of Waseda's texts are available with IIIF (International Image Interoperability Framework) functionality, whereas those from the other repositories are not. The BL/NINJAL project is the only one to provide full transcriptions of their texts,[61] although the NDL has recently released transcriptions produced through optical character recognition (OCR) technology of many of its public domain holdings through its *Next Digital Library*.[62] This is a significant point since it will likely require a significant amount of time and monetary investment in order to make the texts found in the other repositories machine readable through human or computerized transcription.

    OCR technology has only limited accuracy when used with pre-modern printed and handwritten Japanese texts meaning that the tools available on the market may not be suitable for automating the transcription of *Kirishitan-ban* or other texts related to Christianity in early modern Japan. I tried using the application Miwo

---

61 *Nihongoshi Kenkyūyō Tekisuto Dētashū* 日本語史研究用テキストデータ集, https://www2.ninjal.ac.jp/textdb_dataset/amhk/.
62 Next Digital Library, https://lab.ndl.go.jp/dl/.

(version 1.0),⁶³ a popular mobile application for transcribing printed early modern Japanese texts, to automatically transcribe the first page of *Hidesu no kyō* and checked this against the transcription provided by Orii Yoshimi, Shirai Jun, and Toyoshima Masayuki (with elements not present in the original source redacted).⁶⁴ As might be expected, the platform did not recognize the Latin that appeared on the page or the ligature "DS." Additionally, it did not transcribe the *furigana*, a purposeful decision made by the creators of Miwo and the browser based KuroNet⁶⁵ to avoid problems associated with transcribing small characters and to distinguish between the main text and annotations.⁶⁶ The first portion of the transcription (the title of the book's first chapter) reads:

御作の物を似てDSと称じ奉る御作者と其御善徳を
見知り奉るの経巻第一　并序⁶⁷

I took three sample photographs of this passage with my phone from my computer screen and used Miwo to transcribe them. The result was the following three transcriptions. I have underlined characters that differ from the human transcription of the text noted above.

Attempt 1:
御作の物をいてせと淫し奉る御作者と其御若曲を
見やりせるの経巻第一　に序

Attempt 2:
御作の物をいてせと淫し有る御作者と其御石曲を
見やりするの住長巻第一　安序

Attempt 3:
御作の物をいて世と淫し奉る御作者と去御善曲を
見知り奉るの経巻第一　安序

Excluding the incorrect transcription for the ligature, Miwo accurately transcribed between 66.7% and 84.85% of the sentence across the three trials. For KuroNet, on the other hand, tests undertaken by its developers using a sample of 15 books found

---

63 Version 1.1 was released in October 2022, see: *Miwo* みを, http://codh.rois.ac.jp/miwo/index.html.en.
64 Orii, Shirai, and Toyoshima, eds., *Hidesu no kyō*, 11, 10.
65 KuroNet (*KuroNet Kuzushiji Ninshiki Sābisu* KuroNet くずし字認識サービス), http://codh.rois.ac.jp/kuronet/.
66 Lamb, Clanuwat, and Kitamoto, "KuroNet: Regularized Residual U-Nets for End-to-End Kuzushiji Character Recognition," 6.
67 Orii, Shirai, and Toyoshima, eds., *Hidesu no kyō*, 11.

that it had an F1 score of 80–100%,[68] though we might expect similar results given that the platforms use the same datasets and recognition systems. Of course, my small experiment is hardly conclusive, but it is important to note that tools such as Miwo and KuroNet, despite being extremely useful, do not guarantee accuracy. The ability of an OCR platform to accurately transcribe a text is inextricably linked to its dataset, the quality of the image used, and the qualities of the text (i.e., size and clarity of characters),[69] and therefore the accuracy of OCR will vary according to the chosen tool and the texts on which said tool is used. Despite issues of accuracy, using platforms such as Miwo and KuroNet may help to decrease the time spent on keyboarded transcription although careful proof reading is needed to correct the mistakes that OCR software makes and ensure that a transcription is accurate.[70]

Many *Kirishitan-ban* and other texts (particularly documents relating to the persecution of Christianity in different locales) have already been transcribed and reprinted in modern typeface, and therefore, it might not be necessary to transcribe the digitized images of the source material or perform OCR on them. It is theoretically possible for a scholar to scan the modern reprints of *Kirishitan-ban* or other texts and perform more accurate OCR on these modern transcriptions. Since the accuracy of printed character OCR for modern Japanese is over 99%[71] it would be a comparatively quick process to scan, automatically transcribe, and then check the transcribed versions of these modern day reprints. There may, of course, be some copyright issues at play. Additionally, modern transcriptions often include the addition of notes and punctuation, and the underlining of key terms that does not exist in the original text, so some editing of the transcriptions would likely be

---

68 Lamb, Clanuwat, and Kitamoto, "KuroNet: Regularized Residual U-Nets for End-to-End Kuzushiji Character Recognition," 3, 7–13.
69 Writing on the limitations of KuroNet, Alex Lamb, Tarin Clanuwat, and Asanobu Kitamoto note the issues associated with performing OCR on very small and very large text, and problems associated with the large number of characters in Japanese and the layout of a text and its characters, see: Lamb, Clanuwat, and Kitamoto, "KuroNet: Regularized Residual U-Nets for End-to-End Kuzushiji Character Recognition," 6, 11. On the limitations of OCR also refer to: Melissa Terras, "Digitization and digital resources in the humanities," in *Digital humanities in practice*, ed. Claire Warwick, Melissa Terras, and Julianne Nyhan (London: Facet Publishing, 2012)," 48.
70 Yamamoto Sumiko and Ōsawa Tomejirō propose a system by which OCR technology automates processes of transcription and input, with the output being corrected by non-specialists before undergoing correction and editing by a scholar. This would seemingly reduce the scholar's workload by removing the need to transcribe and input the text manually, and perform the initial checks themselves. See: Yamamoto Sumiko 山本純子 and Ōsawa Tomejirō 大澤留次郎, "Kotenseki honkoku no shōryokuka: Kuzushiji o fukumu shinhōshiki OCR gijutsu no kaihatsu" 古典籍翻刻の省力化：くずし字を含む新方式OCR技術の開発, *Jōhō kanri* 情報管理 58, no. 11 (2016), 821.
71 Yamamoto and Ōsawa, "Kotenseki honkoku no shōryokuka: Kuzushiji o fukumu shinhōshiki OCR gijutsu no kaihatsu" 820.

required. The above passage from *Hidesu no kyō* is transcribed by Orii as follows with a number of additional elements that I have underlined:

御作の物を似てDSと称^{せう}<u>⑴</u>じ奉る御作者と、<u>其御善徳を見知り奉るの経、巻第一、并序</u>[72]

In Orii, Shirai and Toyoshima's edition, on the other hand, the text is rendered with a much greater number of additions as follows:

<u>御作^{ごさく}の物を似てDS（デウス）</u>と称^{せう}⑴じ奉る御作者^{ごさくしゃ}と、其御善徳^{そのごぜんどく}を⁰¹」見知り奉るの経、巻第一、并序⁰²」[73]

In Orii's version commas and references have been added to the text, whilst Orii, Shirai and Toyoshima's transcription includes not only additional commas and references, but additional *furigana* and symbols for line breaks that are not present in the source text. These would need to be removed before analysis of the source text could begin. Some of these elements could be removed with data cleaning software such as OpenRefine,[74] such as the *tōten* 読点 (Japanese commas). Alongside the issue of removing new information inserted into the text by transcribers is the issue of information that the transcribers may have omitted. For instance, the transcription of *Sakaramenta teiyō furoku* サカラメンタ提要付録 (Manuale ad Sacramenta, 1605) by Hubert Cieslik, Doi Tadao, and Ōtsuka Mitsunobu omits Latin passages (excluding short quotations) providing brief summarizes in the notes in their stead.[75] Similarly, in his transcription of Sessō Sōsai's 雪窓宗崔(1589–1649) anti-*Kirishitan*, *Taiji jashūron* 対治邪執論, Ebisawa decided to abbreviate some passages rather than provide full transcriptions.[76] In other words, although it is theoretically a potentially simple task to create machine readable transcriptions to work with by performing OCR on modern reprints, other issues are at play meaning

---

72 Orii, ed. *Hidesu no kyō*, 17.
73 Orii, Shirai, and Toyoshima, eds., *Hidesu no kyō*, 10.
74 OpenRefine, https://openrefine.org/. An explanation of this process with Chinese language sources is given by: Lu Wang, "Data Clearing Chinese Text with OpenRefine: Punctuation Removal," *The Digital Orientalist*, December 25, 2020, https://digitalorientalist.com/2020/12/25/data-cleaning-of-chinese-text-by-open-refine/.
75 Hubert Cieslik H. チースリク, Doi Tadao 土井忠生, and Ōtsuka Mitsunobu 大塚光信, eds., "Sakaramenta teiyō furoku" サカラメンタ提要付録, in *Kirishitan sho; Haiya sho* キリシタン書; 排耶書, ed. Ebisawa Arimichi 海老沢有道, Hubert Cieslik H.チースリク, Doi Tadao 土井忠生, and Ōtsuka Mitsunobu 大塚光信 (Tokyo: Iwanami Shoten, 1970), 182, 185–186, 189–190, 193, 195, 197–200, 202–204, 208, 213, 219.
76 Ebisawa Arimichi 海老沢有道, ed. "Taiji jashūron" 対治邪執論, in *Kirishitan sho; Haiya sho* キリシタン書; 排耶書, ed. Ebisawa Arimichi 海老沢有道, Hubert Cieslik H.チースリク, Doi Tadao 土井忠生, and Ōtsuka Mitsunobu 大塚光信 (Tokyo: Iwanami Shoten, 1970), 462–463, 465, 473–476.

that beyond potential copyright concerns careful text selection, proof reading, and processing are necessary before these materials would be ready to use.

There might also be the possibility of developing accurate OCR models for personal use with platforms such as Transkribus[77] or kraken.[78] The nature of *Kirishitan-ban* lends itself to this task. The use of moveable type printing means that although there are variations, the characters that appear in *Kirishitan-ban*, are quite consistent with each other.[79] Furthermore, line spacing and format is fairly consistent.[80] With a little time and effort a model could be built quite easily for *katakana* and small print *hiragana* texts since both types of text lack extensive use of *kanji*. Arai Toshi provides the following data:

Tab. 5: The types of characters in *Kirishitan-ban*.[81]

	Katakana Printing	Small Print Hiragana	Large Print Hiragana
Kanji	7	188	2300
Kana	46	79	110
Joined Characters (2)	1	2	294
Joined Characters (2)	0	0	20
Dakuten Characters	20	22	36
Handakuten Characters	4	0	9

As such, to produce a model capable of performing OCR for *katakana* print texts the computer only needs to learn to recognize 78 different basic characters (special symbols are not included in the table). The question, of course, remains whether it would be worth training a model to perform OCR for a total of four texts (in the case of *katakana* print texts) some of which would be transcribed during the process of creating the model or if these four texts would even provide enough data to make a model. Nevertheless, it is not outside the realms of possibility that individuals with some familiarity of Transkribus or kraken could develop a fairly accurate OCR model for these sorts of texts. A private company or research center may be able

---

77 Transkribus, https://readcoop.eu/transkribus/.
78 Kraken, https://kraken.re/.
79 Arai Toshi 新井トシ, "Kokuji katsuji ni tsuite" 国字活字について in *Kirishitanban no kenkyū: Tominaga sensei koki kinen* きりしたん版の研究: 富永先生古希記念, ed. Tenri Toshokan 天理図書館 (Tenri: Tenri Daigaku Shuppanbu, 1973), 87–89.
80 See the number of lines across different documents recorded in: Arai, "Junsatsushi Varinyānoshi to Kirishitanban no shuppan," 28.
81 Arai, "Junsatsushi Varinyānoshi to Kirishitanban no shuppan," 29; Arai, "Kokuji katsuji ni tsuite," 81–87.

to produce much more sophisticated models to tackle not only *katakana* and small print *hiragana* texts, but big print *hiragana* texts too.

I trained some of my own experimental models in Transkribus for use with *Kirishitan-ban* written in Latin script. The first model, which I trained on BL/NINJAL's *Heike Monogatari, Isoho Monogatari* and *Kinkushū*, had a character error rate (CER) of 1.29% on its validation set, whereas an expanded model which included transcriptions from Diego Collado's *Dictionarium sive thesauri linguae Japonicae compendium*, and *Niffon no cotōbani yô confesion* and *Modus confitendi et examinandi Poenitentem Iaponensem*, and João Rodrigues's *Arte da Lingoa de Iapam* (1604)[82] had a CER of 2.68%.[83] Looking at some extracts from page 62 of Collado's *Niffon no Cotōbani Yô Confesion* and *Modus Confitendi et Examinandi* transcribed using different methods (Tab. 6) we can see that this model is much more accurate than those available through Internet Archive (which uses ABBYY FineReader 11) or through using the OCR functionality in Google Docs.

Tab. 6: A comparison of OCR platforms.

Human Transcription	*Transkribus* Model (Validation Set)	ABBYY FineReader 11.0 (Internet Archive)	Google
Fido no ribai vo tòri motomoru va von imaximè de gozà-	Fido no ribai vo tòri motomoru va von imaximè de gozà-	Kdo no ribal vo t6ri motomoru va vonimaximedegozd-	Fido no ribai vo tori motomoru va von imaximè de gozd
Saiban meſaruru damiŏ no cacurete tòtta mòno vo caie-	Saiban meſaruru damiŏ no cacurete tòtta mòno vo caie-	Saiban mefaruru damid no cacurete totra mono vocaic-	Saiban mefaruru damió no cacurete tòtra mono vo caie
Màta fito no vie vo jaſui xi, ſòno còto vŏba varŭ ſata tò-	Màta fito no. vie vo iaſui xi, ſòno còto vŏba varŭ ſata tò-	Mata fito no vie vo jafui xi, funo coto voba varu fatato-	Màta fito no vie vo jasui xi, sono còto vóba varŭ fata to

It was surprising to notice that major OCR software was unable to adequately transcribe *Kirishitan-ban* in Latin script. Although some other scholars are also starting to work on OCR models for *Kirishitan-ban*,[84] this might indicate that there is a

---

[82] João Rodriguez, *Arte da Lingoa Iapam composta pello João Rodriguez Portugues da Cõpanhia de Iesu, dividida em tres livros* (Nangasaqui: Collegio de Iapão da Companhia de Iesu, 1604).
[83] A lengthier description is given in James Harry Morris "Transkribus and Kirishitanban: Some Initial Experiments," *The Digital Orientalist*, February 18, 2022, https://digitalorientalist.com/2022/02/18/transkribus-and-kirishitanban-some-initial-experiments/.
[84] Sophie Nuetzler ノイツラ・ゾフィー and Miyagawa Sō 宮川創, "HTR puroguramu Transkribus ni yoru Nihongo Kirishitan-ban 'Kontemutsusu munji' no dejitaru ākaibuka" HTRプログラム

huge amount of work remaining to create machine readable transcriptions even if they are written in scripts which most digital tools are designed to work with. Nevertheless, since making models on Transkribus is a relatively simple task, the platform may offer an accessible way for casual and more involved users to begin creating models to transcribe *Kirishitan-ban*.

In conclusion, although a modest corpus of *Kirishitan-ban* and texts relating to Christianity in early modern Japan have been digitized (photographed) and are available to view online very few have been transcribed. Transcribing these texts is a potential difficult task due to the size of the corpus and the challenges associated with performing OCR on texts of this nature. Nevertheless, although there are ethical issues to consider, it might be possible to take a shortcut and perform OCR on modern day transcriptions. Furthermore, it may be possible to build OCR models capable of dealing with *Kirishitan-ban* written in Japanese or Latin script with relative ease as illustrated by my own experimentation with the Transkribus.

Conclusions

In *Computers in Humanities Research*, Philip H. Smith reminds his readers that the use of computers in the humanities is not confined to quantitative research as is commonly assumed. Rather the interaction between humanists and computers may be qualitative and involve little more "than arranging raw data into a slightly less raw and more usable form."[85] Nevertheless, this interaction may open "up new horizons for studies which the scholar might never have attempted."[86] This, I believe, aptly describes the state of what we might term a Japanese *Digital Missiology* — what is needed first and foremost is a wholescale effort to create and organize data through transcribing texts and creating dictionary resources. Most of the available tools are inadequate for approaching texts pertaining to Christianity in early modern Japan particularly for casual users with little training in the digital humanities and it is only through the ordering of data, and the creation of new resources and tools tailored towards our specific needs that we will be able to interact with these texts on the digital plane.

Transkribusによる日本語キリシタン版『コンテムツス・ムンヂ』のデジタルアーカイブ化, *Dejitaru Ākaibu Gakkaishi* デジタルアーカイブ学会誌 6, no. 3 (2022): 123–126.

85 Philip H. Smith, Jr., "The Computer and the Humanist," in *Computers in Humanistic Research: Readings and Perspectives*, ed. Edmund A. Bowles (Englewood Cliffs, NJ: Prentice-Hall Inc, 1967), 16.

86 Ibid.

This chapter has explored some of the issues associated with applying digital tools and methods to texts pertaining to Christianity in early modern Japan. The field of digital humanities in Japan is developing at an incredible rate with new platforms and technologies being released and improved upon each year, but those of us engaged in the interfaces of Japanese studies and the digital humanities continue to face issues that those working in other contexts and with other languages resolved within their own fields many years ago. Literature relating to Christianity is particularly challenging due to the presence of multiple languages, scripts, text directions and other features all within single sources. *Kirishitan-ban* are, after all, neither entirely Japanese, nor entirely European, but a mixture of the two and this creates new challenges and opportunities. Current platforms simply aren't designed to deal with this level of variation and multiplicity. Furthermore, the now rare vocabulary used in publications related to Christianity poses significant problems for text segmentation software and most digital dictionaries. There is, of course, hope. These texts provide the opportunity to collaborate with digital humanists working with other languages and scripts, they provide the opportunity to explore new questions, and they provide (as did their creation) a potential bridge between Europe and Asia.

Bibliography

Arai Toshi 新井トシ. "Junsatsushi Varinyānoshi to Kirishitanban no shuppan" 巡察使ヴァリニャーノ師ときりしたん版の出版. In *Kirishitanban no kenkyū: Tominaga sensei koki kinen* きりしたん版の研究: 富永先生古希記念, edited by Tenri Toshokan 天理図書館, 9–46. Tenri: Tenri Daigaku Shuppanbu, 1973.

Arai Toshi 新井トシ. "Kokuji katsuji ni tsuite" 国字活字について. In *Kirishitanban no kenkyū: Tominaga sensei koki kinen* きりしたん版の研究: 富永先生古希記念, edited by Tenri Toshokan 天理図書館, 79–89. Tenri: Tenri Daigaku Shuppanbu, 1973.

Cieslik, Hubert, H. チースリク, Doi Tadao 土井忠生, and Ōtsuka Mitsunobu 大塚光信, eds. "Dochirina Kirishitan" どちりなきりしたん. In *Kirishitan sho; Haiya sho* キリシタン書; 排耶書, edited by Ebisawa Arimichi 海老沢有道, Hubert Cieslik H. チースリク, Doi Tadao 土井忠生, and Ōtsuka Mitsunobu 大塚光信, 14–81. Tokyo: Iwanami Shoten, 1970.

Cieslik, Hubert, H. チースリク, Doi Tadao 土井忠生, and Ōtsuka Mitsunobu 大塚光信, eds. "Sakaramenta teiyō furoku" サカラメンタ提要付録. In *Kirishitan sho; Haiya sho* キリシタン書; 排耶書, edited by Ebisawa Arimichi 海老沢有道, Hubert Cieslik H. チースリク, Doi Tadao 土井忠生, and Ōtsuka Mitsunobu 大塚光信, 181–223. Tokyo: Iwanami Shoten, 1970.

Collado, Diego. *Ars Grammaticae Iaponicae Linguae in Gratiam et Adiutorium eorum, qui praedicandi Evangelij causa ad Iaponiae Regnum se voluerint conferre*. Romae: Typis & impensis Sac. Congr. de Propag. Fide, 1632.

Collado, Diego. *Dictionarium sive thesauri linguae Iaponicae compendium*. Romae: Typis & impensis Sacr. Congr. de Prop. Fide, 1632.

Collado, Diego. *Niffon no cotōbani yô confesion: vo mósu yōdai to màta Confesor yori gòxensà cu mesarùru tàme nò canyônàru giô giô nocòto dànguixà no monpa no Fr. Diego Collado to yu xucqe Roma ni voite còre voxitàte mòno nàri, 1632. Modus confitendi et examinandi Poenitentem Iaponensem, formula suamet lingua Iaponica.* Romae: Typis & impensis Sacr. Congreg. de Propag. Fide, 1632.

Daiei Toshokan shozō Amakusaban 'Heike monogatari' 'Isoho monogatari' 'Kinkushū' gazō 大英図書館所蔵 天草版「平家物語」「伊曽保物語」「金句集」画像, https://dglb01.ninjal.ac.jp/BL_amakusa/en.php.

Ebisawa Arimichi 海老沢有道. *Nanban bunka: Nichiō bunka kōshō* 南蛮文化: 日欧文化交渉. Tokyo: Shibundō, 1958.

Ebisawa Arimichi, ed. *Christianity in Japan: A Bibliography of Japanese and Chinese Sources, Part I (1543–1858).* Tokyo: Committee on Asian Cultural Studies, International Christian University, 1960.

Ebisawa Arimichi 海老沢有道, ed. "Taiji jashūron" 対治邪執論. In *Kirishitan sho; Haiya sho* キリシタン書; 排耶書, edited by Ebisawa Arimichi 海老沢有道, Hubert Cieslik H. チースリク, Doi Tadao 土井忠生, and Ōtsuka Mitsunobu 大塚光信, 460–479. Tokyo: Iwanami Shoten, 1970.

Ebisawa Arimichi 海老沢有道. *Kirishitan Nanban bungaku nyūmon* キリシタン南蛮文学入門. Tokyo: Kyōbunkan, 1991.

Ebisawa Arimichi 海老沢有道, Hubert Cieslik H. チースリク, Doi Tadao 土井忠生, and Ōtsuka Mitsunobu 大塚光信, eds. "Yōgo ichiranhyō" 洋語一覧表. In *Kirishitan sho; Haiya sho* キリシタン書; 排耶書, edited by Ebisawa Arimichi 海老沢有道, Hubert Cieslik H. チースリク, Doi Tadao 土井忠生, and Ōtsuka Mitsunobu 大塚光信, 1–10. Tokyo: Iwanami Shoten, 1970.

Edo jidai ni okeru jinkō bunseki shisutemu (Danjuro 7.0) 江戸時代における人口分析システム (Danjuro 7.0), http://danjuro.jp/.

fugashi, https://pypi.org/project/fugashi/.

Fukushima Kunimichi 福島邦道. *Kirishitan shiryō to kokugo kenkyū* キリシタン資料と国語研究. Tokyo: Kasama Shoin, 1973.

Gonoi Takashi 五野井隆史. *Kirishitan no bunka* キリシタンの文化. Tokyo: Yoshikawa Kōbunkan, 2012.

Gottlieb, Nanette (née Twine), "The Genbunitchi Movement. Its Origin, Development, and Conclusion." *Monumenta Nipponica* 33, no. 3 (1978): 333–356.

Gottlieb, Nanette. *Language and Society in Japan.* Cambridge: Cambridge University Press, 2005.

JapanKnowledge, https://japanknowledge.com/.

Jisho, https://jisho.org/.

"JL-JMS-1580-KB2," Laures Kirishitan Bunko Database, https://digital-archives.sophia.ac.jp/laures-kirishitan-bunko/view/kirishitan_bunko/JL-JMS-1580-KB2.

"JL-KOSATSU-1711-KB1," Laures Kirishitan Bunko Database, https://digital-archives.sophia.ac.jp/laures-kirishitan-bunko/view/kirishitan_bunko/JL-KOSATSU-1711-KB1.

"JL-1591-KB7-7-3a," Laures Kirishitan Bunko Database, https://digital-archives.sophia.ac.jp/laures-kirishitan-bunko/view/kirishitan_bunko/JL-1591-KB7-7-3a.

"JL-1599-KB22-21-17," Laures Kirishitan Bunko Database, https://digital-archives.sophia.ac.jp/laures-kirishitan-bunko/view/kirishitan_bunko/JL-1599-KB22-21-17.

"JL-1605-KB30-29-24," Laures Kirishitan Bunko Database, https://digital-archives.sophia.ac.jp/laures-kirishitan-bunko/view/kirishitan_bunko/JL-1605-KB30-29-24.

Kawai Tadanobu 河合忠信 and Muramoto Masato 村本正人. "Kirishitanban no shoshi kaisetsu" きりしたん版の書誌解説. In *Kirishitanban no kenkyū: Tominaga sensei koki kinen* きりしたん版の研究: 富永先生古希記念, edited by Tenri Toshokan 天理図書館, 128–163. Tenri: Tenri Daigaku Shuppanbu, 1973.

Kirishitan Ligatures Font, https://github.com/kirishitanbank/KirishitanLigaturesFont.
Kornicki, Peter F. *The Book in Japan: A Cultural History from the Beginnings to the Nineteenth Century*. Leiden: Brill, 1998.
Kotenseki Sōgō Dētabēsu 古典籍総合データベース, https://www.wul.waseda.ac.jp/kotenseki/.
Kotobanku コトバンク, https://kotobank.jp/.
Kraken, http://kraken.re/.
Kuromoji, https://www.atilika.org/.
KuroNet Kuzushiji Ninshiki Sābisu KuroNetくずし字認識サービス, http://codh.rois.ac.jp/kuronet/.
Lamb, Alex, Tarin Clanuwat, and Asanobu Kitamoto. "KuroNet: Regularized Residual U-Nets for End-to-End Kuzushiji Character Recognition." *SN Computer Science* 1: 177 (2020): 1–15.
Laures, Johannes. *Kirishitan Bunko: A Manual of Books and Documents on the Early Christian Mission in Japan*. 3rd edition. Tokyo: Sophia University, 1957.
Laures Kirishitan Bunko Database, https://digital-archives.sophia.ac.jp/laures-kirishitan-bunko/.
Lu Wang. "Data Clearing Chinese Text with OpenRefine: Punctuation Removal," *The Digital Orientalist*, December 25, 2020, https://digitalorientalist.com/2020/12/25/data-cleaning-of-chinese-text-by-open-refine/.
Masamune Atsuo 正宗敦夫, ed. *Giya do pekadoru* ぎや・ど・ぺかどる, *Jōkan* 上巻. Tokyo: Nihon Koten Zenshū Kankōkai, 1929.
McCann, Paul. "fugashi, a Tool for Tokenizing Japanese in Python." *Proceedings of Second Workshop for NLP Open Source Software (NLP-OSS)* (2020): 44–51.
Miwo みを, http://codh.rois.ac.jp/miwo/index.html.en.
Moretti, Laura. *Pleasure in Profit: Popular Prose in Seventeenth-Century Japan*. New York, NY: Columbia University Press, 2020.
Morris, James Harry. "Transkribus and Kirishitanban: Some Initial Experiments," *The Digital Orientalist*, February 18, 2022, https://digitalorientalist.com/2022/02/18/transkribus-and-kirishitanban-some-initial-experiments/.
Nakagawa, Tetsuji. "Chinese and Japanese word segmentation using word-level and character-level information." *COLING '04: Proceedings of the 20th International Conference on Computational Linguistics* (2004): 466–471. DOI: https://doi.org/10.1587/transinf.E92.D.2298.
National Diet Library Digital Collections, https://dl.ndl.go.jp/.
Next Digital Library, https://lab.ndl.go.jp/dl/.
Nihongoshi Kenkyūyō Tekisuto Dētashū 日本語史研究用テキストデータ集, https://www2.ninjal.ac.jp/textdb_dataset/amhk/.
Nuetzler, Sophie ノイツラ・ゾフィー and Miyagawa Sō 宮川創. "HTR puroguramu Transkribus ni yoru Nihongo Kirishitan-ban 'Kontemutsusu munji' no dejitaru ākaibuka" HTRプログラムTranskribusによる日本語キリシタン版『コンテムツス・ムンヂ』のデジタルアーカイブ化. *Dejitaru Ākaibu Gakkaishi* デジタルアーカイブ学会誌 6, no. 3 (2022): 123–126.
OpenRefine, https://openrefine.org/.
Orii Yoshimi 折井喜果, ed. *Hidesu no kyō* ひですの経. Tokyo: Kyōbunkan, 2011.
Orii Yoshimi 折井喜果, Shirai Jun 白井純, and Toyoshima Masauki 豊島正之, eds. *Hidesu no kyō* ひですの経. Tokyo: Yagi Shoten, 2011.
Oyler, Elizabeth. *Swords, Oaths, and Prophetic Visions: Authoring Warrior Rule in Medieval Japan*. Honolulu, HI: University of Hawai'i Press, 2006.
"Part VI: Christian Artefacts," Laures Kirishitan Bunko Database, https://digital-archives.sophia.ac.jp/laures-kirishitan-bunko/search?ct=kirishitan_bunko&cat=02_06.
Popescu, Florin. "'Kōgi yōkō' ni okeru goji hongo ni tsuite" 「講義要綱」における合字本語について. *Kyōto Daigaku Kokubungaku Ronso* 京都大学國文學論叢 12 (2004): 1–24.

Rodriguez, João. *Arte da Lingoa Iapam composta pello João Rodriguez Portugues da Cōpanhia de Iesu, dividida em tres livros.* Nangasaqui: Collegio de Iapão da Companhia de Iesu, 1604.

Shinmura Izuru 新村出 and Hiragi Genichi 柊源一, eds. *Kirishitan bungakushū* 1 吉利支丹文学集 1. Tokyo: Hebonsha, 1993.

"Shiteisho ichiran 指定書一覧," Tenri Toshokan 天理図書館, https://www.tcl.gr.jp/collection/designation-book/.

Smith, Jr., Philip H. "The Computer and the Humanist." In *Computers in Humanistic Research: Readings and Perspectives*, edited by Edmund A. Bowles, 16–28. Englewood Cliffs, NJ: Prentice-Hall Inc., 1967.

Solier, François. *Histoire ecclésiastique des isles et royaumes du Iapon*, 2 vols. Paris: Chez Sebastien Cramoisy, 1627–1629.

Terras, Melissa. "Digitization and digital resources in the humanities." In *Digital humanities in practice*, edited by Claire Warwick, Melissa Terras, and Julianne Nyhan, 47–70. London: Facet Publishing, 2012.

The Marega Collection Database, https://base1.nijl.ac.jp/~marega/en/.

The Max Besson Library of "Japonica" Collection, http://www.tulips.tsukuba.ac.jp/pub/tree/besson.php.

Tominaga Makita 富永牧太. "Kirishitanban no insatsujutsu" きりしたん版の印刷術. In *Kirishitanban no kenkyū: Tominaga sensei koki kinen* きりしたん版の研究: 富永先生古希記念, edited by Tenri Toshokan 天理図書館, 47–78. Tenri: Tenri Daigaku Shuppanbu, 1973.

Tominaga Makita 富永牧太. "Ôbun moji kō" 欧文文字攷. In *Kirishitanban no kenkyū: Tominaga sensei koki kinen* きりしたん版の研究: 富永先生古希記念, edited by Tenri Toshokan 天理図書館, 90–127. Tenri: Tenri Daigaku Shuppanbu, 1973.

Transkribus, https://readcoop.eu/transkribus/.

UTokyo Academic Archives Portal, https://da.dl.itc.u-tokyo.ac.jp/portal/.

Voyant Tools, https://voyant-tools.org/.

Web ChaMame Web 茶まめ, https://chamame.ninjal.ac.jp/.

Weblio, https://www.weblio.jp/.

Yamamoto Sumiko 山本純子 and Ōsawa Tomejirō 大澤留次郎. "Kotenseki honkoku no shōryokuka: Kuzushiji o fukumu shinhōshiki OCR gijutsu no kaihatsu" 古典籍翻刻の省力化: くずし字を含む新方式OCR技術の開発. *Jōhō kanri* 情報管理 58, no. 11 (2016): 819–827.

Social Media

Kusumita Datta
Gonojagoron Monchos of the 2013 Shahbag Protests in Bangladesh: "Religions" and Digital Media

Gonojagoron Monchos: Definition, Expansion and Appropriation

News media in Bangladesh and beyond have defined the *gonojagoron moncho* as a platform for popular rising[1] centered around the 2013 Shahbag protests in Dhaka which called for justice against the perpetrators of war crimes in the Bangladesh Liberation War of 1971. While the term has been used by pro-Shahbag protesters and their leader Imran H. Sarkar (and blogger Arif Jebtik when Sarker was ill in 2014), the term has also been extended to similar platforms in all of Bangladesh's sixty-four districts, right down to the village level, particularly on and through digital media. The term was used to designate an official platform for protesters and online activists, but the platform was thought to be tainted by governmental backing which appeared to be confirmed by nationwide transport strikes that would not allow protesters from the opposition faction, Hefazat-e-Islam, to come to the center of the capital city.[2] These protesters, as well as ordinary people in Bangladesh's remote villages, were influenced by the spirit of this uprising, congregating in sit-ins in their local areas and gaining widespread exposure on digital platforms, particularly in 2013. Some districts have official social media pages like Sreepur,[3] Sylhet,[4] Khulna,[5] and Mymensingh.[6] These social media pages were used

---

[1] Canada: Immigration and Refugee Board of Canada, "Bangladesh: *Gonojagoron Moncho*, including origin, purpose, structure, membership, areas of operation and activities (April 2013–January 2014)," January 24, 2014, https://www.refworld.org/docid/542a80df4.html.
[2] Manosh Chowdhury, "Hefazat & Casual Middle Class's Politics-Desire," Alal O Dulal (blog), April 13, 2013, https://alalodulal.org/2013/04/13/middle-class/.
[3] Srepur Gonojagoron moncho.org, Facebook, https://www.facebook.com/Srepur-Gonojagoron-moncho-org-391512831201492/. Archived links for all Facebook content can be found at DOI: https://doi.org/10.5281/zenodo.8132446.
[4] Gonojagoron Mancho, Sylhet, Facebook, https://www.facebook.com/GonojagoronManchoSylhet/?p aipv=0&eav=AfaZ6bBoxu0OOpJCsPNlOT3ymAvbcni90QzAfdGVlkj0Sp4i6K8Cxzt-9pFo-Xqu9xQ&_rdr.
[5] Gonojagoron Moncho (@KhulnaMoncho), Twitter, https://twitter.com/KhulnaMoncho. Archived versions of Twitter content can be found within the bibliography.
[6] Gonojagoron moncho (@Gonojagoron_13), Twitter, https://twitter.com/Gonojagoron_13.

to post about the local stages of the uprising through cultural center outlets[7] and some individuals even reached out to the Shahbag uprising through its online local news portals and society and culture websites.[8] The social media pages of these district units highlight the actions of the groups or individuals who create or follow the respective groups. Individuals appropriate the *gonojagoron* tag in multiple ways — staging pro-Shahbag protests,[9] uploading of photographs[10] including those taken on mobile phones (i.e. mobile uploads).[11] This study explores these expanded sites of popular uprising and their invocation of variant "religions" on digital media.

While the Shahbag movement began as a coordinated uprising online, people responded to its call and gathered at an area known as Shahbag in the capital city of Dhaka. Studies exist on analyzing the Shahbag crowds from an economic perspective. Razia Shariff records about the funding of the movement through individuals, businesses and crowdsourcing of the movement aimed at generating economic well-being for the movement later.[12] However, Shariff's study does not explore the role of regional non-profit organizations in facilitating individuals, both rich and poor. The voices of these people found outlet through more populist digital modes as regional discrimination in network support continued to decrease.[13] This study, therefore, probes into the role of digital media as an egalitarian tool in representing the regional voices of *gonojagoron monchos*.

---

[7] See the following example from Noakhali: NOA TV Live, "Gonojagoron moncho, noakhali," Facebook, December 17, 2013, https://www.facebook.com/swojon4/photos/a.152987438213481/225648847614006/?type=3&paipv=0&eav=AfbO8Tj0pYqaCq8sK0IovVdRYcIUXtfG6B6VgmumhMDg9vcH8LOEiPuoP-PuoQ5o6-o&_rdr.

[8] See the following example from the Facebook page of the *gonojagoron moncho* from Chittagong: Gonojagoron mocho, Chittagong, Facebook, https://www.facebook.com/GonojagoronMonchoChittagong.

[9] See example from Noakhali: Gonojagoron Companigonj, Facebook, https://www.facebook.com/gonojagoron.companigonj?paipv=0&eav=Afb-uTurh1R8XdPu5V6Pj8aWQCKv-EiTkU-MjrBbBjaWtlOnLiSXntD0HCXi2OwHBBs&_rdr.

[10] See example from Narsingdi: Ohiduzzaman Sapan, "Gonojagoron monch, Baroicha Bus-stand. Belabo, narsingdi," Facebook, February 16, 2016, https://m.facebook.com/photo.php?fbid=1714243438799094&id=100006403633805&set=a.1714243425465762.

[11] See example from Jessore: Mahamud Hassan Bulu, "Gonojagoron moncher prothom janmodiner jessore," Facebook, February 6, 2014, https://m.facebook.com/photo.php?fbid=213167412218695&id=100005763122580&set=a.159103837625053.

[12] Razia Shariff, "Collective Agency Capability: How Capabilities Can Emerge in a Social Moment," in *New Frontiers of the Capability Approach*, ed. Comin, Fennell and Anand (Cambridge: Cambridge University Press, 2018), 169.

[13] Muhammad Nazrul Islam and Toki Tahmid Inan, "Exploring the Fundamental Factors of Digital Inequality in Bangladesh," *SAGE Open* (April 2021): 3. DOI: https://doi.org/10.1177/21582440211021407.

Gonojagoron Monchos of the Regions: Differential Digital Accessibility, Regional Media, and Associational Content

Narratives percolate to users through differential digital user access. When *gonojagoron monchos* are created at the level of the grassroots, people come to know about the Shahbag movement through forwarded messages, tagged tweets and shared videos. As such, it is pertinent to undertake a content analysis of a purposive sampling of textual, image and video posts on digital platforms such as blogs, Twitter, Facebook, YouTube, SoundCloud, etc. in 2013 to probe the expansion and appropriation of the term *gonojagoron monchos* in the districts of Bangladesh. New narratives about common interests and affiliations emerge when district *gonojagoron monchos* give voice to pro- and anti- Shahbag content in their posts. Some Facebook or Twitter pages supporting anti-*gonojagoron moncho* stances are delimited through limited visibility, though this does not mean that such accounts have fewer followers or less posts. The visibility of these posts and tweets is protected by the account holders so that only tagged people may share them.[14] Any user who may have accessed the post in the past immediately understands the inhibition in a ubiquitous circulation. The post is thence circulated in select groups who further share and retweet the content.

When *gonojagoron monchos* celebrate the martyrdom of people associated with the pro-Liberation War forces, they are more accessible because they espouse the freedom of the nation from fundamentalist forces. Account profile pictures use slogans such as *"Joy Bangla"* ("Hail to Bengal") while header images feature the sculpture of "Undefeated Bangladesh," a sculpture dedicated to the fighters of the Liberation War. The affiliation of the account holder is thereby made clear through verbal and visual modes. Twitter display names substantiate this patriotic stance. For example, alongside political taglines, display names such as *"Mongol Alok"* ("An Auspicious Ray of Light") indicate that the account holder is not impartial but only on the side of the pro-Liberation forces in the 1971 War. Through associational content analysis, interpretation of account profile and cover pictures and local media content, this study will explore the role of variant "religions" in the regions of Bangladesh during the 2013 Shahbag movement.

---

14 Note for example the following Tweet: "This Tweet is unavailable," Twitter, https://twitter.com/AshfaqHoque/status/268757025637425152?s=20.

Gonojagoron Monchos and Variant Religio-Political Affiliations

Although the term *gonojagoron* has been used to refer to pro-Shahbag protests, there are also instances where it is used to refer to anti-Shahbag protests. Shariff explained the positions of political parties in relation to the Shahbag protests writing that "political structures and parties reacted positively (AL), negatively (JI) and tried to ignore Shahbag (BNP)."[15] The Shahbag protesters were often associated with left-wing political views, whilst those who reacted negatively were often associated with the Jamaat-e-Islami (JI), an Islamist party, which brands communists as anti-religious. Though taking a divergent opinion the communists are also located at par with both their religious opposition — Hindus — and their political opposition — the ruling party, the Awami League (AL) — in mass rallies organized in districts like Chittagong. Social media pages based in Chittagong represent conflicting religio-political interests. Mass demonstrations on the streets with the flag of Bangladesh fluttering behind had been organized by Chittagong *Gonojagoron* Manch and images of this were posted on Facebook.[16] Through displaying the national flag, the pro-Shahbag faction appeared as patriotic and pro-nation. The username of this Facebook page "*Pra Janma*" or "New Generation" is a term used by the Shahbag protesters to refer to the location of Shahbag square — the "*Projonmo Chottor*" ("Space of the New Generation"). Through the username the user thus makes us conscious that the posts on this page will be pro-Shahbag in nature. Other users posting about the demonstration organized by the Chittagong press club *gonojagoron moncho* also make overt pro-Shahbag statements through their photographs. One user, for instance, appears with a bandana stating "[I] want death penalty" on his forehead.[17] Another Facebook page entitled *Gonojagoron Chittagong* makes their anti-Shahbag stance systematically clear by arguing that the perpetrators of injustice will not be punished, an all-party united council to challenge ruling party autocracy will not be formed, and the trial of war criminals by the International Crimes Tribunal (ICT) will be biased. It is filled with posts where those awarded capital punishments are hailed as martyrs who sing

---

[15] Razia Shariff, "Shahbag: A Critical Social Moment: A Collective Agency Capabilities Analysis," Doctoral thesis (Canterbury Christ Church University, 2019), 193.
[16] Pra Janma, "Ganamichil — Chittagong *Gonojagoron* Manch," Facebook, February 23, 2013, https://m.facebook.com/photo.php/?fbid=115742108610927.
[17] Rafiqul Mowla, "In chittagong press club gonojagoron moncho. . .," Facebook, February 12, 2013, https://m.facebook.com/photo.php?fbid=10200559261044658&id=1252663262&set=a.1872807020559.

of victory on the pulpit of their execution[18] or with posts hailing the contributions (both to religious scholarship and secular politics) of ICT deemed war criminals and Jamaat leaders like Allama Sayeedi. The admins of the page want these points of view to be circulated widely on digital media. The page even states: "Get to new updates plz LIKE our page Cyber group of Bangladesh."[19] This language of digital dissemination incorporates the "like" of Facebook and YouTube, whereas the term "Cyber group" refers to the wide world of social media, weblogs, online discussion portals and cyber solidarity units. These overlapping online strategies of both supposedly secular and religious factions, even when based in the same district, further blurs their oppositional stances.

Shaffer studies the apparent conflict between religious bigotry and secular rationalism citing Ali Riaz's 2008 work on the better organization of rightist and Islamic political parties in comparison to the apparently secular parties like the Awami League and the Bangladesh Nationalist Party.[20] However, even during the Shahbag protests, the Awami League continued to utilize religious language even as they tried to maintain a distinction with the fundamentalist language of the Jamaat-i-Islami. Shahriar Kabir, a noted human rights activist points out that when the Jamaat was in power, they did not introduce the Blasphemy Law, but subsequently created pressure for the Awami League to do so.[21]

Beyond these religio-political associations, was the concrete appropriation of the *gonojagoron moncho* by the Awami League, whose governmental modes the protesters had denied. Nusrat Sabina Chowdhury writes:

> For many people, the idea that the government had co-opted part of the movement's leadership signalled the beginning of the end. That public gatherings as large as these were subject to metal detectors and closed-circuit surveillance, and the fact (equally, the rumour) that

---

18 Gonojagoron Chittagong, "Shahid Muhammad Kamruzzaman: Phasir Monche dariye ami bijoyer joy gaan gai" [Martyr Muhammad Kamruzzaman: I sing of Victory on the Pulpit of Execution], Facebook, April 11, 2021, https://www.facebook.com/416935725045874/posts/5293962627343135/.
19 Gonojagoron Chittagong, "Allama Sayeedi Rajnoitik Protihingshar Shikar" [Allama Sayeedi Victim of Political Vendetta], Facebook, February 14, 2013, https://m.facebook.com/story.php?story_fbid=445790788827034&substory_index=0&id=416935725045874.
20 Ryan Shaffer, "Islamist Attacks against Secular Bloggers in Bangladesh," in *Violence in South Asia: Contemporary Perspectives*, eds. Pavan Kumar Malreddy, Anindya Sekhar Purakayastha and Birte Heidemann (London: Routledge, 2020), 212.
21 In an interview given to *ANI* News for its show "Bangladesh Today" a few months after the Shahbag uprising, Shahriar Kabir explained that when the Jamaat-e-Islami and the Bangladesh National Party were in a coalition in 1993, the Jamaat chief and national Minister Motiur Rahman Nizami did not bring the draft bill of the Blasphemy Law before parliament because they knew that it would be outrightly rejected. However, they subsequently created pressure for the Awami League to do so only to create chaos.

free food was being distributed among protestors, led others to suspect powerful third-party involvement.[22]

Awami League platforms based in Chittagong appropriated the poetic narrative of the *gonojagoron moncho* Chittagong protester, metaphorically writing of why some are quiet in the face of the sentencing of Kader Molla, accused of 1971 war crimes, to death, using the opposition political party leader Khaleda Zia as a poetic character. The political voices of the districts are more vocal in relation to this sort of appropriation and castigation, especially on digital media.

On the other end of unsolicited appropriation by political parties, is the vehement denial of any political association by the anti-*gonojagoron moncho*. From bases in madrasas and mosques, Jamaat and other religio-political groups clashed with the protesters at *gonojagoron moncho* after their Friday prayers on February 23, 2013, and claimed that they were common people, assaulted by governmental apparatuses like the police. A television broadcast of this, subsequently uploaded on YouTube,[23] portrays the specter of innumerable religio-political affiliates who would bear down upon the pro-Shahbag protesters at the city center. In other words, the religio-political affiliations of the *gonojagoron moncho* created a more spectacular visual specter on digital media.[24] Every religio-political affiliation is marked by a tendency to attempt to create mass gatherings often comprised of people from the districts like those young children from Gazipur who came for a protest march against the bloggers without quite knowing what the protest was all about.[25]

Gonojagoron Monchos and Regional Rituals in the Shahbag Movement

Religion is a major tenet at the root of the Shahbag movement since the bloggers initiated a war on religious extremism. Islamic religiosity is seen as a local lived religion in Bangladeshi culture and society but when it comes to Islamic

---

22 Nusrat Sabina Chowdhury, "Death, Despair and Democracy in Bangladesh," in *Emotions, Mobilisations and South Asian Politics*, eds. Amélie Blom and Stéphanie Tawa Lama-Rewal (London: Routledge, 2020), 274.
23 Hossain Iqbal, "Anti-*gonojagoron moncho* clash 23 02 2013," YouTube, February 25, 2018, https://www.youtube.com/watch?v=VfbzeTRyeJ4.
24 Chowdhury, "Hefazat & Casual Middle Class's Politics-Desire."
25 Chowdhury, "Death, Despair and Democracy in Bangladesh," 275.

fundamentalist forces like Hefazat-e-Islam becoming active political actors, the path forward appears to lead to an era of post-secularism.[26]

When the Shahbag protesters demanded capital punishment for the war criminals of the 1971 Liberation War, they were accused of being anti-Muslim and atheists. The Bloggers and Online Activists Network (BOAN) coordinated the actions of the protesters which enabled *gonojagoron monchos* to spring up everywhere overnight. At a time when Facebook had yet to arrive in Bangladesh, blogs like *Somewhereinblog* served as spaces to express thoughts on religious freethinking nurtured by young bloggers like Kowshik from districts like Barishal. *Muktomona* is a Bengali language blog[27] for secularists, atheists, and freethinkers founded in 2001 by Avijit Roy whose murder in 2013 was claimed by a Twitter account belonging to the Ansarullah Bangla Team, an Islamic militant group.[28] Jamaat-i-Islam and twelve other like-minded Islamic parties claimed that the bloggers insulted Islam and Prophet Mohammad. They utilized religious modes like prayer to consolidate crowds at Shahbag. Islami Andolan Bangladesh is one of the biggest political parties in Bangladesh and their official Facebook posts included numerous international media reports with visuals of tens of thousands of Islamic activists saying Jummah Prayer together on the street at Motijheel Square in Dhaka together. Individual voices also tag other media reports[29] with panoramic visuals[30] of thousands attending Friday prayers during a rally in Dhaka, calling for new blasphemy laws and making hateful statements about the blasphemous blogs of the Shahbag bloggers and online activists who insult Islam. Such panoramic visuals foreground the concept of "vicarious religion" where people are tangibly displaying a belief in their call to *Allah* despite not quite belonging to the dominion of

---

26 Abdul Wohab, "'Secularism' or 'No-Secularism'? A Complex Case of Bangladesh," *Cogent Social Sciences* 7, no. 1 (2021): 1–21. DOI: https://doi.org/10.1080/23311886.2021.1928979.
27 There is also an English counterpart to the Bengali blog at: MuktoMona English Blog, https://en.muktomona.com/.
28 Samanth Subramanian, "The Hit List: The Islamist war on secular bloggers in Bangladesh," *The New Yorker*, December 13, 2015, https://www.newyorker.com/magazine/2015/12/21/the-hit-list.
29 Daily Mail Reporter, "'Arrest the atheists who insulted Islam!' Tens of thousands of Muslim activists hold prayers on streets of Bangladesh capital to call for new blasphemy laws against bloggers," Mail Online, March 30, 2013, https://www.dailymail.co.uk/news/article-2301138/Tens-thousands-Islamic-activists-hold-prayers-streets-Bangladesh-capital-new-blasphemy-laws.html?ito=feeds-newsxml&fbclid=IwAR1OQZWf9g9elrS7OKJttMgpyymgX_1bXSf-cGbELThgYAQYpdKLLk5ESpc.
30 Huma Yusuf, "Islamist rise against Shahbag Bloggers," Facebook, March 30, 2013, https://tinyurl.com/ycytuvcp.

religious conservatism.[31] This digital media not only enables an easy and related sharing of such media posts but gives people time to ponder on the force of the physically coordinated gathering together of the rural and urban masses through calls for prayers at the Baitul Mukarram National Mosque at Dhaka. Comments also bring in divergent voices castigating the country's media houses as atheistic and calling upon Allah to protect the Islamic activities and disburse punishment to atheists.

In Shahbag square, the voices supporting religious advocacy presented a charter of demands for a progressive society. Yet even as the city center in Dhaka was alive with the cries of capital punishment for the Jamaat-i-Islami leaders, namely Abdul Quader Molla and Maulana Motiur Rahman Nizami, digital media utilized the official pages of district branches to highlight work being undertaken on the grassroots by these leaders. The Facebook page for Martyr Maulana Nizami (2013),[32] enumerated his works and spread across districts like Chapainawabganj, where sit-ins and protest movements spontaneously erupted in parallel to the Shahbag demonstrations. These Facebook posts were being made in June 2013, at the same time that the free Nizami campaign was being conducted. Local stages of protest on social media thereby constituted comprehensive crowdsourcing campaigns — for political demands, social initiatives, and judicial demands — transforming the anti-Shahbag rallies into a countrywide phenomenon. It is also significant that the crowdsourcing of religious political parties enmeshes social work with religious ethicality. Regional piety of lived religion perpetuates its digital legacy through a mass rejoinder of calls to the Prophet Mohammed whenever socio-political-judicial claims are posted.

---

31 Grace Davie, "Vicarious Religion: A Response," *Journal of Contemporary Religion* 25, Issue 2 (2010): 266, DOI: https://doi.org/10.1080/13537901003750944. Davie explains "vicarious religion" as "the notion of religion performed by an active minority but on behalf of a much larger number, who (implicitly at least) not only understand, but, quite clearly, approve of what the minority is doing." The crowds here emblematize the active minority on behalf of a religious-minded larger group, except that their understanding of what religion entails, ranges from the Islamic state, blasphemy laws, local piety and congregational prayers, all posited in opposition to the pro-Shahbag ideals of the *gonojagoron moncho*.
32 Je Tyag Preronar [The Sacrifice for Motivation], Facebook, https://www.facebook.com/profile.php?id=100050602864323.

Gonojagoron Monchos, "Religions" and Digital Modes of District Dissemination

When individuals appropriate the *gonojagoron* username, the pulpit of popular uprising is emblematized at the level of the local sub-district and village. Local stages are organized to enable crowdsourcing in various nearby sub-districts, educational and administrative institutions. The Companigonj *Gonojagoron Moncho* brought together its initiator Hasan Imam Russell, the mayor of Basurhat Corporation, Liberation War fighter Abunacher, and others in a solidarity meeting organized by students at Government Mujib College in Basurhat. Companigonj is a sub-district of the Noakhali district. Social media posts not only create an awareness that the Shahbag uprising has permeated multiple institutions but also bring in local print news media like *Noakhali Pratidin* (Daily Noakhali) into the digital domain.[33] This marks a new mode of datafiction through web retrieval. Pauline Hope Cheong notes that web retrieval and weblogs extract user statistics and enable the posting of related comments.[34] This leads to the creation of a related religious vocabulary of martyrdom and morality. Thus, permeation brings out information about those who had sacrificed their lives in the 1971 Liberation War from Noakhali.[35] For some in this region, the Shahbag movement would avenge their martyrdom. In the thread from the *Noakhali Pratidin*'s post, there are comments of those who oppose the secular polity in Bangladesh. Merging history and religion, religious datafiction thrives through such comments. Even though the local unit proclaims that their struggle is not against any religion, the language of religion interjects comments on seeking justice for those who sacrificed their lives during the 1971 war. Users supporting the Pakistan side in the conflict claim that true Muslims ought to demand justice for those who murdered the pro-Pakistan martyrs. Religious identity, justice in the war crimes tribunal and conflicting interests of martyrs and criminals thus become deliberately intermeshed. One comment specifically mentions the father of a person from Natore, near Noakhali, even though there is no specific context of a discussion regarding this person nor any reference to the place in the comment thread. The idea of religion on digital media is characterized by such imposition and randomness.

---

33 Gonojagoron Companigonj, "n k barta news," Facebook, March 17, 2013, https://tinyurl.com/5n74xeeb.
34 Pauline Hope Cheong, "Religious Datafiction: Platforms, Practices and Power," in *The Routledge Handbook of Religion and Journalism*, eds. Kerstin Radde-Antweiler and Xenia Zeiler (London: Routledge, 2021), 401.
35 Gonojagoron Companigonj, "GONOJAGORON COMPANIGONJ NOAKHALI," Facebook, March 1, 2013, https://tinyurl.com/uznwf4re.

Gonojagoron Monchos on the Move and Digital Democracy

The varying locations of the different stages of mass uprising constitute the topic of the greatest number of social media posts. Mass gatherings at Shahbag square have been the subject of recent studies such as Nusrat Sabina Chowdhury's 2019 work on the body of the protesters.[36] She noted the crucial difference between the *Gonojagoron Moncho*, the official name of the Shahbag platform, and the spontaneous crowds that gathered at Shahbag for weeks on end. While mass gatherings at the capital's city center seemed to indicate political patronage and governmental crowdsourcing, gatherings in far-flung districts could not and did not have these associations. *Gonojagoron monchos* in the districts are not offshoots of this official platform but spontaneous street protests which gained digital footprints when their participants or bystanders uploaded photos on social media. Ohiduzzaman Sapan is a proprietor and contractor from Narsingdi who uploaded a photo of himself giving a speech at the *gonojagoron moncho* at Baroicha bus stand. Under a tree, in front of a makeshift stage, with some looking for a bus rather than engaging in the speech, he makes a Shahbag square of his own.[37] With forty-eight likes and two shares, this post does not make a remarkable digital statement but it does reflect the attempt by small-town internet users to gradually enter the digital world. Three years after the Shahbag protests, this post is a witness to the belated, persistent reach of mass awakening ethos, as well as the relatively slow acquisition of digital knowledge, amongst those engaged in the district and village uprisings.

From bus stands to school courtyards, popular voices came together in the most commonplace sites of amalgamation. The grounds of Shahid Syed Nazrul Islam College, its students and staff become the *projonmo* ("new generation") square at Mymensingh, reminiscent of the *Projonmo Chottor* at Shahbag. An image of this protest posted on social media shows a banner that not only proclaims solidarity with the Shahbag cause but specifically calls out for religion devoid of politics. Other than the printed banner, which is of central focus, a paper placard held by some people proclaims, "Faith be stronger."[38] In district locales, an admixture of the archetypal Bangla language slogan *"Kasai Kader Mollar Phashi Chai"* ("Hang Butcher Kader Molla") and the English statement "Faith be stronger" on placards

---

36 Nusrat Sabina Chowdhury, *Paradoxes of the Popular: Crowd Politics in Bangladesh* (Stanford, CA: Stanford University Press, 2019), 161–198.
37 Sapan, "Gonojagoron monch, Baroicha Bus-stand, Belabo, narsingdi."
38 Tipu Sultan Ronit, *"Gonojagoron mymensingh,"* Facebook, February 12, 2013, https://m.facebook.com/photo.php?fbid=416180631802611&id=100002320348244&set=a.414444745309533.

is indicative of the *gonojagoron* of the new generation. It was not only in the cities that the educated youth were participating in the online Shahbag activism. In the districts, the youth were becoming aware of an online call for protests and played their part in local gatherings which then found their space in social media through individuals' posts. At a time when these areas had limited access to the internet and internet education, minimal knowledge of tagging and sharing posts enabled blatant statements on religiosity in the Shahbag movement and its figuration in the digital domain.

Gonojagoron monchos are not only found in various locations but are also variously named. Nomenclature reveals the exact terms in which local people understand its meaning and implications. Beyond religious conflicts and political biases, these stages called out for the death of the war criminals. At Rajshahi, a storeroom becomes the stage of calls for execution where the Vice-Chancellor of the University of Rajshahi expresses solidarity with the ideals of the Shahbag movement. While local environs like the bus stand and the school courtyard are more banal, this storeroom is a storehouse for art ephemera related to the Shahbag movement.[39] From painted parody images of war criminals and paintings of Jahanara Imam (the mother of martyr Rumi who died in the 1971 war) to slogans of protest painted on the walls, the room becomes a site of art activism. When a photographer based in Rajshahi uploads an image of the site on Facebook, it is a marketing of his art of photography. Yet the photograph is also a witness to the locations in which stages of uprising turn up where the educated elite and the working classes come together to nurture the narrative of protest. Digital democracy entails people from varying classes utilizing digital media and making everyday demands of livelihood.

Everyday social injustices are also protested from district *gonojagoron monchos* like the one based in Faridpur. Since this stage is concerned with gaining justice for indiscriminate killings, local users parallelly highlight deaths at a Faridpur municipal corporation, that are to be deemed as no less important.[40] The march for social justice uses the same tropes of protest such as a human chain. Through a mobile upload, an individual who lives in the capital city of Dhaka posts a photograph of this post from Faridpur and terms it *gonojagoron moncho*. People throughout the country thereby continue the democratic legacy of the 2013 platforms of popular uprising long after on social media. Such posts evoke remembrances of the 2013 Shahbag *gonojagoron moncho* and what it stood for. This post[41] features a poem where people may

---

39 Storyteller of Life, "Former Vice chancellor of Rajshahi University who is also a freedom fighter came to support us," Facebook, February 13, 2013, https://tinyurl.com/3zvudc3d.
40 Kamruzzaman Zmn, "*Gonojagoron moncho*," Facebook, April 10, 2016, https://m.facebook.com/photo.php?fbid=10208989585355204&id=1183881965&set=a.10203532339127459&source=57.
41 Ibid.

be on a "long march" to Faridpur or Shahbag. During these marches, they upload photographs. On the move in a road procession, mobile uploads are the most pertinent way of upholding the digital democracy of *gonojagoron monchos*.

Gonojagoron Monchos and Days of Religiosity in Digital Media

The official platform of the Shahbag movement held marches and protest meetings all through the day and night. All-night vigils of the candlelight marches and slogans made the *gonojagoron monchos* sites of vibrant mass gathering where people from old Dhaka and the districts flocked in. Whether on *"Jumma bar"* (Friday, when Muslims offer the congregational prayer) or *"Budh bar"* (Wednesday), the butcher, Quader Molla, will be hanged, screams the crowds. Sacred days will not be able to save sacred people because they are not sacred anymore. Religious leaders like Molla delivered speeches on these sacrosanct days and the new generation at Shahbag challenged these norms. Lived religiosity permeates the language of the people. Such language of *gonojagoron monchos*, with the accent of old Dhaka appealing to the masses, made "Chorompotro 2013" a popular program on digital media. It was circulated widely through SoundCloud. Digital media dissemination is simultaneously inhibited by a lack of digital literacy and Bangla interface, and spread through= widely circulated local language videos.

From days to dates, from the religiously sacred to the politically sacred, *gonojagoron monchos* are a witness to varied modes of religiosity, celebrated at the local level. Martyrdom is a form of the politically sacred, wherein the martyr, executed for war crimes is deemed to have reached paradise. To be granted capital punishment is a ticket to the martyr's paradise. March 11 has been used to commemorate the martyrdom of members of the anti-Shahbag faction thus allowing the said commemoration to gain more visual space. On Twitter, Omar Fokran,[42] a member of the Bangladesh Islami Chhatra Shibir based in Noakhali, uploaded a tweet celebrating the martyrdom of members of this organization, which is a student wing of Jamaat-i-Islami. The organization's Twitter account has 65.2K followers and has newly opened a Telegram page (with about 14K followers)[43] to reach out to users through mobile applications. Similar posts emanate each year, contending with the hashtag world of a parallel martyrs' day,

---

42 Omar Fokran, "#11MarShahidDibosh," Twitter, March 11, 2021, https://twitter.com/omar_forkan_bd/status/1369887690578006019.
43 @bangladeshislamichhatrashibir, Telegram, https://t.me/bangladeshislamichhatrashibir.

December 14. #MartyredIntellectualDay generates multiple posts each year, spanning across Twitter and Facebook, featuring black and white photographs of the martyrs, with a memorial commemorating this event at Rayerbazar, Dhaka and a sculpture at the Mujibnagar Memorial Complex in the Meherpur District. When remembrance days are associated with memorial monuments, they appear to gain greater space on digital media, with a single tagged image generating a web of awareness.

Gonojagoron Monchos and Cultural Religiosity of the Regions on Digital Media

Gonojagoron monchos were centers of a cultural awakening, mostly based in the city center of Shahbag. There are scattered references to slogans like *"Tui Rajakar"* ("You Razakar!") which appeared in songs that were compiled on new media platforms and spread rapidly. Sanchari De cites a video clip which was made from a television drama and circulated through YouTube during the protests along with slogans from the physical sphere and a newly made song by the Bangla band *Chirkut*,[44] but a sustained exploration of folk artists performing at Shahbag, images of regions participating through cultural events, edited videos circulating on YouTube and social media foregrounding voices of the districts and based therein, presents *gonojagoron monchos* as sites of a cultural awakening, particularly in the regions. The album, *Songs from Shahbag*, released on March 26, 2013, mostly celebrates city-based artists, re-negotiating the realities of the 1952 language movement, the 1969 mass uprising and the 1971 Liberation War in terms of their 2013 awakening. The official song of the *gonojagoron* on YouTube includes visual clips of journeys to villages and digitized images of the National Martyrs' Monument and the Shahid Minar. Lyrics hailing a Bangladesh where no divisions will be allowed find their representation in such audio-visual compilations.[45] Kalika Prasad of Bangla folk band *Dohar* and visual artist Sudipto Chakraborty present a song of Shahbag with the folk music of Baul singers accompanied by visuals of the *gonojagoron moncho* on wheels organizing marches in various villages.[46] Shahbag becomes a symbol of the mediaeval Bengali lyrical poetry of Chandidas and the mystic songs of social

---

[44] Sanchari De, "Context, Image and the Case of the Shahbag Movement," in *The People and the State — Twenty-First Century Protest Movement*, ed. Thomas O'Brien (London: Routledge, 2018), 55.
[45] Imran H. Sarker Official, *"Gonojagoron*/Shahbag Movement Official Theme Song," YouTube, December 18, 2014, https://www.youtube.com/watch?v=7JmyKCs_Wj8.
[46] Sudipto Dohar, "Dohar I Shahbag er Gan" [Dohar | - straight line. Song of Shahbag], YouTube, February 17, 2013, https://www.youtube.com/watch?v=DchyNuBr1bY.

reform of Fakir Lalon Shah, whose poetry nurtured the folk culture of Bangladesh for generations. Beyond organized musical bands are musical gatherings that abound in district *gonojagoron monchos*, whose pictures are uploaded on social media pages by individuals, like the one in Narsingdi.[47]

In opposition to the cultural events of the *gonojagoron moncho* are the mass marches and rallies organized by Hefazat-e Islam (HI), an organization that gained prominence on a national level in the spring of 2013. They brought together the masses through religious teachings and *waz mahfils* (an Arabic term referring to a genre of framed songs and announcements as religious instructions in an assembly for preaching). Organized mostly in rural areas, they gained resurgence during 2013, as a counter to the gatherings at the *gonojagoron moncho* in the city. Max Stille explains the remarkable range:

> As most *waz mahfils* are announced only locally and depend on a multitude of decentralized actors, it is impossible to measure exactly how many are held in Bangladesh. My impression was that during the peak season it is nearly impossible to avoid them. When driving through the country by night bus from Dhaka to Gaibandha in January 2013, I counted no less than six *mahfils* next to the highway. When a student compiled a (non-comprehensive) list of *mahfils* in and around Sylhet town in March 2014 (the end of the season), he listed at least two for every evening, despite the fact that the AL government had already in that year effectively decreased *mahfils* openly organized by the BJI.[48]

Their images and recordings were uploaded on social media in 2013 by individuals at Narsingdi,[49] student organizations at Burunga[50] and media groups at Gazipur.[51] Even *waz mahfils* organized by the Bangladesh Jamaat-i-Islami (BJI), especially those delivered by Delwar Hossain Sayeedi (a person accused of war crimes) at Sylhet in 2009 were circulated as YouTube videos during 2013 and have been viewed over 5.5 million times till date.[52]

---

[47] Mir Lokman Hossain, "Untitled Album," Facebook, December 17, 2013, https://m.facebook.com/photo.php?fbid=238203559688425&id=100004963480280&set=a.238202873021827.

[48] Max Stille, *Islamic Sermons and Public Piety in Bangladesh: The Poetics of Popular Preaching* (London: I.B.Tauris, 2020), 42.

[49] USU Mahmudabad, Narsingdi, Facebook, https://www.facebook.com/groups/167539003324880/permalink/546585332086910/?paipv=0&eav=Afa3q1N1Uo2imkCdHERz66VuMEYfyB4YWCcvCJ6X9B-DcqdVIJ_k8OzRlk0Z0ZgACUUc&_rdr.

[50] Iqbal Ahmed, "Al-Farah Islami Shomaj Kollan Songo," Facebook, March 10, 2013, https://m.facebook.com/photo.php?fbid=317674101688030&id=100003363283122&set=a.299558176832956.

[51] Jatiya Sangbadik Sangstha, "Jatiya Sangbadik — Lion Gani Miah Babul chief guest on Was & Doa mahfil at gazpiur on 22 November-2013," Facebook, November 23, 2013, https://m.facebook.com/photo.php?fbid=235331489959784&id=100004488034216&set=a.235331116626488&source=48.

[52] Saidi Waz, "Bangla Waz by Allama Delwar Hossain Sayeedi Sylhet 2009 day 3 Part 2 bangla waj HD)," YouTube, July 22, 2013, https://www.youtube.com/watch?v=U7hjPPQ5jlU.

Gonojagoron Monchos and the Indigenous Religiosity in Digital Media

"*Shabage Saothal, Garo aar Bangali*" ("Santhals, Garo and Bengalis at Shahbag") in the song "*Shimana Chariye Jak Shahbag*" ("Borders be crossed, Shahbag") by *RaRo* is an instance of lyrics dedicated to the Garo and Santals (indigenous ethnic minorities) residing in Dinajpur, Koikhali, Mymensingh, Netrakona, Gazipur, Sherpur and Tangail. Their participation in the Shahbag demonstrations is a witness to the attempts by the city-based activist elite to give due recognition to the tribal voices of the districts. Muktasree Chakma Sathi writes of indigenous freedom fighters from the Santal, Garo, Chakma, Marma, Tripura, Oraon Chak and other indigenous communities who were martyred in the 1971 Liberation War and were given an inclusive space in the *gonojagoron moncho* at Shahbag. The image of the banner carried by members of these communities on February 20, 2013, is now a digital image archived in Shahbag literature where governmental documents and printed literature on the role of indigenous communities in the 1971 Liberation War are scarce.[53] Media reports and social media updates played a major role and were fueled by the context of Shahbag. Social media posts not only focus on the participation of Indigenous Students Council members at the *Projonmo Chottor* but also on their distinct cultural participation with tribal musical instruments, such as *tamak* and *tumdak* (typical drums of the Santhal people),[54] and identity-specific slogans — "*Tumi ke, ami ke, Garo, Chakma, Bangali*" ("Who are you, who am I, Garo, Chakma, Bangali").[55] Their equanimity with the Bangali is ironic given that they were equated to "razakars" (members of an East Pakistani anti-Bangladesh paramilitary force) by the freedom fighters of 1971 and killed after the Liberation War. Dubbed as informants of the West Pakistan army, they are simultaneously

---

53 Muktasree Chakma Sathi, "The Liberation War and indigenous freedom fighters," Dhaka Tribune, December 15, 2013, https://archive.dhakatribune.com/uncategorized/2013/12/15/the- liberation-war-and-indigenous-freedom-fighters#:~:text=The%20freedom%20fighters%20named%20 were,Michael%20Sujay%20Rema%20of%20Netrokona.
54 Bivuti Bhuson Mahato, "Projonmo Chottor — Shahbag a "Indigenous Students Council" ar member ra (15-02-2013)" [Projonmo Chottor — Indigenous Students Council members at Shahbag], Facebook, February 26, 2013, https://tinyurl.com/3ay6ma22.
55 Muktasree Sathi. Chakma, "Shahbag Slogans: Inclusion of Diversity," Alal O Dulal, February 15, 2013, https://alalodulal.org/2013/02/15/shahbag-5/. Also referred to by: Nasrin Khandoker Sexism in 'Online War': An Analysis of Online Discursive Battle of Shahbag Protest 2013 in Bangladesh," Master's thesis (Central European University, 2014), 26.

deemed as "non-Muslims" by the local communities of socially marginal people like the Mojahirs.[56] The Shahbag movement spoke of their rights at par with the pro-Shahbag protesters[57] and utilized the same tropes of the *gonojagoron moncho* like a human chain, in demanding justice for the kidnapped Kalpana Chakma.[58] The online activism of the *gonojagoron moncho* may have appropriated their demands into the larger narrative of national justice and provided a scope to present their claims to a larger audience. Related social media profiles were created. For instance, the Facebook page of Rangabel[59] was launched on March 18, 2013, and sought to produce and publish works on Chittagong Hill Tracts' culture, society and prosperity and preserve their stories digitally, even via YouTube.[60]

Gonojagoron Monchos and Fiction

Anti-Shahbag protests which penetrated the villages of Bangladesh find a multifaceted voice in the fiction of 2013. Mashiul Alam published a collection of short stories in Bengali entitled *Blogger o Onnanno Golpo* (Blogger and Other Stories). The title story is based both in the city of Dhaka where the narrator Rafique is studying social science and the village of Madhupur from where Rafique hails. News of rallying cries at Shahbag demanding capital punishment for Delawar Hussain Sayeedi reached the village. Having seen Rafique on television, the villagers immediately surmise that he is a blogger, and thereby an atheist. For the people of the village, becoming university-educated in the city leads one to becoming a non-Muslim and almost a Jew. It is such a person who can claim the death penalty for a religious leader like Sayeedi. Remarkably, this religious prejudice is closely allied to digital distortions. Rafique is not an atheist or a blogger. He explains that Sayeedi cannot be a scholar of sacred theology if he has committed adultery and murder, and makes the imam of the local village masjid hear the audio clips as digital proof. What follows thereon shows how digital distortions are rooted in people's psyche and religious stances. It does not matter that such audio clips have circulated all over

---

56 Alexander Claire, Joya Chatterji and Annu Jalais, *The Bengali Diaspora: Rethinking Muslim Migration* (London: Routledge, 2016), 85–86.
57 Munazir Hussain Syed (@Munazir43rd), "When will all Bangladeshis. . ." Twitter, March 18, 2015, https://twitter.com/Munazir43rd/status/578024872078487552
58 Kapaeeng Fdn, "Indigenous Jumma women demanding justice for Kalpana Chakma in an human chain formed on 5 January 2013 at Shahbag, Dhaka," Facebook, January 6, 2013, https://tinyurl.com/wfz75dzv.
59 Rangabel Media, Facebook, https://www.facebook.com/RangabelMedia.
60 Rangabel, YouTube, http://www.youtube.com/Rangabel.

Bangladesh through digital media. Rafique's phone, a lone witness in the village of Madhupur, has to be destroyed. He is assaulted by his brother, one who has now attained the proportion of a religious fanatic. Alam represents religious prejudice and regional parochialism as they encounter digital modes like television screens and mobile phones in such spontaneous mass uprisings.

Even as digital media became central tropes in Shahbag fiction, it also enabled publication, withdrawal and irrevocable mass circulation. A local blog based in Bangladesh called *Jolbhumi* published the controversial story by Hasnat Abdul Hye in its web magazine on April 16, 2013 along with the withdrawal comments by *Prothom Alo*, a premier newspaper in the country and an apology statement by the author himself, both on the same day. This newspaper withdrew the story from its online version within a day. The blog, however, enabled one to encounter the debatable literary fiction and the debates surrounding it. Significantly, the blog uses the word *gonojagoron* in its public statement to explain the reasons for the re-publication of *"TV camerar shamne meyeti"* ("Girl in front of TV cameras") to signify mass awareness regarding the debates of this controversial story. Shahaduzzaman, in *Shahbag 2013*, writes of Hasnat as a literary writer who has sided with the opposing forces of Shahbag and whose revoking of the story could not prevent its circulation through digital media.[61] This story lays bare what the anti-Shahbag protesters understood as "atheism" — manipulation of young educated girls who come from villages like Pabna for education and work but are drawn into the vociferous demands of Shahbag activism. If Alam's story foregrounds religious sectarianism as menacing, Hye's story shows secular liberalism as equally destructive. It was castigated for representing pro-Shahbag protesters as power-hungry and hedonistic. What is significant is the use of media as a trope in a story, which itself generated media debates. In front of the television camera, desiring to become a news anchor, the young female protagonist becomes subject to media afterlives. *Somewhereinblog*, branded by some as blasphemous, published the piece again if only to distance themselves from madrasa-educated Hefazat-e-Islam workers who denounce blogs without understanding about them.[62] From television and cameras to social media and blogs, Shahbag fiction appropriated digital media with religiosity. Whether direct or indirect, clear or confused, the relation between the two led to new understandings among the masses, especially those who hailed from the villages and entered the precincts of the city through Shahbag protest ventures.

---

61 Shahaduzzaman, "Otopor ekti golpo," ("Then a story") in *Shahbag 2013*, ed. Shahaduzzaman (Dhaka: Agamee Prakashani, 2014), 29.
62 Betan, "TV Camerar Shamne Meyeti" [Girl in Front of TV Cameras], Somewhereinblog, April 23, 2013, https://www.somewhereinblog.net/mobile/blog/tanblog/29821758.

Shahbag fiction derived much from digital media debates even as it contributed to many of them. Alam's story represented the controversy of seeing Sayeedi on the moon. This was not just a case of a rumour finding literary representation. The digital media could spread these rumours quickly with added religious distortions. Al-Jāmiʿah Al-Islāmiyyah Patiya Maulana Mufti commented that with the help of modern technologies[63] such things could be created. What he implied was ironically explicated by random members of *Somewhereinblog*. A thread[64] created on March 3, 2013 commented on multiple images "projected" onto the face of the moon ranging from Sayeedi to celebrity model Arif Khan, on photoshop-71[65] as a metaphorical spacecraft to reach the moon, and on young people pacifying their elders by depicting them as being on the moon through photoshop editing. While newspapers reported thousands who came out in support of the release of Sayeedi in the wake of this announcement in the local masjids in the villages of Hatiarpul, Gatiadanga, Khalifa para, etc., such comments also revealed how people reacted with digital distortions. At the level of the grassroots, religious ideas are not only circulated through digital modes, they are spread through digital misconceptions. Alam highlighted the misconception regarding the term "blogger" in his story, which was a trope for similar digital distortions raging in real-time experiences. Such distortions were commonplace in the villages where people knew about the oncoming digital technologies but understood them in terms of their established belief systems.

Gonojagoron Monchos, Parody and Digital Media Interactions

Global digital platforms used district dialects to discuss diurnal activities. During the Liberation War, a radio program *Chorompotro*, based in Chittagong's Kalurghat, aired everyday updates on the struggle and the role of common people, mostly

---

63 "Gojob: Sayeedi Chande" [Rumour: Sayeedi in the Moon], Ittefaq, March 8, 2013, https://archive.ittefaq.com.bd/index.php?ref=MjBfMDNfMDRfMTNfMV8yXzFfMjM1NjI= .
64 Nostochele Tanim, "Proshongo: Sayeedi Saheber Chande Gomon" [In Context: Sir Sayeedi's Passage to the Moon], Somewhereinblog, March 3, 2013, https://m.somewhereinblog.net/mobile/blog/tanimkhan121/29788368.
65 A blogger on *Somewhereinblog* critiques the martyrdom of Delwar Hossain Sayeedi. Sayeedi's followers spread a rumour that his face was seen on the moon and that his enlightened self granted light to the moon. However, the blogger exposes this as the result of photoshop editing. The blogger thus names the metaphorical spacecraft as photoshop-71 creating the term from the words "photoshop" (the popular photo editing software) and "71" (a reference to the Liberation War of 1971).

through parody. In February 2013, when the Shahbag uprising began demanding maximum punishment for war criminals, a UK-based online radio, under the name *"Shadhin Bangla Betar Kendra"* ("Independent Bengal Radio Station") aired patriotic songs, poems and live updates from "Projonmo Chattar."[66] Made by the Facebook group *Shahbag Protibad* with inspiration from the original program, it streamed on SoundCloud in episode form. The Dhakaiya (old Dhaka) dialect, parodying the excessive religiosity of the Jamaat leaders with its hyperbolic assertions, represent the ways of incorporating religion in everyday life. It thus transforms religious references into banal statements of everyday life: "Let the bananas ripen in Munshiganj, it will only enable the making of ropes from the plant fiber for the execution of war criminals" (*Chorompotro 2013* Part 1). Religious tropes are appropriated by the people for their wishes — offering prayers for execution and not just the natural death of the accused. From fake IDs to mobile commodes, *gonojagoron monchos* are witness to variant forms of the online banality on the part of the pro- and the anti-Shahbag factions (Part 3). According to the former, the latter create dubious profiles on the internet. Protesting for days on end, they make mobile commodes out of wooden carts, each of which they name after a "rajakar" (also "razakar" — see definition earlier in this chapter). Otherwise, the sacred stage of the *gonojagoron moncho* would be desecrated with feces of the protesters. These are not merely banal references but practical matters of survival uttered by regional voices, challenging a literature of abstract religiosity which was associated with this pulpit of popular uprising. Slogans sound through the *gonojagoron monchos* and make them vital sites of contestation. Anti-Shahbag factions dub the pro-Shahbag protesters as Awami League cadres because they use *"Joy Bangla"* as their slogan. In *Chorompotro 2013* Part 3, the narrator adds that to use the slogan *"Allah hu Akbar"* ("Allah is the greatest") would make a person a "rajakar" then. Such politically and religiously subversive comments were commonplace among the people, and it is only the digital space where they could be circulated unrestrained, especially in the garb of humor and parody.

Gonojagoron Monchos and Digital Misinformation and Disinformation

Sayeed Al-Zaman writes of interest groups in Bangladesh playing with digital disinformation conjoining religious sentiment. The online activism of the *gonojagoron*

---

[66] "Did You Know?" The Daily Star, March 15, 2013, https://www.thedailystar.net/news/did-you-know-2.

monchos ranges from blasphemous blogs to hitlists posted by the fanatic factions. While Al-Zaman writes of the digital public sphere as a more democratic, common, and effective ground,[67] increasing media control has also resulted in the rise of fake news, like the branding of all free-thinking or secular bloggers as "atheists."[68] Ahmed quotes Hossain (2013) where the latter refers to *gonojagoron moncho* spokesperson Imran H Sarker, who points out that a few days before the murder of Ahmed Rajib Haider (an atheist blogger), a post appeared in a blog named *Shonar Bangla* where he was associated with the *gonojagoron moncho*. Such case studies of intentionally circulated digital disinformation foreground that the *gonojagoron monchos* were not declaredly atheist in their struggle against religious fundamentalism and were forcefully subject to religious divisiveness and centers of atheism. They were rooted in regions, in everyday conflicts, antagonistic factions and wide-ranging posts. This study only traces the trajectory of Bangladesh's lack of a national history based on research-based facts, which persistently constructs affective histories where assumptions become information.[69]

Bibliography

Archived versions of Twitter content were created using the Internet Archive's Way Back Machine and can be found within this bibliography. Archived links for all Facebook content, on the other hand, can be found on Zenodo at DOI: https://doi.org/10.5281/zenodo.8132446.

Ahmed, Iqbal. "Al-Farah Islami Shomaj Kollan Songo," Facebook, March 10, 2013, https://m.facebook.com/photo.php?fbid=317674101688030&id=100003363283122&set=a.299558176832956.

Ahmed, K. Anis. "In Bangladesh: Direct Control of Media Trumps Fake News." *The Journal of Asian Studies* 77, no. 4 (2018): 909–922. DOI: https://doi.org/10.1017/S0021911818002516.

Al-Zaman, Md. Sayeed. "Religious Communication in Digital Public Sphere." *Penelitian* 17, no. 1 (2020): 29–42. DOI: https://doi.org/10.28918/jupe.v17i1.2450.

@bangladeshislamichhatrashibir, Telegram, https://t.me/bangladeshislamichhatrashibir.

Betan, "TV Camerar Shamne Meyeti" [Girl in Front of TV Camera]. Somewhereinblog, 23 Apr 2013. https://www.somewhereinblog.net/mobile/blog/tanblog/29821758.

---

[67] Md. Sayeed Al-Zaman, "Religious Communication in Digital Public Sphere," *Penelitian* 17, no. 1 (2020): 32. DOI: https://doi.org/10.28918/jupe.v17i1.2450.

[68] Anika Hossain, "A Call to Rise." The Daily Star, February 22, 2013, http://archive.thedailystar.net/magazine/2013/02/04/cover.htm. Quoted by K. Anis Ahmed, "In Bangladesh: Direct Control of Media Trumps Fake News," *The Journal of Asian Studies* 77, no. 4 (2018): 911, DOI: https://doi.org/10.1017/S0021911818002516.

[69] Afsan Chowdhury, "Itihasher Sondhane na Sonkhar Sondhane" [In Search of History or Numbers], bdnews, December 4, 2014, https://opinion.bdnews24.com/bangla/archives/22787.

Bulu, Mahamud Hassan. "Gonojagoron moncher prothom janmodiner jessore," Facebook, February 6, 2014, https://m.facebook.com/photo.php?fbid=2131674122186958&id=100005763122580&set=a.159103837625053.

Canada: Immigration and Refugee Board of Canada, "Bangladesh: *Gonojagoron Moncho*, including Origin, Purpose, Structure, Membership, Areas of Operation and Activities (April 2013–January 2014)," RefWorld, January 24, 2014, https://www.refworld.org/docid/542a80df4.html.

Cheong, Pauline Hope. "Religious Datafiction: Platforms, Practices and Power." In *The Routledge Handbook of Religion and Journalism*, edited by Kerstin Radde-Antweiler and Xenia Zeiler, 397–410. London: Routledge, 2021.

Chowdhury, Afsan. "Itihasher Sondhane na Sonkhar Sondhane" [In Search of History or Numbers], bdnews, December 4, 2014, https://opinion.bdnews24.com/bangla/archives/22787.

Chowdhury, Manosh. "Hefazat & Casual Middle Class's Politics-Desire." Alal O Dulal, April 13, 2013, https://alalodulal.org/2013/04/13/middle-class/.

Chowdhury, Nusrat Sabina. "Death, Despair and Democracy in Bangladesh." *Emotions, Mobilisations and South Asian Politics*, edited by Amélie Blom and Stéphanie Tawa Lama-Rewal, 264–280. London: Routledge, 2020.

Chowdhury, Nusrat Sabina. *Paradoxes of the Popular: Crowd Politics in Bangladesh*. Stanford, CA: Stanford University Press, 2019.

Claire, Alexander, Joya Chatterji and Annu Jalais. "Belonging, Status and Religion: Migrants on the 'Peripheries'." In *The Bengali Diaspora: Rethinking Muslim Migration*. London: Routledge, 2016.

Daily Mail Reporter. "'Arrest the atheists who insulted Islam!' Tens of thousands of Muslim activists hold prayers on streets of Bangladesh capital to call for new blasphemy laws against bloggers," Mail Online, March 30, 2013. https://www.dailymail.co.uk/news/article-2301138/Tens-thousands-Islamic-activists-hold-prayers-streets-Bangladesh-capital-new-blasphemy-laws.html?ito=feeds-newsxml&fbclid=IwAR1OQZWf9g9eIrS7OKJttMgpyymgX_1bXSf-cGbELThgYAQYpdKLLk5ESpc.

Davie, Grace. "Vicarious Religion: A Response." *Journal of Contemporary Religion* 25, no. 2 (2010): 261–266. DOI: https://doi.org/10.1080/13537901003750944.

De, Sanchari. "Context, Image and the Case of the Shahbag Movement." In *The People and the State — Twenty-First Century Protest Movement*, edited by Thomas O'Brien, 47–57. London: Routledge, 2018.

"Did You Know?" The Daily Star, March 15, 2013, https://www.thedailystar.net/news/did-you-know-2.

Dohar, Sudipto. "Dohar I Shahbag er Gan" [Dohar I Song of Shahbag] YouTube, February 17, 2013, https://www.youtube.com/watch?v=DchyNuBr1bY.

Fokran, Omar (@omar_forkan_bd). "#11MarShahidDibosh," Twitter, March 11, 2021, https://twitter.com/omar_forkan_bd/status/1369887690578006019. Archived version: https://web.archive.org/web/20230710175324/https://twitter.com/omar_forkan_bd/status/1369887690578006019.

"Gojob: Sayeedi Chande" [Rumour: Sayeedi in the Moon] Ittefaq, March 8, 2013, https://archive.ittefaq.com.bd/index.php?ref=MjBfMDNfMDRfMTNfMV8yXzFfMjM1NjI=.

Gonojagoron Chittagong, "Allama Sayeedi Rajnoitik Protihingshar Shikar" [Allama Sayeedi Victim of Political Vendetta], Facebook, February 14, 2013, https://m.facebook.com/story.php?story_fbid=445790788827034&substory_index=0&id=416935725045874.

Gonojagoron Chittagong, "Shahid Muhammad Kamruzzaman: Phasir Monche dariye ami bijoyer joy gaan gai" [Martyr Muhammad Kamruzzaman: I sing of Victory on the Pulpit of Execution], Facebook, April 11, 2021, https://www.facebook.com/416935725045874/posts/5293962627343135/.

Gonojagoron Companigonj, Facebook, https://www.facebook.com/gonojagoron.companigonj?paipv=0&eav=Afb-uTurh1R8XdPu5V6Pj8aWQCKv-EiTkU-MjrBbBjaWtlOnLiSXntD0HCXi2OwHBBs&_rdr.

Gonojagoron Companigonj, "GONOJAGORON COMPANIGONJ NOAKHALI," Facebook, March 1, 2013, https://tinyurl.com/uznwf4re.

Gonojagoron Companigonj, "n k barta news," Facebook, March 17, 2013, https://tinyurl.com/5n74xeeb.

Gonojagoron mocho, Chittagong, Facebook, https://www.facebook.com/GonojagoronMonchoChittagong.

Gonojagoron mocho, Sylhet, Facebook, https://www.facebook.com/GonojagoronManchoSylhet/?paipv=0&eav=AfaZ6bBoxu0OOpJCsPNIOT3ymAvbcni90QzAfdGVlkj0Sp4i6K8Cxzt-9pFo-xqU9xQ&_rdr.

Gonojagoron moncho (@Gonojagoron_13), Twitter, https://twitter.com/Gonojagoron_13. Archived version: https://web.archive.org/web/20230705080247/https://twitter.com/Gonojagoron_13.

Gonojagoron Moncho (@KhulnaMoncho), Twitter, https://twitter.com/KhulnaMoncho. Archived version: https://web.archive.org/web/20230705080029/https://twitter.com/KhulnaMoncho.

Gonojagoron Monchos Files [Archived Facebook Pages and Images], DOI: https://doi.org/10.5281/zenodo.8132446.

Hossain, Anika. "A Call to Rise." The Daily Star, February 22, 2013, http://archive.thedailystar.net/magazine/2013/02/04/cover.htm.

Imran H. Sarker Official. "*Gonojagoron*/Shahbag Movement Official Theme Song," YouTube, December 18, 2014, https://www.youtube.com/watch?v=7JmyKCs_Wj8.

Islam, Muhammad Nazrul, and Toki Tahmid Inan. "Exploring the Fundamental Factors of Digital Inequality in Bangladesh." *SAGE Open* (April 2021): 1–12. DOI: https://doi.org/10.1177/21582440211021407.

Iqbal, Hossain. "Anti-*gonojagoron moncho* clash 23 02 2013," YouTube, February 25, 2018, https://www.youtube.com/watch?v=VfbzeTRyeJ4.

Jatiya Sangbadik Sangstha, "Jatiya Sangbadik — Lion Gani Miah Babul chief guest on Was & Doa mahfil at gazpiur on 22 November-2013," Facebook, November 23, 2013, https://m.facebook.com/photo.php?fbid=235331489959784&id=100004488034216&set=a.235331116626488&source=48.

Je Tyag Preronar [The Sacrifice for Motivation], Facebook, https://www.facebook.com/profile.php?id=100050602864323.

Khandoker, Nasrin. "Sexism in 'Online War': An Analysis of Online Discursive Battle of Shahbag Protest 2013 in Bangladesh." Master's thesis, Central European University, 2014.

Mahato, Bivuti Bhuson. "Projonmo Chottor — Shahbag a "Indigenous Students Council" ar member ra (15-02-2013)" [Projonmo Chottor — Indigenous Students Council members at Shahbag], Facebook, February 26, 2013, https://tinyurl.com/3ay6ma22.

Mowla, Rafiqul. "In chittagong press club *gonojagoron moncho*. . .," Facebook, February 12, 2013, https://m.facebook.com/photo.php?fbid=10200559261044658&id=1252663362&set=a.1872807020559.

MuktoMona English Blog, https://en.muktomona.com/.

NOA TV Live, "Gonojagoron moncho, noakhali," Facebook, December 17, 2013, https://www.facebook.com/swojon4/photos/a.152987438213481/225648847614006/?type=3&paipv=0&eav=AfbO8Tj0pYqaCq8sK0IovVdRYcIUXtfG6B6VgmumhMDg9vcH8LOEiPuoP-PuoQ5o6-o&_rdr.

Nostochele Tanim. "Proshongo: Sayeedi Saheber Chande Gomon" [In Context: Sir Sayeedi's Passage to the Moon], Somewhereinblog, March 3, 2013, https://m.somewhereinblog.net/mobile/blog/tanimkhan121/29788368.
Pra Janma. "Ganamichil — Chittagong *Gonojagoron* Manch," Facebook, February 23, 2013, https://m.facebook.com/photo.php/?fbid=115742108610927.
Rangabel, YouTube, http://www.youtube.com/Rangabel.
Rangabel Media, Facebook, https://www.facebook.com/RangabelMedia.
Ronit, Tipu Sultan. "*Gonojagoron* mymensingh," Facebook, February 12, 2013, https://m.facebook.com/photo.php?fbid=416180631802611&id=100002320348244&set=a.414444745309533.
Sapan, Ohiduzzaman. "Gonojagoron monch, Baroicha Bus-stand. Belabo, narsingdi," Facebook, February 16, 2016, https://m.facebook.com/photo.php?fbid=1714243438799094&id=1000064036 33805&set=a.1714243425465762.
Sathi, Muktasree Chakma, "Shahbag Slogans: Inclusion of Diversity," Alal O Dulal, February 15, 2013, https://alalodulal.org/2013/02/15/shahbag-5/.
Sathi, Muktasree Chakma. "The Liberation War and indigenous freedom fighters," Dhaka Tribune, December 15, 2013, https://archive.dhakatribune.com/uncategorized/2013/12/15/the-liberation-war-and-indigenous-freedom-fighters#:~:text=The%20freedom%20fighters%20 named%20were,Michael%20Sujay%20Rema%20of%20Netrokona.
Shaffer, Ryan. "Islamist Attacks against Secular Bloggers in Bangladesh." In *Violence in South Asia: Contemporary Perspectives*, edited by Pavan Kumar Malreddy, Anindya Sekhar Purakayastha and Birte Heidemann, 209–223. London: Routledge, 2020.
Shahaduzzaman. "Otopor ekti golpo" [Then a story]. In *Shahbag 2013*, edited by Shahaduzzaman, 29–31. Dhaka: Agamee Prakashani, 2014.
Shariff, Razia. "Collective Agency Capability: How Capabilities Can Emerge in a Social Moment." In *New Frontiers of the Capability Approach*, edited by Flavio Comim, Shailaja Fennell and P. B. Anand, 153–175. Cambridge: Cambridge University Press, 2018.
Shariff, Razia. "Shahbag: A Critical Social Moment: A Collective Agency Capabilities Analysis." Doctoral dissertation, Canterbury Christ Church University, 2019.
Srepur Gonojagoron moncho.org, Facebook, https://www.facebook.com/Srepur-Gonojagoron-mon-cho-org-391512831201492/.
Stille, Max. *Islamic Sermons and Public Piety in Bangladesh: The Poetics of Popular Preaching.* London: I.B.Tauris, 2020.
Storyteller of Life, "Former Vice chancellor of Rajshahi University who is also a freedom fighter came to support us," Facebook, February 13, 2013, https://tinyurl.com/3zvudc3d.
Subramanian, Samanth. "The Hit List: The Islamist war on secular bloggers in Bangladesh," The New Yorker, December 13, 2015, https://www.newyorker.com/magazine/2015/12/21/the-hit-list.
Syed, Munazir Hussain (@Munazir43rd). "When will all Bangladeshis. . ." Twitter, March 18, 2015, https://twitter.com/Munazir43rd/status/578024872078487552 Archived version: https://web.archive.org/web/20230710175648/https://twitter.com/Munazir43rd/status/578024872078487552.
"This Tweet is unavailable," Twitter, https://twitter.com/AshfaqHoque/status/268757025637425152?s=20. Archived version: https://web.archive.org/web/20230705084347/https://twitter.com/AshfaqHoque/status/268757025637425152?s=20.
USU Mahmudabad, Narsingdi, Facebook, https://www.facebook.com/groups/167539003324880/permalink/546585332086910/?paipv=0&eav=Afa3q1N1Uo2imkCdHERz66VuMEYfyB4YWCcvCJ6X9 BDcqdVlJ_k8OzRlk0Z0ZgACUUc&_rdr.

Waz, Saidi. "Bangla Waz by Allama Delwar Hossain Sayeedi Sylhet 2009 day 3 Part 2 bangla waj HD)," YouTube, July 22, 2013, https://www.youtube.com/watch?v=U7hjPPQ5jIU.

Wohab, Abdul. "'Secularism' or 'No-Secularism'? A Complex Case of Bangladesh." *Cogent Social Sciences* 7, no. 1 (2021): 1–21. DOI: https://doi.org/10.1080/23311886.2021.1928979.

Yusuf, Huma. "Islamist rise against Shahbag Bloggers," Facebook, March 30, 2013, https://tinyurl.com/ycytuvcp.

Zmn, Kamruzzaman. "*Gonojagoron moncho,*" Facebook, April 10, 2016, https://m.facebook.com/photo.php?fbid=10208989585355204&id=1183881965&set=a.10203532339127459&source=57.

Paula R. Curtis
On Kami and Avatars: Social Media Literacy and Academics as Public Intellectuals

With digital media at the forefront of our changing academic landscape, the visibility of the work being done by a wide variety of researchers is on the rise. This is, of course, a double-edged sword. The "digital shift," whether speaking of the growth of digital humanities as a discipline or the accelerated demands for online teaching, research, and learning in the face of COVID-19, has brought enhanced exposure to scholars who face systemic inequities related to their identities, institutions, or work. It has generated new enthusiasm for digitizing sources of knowledge and making them more accessible. It has encouraged more of us to connect and start dialogues across long distances. And yet it has also exacerbated the spread of misinformation, encouraged overwork and uncompensated labor to make up for institutions with inadequate infrastructures to cope with these changes, and made many vulnerable to new forms of hate speech, radicalization, and online aggression, sometimes at the cost of careers and mental health.

Most universities and colleges are still stumbling through the process of adapting to the digital shift. Despite dedicated efforts to integrate digital scholarship into their curricula, they struggle to evaluate these new modes of research and engagement in hiring and tenure evaluation processes, let alone grapple with the ramifications of highly visible public dialogues on their institutional failures.[1] Decisions that would have stayed largely behind closed doors and passed through whisper networks, like Nikole Hannah-Jones's tenure denial or decades-long allegations of sexual harassment in Ivy League universities now garner attention from *The New York Times* and spark public outrage.[2] In addition, educational institutions must contend with more and more departments, libraries, area centers, instructors, and students creating social media profiles as a primary means of helping their

---

[1] On the subject of evaluating digital scholarship, see Grunow, "'Making it Count'," which helpfully summarizes some organizational responses to the digital shift. Tristan R. Grunow, "'Making it Count': The Case for Digital Scholarship in Asian Studies," #AsiaNow, June 9, 2020, https://www.asianstudies.org/making-it-count-the-case-for-digital-scholarship-in-asian-studies.
[2] See: Katie Robertson, "Nikole Hannah-Jones Denied Tenure at University of North Carolina," The New York Times, May 19, 2021, https://www.nytimes.com/2021/05/19/business/media/nikole-hannah-jones-unc.html and James S. Bikales, "Protected by Decades-Old Power Structures, Three Renowned Harvard Anthropologists Face Allegations of Sexual Harassment," The Harvard Crimson, May 29, 2020, https://www.thecrimson.com/article/2020/5/29/harvard-anthropology-gender-issues.

https://doi.org/10.1515/9783110747607-012

intellectual endeavors reach the public, which increases the possibility that they may become targets of mobilized harassment campaigns.

A significant part of bringing academic labor and research to the public has been achieved through scholars writing op-eds, running departmental or institutional social media accounts, and translating both analog and digital research into easily shared formats for broad circulation. As a result, we have also seen more engagement in ever-intensifying debates that previously happened in highly localized settings, whether heated disagreements over the installation of comfort women statues that acknowledge the wartime atrocities of the Japanese empire, textbook wars over the causes of the Civil War, or any number of other controversial histories that become political and cultural flashpoints with public exposure.[3] These battles have been going on for decades, but have found new life on social media, where many feel invigorated by the power of online communities and the security of anonymity. Now that these discussions are happening beyond the printed page, scholars, too, often find themselves sending their work out in the world, gaining greater buzz and recognition than they might have received in conventional academic publications, only to face internet backlash that they and their institutions are not prepared to handle.[4] What, then, are the professional and personal stakes of being a public intellectual? How do we continue to engage?

This chapter will discuss a series of online exchanges between scholars of East Asian religion, history, and culture and an anonymous Twitter (known as "X" since mid-2023) espousing ethnonational and discriminatory positions. This event, which took place over several days in July 2021, serves as an instructive case study of both the possibilities and perils of public engagement on social media. These interactions bring into relief the methods that online antagonizers use to promote extremist, racist, and anti-intellectual agendas, as well as the connections between seemingly disparate communities of harassers across many political and popular realms. Familiarizing ourselves and learning to cope with such actors in online spaces is an increasingly crucial form of knowledge that, now more than ever, academics and their employers cannot afford to ignore.

---

3 For example, Andrea Pető discusses the anti-gender studies movements in Hungary and death threats she received via Academia.edu in response to an article she wrote on the history of abortion regulation. Andrea Pető, "Academic Freedom and Gender Studies: An Alliance Forged in Fire," *Gender and Sexuality: Journal of the Center of Gender Studies* (2020): 9–24.

4 See: Abby L. Ferber, "Are You Willing to Die for This Work?" Public Targeted Online Harassment in Higher Education: SWS Presidential Address. *Gender & Society* 32, no. 3 (2018): 301–320.

Public Engagement: Addressing Religiocultural Essentialism in the Twitterverse

Academics use social media in diverse ways. Some primarily post personal photos and experiences, some stick to scholarly topics, and others strike a balance somewhere in between. Many take refuge in and network through global communities via hashtags, whether broad topics (such as #academictwitter or #PhDChat) or more specialized fields (such as #medievaltwitter or #librarytwitter). Those who choose to produce academic content often see the benefit of reaching a wider, public audience, not simply for purposes of self-promotion but to demonstrate the relevance of their research to the everyday world. With more and more information, misinformation, and disinformation circulating through social media channels, applications like Twitter can be an invaluable tool to address questionable information or historical inaccuracies spread intentionally or unintentionally by popular news outlets or other online venues. Although platforms like Facebook and Instagram are also often used by academics and academic institutions, Twitter functions distinctly as a space in which information disseminates rapidly; users' goals are typically to make their content and profile as visible and readily shared as possible. Although the future of Twitter and free speech on the platform has been in limbo since Elon Musk's takeover in late 2022, it remains a digital venue through which academic specialists can communicate their knowledge to the public with ease.[5] It was with these advantages in mind that in the summer of 2021 the scholars featured in this case study set out to present an accessible analysis of recent events and their connections to Religious Studies on Twitter.

On July 8, 2021, with the delayed 2020 Olympics in Tokyo on the horizon, Jolyon Thomas (Associate Professor, Department of Religious Studies, University of Pennsylvania), wrote a thread of thirty-nine tweets that addressed essentialism, nationhood, and their connection to Japan as seen through representations of religion, particularly tourism advertisements in anticipation of the games.[6] Thomas included the hashtag #SmartInPublic and tagged the Twitter account for *Sacred Writes*, a 5-year project funded by the Henry Luce Foundation to promote public-facing scholarship on religion, which would allow his thread to be indexed and

---

[5] Adam Serwer, "Elon Musk's Free-Speech Charade Is Over," The Atlantic, April 12, 2023, https://www.theatlantic.com/ideas/archive/2023/04/elon-musk-twitter-free-speech-matt-taibbi-substack/673698.
[6] Jolyon Thomas (@jolyonbt), "The Tokyo Olympics," Twitter, July 8, 2021, 12:32 p.m., https://twitter.com/jolyonbt/status/1413219538997587980. For the sake of clarity and ease of access, hotlinks to the original tweets cited are provided in footnotes. To preserve any content that may be deleted at a later date, archived links to all tweets are available as an appendix.

easily discoverable.⁷ In his thread, Thomas thoroughly explored the Japanese government's eagerness to promote "real Japan" and "traditional culture" for foreign visitors as intimately linked to Buddhist pilgrimage, Shinto shrines and festivals, and performance arts that have histories of spiritual practice. These consciously created images, he argued, target Western audiences by "[providing] a sanitized version [of "Japanese culture"] that appeals to Orientalist fantasy and nationalist pride alike."⁸

This tweet caught the attention of another Twitter user, whose handle (username) is @Indologyteacher, with their name listed at the time as "Professor of Buddhology." Their biographical description claimed they were a tenured professor. This user responded with a string of banal and unsubstantiated statements: that Buddhism was taken "even more seriously" than Shinto, that Kyoto has more temples than shrines, that Buddhism represents Japan's soft power as a major world religion, and that Shinto traditions represent Japan far better than churches or mosques.⁹ The tweet received no engagement.

When Bryan D. Lowe (Assistant Professor, Department of Religion, Princeton University), retweeted Thomas's thread with a statement of praise, @Indologyteacher re-appeared within the hour, replying:

> It is essential for Japan to promote its rich Buddhist and Shinto culture and heritage as well as its kimonos and ethnic traditions. We do not want the entire world to be all about McDonalds and the Kardashians. America has no culture, Japan must strongly preserve her uniqueness.¹⁰

This commentary raised further problematic assumptions, notably the very essentialism and advertisement that both Thomas and Lowe warned against, with the user urging the promotion of a monolithic religious "heritage" while reducing Japan's culture to the popular image of kimono and framing these as symbols of

---

7 A prime example of efforts to generate accessible public-facing scholarship, the stated goals of *Sacred Writes* according to their "About" page are: "[providing] support, resources, and networks for scholars of religion committed to translating the significance of their research to a broader audience. Over the life of the project (2018–2022), we will host trainings for scholars, create and fund partnerships between scholars and media outlets, and convene meetings to discuss best practices for public scholarship." "About." Sacred Writes: Public Scholarship on Religion, https://www.sacred-writes.org/about.
8 Thomas, "But just as the videographers," July 8, 2021, 12:54 p.m., https://twitter.com/jolyonbt/status/1413224941353308160.
9 @Indologyteacher, "In Japan Buddhism," Twitter, July 8, 2021, 2:07 p.m., https://twitter.com/Indologyteacher/status/1413243345804070913.
10 Bryan D. Lowe (@bryandaniellowe), "The always brilliant," Twitter, July 8, 2021, 1:04 p.m., https://twitter.com/bryandaniellowe/status/1413227481067360263; @Indologyteacher, "It is essential for Japan," July 8, 2021, 2:25 p.m., https://twitter.com/Indologyteacher/status/1413247831952052228.

"Japaneseness" as "ethnic traditions." @Indologyteacher juxtaposes Japan's supposedly timeless and time-honored culture with that of the United States' popular culture, thereby situating Japan as a nation under threat by evils of the Western, modern world. Japan becomes both feminized (seen as in need of protection and falling into long-held nationalist dialogues on Japanese culture, language, and their origins) and hailed as "unique" in keeping with essentialist *Nihonjinron* ("theories of the Japanese") tropes of Japanese exceptionalism.[11] The above tweet was also ignored. However, it showed that @Indologyteacher was now following the posts of these scholars with interest, and that they hoped to advance their own questionable ideas of what was and was not "Japanese."

Taking Thomas's original post as inspiration, four days later, on July 12, Lowe wrote an extensive thread on the relationship between representations of Shinto as Japan's "indigenous" religion and cultural essentialism, citing primary sources and secondary scholarship on art objects.[12] @Indologyteacher did not appear. One day later, Lowe praised a recent article by Wai-ming Ng, "The Shintoization of Mazu in Tokugawa Japan," reflecting on how the Chinese god Mazu became worshipped as a Shinto deity and stating that it demonstrated how Shinto was in fact transnational. @Indologyteacher surfaced again to argue that such examples were an exception, and the "the MAJOR deities such as Amaterasu et all [sic] are distinctively Japanese," (emphasis theirs) thus reiterating an essentialist stance.[13]

This exchange prompted Lowe to write yet another thread in response, addressing how we might interpret Amaterasu, the sun goddess of Japanese mythology from whom the emperor is said to have descended, through a lens beyond modern national borders. He used the term "transnational" to refer to these interregional and intercultural connections. Lowe referred to work by Michael Como on the importation of continental deities and concepts, medieval syncretic interpretations of kami through Buddhism, and several other examples of engagement with and the development of Amaterasu imagery through extra-archipelagic interaction, citing

---

11 On the connection between the development of Japanese language, culture, and the feminine as "national," see Tomiko Yoda, "Literary History against the National Frame, or Gender and the Emergence of Heian Kana Writing," *positions: east asia cultures critique* 8, no. 2 (Fall 2000): 465–497. On *Nihonjinron*, see: Tessa Morris-Suzuki, *Re-inventing Japan: Time, Space, Nation* (Armonk, NY: M. E. Sharpe, 1998) Chapters 7 and 8 and Oguma Eiji, *A Genealogy of 'Japanese' Self-images* (Melbourne: Trans Pacific Press, 2002) are particularly useful.
12 Lowe, "Last week, @jolyonbt wrote," July 12, 2021, 4:52 a.m., https://twitter.com/bryandaniellowe/status/1414553281049808897.
13 Lowe, "Catching up on recent issues," July 13, 2021, 6:57 p.m., https://twitter.com/bryandaniellowe/status/1415128243687075842; Wai-ming Ng, "The Shintoization of Mazu in Tokugawa Japan," *Japanese Journal of Religious Studies* 47, no. 2 (2020): 225–246; @Indologyteacher, "Technically, some Kami," July 14, 2021, 12:19 a.m., https://twitter.com/Indologyteacher/status/1415209202323234816.

the most recent scholarship on the subject.[14] Within an hour, @Indologyteacher responded with a series of arguments that offered whataboutist and oversimplified logical fallacies "that one could question the 'uniqueness' of any religion" by focusing on mythology, and that the dispute over Amaterasu's transnational characterization could be solved by simply asking which country has the most shrines dedicated to Amaterasu.[15] @Indologyteacher continued to reply with what then turned to tangents on academics risking making their work irrelevant, at which point Lowe politely disengaged, stating that he would let readers decide which was more compelling: "the evidence [he] presented or the argument that Japan has lots of shrines."[16] @Indologyteacher reiterated their "Shinto is distinctly Japanese" argument and suggested that Lowe spoke only within an echo chamber. After the exchange with Bryan Lowe, others, such as Hiromu Nagahara (Associate Professor, Department of History, Massachusetts Institute of Technology), replied in Lowe's defense, calling out @Indologyteacher for anachronistic and reductive claims, which resulted in further pushback and a repetition of the "echo chamber" accusation.[17] This turn marks a style of engagement commonly used in online spaces to undermine and attack legitimate argumentation.

Many of the scholars who witnessed or were involved in these interactions wondered who this @Indologyteacher was and why they were so invested in promoting these distorted, nationalist views, particularly if they were, in fact, the professor they claimed to be. Some took a deeper dive into @Indologyteacher's other tweets before July 2021 and found a disturbing trove of hateful interactions. Even a brief review of prior posts showed that the profile was seemingly created for the express purpose of heckling accounts that promoted Buddhism- and Hinduism-related information and events.

Specifically, @Indologyteacher had spent months promoting anti-Indian and anti-Hindu content, stating that Hindus "have no civilization," having "stolen" any redeeming aspects of Hinduism from Buddhism and that "No genocide in history compares in magnitude and scale to what Hindus did to Buddhists in India — fully erasing their civilization and stealing their temples. The Hindu persecution of

---

14 Lowe, "Of course an exception," July 14, 2021, 4:53 a.m., https://twitter.com/bryandaniellowe/status/1415278246934061057.
15 @Indologyteacher, "Thx for your response," July 14, 2021, 7:53 a.m., https://twitter.com/Indologyteacher/status/1415323549196226564; "I appreciate your research," July 14, 2021, 7:57 a.m., https://twitter.com/Indologyteacher/status/1415324491559931908.
16 Lowe, "Thank you for taking the time," July 14, 2021, 9:01 a.m., https://twitter.com/bryandaniellowe/status/1415340618583351301.
17 Hiromu Nagahara (@HiromuNagahara), "Um, you started out," Twitter, July 14, 2021, 9:11 a.m., https://twitter.com/HiromuNagahara/status/1415343114039005186.

Buddhists is worst genocide in history."[18] Even the header image on their account profile at the time was a roughly-sketched picture of the Buddha decapitated by one of the most widely worshipped Hindu deities, Ganesh. Although @Indologyteacher appeared to perhaps have some form of specialist knowledge in Asian religions, citing specific deities and practices in their arguments, the claims themselves were largely ahistorical and motivated by the desire to proclaim all of India a "land of filth and beggars" in the absence of Buddhism.[19] Scholars of Asian Studies were baffled by the content, and with many of them having recently come under fire by ultranationalist Twitter communities denying Japan's wartime atrocities, they stayed vigilant as the @Indologyteacher account continued to engage.[20]

The "Professor of Buddhology": Crafting a Specialist Identity

Anonymity online has both given voice to those otherwise unable to address inequities and enabled untold numbers of less altruistic individuals to air their most sordid and repugnant thoughts. Just as often as good-faith actors cross social media feeds, we find bots, nameless trolls, and fake accounts engaging in malicious behavior. In recent years, social media has also been at the forefront of public reckonings for dubious identities offline and online, such as Rachel A. Dolezal or Jessica A. Krug falsely claiming Black heritage, Thomas A. Macmaster pretending to be a Syrian-American lesbian kidnapped in Damascus, or BethAnn McLaughlin posing as a fictitious bisexual indigenous STEM researcher who died of COVID-19.[21] In the

---

18 @Indologyteacher, "You've never been to university," June 19, 2021, 9:59 a.m., https://twitter.com/Indologyteacher/status/1406295553361723396; "No genocide in history compares," July 4, 2021, 4:46 a.m., https://twitter.com/Indologyteacher/status/1411652623426637825.
19 @Indologyteacher, "Laughable nonsense," June 20, 2021, 4:26 a.m., https://twitter.com/Indologyteacher/status/1406574210575699968.
20 Many scholars of Asian Studies experienced online harassment as of early 2021 for criticisms of J. Mark Ramseyer's historically inaccurate publications on "comfort women" during World War II. This harassment is summarized in multiple public-facing articles, including Paula R. Curtis, "Taking the Fight for Japan's History Online: The Ramseyer Controversy and Social Media," *The Asia-Pacific Journal: Japan Focus* 19, no. 22 (December 1, 2021), https://apjjf.org/2021/22/Curtis.html and Chelsea Szendi Schieder, "The History the Japanese Government Is Trying to Erase," *The Nation*, May 26, 2021, https://www.thenation.com/article/world/ramseyer-comfort-women-japan-nationalism.
21 Michael Levenson and Jennifer Schuessler, "University Investigates Claim That White Professor Pretended to Be Black," *The New York Times*, September 3, 2020, https://www.nytimes.com/2020/09/03/us/jessica-krug-gwu-race.html; Jessica A. Krug, "The Truth, and the Anti-Black Violence of My Lies,"

case of @Indologyteacher, the scholars embroiled in these exchanges took careful note of the user's conscious efforts to create a persona that would seem, on its surface, authoritative in the academic realm.

Fig. 1: The stock illustration used for @Indologyteacher's profile picture (avatar), originally from Shutterstock and now featured in other online image libraries. iStock license no. 5759950. (From Morris and Van Lit).

When replied to or messaged by a Twitter user, one of the first things one sees is their avatar—the circular user image that accompanies all their messages. The picture chosen by @Indologyteacher is a stock illustration of a white woman with a short blonde bob wearing glasses, originally a Shutterstock image entitled

Medium, September 3, 2020, https://medium.com/@jessakrug/the-truth-and-the-anti-black-violence-of-my-lies-9a9621401f85; Helen Lewis, "The Identity Hoaxers," The Atlantic, March 16, 2021, https://www.theatlantic.com/international/archive/2021/03/krug-carrillo-dolezal-social-munchausen-syndrome/618289; Kevin Young, "How to Hoax Yourself: The Case of A Gay Girl in Damascus," The New Yorker, November 9, 2017, https://www.newyorker.com/books/page-turner/how-to-hoax-yourself-gay-girl-in-damascus; Melissa Bell and Elizabeth Flock, "'A Gay Girl in Damascus' Comes Clean," The Washington Post, June 12, 2011, https://www.washingtonpost.com/lifestyle/style/a-gay-girl-in-damascus-comes-clean/2011/06/12/AgkyH0RH_story.html; Jonah E. Bromwich and Ezra Marcus, "The Anonymous Professor Who Wasn't," The New York Times, August 4, 2020, https://www.nytimes.com/2020/08/04/style/college-coronavirus-hoax.html.

"Young blonde woman in black shirt writing on a document." (Fig. 1).[22] On Twitter, the image was cut off at the neck to avoid the watermark and highlight the face. @Indologyteacher's short profile biography read "Tenured Professor. Here to debate colonialism, groupthink & echo chambers in academia. Anonymity helps me tell it like it is, sans sugarcoating facts. She/Her."

Both the image and the bio consciously signal particular and overlapping claims to academic identity and authority; first, academic credentials as a tenured professor and, by virtue of that designation, an expert on the topic of "Buddhology," (so stated in the "Professor of Buddhology" title); second, a female gender identity, thereby better granting them, as we shall see below, the latitude to participate in academic cultures of critique on sexism, racism, colonialism, and more; and a racial identity as white, thereby enhancing one's perceived positionality to "call out" others for seemingly inappropriate statements on race and ethnicity by modeling self-deprecating allyship. Note the strategic mention of colonialism, as well as the circular justification that being anonymous (as with the username, title, and profile image) allows @Indologyteacher to speak freely. These statements attempt to preempt any criticism of their academic qualifications, written statements, and refusal to name themselves. All these self-identified markers came into play as @Indologyteacher's campaign against scholars who rejected their essentialist views devolved and their academic mask of expertise began to slip.

Mediaspeak Devolutions and the Co-opting of "Woke" Language

As scholars and educators, we are trained to evaluate arguments and language in relation to their authors, subjects, and sociocultural contexts. Twitter, like academic articles or conferences, has its own communities and ecosystems that inform how users respond to one another. As exchanges with @Indologyteacher continued over several days, those who interacted with them were increasingly convinced of their initial evaluations that this user was likely not who they made themselves out to be but was rather an internet provocateur with an axe to grind because of their own anti-Hindu and, more broadly, anti-academic biases. The more heated interactions

---

22 The image "Young blonde woman in black shirt writing on a document" has since been removed from Shutterstock, but is available through other stock image services. The image was purchased for use in this chapter from iStock under the title "Serious woman in glasses stock illustration," https://www.istockphoto.com/vector/serious-woman-in-glasses-gm493740084-77064275. The license holder is De Gruyter.

became, the more indicators emerged that @Indologyteacher fit into popular internet cultures of intolerance and extremism, attempting to gain credibility by masquerading as a white female academic.[23] These signs, complex and interrelated, are broken down into broad categories below.

Over-Insistence on One's Credentials

The anonymity of @Indologyteacher's digital presence presented them with both an advantage, in that they could make as many heinous remarks as they pleased without real-life consequences, and a disadvantage, in that having their statements taken seriously required that their online identity be recognized as legitimate. Their apparent insecurity in this regard, underscored by overblown attempts at credentialism, further suggested the improbability of their assertions and that their comments were merely ill-informed attempts at provocation.

Throughout the exchanges, largely with scholars of East Asia, @Indologyteacher repeatedly attempted to garner validity to their claims by insisting upon their academic status as an authority in Religious Studies of Asia and a tenured professor. In the case of the former, @Indologyteacher attempted to push back against Lowe's transnational Amaterasu tweets by insisting they had translated Buddhist texts from Sanskrit and visited temples, with no Amaterasu to be found.[24] As with @Indologyteacher's previous tweets, this was a willful disengagement from the actual arguments at hand about syncretic practice and transregional exchange in the premodern world. In less specific attempts, @Indologyteacher simply blustered in response to other tweets, "No one can match my knowledge on Asian religions and cultures."[25]

A glimpse at previous tweets before the transnational Amaterasu incident reveals that @Indologyteacher frequently leaned on this authority they hoped to project when harassing other accounts (with an insistence that had the opposite effect), purporting they are an "actual professor" in contrast to others: "I am an actual professor of Indology, you surely are not."[26] Other obvious attempts at

---

23 Joel Stein, "How Trolls Are Ruining the Internet," Time, August 18, 2016, https://time.com/4457110/internet-trolls.
24 @Indologyteacher, "Similarly the sources you cited," July 14, 2021, 5:24 p.m., https://twitter.com/Indologyteacher/status/1415467283577720840.
25 @Indologyteacher, "You are showing how evil," July 19, 2021, 12:32 a.m., https://twitter.com/Indologyteacher/status/1417024609170468866.
26 @Indologyteacher, "I am an actual professor," July 17, 2021, 5:34 a.m., https://twitter.com/Indologyteacher/status/1415288504393867264; "I am an actual Professor," August 18, 2021, 9:18 p.m., https://twitter.com/Indologyteacher/status/1428209761477070849.

credentialing themselves when offensive statements were challenged relied on suggesting their degrees from or connections to elite universities. Disparaging the qualifications of others, they stated that a given opponent "[was] not a professor but a lowly graduate from a 3rd class university that is not even ranked," while adding "My peers at Oxford, Harvard and Yale agree with me."[27]

In the context of disputes with scholars who are, in fact, employed by well-known research institutions, @Indologyteacher felt the need to compensate, becoming fixated on their claim to be a tenured professor of some renown (albeit one still unwilling to identify themselves). Yet, the longer @Indologyteacher was challenged, the more desperate their attempts to show academic superiority became, devolving into ad hominem attacks that also revealed a fundamental ignorance of the academic system.

They began by challenging criticisms of anonymity by stating that others would surely "know who [they] are or at least have heard of [them]," thus trying to reinforce the constructed tenured professor and specialist image seen on their profile. At the outset of engagements with the account, which was originally focused on anti-Hindu and pro-Buddhist content, their descriptive title (where normally one's name would appear) was given as "Professor of Buddhology." Over the several days @Indologyteacher interacted with Asian Studies scholars, they changed this title to "Professor (Tenured, Debater)," presumably to validate their academic status and desire to maintain anonymity in the name of debate. This was followed by "Professor (Tenured, not assistant)," an intentional insult in line with their attempts to undermine (verified) professors who contested their misinformation, and, finally, "Professor (Asian Studies)," ostensibly an endeavor to make more broad-reaching claims to expertise beyond Buddhist Studies.

@Indologyteacher later added paternalistic claims that they were being bullied for their superior intelligence and gender, attempting to enhance the grounds of their arguments based on academic status: "I was simply educating & correcting my juniors is because they hate the fact, that while I am a Tenured professor despite being a female, these aging White men still are assistants."[28] Notably, Hiromu

---

27 @Indologyteacher, "Yes, but who will I debate?" July 4, 2021, 11:11 p.m., https://twitter.com/Indologyteacher/status/1411930629881610241.
28 It is also worth highlighting that @Indologyteacher frequently drew attention to their purported gender to assert their positionality and ability to "defeat" others by being superior in spite of perceived affronts, using phrases like "despite being a female" or "despite being a woman," which, arguably, read as poor, awkward, and unnecessary attempts to assert one's gender identity as a part of their credentials. @Indologyteacher, "Further, the reason why," July 17, 2021, 8:04 p.m., https://twitter.com/Indologyteacher/status/1416594581160964097; "You started it," July 16, 2021, 9:27 a.m., https://twitter.com/Indologyteacher/status/1416071897721212928.

Nagahara (Associate Professor of History, MIT), also involved in the exchange, is neither an assistant professor nor a white man. These insults devolved even further into aspersions that researchers who had vocally objected to @Indologyteacher's statements were "bottom-tier, lifetime assistants jealous of tenured professors," with each subsequent attack growing more ugly and personal.

The user then began to lash out against the job status of more junior scholars, focusing their attention on me for pressuring them to reveal their identity.[29] When I responded to @Indologyteacher that the scholars they argued with would be happy to read an evidenced refutation—with their name on it—that proved their racist and essentialist accusations, they shifted their focus to my lack of a tenure track position, replying, "You surely will as I hear you have a lot of extra time on your hands. More than any of us and that's very telling. I won't go into your job status here (at least you have the cajones [sic] to engage [. . .])."[30] Despite clearly indicating in my response that I was not unemployed, but about to begin a second competitive position as a postdoctoral researcher and lecturer at a large research institution, @Indologyteacher focused in on their (perhaps willful) ignorance of this fact, referring to me in subsequent threads as "an *unemployed* troll" (emphasis theirs) and "unemployed nobody," further attempting to leverage their own fantastical identity as a prestigious tenured professor.[31] No doubt there are those in academia and beyond who hold their juniors in such contempt and are convinced of their own importance, whether they choose to publicly air those ill-informed beliefs or not; however, in the case of @Indologyteacher, comments like "Paula Curtis [. . .] won't even get past the intern level!" which suggest a basic lack of knowledge about academic employment (one does not in any typical circumstance pass through an "intern" stage to become a professor in the humanities).[32] Assuming @Indologyteacher did actually understand that postdoctoral positions are a form of employment and was simply going out of their way to misbehave by denying reality, this act in and of itself is grossly childish behavior hardly fitting for the prestigious role to which they so ardently clung. Similar personal attacks were flung at other respondents, suggesting they were too ignorant or poor to be @Indologyteacher's

---

29 @Indologyteacher, "You certainly know who I am," July 14, 2021, 5:27 p.m., https://twitter.com/Indologyteacher/status/1415468070408175617, "You're panicking now," July 18, 2021, 11:20 p.m., https://twitter.com/Indologyteacher/status/1417006411452715008.
30 @Indologyteacher, "You surely will," July 15, 2021, 1:27 p.m., https://twitter.com/Indologyteacher/status/1415770054336172033.
31 @Indologyteacher, "So you are relying on your status," July 25, 2021, 10:24 p.m., https://twitter.com/Indologyteacher/status/1419528977253867522; "I've never seen anyone so needy," July 16, 2021, 5:07 p.m., https://twitter.com/Indologyteacher/status/1416187763444133888.
32 @Indologyteacher, "Not lemons but lemmings," July 16, 2021, 11:02 p.m., https://twitter.com/Indologyteacher/status/1416277011627188226.

students, insulting their language abilities as non-native speakers, or simply calling them "losers." The guise of professionalism was long gone.[33]

It goes without saying that the more one insists upon their credentials and competence as a matter of course instead of a matter of demonstrated expertise, sound reason, and collegial engagement, the more likely it is that their stated qualifications are but a feat of ego, deception, and insecurity.

Engagement in Mediaspeak Common to Anti-Intellectual Punditry

Throughout these exchanges with @Indologyteacher, they used a variety of hyperbolic rhetoric that in recent years has become associated with news media punditry and social media communities, particularly those engaging in anti-intellectual and inflammatory content intended to provoke extreme responses. Much of this language is used to fashion artificial mentalities of "us" versus "them," creating the spectre of threatening enemies and dangers that must be combatted while suggesting the validity of otherwise unsound arguments.

One technique @Indologyteacher embraced is an appeal to facticity. This premise is first and foremost established in their Twitter biography, which states that their "anonymity helps [them] tell it like it is, sans sugarcoating facts."[34] When challenged on their ignorance of academia, @Indologyteacher repeated this line, stating that "here I just get to say what many of us think, but can't openly enunciate due to professional ramifications. Here I can tell it like it is."[35] Though promises to "tell it like it is" originate in Black popular and activist culture going back decades, more recently the phrase has been used by conservative politicians such as Chris Christie and Donald Trump in response to critiques of their political positions and grandiose suggestions that they alone speak the truth in a world of "fake news."[36] This polarizing effect is similarly utilized in political punditry that invokes war metaphors to suggest an "us/them" dichotomy, a tactic that manifests a sense of urgency

---

33 @Indologyteacher, "I'll let this one pass," July 15, 2021, 5:51 p.m., https://twitter.com/Indologyteacher/status/1415836559723704322; "Good riddance," July 15, 2021, 9:29 p.m., https://twitter.com/Indologyteacher/status/1415891422767632384.
34 @Indologyteacher, https://twitter.com/Indologyteacher.
35 @Indologyteacher, "Nah – here I just get to say," July 15, 2021, 9:35 p.m., https://twitter.com/Indologyteacher/status/1415892833924419585.
36 Geoff Nunberg, "Tracing The Origin Of The Campaign Promise To 'Tell It Like It Is'," NPR, July 15, 2015, https://www.npr.org/2015/07/15/423194262/tracing-the-origin-of-the-campaign-promise-to-tell-it-like-it-is.

and emotional investment to the matter at hand; in the case of @Indologyteacher, they justified their activities by asserting there was a "racist war on Amaterasu."[37]

In a similar vein, @Indologyteacher leaned heavily on "debate me" culture, another outgrowth of conservative media punditry and extremist online communities, particularly among men. Donna Zuckerberg, a specialist in the use of literary classics by the alt-right, notes that demands for debate "are about scoring points and subjugating your opponent. Which means that, no matter what their opponents say, debaters have every reason to spin a confrontation as a victory."[38] @Indologyteacher frequently demanded that they be debated or asserted their prowess as a master of argument, accusing other researchers of being "lemmings" trapped in the "groupthink" and "echo chambers" of academia, in itself another sign of anti-intellectual leanings.[39] "Why are some academics such cowards," they lamented, "that when faced with a champion debater, they just block & run for the hills in disgrace? Shows they can't survive beyond fawning students, back-scratching peers, lazy groupthink & constrained echo-chambers. If you know your stuff, debate me!"[40] Yet, they themselves had little to offer in the way of "debate" on Amaterasu's transnational nature, other than denying it, and merely repeated statements ad nauseum like "debate is my forte" and that they had "eclipsed [their opponents] in debate," though there was no substantial argumentation to be found.[41]

At its core, this "debate me" mentality is a Catch-22. If the target accepts demands for the encounter, they tacitly acknowledge that the argument at hand is valid in the first place. If the target refuses to engage in a "debate" with a faulty premise, they are deemed cowardly or incapable. In the political sphere, this tactic is often seen among conservative talking heads who speak on controversial issues,

---

[37] @Indologyteacher, "The racist war on Amaterasu," July 17, 2021, 7:59 p.m., https://twitter.com/Indologyteacher/status/1416593529254596608; See Stephen J. Flusberg, Teenie Matlock, and Paul H. Thibodeau, "War metaphors in public discourse," *Metaphor and Symbol* 33, no. 1 (2018): 1–18 (especially page 4).

[38] Donna Zuckerberg, "The problems with online 'debate me' culture: If you make an argument online, get ready for someone to throw down a gauntlet," The Washington Post, August 29, 2019, https://www.washingtonpost.com/outlook/whats-wrong-with-online-debate-me-culture/2019/08/29/c0ec8aa2-c9ca-11e9-8067-196d9f17af68_story.html.

[39] @Indologyteacher, "Right! A whole clique," July 15, 2021, 3:38 p.m., https://twitter.com/Indologyteacher/status/1415803022379204610; "You just can't imagine," July 15, 2021, 10:09 a.m., https://twitter.com/Indologyteacher/status/1415720185055612938; https://twitter.com/Indologyteacher/status/1416277011627188226.

[40] @Indologyteacher, "Why are some academics such cowards," July 15, 2021, 3:48 p.m., https://twitter.com/Indologyteacher/status/1415805508515139587.

[41] @Indologyteacher, "Yes, please tell all your friends," July 20, 2021, 9:15 a.m., https://twitter.com/Indologyteacher/status/1417518463791345666.

such as demanding that liberal politicians publicly express support for terminating ectopic pregnancies as damning evidence against pro-life stances, even though such pregnancies are not viable and the reimplantation many pro-life advocates call for is not scientifically possible.[42] Insisting on debates over a fundamentally flawed premise is a rhetorical tactic intended to ensnare an opponent in a no-win situation. It was abundantly clear that @Indologyteacher made these demands merely as a tool for empty bravado; in the course of these ongoing disagreements, they even changed the header of their profile to a vector graphic of two people pointing at one another with the phrase "DEBATE!" displayed between them.

The Co-Opting of Perceived "Wokeness"

The co-opting of activist language to project a sense of infallibility was also a central part of @Indologyteacher's over-insistence on their own identity. This, too, is a rhetorical strategy often found among conservative and anti-intellectual agitators that has become pervasive in recent years. Here the Black Lives Matter movement provides a particularly useful example. The phrase "Stay woke," which came into popular use in the mid-2010s after Michael Brown's murder by a white police officer, became part of a widespread call for people to be aware of and actively combat racial injustice and other forms of oppression. However, much as with the contrarian "Blue Lives Matter" response, the term "woke" has been contorted by its critics into an intentional mockery of its original meaning. Conservative politicians and their supporters now decry "woke indoctrination" as they attempt to eliminate any discussions of race in public schools and remove diversity, equity, and inclusion training from the workplace.[43] As Nathalie Baptiste explains, such concepts become "flipped on their head, turned inside out, repurposed to sneer at the people they were meant to rally, and generally made to seem comical and ridiculous—a rhetorical minstrel act, essentially, whose theme is the old American standby that there's no greater racist than the anti-racist [. . .] "[44] For @Indologyteacher, these precise

---

42 Kayla Epstein, "A sponsor of an Ohio abortion bill thinks you can reimplant ectopic pregnancies. You can't," The Washington Post, May 10, 2019, https://www.washingtonpost.com/health/2019/05/10/sponsor-an-ohio-abortion-bill-thinks-you-can-reimplant-ectopic-pregnancies-you-cant.
43 "Governor DeSantis Announces Legislative Proposal to Stop W.O.K.E. Activism and Critical Race Theory in Schools and Corporations," Ron DeSantis: 46th Governor of Florida, December 15, 2021, https://www.flgov.com/2021/12/15/governor-desantis-announces-legislative-proposal-to-stop-w-o-k-e-activism-and-critical-race-theory-in-schools-and-corporations.
44 Nathalie Baptiste, "The Worst People Keep Stealing the Language of Black Struggle," Mother Jones, March 29, 2021, https://www.motherjones.com/crime-justice/2021/03/the-worst-people-keep-stealing-the-language-of-black-struggle. See also: Tahema Lopez Bunyasi and Candis Watts Smith's

strategies were employed to both brand their identity as what they perceived to be a representation of the stereotypical "white woman academic," a person who surely would fit into the ironic sense of "wokeness," and also to discredit those who disagreed with them by suggesting they were party to a variety of systems of oppression and discrimination, despite no evidence thereof.[45]

This mobilization of advocacy language was primarily characterized by a forced, performative self-awareness about one's positionality and an ad hoc usage of accusations that escalated in aggressiveness the longer exchanges occurred. In keeping with the previous emphasis on the realness of their identity, @Indologyteacher drew on phrases intended to demonstrate allyship and humbleness, despite doing so to endorse essentialist narratives. For example, in insisting that Amaterasu could never be transnational, they argued that Nagahara and Lowe were committing cultural erasure of the Japanese and that

> We Caucasians did [cultural erasure] to the Natives & African Americans & Asians & must correct our ways. Telling POCs they have no culture or identity was a hallmark of colonialism that must be combated. Instead we should celebrate the uniqueness & diversity of Asians — especially Japanese[46]

Note the escalation from Lowe's original idea that "Japanese" deities underwent multicultural generation, transformation, reinterpretation, and relocation over centuries of practice to an oversimplified "transnationalism = cultural erasure." This accusation is leveled purposefully within @Indologyteacher's supposed register as a white person, creating a whataboutist logical fallacy that deflects the subject to other instances of historical wrongdoings by white communities. In doing so, they situate themselves as an apologetic ally and their dissenters as complicit in colonialist agendas.

As @Indologyteacher became increasingly frustrated with resistance to their statements, the co-opting of activist language became more extreme; they began to claim that Nagahara and Lowe were "Whitesplaining revisionists" from which

---

Stay Woke: A People's Guide to Making All Black Lives Matter (New York University Press, 2019), especially Chapter 2.
[45] Francesca Sobande has addressed this co-opting of social justice activism language in the context of marketing, which demonstrates similar misinterpretations and misuses of the core concepts of these movements to benefit from their visibility. See: Francesca Sobande, "Woke-washing: 'intersectional' femvertising and branding 'woke' bravery," *European Journal of Marketing* 54, no. 11 (2019): 2723–2745.
[46] @Indologyteacher, "We Caucasians did this," July 14, 2021, 5:33 p.m., https://twitter.com/Indologyteacher/status/1415469575316123649; "Stop cultural appropriation," July 22, 2021, 8:41 p.m., https://twitter.com/Indologyteacher/status/1414429749460492291.

"Asian heritage" must be defended while generally railing against "white professors" for promoting what they deemed to be "racist propaganda."[47] After one scholar critiqued their comments on racial science with a reference to Nazis, @Indologyteacher quickly began drawing on this as well, sarcastically accusing a female historian of trying to "feign Aryan supremacy" with dyed hair and calling the scholars in disagreement with them a "Neo-Nazi gang."[48] After several days, @Indologyteacher's feed boasted a fascinating amalgam of these phrases, entirely divorced from any germane context other than an attempt to use them as insults:

> You're panicking now that I've exposed your Neo-Nazi cabal of White Supremacists, colonialists & revisionists promoting anti-Asian hate; as well as patriarchal misogynists that attack Amaterasu for being a Goddess, & bottom-tier, lifetime assistants jealous of tenured professors.
>
> Never said anything about biological differences you White trash Nazi! Did you not learn anything from BLM? We must tackle racism but trailer park KKK Nazis like you want to pretend racism does not exist so that you can continue your White Supremacy, Nazism, colonialism & racism.
>
> I am the one who rattled the Nazi, colonialist, imperialist, xenophobic, misogynist, patriarchal clique of White *assistant* professors & jobless wannabe scholars who promote anti-Asian & anti-Japan hate. Now who (or what) are you & whose side are you on?[49]

The terminology one might perceive as the favorite of "woke" circles, descriptors purportedly prevalent in liberal academic environments, was used with increasing desperation to denigrate enemies who challenged @Indologyteacher's constructed virtual identity. The belabored attempt to deploy these concepts, concepts that have become a part of public discourses appropriating and mocking them, ultimately demonstrated a profound ignorance of their meaning. They were used solely as childish, pretentious placeholders for ridicule without real nuance or substance.

---

[47] @Indologyteacher, "You just can't imagine," July 15, 2021, 10:09 a.m., https://twitter.com/Indologyteacher/status/1415720185055612938; "And yes, it's nauseating," July 15, 2021, 10:50 a.m., https://twitter.com/Indologyteacher/status/1415730381123473412.
[48] @Indologyteacher, "Bottled blonde," July 16, 6:15 p.m., https://twitter.com/Indologyteacher/status/1416204926070530049.
[49] @Indologyteacher, "You're panicking now," July 18, 2021, 11:20 p.m., https://twitter.com/Indologyteacher/status/1417006411452715008 ; "Never said anything," July 19, 8:03 p.m., https://twitter.com/Indologyteacher/status/1417319248179998724; "I am the one who rattled," July 20, 2021, 8:28 a.m., https://twitter.com/Indologyteacher/status/1417506671887323142.

The Attention-Seeking Rejection of Reality and Interwoven Right-Wing Networks

After several days, the mask of a seasoned, professional academic became heavy to wear. @Indologyteacher's pretense at civility deteriorated almost entirely, replaced with increasingly bizarre insults and unreal claims to "victory" in so-called debates that never took place. @Indologyteacher began referring to scholars as "[hunting] in packs like hyenas" who "[coddled] & [shielded] the other" while @Indologyteacher "[strutted] alone like a lioness."[50] The academics involved were labeled as instigators of harassment who then "fled the scene like a disgraced Daimyo."[51] By this point, most Asian Studies researchers had ceased responding to the account and its strange proclamations with anything but animated gifs and joking replies, no longer taking any of the interactions seriously.

Seeing that the overwhelming majority of those replying on threads by or about them were not further engaging with their absurdist claims and insults as they hoped, @Indologyteacher began posting at random about their purported defeat of their enemies, claiming to have "just defeated an army of trolls" and using these hostile exchanges to garner the attention of Japanese cybernationalists who had already been harassing several East Asia scholars since February of 2021 (and thus gradually took notice of the dispute).[52] Once these two threads of trolling intertwined, they became a mutually reinforcing dialogue, with one particularly virulent cybernationalist taking the fictitious identity of @Indologyteacher and their boasting at face value, retweeting @Indologyteacher to her 14,000+ followers with the note: "This Professor @Indologyteacher is taking on anti-Japanese researchers and it's incredibly revealing. Definitely support [@Indologyteacher]! I thank them for revealing how these anti-Japanese are racists who don't treat Japanese people as human beings!"[53] @Indologyteacher was quick to reply in a way that positioned themselves as a superior academic authority and advocate for Japanese essentialist ideas about uniqueness and tradition: "Yes, please tell all your friends that I have rattled and scared that racist clique like never before. I know all of their games, their strategies,

---

50 @Indologyteacher, "Glad you admit," July 16, 2021, 3:17 p.m., https://twitter.com/Indologyteacher/status/1416160010753777664; "See Paula is DMing," July 15, 2021, 6:37 p.m., https://twitter.com/Indologyteacher/status/1415847978158465025.
51 Paula R. Curtis (@paularcurtis), "Lessons in how attacks unfold in Twitter," Twitter, July 20, 2021, 5:36 a.m., https://twitter.com/paularcurtis/status/1417463341505724422.
52 @Indologyteacher, "You started it," July 16, 2021, 9:27 a.m., https://twitter.com/Indologyteacher/status/1416071897721212928; Curtis, "Taking the Fight."
53 Sachi Hirayama (@sachihirayama), "こちらのProfessorさん," Twitter, July 20, 9:04 a.m., https://twitter.com/sachihirayama/status/1417515665183842304.

their tactics & schemes. They can never beat me in debate. Be proud to be Japanese & celebrate your great Shinto Buddhist heritage."[54] @Indologyteacher's comments finally had a captive audience, as well as an ally who could amplify their ideas. This encounter prolonged the harassment of researchers by other extremist users with intersecting interests in promoting ethnonationalist ideologies about Japan.

Shortly after these attacks slowed down @Indologyteacher was temporarily suspended from Twitter, though it is unclear whether this was a result of the ongoing harassment of Asia scholars or because of their other hateful anti-Hindu and anti-Indian content. When their account was reinstated in mid-August 2021, they proclaimed the ban was a result of "taking on an entire cabal of Neo-Nazi "scholars," and that they looked forward to "correcting false narratives," a goal that further pushed their online agenda towards the Japanese cybernationalist (and historical denialist) communities that had spent months attacking many of the same scholars.[55] @Indologyteacher also announced that they were working with the aforementioned right wing Japanese activist to "create a YouTube where we will expose these trash professors/journalists and their poor scholarly and also counter their anti-Japan narratives."[56] Although @Indologyteacher noted plans to continue pursuing this online harassment in collusion with existing ultraconservative communities, to date, such projects have not materialized. The account is now only periodically active, replying to various tweets about religion to accuse Hindus of genocide.

Virtual Engagement and the Need for Strategic Advocacy

Many social media users remind their friends and colleagues of the golden rule of virtual engagement: "Do not feed the trolls." When it becomes clear that a person is a bad-faith actor with no investment in discussing a topic on respectful

---

54 @Indologyteacher, "Yes, please tell all your friends," July 20, 2021, 9:15 a.m., https://twitter.com/Indologyteacher/status/1417518463791345666; "I gave those racist thugs," July 21, 2021, 3:25 a.m., https://twitter.com/Indologyteacher/status/1417792968644247552.
55 One such harasser spent months tweeting at and about several Asian Studies scholars who challenged their historical revisionist views in order to whip their large number of followers into a frenzy of targeted harassment, tweeting on one scholar as many as 60 times in a single day. Curtis, "Here is the data," September 14, 2021, 8:50 a.m., https://twitter.com/paularcurtis/status/1437806066515857409; @Indologyteacher, "So recently I was locked out," August 18, 2021, 9:43 p.m., https://twitter.com/Indologyteacher/status/1428216062693322755.
56 @Indologyteacher, "We are in talks," August 31, 2021, 6:40 a.m., https://twitter.com/Indologyteacher/status/1432699910151983116.

or reasonable grounds, it is best to walk away. The travails of interacting with @Indologyteacher provide an apt demonstration of this model. Yet, as researchers and educators, many of us, despite our suspicions, attempted to respond sensibly and give the benefit of the doubt, if not provide an instructive example by responding to problematic statements. Herein lies a fundamental conflict for researchers: we face increasing demands to engage virtually and often attempt to counter false or dubious narratives in public spaces, but these practices do not come easily or naturally to anyone. Handling irrational individuals, managing digital exchanges, and protecting oneself from potential harm are learned skills; despite our increasingly plugged-in world, there is no such thing as a digital native. How, then, can we engage responsibly on social media such as Twitter, and promote best practices? And how can institutions rise to the occasion to support scholars who represent them in the online world? Academics and their administrators are direly in need of focused instruction on virtual engagement.

Public-Facing Research

At a methodological level, graduate students and established faculty alike must receive instruction on how to effectively create and present public-facing work intended for a general audience. Whether or not they choose to use open-access or popular venues to disseminate their work, these modes of presentation and writing are essential for academics to understand the labor, outcomes, and influence of digital media. Whether collaborating with information specialists to create metadata or negotiating one's writing for an op-ed, these knowledge gaps hinder our ability to fully understand how our research demands and findings impact others beyond our colleagues and classrooms. It is easy to be an armchair critic of museum search engines or talking heads when we ourselves have no training in these methods of knowledge production and circulation. Just as graduate students learn to tailor their writing and arguments to disciplinary academic journals, we must facilitate education on virtual forms of media. Our inability to speak to non-specialist audiences only widens the gap between informed insights and those who would otherwise misuse or misrepresent them. In the age of the internet, anyone may peek into the windows of the Ivory Tower and report back what they think they see; it is up to us to open those windows and share dialogues with our neighbors.

Personal Safety and Institutional Advocacy

Being online, particularly when using one's real name and credentials, exposes individuals and their employers to any person with an internet connection. Cyberbullying and cyberstalking have been in the public discourse and popular imagination for nearly fifty years now. Although social media like Twitter is often used to amplify educational content and is a critical tool for activists, journalists, and others who would use the platform for good, in doing so, the dangers of visibility are also magnified.

Examples of these dangers can be found across disparate academic circles. The #medievaltwitter community on Twitter has been particularly vocal about exposing how right-wing nationalism manifests in internet communities and appropriates the medieval European pasts to promote interlocking ethnocentric, revisionist narratives and conspiracy theories.[57] Dorothy Kim, a junior scholar of color, was targeted by the alt-right at the direction of a white senior scholar whose public writings Kim critiqued as a part of her work on anti-racist teaching in Medieval Studies. Kim had to take a variety of digital and in-person measures for her safety in the face of violent threats, the circulation of her photo, and the sharing of her work address online.[58] Dr. Kelly J. Baker, a historian of American religious history, wrote an op-ed on white nationalism and the alt-right that was picked up by MSNBC, resulting in a barrage of hostile responses on Twitter and threats on her life (including a detailed plan to murder her that was left on her Facebook author page). She was even mentioned by name in a Klan newspaper. In 2021, she declined to write a piece for a major news outlet on the January 6 insurrection in Washington, not wishing to expose herself or her family to the backlash often experienced by those who engage in public scholarship on controversial topics.[59] There is also danger, however, in scholars withdrawing from the public eye and allowing misinforma-

---

[57] An excellent series on this topic is "Race, Racism, and the Middle Ages," which covers topics from Pizzagate and Confederate monuments to medievalism in the KKK. "Race, Racism and the Middle Ages: Table of Contents," The Public Medievalist, https://www.publicmedievalist.com/race-racism-middle-ages-toc.

[58] Dorothy Kim, "Medieval Studies Since Charlottesville," Inside Higher Ed, August 29, 2018, https://www.insidehighered.com/views/2018/08/30/scholar-describes-being-conditionally-accepted-medieval-studies-opinion.

[59] Kelly J. Baker, "The New White Nationalists?" Religion & Politics, October 20, 2016, https://religionandpolitics.org/2016/10/20/the-new-white-nationalists; Kelly J. Baker (@kelly_j_baker), "So, I was asked to write down," Twitter, January 10, 2021, 4:36 p.m., https://twitter.com/kelly_j_baker/status/1348307698278932480. For more on how digital engagement and online harassment impact scholars of Asian Studies in particular, see the videos and reading lists produced as a part of the 2022 Association for Asian Studies Digital Dialogues Series: Paula R. Curtis, "Association for Asian

tion and ahistorical materials created for malicious purposes to have free reign in popular circulation.

For this reason, professionalization efforts also need to address privacy and safety. Researchers need to be aware of methods for protecting personal information data mined by online companies, of how to interact safely and appropriately in virtual spaces (particularly when representing an organization or institution directly), and of how the policies of employers do or do not protect information about their scholars and students (such as email communications).[60] This training is not only vital for educators to safeguard themselves but their students as well. Even well-meaning instructors may not think twice before they post screenshots of their Zoom classrooms, never knowing if one of their students resists using social media because of real-life dangers that might require restraining orders, relocation, or name changes. Teachers are rarely trained in FERPA restrictions that require they preserve student privacy.

Most universities and colleges are ill-equipped to provide advice or protections for their faculty and students, despite the "digital shift" and the COVID-19 pandemic driving most educators online.[61] Few are aware of the efforts begun by the American Association of University Professors (AAUP) in early 2017 to create resources on the targeted online harassment of faculty, which need more sustained circulation and continued development.[62] This education on virtual engagement is equally important for the administrators who enact change at the institutional level. For better or for worse, it has become increasingly popular to "doxx" individuals who operate on the internet, sharing their personal contact information for mass audiences on social media or internet forums, and encouraging others to (rightfully, or

---

Studies Digital Dialogues Series: *Academics Online*," Paula R. Curtis, http://prcurtis.com/events/AASDD2022.

60 On Twitter safety, see Paula R. Curtis, "A Guide to Twitter and Social Media Safety for Academics (and Everyone Else)," Paula R. Curtis, May 20, 2022, http://prcurtis.com/docs/twitterguide2.

61 The discussion of institutional responsibility and preparedness predates the acceleration of the digital shift. On institutional responses to digital harassment of faculty and its repercussions, see: Joan Wallach Scott, "Targeted Harassment of Faculty: What Higher Education Administrators Can Do," *Liberal Education* 104, no. 2 (Spring 2018): 50–55. Recent studies have also shown that there is a significant gap in support for scholars who experience online harassment at the level of one's academic institution and the infrastructure of the digital platforms themselves, leaving many feeling unable to cope with such attacks. On this see: Shandell Houlden et al., "Support for scholars coping with online harassment: an ecological framework," *Feminist Media Studies* 22, no. 5 (2022): 1120–1138.

62 "Fighting Targeted Harassment of Faculty," American Association of University Professors, https://www.aaup.org/news/targeted-online-harassment-faculty#.YuteorhKhnI; "Targeted Online Harassment of Faculty," American Association of University Professors.

not) contact their employers. In the most extreme cases, some cyber harassment through doxxing has resulted in deaths.[63] Large companies and academic institutions are often driven by online campaigns to respond to uncomfortable subjects, and though this can put flummoxed administrators (concerned about donors and often unfamiliar with virtual landscapes of exchange) in a difficult spot, ultimately it is their employees who suffer the most personal and professional damage.

How, then, should institutions respond? One recent example took place in September 2021. Political scientist Jenn Jackson of Syracuse University wrote a series of tweets criticizing 9/11 coverage by white correspondents and pundits, saying that they did not consider fear and military violence prior to the attacks from intersectional perspectives. Her comments provoked a strong response on social media and garnered news coverage, notably including Fox News. On September 13, 2021, Syracuse Chancellor and President Kent Syverud and Dean of the Maxwell School of Citizenship and Public Affairs David Van Slyke issued a joint statement condemning calls for Jackson to be fired, stating that they would not tolerate the "harassment and violent threats that we have seen in response that have been directed at this professor. Our Department of Public Safety is in contact with the professor and has engaged the support of federal, state and local law enforcement agencies."[64] The unequivocal public support of Jackson by her university and colleagues is an important statement of solidarity with the work academics do and academic freedom at large. Contrast this example with recent failures, such as the University of Mississippi's termination of Garrett Felber, historian of racial inequality and the carceral state, after he publicly criticized their refusal to accept a $42,000 grant awarded for an education project on mass incarceration and immigrant detention. According to Felber, his chair cited concerns that it could impact their departmental funding, being too "political."[65] Historian Lora D. Burnett was forced out of Collin College after mocking Mike Pence on Twitter, while two of her

---

[63] For an overview of notable legal cases of cyber harassment in the form of swatting from the last decade, see Elizabeth M. Jaffe, "Swatting: the New Cyberbullying Frontier After Elonis v. United States," *Drake Law Review* 64 (2016): 455–483 .
[64] Colleen Flaherty, "'What Cannot Be Tolerated'," Inside Higher Ed, September 14, 2021, https://www.insidehighered.com/news/2021/09/14/syracuse-offers-unequivocal-support-targeted-professor; Kent Syverud and David Van Slyke, "Message from Chancellor Kent Syverud and Dean David Van Slyke," September 13, 2021, https://news.syr.edu/blog/2021/09/13/message-from-chancellor-kent-syverud-and-dean-david-van-slyke.
[65] Colleen Flaherty, "Ole Miss Settles With Professor," Inside Higher Ed, July 30, 2021, https://www.insidehighered.com/news/2021/07/30/ole-miss-settles-professor.

colleagues received the same treatment for openly criticizing administrators on their COVID-19 policies after the death of a colleague.[66]

Academics now have the difficult task of balancing both their personal and professional identities in virtual spaces. But if institutions want their best researchers to be visible and emblematic of all that is great about their school, labor that is increasingly public-facing, then those same administrators must themselves be educated in virtual engagement and learn how to best stand in solidarity with their workers when negative consequences arise.

Ethics and the Amplification of the Digital

In addition to considerations of privacy and safety, interacting online also merits many interrelated ethical considerations that are worth briefly touching on. At the same time as social media presence and digital projects can create new venues of representation for underserved communities—both scholars themselves and the promotion of resources on marginalized topics—academics must be cognizant of whose voice is being heard and how certain narratives are controlled and represented. This is particularly important when working on living traditions and communities. Furthermore, we cannot ignore the need to be transparent about our sources of funding and the platforms that support our scholarship, not only to give credit to those organizations and institutions that make our research possible but also because the form that public-facing scholarship takes must be evaluated in the holistic context of the means through which it was created.

Furthermore, the immediacy of the internet demands that academics learn principles of intellectual property, both to protect themselves and participate in ethical attribution practices. Whether presenting scholarly knowledge on a topic through an official website or in a personal Twitter thread, the aim of sharing our work with the public should demonstrate, insofar as is possible, the integrity of our academic practices. If one is a tenured professor, for example, but regularly reproduces others' content without proper credit or presents data or images without context and attribution, then the entirety of one's expertise (and, indeed, professionalism and collegiality itself) is undermined. Who will trust the work of a researcher who

---

[66] L.D. Burnett, "What a Public-Information Act Request Revealed About My College President," The Chronicle of Higher Education, February 16, 2021, https://www.chronicle.com/article/what-a-public-information-act-request-revealed-about-my-college-president; Michael Vasquez, "Fired for Tweeting? A Professor Says She Was Cut Loose in Retaliation," The Chronicle of Higher Education, February 25, 2021, https://www.chronicle.com/article/fired-for-tweeting-a-professor-says-she-was-cut-loose-in-retaliation.

regularly violates the very tenets of the integrity that they demand of their students while actively disrespecting the labor of others? Such practices harm academia as a whole and sow mistrust among colleagues and the wider public.

Finally, one of the most serious ethical considerations for virtual engagement, aptly illustrated by the production of this chapter, is whether or not your own participation in arguments with bad-faith actors ultimately amplifies their voices. Interacting with trolls and their followers provides more fodder for their baseless criticisms and ongoing harassment, and there is always the risk that something you say will be twisted and misrepresented. Twitter users often go out of their way to avoid directly provoking further negative engagement by using screenshots of a user's comment or "subtweeting" (tweeting about someone without using their name) instead of quote-tweeting them directly, which would result in the person being alerted to the response. In even writing this chapter, I thought hard about whether it was ethical to potentially drive traffic to @Indologyteacher's tweets by putting them into publication, or if quoting their hateful contents directly was tantamount to overemphasizing the voice of abusers over that of victims.

Yet, it is our professional responsibility to properly cite the content we discuss, even when problematic, and simply ignoring that content does not make it go away. Those of us entangled in @Indologyteacher's web will not be the first or the last, but we can lead by example, learn from that interaction, and subsequently educate others through it. These issues, and what we can and should do about them, are best understood through the real-life experiences that scholars endure. Though not everyone can or should take up such battles (for they come at a high cost of mental and emotional labor), it is not enough to completely ignore what happens in these public-facing spaces with no critical engagement.

Why Do We Care About What Happens on the Internet?

For all the good, the bad, and the ugly, the internet is here to stay. Social media is a medium through which most people now obtain their information. Whether the struggle between print and digital platforms, Wikipedia wars, or attempts to clarify muddled assertions of "fake news," digital literacy has never been more urgent. This is especially true for scholars, who have a moral and ethical responsibility to share accurate, properly sourced information. All academics—be they specialists in religious studies or history, premodern or modern periods, East Asia or other areas—must contend with these new modes of interaction that are capable of spreading falsehoods and radicalizing individuals far more easily than a published article or book.

The most recent digital shift is just beginning to reveal its manifold impacts on how scholars conduct their teaching and research. With increasing demands by academics for their institutions to take digital scholarship and engagement seriously in tandem with institutional demands that their academics engage popular audiences, we must be prepared to support all that it means to be a public intellectual. Students, faculty, and administrators all need an introductory, if not comprehensive, digital literacy education. We can no longer afford to wage intergenerational and internecine battles over whether or not virtual engagement and digital scholarship are relevant; there is no such thing as being entirely analog anymore. We cannot simply power down and let these exchanges with global ramifications pass us by. Academics who are embracing their roles as public-facing intellectuals are responding to active demonstrations of why our work matters now more than ever. If we are to fulfill our goals of promoting academic freedom, training our students to be responsible global citizens, supporting innovative work by diverse scholars, and sharing knowledge built on a foundation of academic integrity, then we and the institutions that employ us must also embrace that many of these battles will be fought on virtual grounds.

Bibliography

"About," Sacred Writes: Public Scholarship on Religion, https://www.sacred-writes.org/about [Accessed September 25, 2021].

Baker, Kelly J. "The New White Nationalists?" Religion & Politics, October 20, 2016, https://religionandpolitics.org/2016/10/20/the-new-white-nationalists.

Baptiste, Nathalie. "The Worst People Keep Stealing the Language of Black Struggle," Mother Jones, March 29, 2021, https://www.motherjones.com/crime-justice/2021/03/the-worst-people-keep-stealing-the-language-of-black-struggle.

Bell, Melissa and Elizabeth Flock. "'A Gay Girl in Damascus' Comes Clean," The Washington Post, June 12, 2011, https://www.washingtonpost.com/lifestyle/style/a-gay-girl-in-damascus-comes-clean/2011/06/12/AgkyH0RH_story.html.

Bikales, James S. "Protected by Decades-Old Power Structures, Three Renowned Harvard Anthropologists Face Allegations of Sexual Harassment," The Harvard Crimson, May 29, 2020, https://www.thecrimson.com/article/2020/5/29/harvard-anthropology-gender-issues.

Bromwich, Jonah E. and Ezra Marcus. "The Anonymous Professor Who Wasn't," The New York Times, August 4, 2020, https://www.nytimes.com/2020/08/04/style/college-coronavirus-hoax.html.

Burnett, L.D. "What a Public-Information Act Request Revealed About My College President," The Chronicle of Higher Education, February 16, 2021, https://www.chronicle.com/article/what-a-public-information-act-request-revealed-about-my-college-president.

Curtis, Paula R. "Association for Asian Studies Digital Dialogues Series: Academics Online," Paula R. Curtis, http://prcurtis.com/events/AASDD2022 [Accessed June 12, 2023].

Curtis, Paula R. "A Guide to Twitter and Social Media Safety for Academics (and Everyone Else)," May 20, 2022, Paula R. Curtis, http://prcurtis.com/docs/twitterguide2.

Curtis, Paula R. "Taking the Fight for Japan's History Online: The Ramseyer Controversy and Social Media," *The Asia-Pacific Journal: Japan Focus* 19, no. 22 (December 1, 2021), https://apjjf.org/2021/22/Curtis.html.

Epstein, Kayla. "A sponsor of an Ohio abortion bill thinks you can reimplant ectopic pregnancies. You can't," The Washington Post, May 10, 2019, https://www.washingtonpost.com/health/2019/05/10/sponsor-an-ohio-abortion-bill-thinks-you-can-reimplant-ectopic-pregnancies-you-cant.

Ferber, Abby L. "Are You Willing to Die for This Work?" Public Targeted Online Harassment in Higher Education: SWS Presidential Address. *Gender & Society* 32, no. 3 (2018): 301–320.

"Fighting Targeted Harassment of Faculty," American Association of University Professors, https://www.aaup.org/news/targeted-online-harassment-faculty#.YuteorhKhnI [accessed September 25, 2021.

Flaherty, Colleen. "Ole Miss Settles With Professor," Inside Higher Ed, July 30, 2021, https://www.insidehighered.com/news/2021/07/30/ole-miss-settles-professor.

Flaherty, Colleen. "'What Cannot Be Tolerated'," Inside Higher Ed, September 14, 2021, https://www.insidehighered.com/news/2021/09/14/syracuse-offers-unequivocal-support-targeted-professor.

Flusberg, Stephen J., Teenie Matlock, and Paul H. Thibodeau. "War metaphors in public discourse." *Metaphor and Symbol* 33, no. 1 (2018): 1–18.

"Governor DeSantis Announces Legislative Proposal to Stop W.O.K.E. Activism and Critical Race Theory in Schools and Corporations," Ron DeSantis: 46th Governor of Florida, December 15, 2021, https://www.flgov.com/2021/12/15/governor-desantis-announces-legislative-proposal-to-stop-w-o-k-e-activism-and-critical-race-theory-in-schools-and-corporations.

Grunow, Tristan R. "'Making it Count': The Case for Digital Scholarship in Asian Studies," #AsiaNow, June 9, 2020, https://www.asianstudies.org/making-it-count-the-case-for-digital-scholarship-in-asian-studies.

Houlden, Shandell, Jaigris Hodson, George Veletsianos, Chandell Gosse, Patrick Lowenthal, Tonia Dousay, and Nathan C. Hall. "Support for scholars coping with online harassment: an ecological framework." *Feminist Media Studies* 22, no. 5 (2022): 1120–1138.

Jaffe, Elizabeth M. "Swatting: the New Cyberbullying Frontier After *Elonis v. United States*." *Drake Law Review* 64 (2016): 455–483.

Kim, Dorothy. "Medieval Studies Since Charlottesville," Inside Higher Ed, August 29, 2018, https://www.insidehighered.com/views/2018/08/30/scholar-describes-being-conditionally-accepted-medieval-studies-opinion.

Krug, Jessica A. "The Truth, and the Anti-Black Violence of My Lies," Medium, September 3, 2020, https://medium.com/@jessakrug/the-truth-and-the-anti-black-violence-of-my-lies-9a9621401f85.

Levenson, Michael and Jennifer Schuessler. "University Investigates Claim That White Professor Pretended to Be Black," The New York Times, September 3, 2020, https://www.nytimes.com/2020/09/03/us/jessica-krug-gwu-race.html.

Lewis, Helen. "The Identity Hoaxers," The Atlantic, March 16, 2021, https://www.theatlantic.com/international/archive/2021/03/krug-carrillo-dolezal-social-munchausen-syndrome/618289.

Lopez Bunyasi, Tehama and Candis Watts Smith. *Stay Woke: A People's Guide to Making All Black Lives Matter*. New York University Press, 2019.

Morris-Suzuki, Tessa. *Re-inventing Japan: Time, Space, Nation*. Armonk, NY: M. E. Sharpe, 1998.

Ng, Wai-ming. "The Shintoization of Mazu in Tokugawa Japan." *Japanese Journal of Religious Studies* 47, no. 2 (2020): 225–246.

Nunberg, Geoff. "Tracing The Origin Of The Campaign Promise To 'Tell It Like It Is'," NPR, July 15, 2015, https://www.npr.org/2015/07/15/423194262/tracing-the-origin-of-the-campaign-promise-to-tell-it-like-it-is.

Oguma Eiji. *A Genealogy of 'Japanese' Self-images*. Trans Pacific Press, 2002.

Pető, Andrea. "Academic Freedom and Gender Studies: An Alliance Forged in Fire." *Gender and Sexuality: Journal of the Center of Gender Studies* (2020): 9–24.

"Race, Racism and the Middle Ages: Table of Contents," The Public Medievalist, https://www.publicmedievalist.com/race-racism-middle-ages-toc [accessed September 25, 2021].

Robertson, Katie. "Nikole Hannah-Jones Denied Tenure at University of North Carolina," The New York Times, May 19, 2021, https://www.nytimes.com/2021/05/19/business/media/nikole-hannah-jones-unc.html.

Scott, Joan Wallach. "Targeted Harassment of Faculty: What Higher Education Administrators Can Do." *Liberal Education* 104, no. 2 (Spring 2018): 50–55.

Serwer, Adam. "Elon Musk's Free-Speech Charade Is Over," The Atlantic, April 12, 2023, https://www.theatlantic.com/ideas/archive/2023/04/elon-musk-twitter-free-speech-matt-taibbi-substack/673698.

Sobande, Francesca. "Woke-washing: 'intersectional' femvertising and branding 'woke' bravery." *European Journal of Marketing* 54, no. 11 (2019): 2723–2745.

Stein, Joel. "How Trolls Are Ruining the Internet," Time, August 18, 2016, https://time.com/4457110/internet-trolls.

Syverud, Kent and David Van Slyke. "Message from Chancellor Kent Syverud and Dean David Van Slyke," September 13, 2021, https://news.syr.edu/blog/2021/09/13/message-from-chancellor-kent-syverud-and-dean-david-van-slyke.

Szendi Schieder, Chelsea. "The History the Japanese Government Is Trying to Erase," The Nation, May 26, 2021, https://www.thenation.com/article/world/ramseyer-comfort-women-japan-nationalism.

"Targeted Online Harassment of Faculty," American Association of University Professors, January 31, 2017, https://www.aaup.org/issues/fighting-targeted-harassment-faculty.

Vasquez, Michael. "Fired for Tweeting? A Professor Says She Was Cut Loose in Retaliation," The Chronicle of Higher Education, February 25, 2021, https://www.chronicle.com/article/fired-for-tweeting-a-professor-says-she-was-cut-loose-in-retaliation.

Yoda, Tomiko. "Literary History against the National Frame, or Gender and the Emergence of Heian Kana Writing." *positions: east asia cultures critique* 8, no. 2 (Fall 2000): 465–497.

Young, Kevin. "How to Hoax Yourself: The Case of A Gay Girl in Damascus," The New Yorker, November 9, 2017, https://www.newyorker.com/books/page-turner/how-to-hoax-yourself-gay-girl-in-damascus.

Zuckerberg, Donna. "The problems with online 'debate me' culture: If you make an argument online, get ready for someone to throw down a gauntlet," The Washington Post, August 29, 2019, https://www.washingtonpost.com/outlook/whats-wrong-with-online-debate-me-culture/2019/08/29/c0ec8aa2-c9ca-11e9-8067-196d9f17af68_story.html.

Archived Tweets

@Indologyteacher. "And yes, it's nauseating," Twitter, July 15, 2021, 10:50 a.m., https://web.archive.org/web/20210913004148/https://twitter.com/Indologyteacher/status/1415730381123473412.
@Indologyteacher. "Bottled blonde," Twitter, July 16, 6:15 p.m., https://web.archive.org/web/20210913004300/https://twitter.com/Indologyteacher/status/1416204926070530049.
@Indologyteacher. "Further, the reason why," Twitter, July 17, 2021, 8:04 p.m., http://web.archive.org/web/20210913005143/https://twitter.com/Indologyteacher/status/1416594581160964097.
@Indologyteacher. "Glad you admit," Twitter, July 16, 2021, 3:17 p.m., https://web.archive.org/web/20210913005309/https://twitter.com/Indologyteacher/status/1416160010753777664.
@Indologyteacher. "Good riddance," Twitter, July 15, 2021, 9:29 p.m., https://web.archive.org/web/20210716043001/https://twitter.com/Indologyteacher/status/1415891422767632384.
@Indologyteacher. "I am an actual professor," Twitter, July 17, 2021, 5:34 a.m., http://web.archive.org/web/20210913005058/https://twitter.com/Indologyteacher/status/1415288504393867264.
@Indologyteacher. "I am an actual Professor," Twitter, August 18, 2021, 9:18 p.m., http://web.archive.org/web/20210913004810/https://twitter.com/Indologyteacher/status/1428209761477070849.
@Indologyteacher. "I am the one who rattled," Twitter, July 20, 2021, 8:28 a.m., http://web.archive.org/web/20210913004524/https://twitter.com/Indologyteacher/status/1417506671887323142.
@Indologyteacher. "I appreciate your research," Twitter, July 14, 2021, 7:57 a.m., http://web.archive.org/web/20210714155923/https://twitter.com/Indologyteacher/status/1415324491559931908.
@Indologyteacher. "I gave those racist thugs," Twitter, July 21, 2021, 3:25 a.m., http://web.archive.org/web/20210913005500/https://twitter.com/Indologyteacher/status/1417792968644247552.
@Indologyteacher. "I'll let this one pass," Twitter, July 15, 2021, 5:51 p.m., https://web.archive.org/web/20210913005201/https://twitter.com/Indologyteacher/status/1415836559723704322.
@Indologyteacher. "In Japan Buddhism," Twitter, July 8, 2021, 2:07 p.m., http://web.archive.org/web/20211008013041/https://twitter.com/Indologyteacher/status/1413243345804070913.
@Indologyteacher. "It is essential for Japan," Twitter, July 8, 2021, 2:25 p.m., http://web.archive.org/web/20210829214731/https://twitter.com/Indologyteacher/status/1413247831952052228.
@Indologyteacher. "I've never seen anyone so needy," Twitter, July 16, 2021, 5:07 p.m., https://web.archive.org/web/20220218070736/https://twitter.com/Indologyteacher/status/1416187763444133888.
@Indologyteacher. "Laughable nonsense," Twitter, June 20, 2021, 4:26 a.m, http://web.archive.org/web/20210913003820/https://twitter.com/Indologyteacher/status/1406574210575699968.
@Indologyteacher. "Nah – here I just get to say," Twitter, July 15, 2021, 9:35 p.m., https://web.archive.org/web/20210913004047/https://twitter.com/Indologyteacher/status/1415892833924419585.
@Indologyteacher. "Never said anything," Twitter, July 19, 8:03 p.m., https://web.archive.org/web/20210913004358/https://twitter.com/Indologyteacher/status/1417319248179998724.
@Indologyteacher. "No genocide in history compares," Twitter, July 4, 2021, 4:46 a.m., http://web.archive.org/web/20210913003745/https://twitter.com/Indologyteacher/status/1411652623426637825.
@Indologyteacher. "Not lemons but lemmings," Twitter, July 16, 2021, 11:02 p.m., https://web.archive.org/web/20210913004951/https://twitter.com/Indologyteacher/status/1416277011627188226.
@Indologyteacher. "The racist war on Amaterasu," Twitter, July 17, 2021, 7:59 p.m., https://web.archive.org/web/20210718030023/https://twitter.com/Indologyteacher/status/1416593529254596608.
@Indologyteacher. "Right! A whole clique," Twitter, July 15, 2021, 3:38 p.m., https://web.archive.org/web/20210715223911/https://twitter.com/Indologyteacher/status/1415803022379204610.

@Indologyteacher. "See Paula is DMing," Twitter, July 15, 2021, 6:37 p.m., http://web.archive.org/web/20210913005250/https://twitter.com/Indologyteacher/status/1415847978158465025.

@Indologyteacher. "Similarly the sources you cited," Twitter, July 14, 2021, 5:24 p.m., http://web.archive.org/web/20210913004613/https://twitter.com/Indologyteacher/status/1415467283577720840.

@Indologyteacher. "So recently I was locked out," Twitter, August 18, 2021, 9:43 p.m., https://web.archive.org/web/20220720173859/https://twitter.com/Indologyteacher/status/1428216062693322755.

@Indologyteacher. "So you are relying on your status," Twitter, July 25, 2021, 10:24 p.m., https://web.archive.org/web/20210913005132/https://twitter.com/Indologyteacher/status/1419528977253867522.

@Indologyteacher. "Stop cultural appropriation," Twitter, July 22, 2021, 8:41 p.m., https://web.archive.org/web/20210913004133/https://twitter.com/Indologyteacher/status/1414429749460492291.

@Indologyteacher. "Technically, some Kami," Twitter, July 14, 2021, 12:19 a.m., http://web.archive.org/web/20210714132732/https://twitter.com/Indologyteacher/status/1415209202323234816.

@Indologyteacher. "Thx for your response," Twitter, July 14, 2021, 7:53 a.m., http://web.archive.org/web/20210714165430/https://twitter.com/Indologyteacher/status/1415323549196226564.

@Indologyteacher. "We are in talks," Twitter, August 31, 2021, 6:40 a.m., https://web.archive.org/web/20210913010434/https://twitter.com/Indologyteacher/status/1432699910151983116.

@Indologyteacher. "We Caucasians did this," Twitter, July 14, 2021, 5:33 p.m., https://web.archive.org/web/20210715012030/https://twitter.com/Indologyteacher/status/1415469575316123649.

@Indologyteacher. "Why are some academics such cowards," Twitter, July 15, 2021, 3:48 p.m., https://web.archive.org/web/20210914144932/https://twitter.com/Indologyteacher/status/1415805508515139587.

@Indologyteacher. "Yes, but who will I debate?" Twitter, July 4, 2021, 11:11 p.m., http://web.archive.org/web/20210913004818/https://twitter.com/Indologyteacher/status/1411930629881610241.

@Indologyteacher. "Yes, please tell all your friends," Twitter, July 20, 2021, 9:15 a.m., https://web.archive.org/web/20210914145330/https://twitter.com/Indologyteacher/status/1417518463791345666.

@Indologyteacher. "You are showing how evil," Twitter, July 19, 2021, 12:32 a.m., http://web.archive.org/web/20210913004729/https://twitter.com/Indologyteacher/status/1417024609170468866.

@Indologyteacher. "You certainly know who I am," Twitter, July 14, 2021, 5:27 p.m., http://web.archive.org/web/20210715002745/https://twitter.com/Indologyteacher/status/1415468070408175617.

@Indologyteacher. "You just can't imagine," Twitter, July 15, 2021, 10:09 a.m., https://web.archive.org/web/20210715171001/https://twitter.com/Indologyteacher/status/1415720185055612938.

@Indologyteacher. "You're panicking now," Twitter, July 18, 2021, 11:20 p.m., http://web.archive.org/web/20210913004405/https://twitter.com/Indologyteacher/status/1417006411452715008.

@Indologyteacher. "You started it," Twitter, July 16, 2021, 9:27 a.m., https://web.archive.org/web/20210913004605/https://twitter.com/Indologyteacher/status/1416071897721212928.

@Indologyteacher. "You surely will," Twitter, July 15, 2021, 1:27 p.m., https://web.archive.org/web/20210715202807/https://twitter.com/Indologyteacher/status/1415770054336172033.

@Indologyteacher. "You've never been to university," Twitter, June 19, 2021, 9:59 a.m., http://web.archive.org/web/20210913003520/https://twitter.com/Indologyteacher/status/1406295553361723396.

Baker, Kelly J. (@kelly_j_baker). "So, I was asked to write down," Twitter, January 10, 2021, 4:36 p.m., https://web.archive.org/web/20221221032204/https://twitter.com/kelly_j_baker/status/1348307698278932480.

Curtis, Paula R. "Here is the data," Twitter, September 14, 2021, 8:50 a.m., https://web.archive.org/web/20220827112011/https://twitter.com/paularcurtis/status/1437806066515857409.
Curtis, Paula R. "Lessons in how attacks unfold in Twitter," Twitter, July 20, 2021, 5:36 a.m., https://web.archive.org/web/20220408231117/https://twitter.com/paularcurtis/status/1417463341505724422.
Hirayama, Sachi (@sachihirayama). "こちらのProfessorさん," Twitter, July 20, 9:04 a.m., https://web.archive.org/web/20210913005340/https://twitter.com/sachihirayama/status/1417515665183842304.
Lowe, Bryan D. (@bryandaniellowe). "The always brilliant," Twitter, July 8, 2021, 1:04 p.m., http://web.archive.org/web/20210708200432/https://twitter.com/bryandaniellowe/status/1413227481067360263.
Lowe, Bryan D. (@bryandaniellowe). "Catching up on recent issues," Twitter, July 13, 2021, 6:57 p.m., http://web.archive.org/web/20210714015725/https://twitter.com/bryandaniellowe/status/1415128243687075842.
Lowe, Bryan D. (@bryandaniellowe). "Last week, @jolyonbt wrote," Twitter, July 12, 2021, 4:52 a.m., http://web.archive.org/web/20220720025307/https://twitter.com/bryandaniellowe/status/1414553281049808897.
Lowe, Bryan D. (@bryandaniellowe). "Of course an exception," Twitter, July 14, 2021, 4:53 a.m., http://web.archive.org/web/20210829222507/https://twitter.com/bryandaniellowe/status/1415278246934061057.
Lowe, Bryan D. (@bryandaniellowe). "Thank you for taking the time," Twitter, July 14, 2021, 9:01 a.m., http://web.archive.org/web/20210714193649/https://twitter.com/bryandaniellowe/status/1415340618583351301.
Nagahara, Hiromu (@HiromuNagahara). "Um, you started out," Twitter, July 14, 2021, 9:11 a.m., http://web.archive.org/web/20210714204908/https://twitter.com/HiromuNagahara/status/1415343114039005186.
Thomas, Jolyon (@jolyonbt). "But just as the videographers," Twitter, July 8, 2021, 12:54 p.m., http://web.archive.org/web/20220415131539/https://twitter.com/jolyonbt/status/1413224941353308160.
Thomas, Jolyon (@jolyonbt). "The Tokyo Olympics," Twitter, July 8, 2021, 12:32 p.m., http://web.archive.org/web/20220423224746/https://twitter.com/jolyonbt/status/1413219538997587980.

Kaitlyn Ugoretz
Consuming Shinto, Feeding the Algorithm: Exploring the Impact of Social Media Software on Global Religious Aesthetic Formations

Introduction

My smartphone starts buzzing in my pocket and immediately, instinctively, I check my notifications to see what is causing such a stir in my social network. Kelly,[1] a newcomer to one of several digital Shinto communities (hereafter DSCs) on Facebook, has just posted a picture of her domestic Shinto altar or *kamidana* (Fig. 1). The caption reads, "After many shipping delays due to the pandemic, finally I received an ofuda to enshrine in my kamidana!" She adds a sparkling heart emoji to emphasize her excitement and sincere intention to ritually venerate the Shinto deities called *kami* now properly enshrined in her altar. A steady stream of likes and comments from other members of the group appear below the photo, congratulating Kelly, complimenting her altar's appearance, asking where she sourced the various elements of her altar, and questioning whether she received the paper *ofuda*—the sacred core of her altar—directly from a shrine instead of an unscrupulous online retailer.

Japan is home to some one hundred thousand Shinto shrines dedicated to the ritual veneration of deities called *kami* 神, scattered across mountains and coasts and occupying grand precincts and narrow alleys. If a person who finds themself in Japan desires to visit a Shinto shrine and pay their respects to the *kami*, perhaps to ask for or express gratitude for their blessings, they may do so without great complication or logistical calculation. It is not a question of if or how they can visit a shrine, but rather a matter of which one and when. Practicing Shinto outside of Japan is not so easy an undertaking, as physical shrines are few and far between, but thousands around the world choose to do so. The primary focus of their everyday ritual practice for these global Shinto practitioners necessarily shifts from shrines to the more accessible material and portable form of the *kamidana*.

---

[1] All names of DSC members are pseudonyms and identifiable information is masked out of respect for their privacy.

Fig. 1: Example of a simple *ofuda* stand style *kamidana*. ("神棚" by sakura100322, Photo AC, Photo ID: 1824565).

Kamidana, an individual household altar or shrine dedicated to the Shinto deities called *kami*, date back to the mid-Edo period (1603–1868).[2] Today, a conventional *kamidana* is comprised of a wooden miniature shrine structure called a *miyagata*, which typically enshrines a sacred object or *shinsatsu* in which the *kami* may reside during ritual veneration. By far the most common type of *shinsatsu* is an *ofuda*, a paper talisman linked to a particular shrine and its deities. The *kamidana* is then surrounded by a number of ritual implements, including several offering dishes (Fig. 2). Regular offerings for the *kami* traditionally include rice, water, and salt, as

---

2 Okada Yoshiyuki, "Kamidana," *Encyclopedia of Shinto*, https://d-museum.kokugakuin.ac.jp/eos/detail/?id=9666.

well as sake and evergreen branches.³ At its most minimal, a *kamidana* may simply include an *ofuda* and a stand (*ofuda-tate*) on which it may rest. Ideally, *kamidana* are to be kept in a clean, bright, and quiet space, elevated on a shelf above eye-level out of respect for the sacred status of the *kami*. A *kamidana* may share space in the home with any number of other altars. DSC members may maintain a *kamidana* alongside *butsudan* and/or domestic altars dedicated to a constellation of divinities, including Greek, Celtic, and Norse deities, Roman household spirits, *orishas* of Yoruba and African diasporic religions, and Catholic saints. The community consensus, however, is that each altar is to be kept separate and given its own space, rather than combining altars and enshrining non-Shinto deities in one's *kamidana*.

Fig. 2: Example of a traditional one-door *kamidana* with offerings. ("神棚" by beauty-box, Photo AC, Photo ID: 23148900).

The photo Kelly shared of her home altar and the attention it received from her fellow global Shinto practitioners in the digital Shinto community is remarkable in the sense that *kamidana* are for the most part an unremarkable part of Japanese

---

3 For more about the glocalization of offerings at *kamidana*, see: Kaitlyn Ugoretz, "Do Kentucky Kami Drink Bourbon? Exploring Parallel Glocalization in Global Shinto Offerings," *Religions* 13, no. 257 (2022): 1–15.

religious material culture today. These miniature shrines are highly formalized and can be found commonly in households, offices, martial arts dojos, and shops. Though Japanese media often feature photos of particularly impressive, cute, or creative materials offered by Shinto shrines and retailers (e.g., protective *omamori* amulets, votive *ema* boards, and commemorative shrine visit stamps), I have never seen people in Japan routinely share digital images of their home altars with others as DSC members do. Studies of the contemporary function of domestic Buddhist altars or *butsudan* in Japan similarly suggest that the altar participates in a process of inward, rather than outward, communication.[4] That is, altars aid in the maintenance of intimate relationships between the practicing individual or family and the deities, ancestors, and living and deceased relatives enshrined in the home.[5] Moreover, altars are dynamic, personal creative assemblages which may act as a site of aesthetic self-expression and religious identity formation.[6]

If domestic altars in Japanese traditions are a deeply private and personal matter, why then do transnational Shinto practitioners make a habit of sharing photos of their *kamidana* online? DSCs are populated by a diverse and dispersed collection of clergy and lay practitioners living around the world who for the most part never communicate face-to-face. The challenges of physical distance are compounded by a lack of access to foundational Shinto texts (particularly those translated into English) and traditional Shinto spaces, such as shrines. As a result, DSCs must make creative use of the sources available to them to establish shared knowledge, aesthetics, belief, and practice.

---

[4] Fabio Rambelli, "Home Buddhas: Historical Processes and Modes of Representation of the Sacred in the Japanese Buddhist Family Altar (Butsudan)," *Japanese Religions* 35, no. 1/2 (2010): 80. See also: John Nelson, "Home Altars in Contemporary Japan: Rectifying Buddhist 'Ancestor Worship' with Home Décor and Consumer Choice," *Japanese Journal of Religious Studies* 35, no. 2 (2008): 305–330.

[5] See: Jane Naomi Iwamura, "Altared States: Exploring the Legacy of Japanese American Butsudan Practice," *Pacific World: Journal of the Institute of Buddhist Studies* 3, no. 5 (2003): 275–291; Nelson, "Home Altars," 2008; Hannah Gould, "Domesticating Buddha: making a place for Buddhist altars (butsudan) in western homes," *Material Religion* 14, no. 4 (2019): 488–510; Hannah Gould, Tamara Kohn and Martin Gibbs, "Uploading the ancestors: Experiments with digital Buddhist altars in contemporary Japan," *Death Studies* 43, no. 7 (2019): 456–465.

[6] See: Kay Turner, *Beautiful Necessity: The art and meaning of women's altars* (New York, NY: Thames & Hudson, 1999); Christina Rocha, "'Can I put this Jizō together with the Virgin Mary in the altar?': Creolizing Zen Buddhism in Brazil," in Issei Buddhism in the Americas, ed. Duncan Ryūken Williams and Tomoe Moriya (Urbana, IL: University of Illinois Press, 2010), 5–26; Gould, "Domesticating Buddha."

Based on a digital ethnography of digital Shinto communities located on Facebook,[7] this chapter explores how the technological structures and affordances of social networking sites mediate the emergence of distinct aesthetic formations among transnational Shinto practitioners. In particular, I examine how and why digital Shinto community members collectively have adopted unusual visual communication practices such as the routine posting of images of personal *kamidana*. Drawing on Bourdieusian field theory, I argue that their prioritization of the production and consumption of digital artefacts reproducing material ritual objects is not only motivated by community-constructed notions of value and capital, but also partially determined by a shared digital habitus and the power of the Facebook newsfeed algorithm. I suggest scholars of digital religion and Asian religion must pay greater attention to the agency of algorithms in the online *and* offline lives of religious communities today.

Genealogy of Digital Shinto Communities

Given that there is limited research on the globalization of contemporary Shinto to date, I will first present an overview of the historical development of digital Shinto communities and the global Shinto practitioners who form them.[8] In the early 2000s, a computer-mediated communication (CMC) software revolution transformed the static archival character of Web 1.0, exemplified by ARPANET and bulletin board systems (BBS), with the dynamic person-to-person interconnectivity characteristic

---

[7] For more information on digital Shinto communities, see: Kaitlyn Ugoretz, "Case Study — World-Wide Shintō: The Globalization of 'Japanese' Religion," in *Bloomsbury Handbook of Japanese Religions*, ed. Erica Baffelli, Andrea Castiglioni, and Fabio Rambelli (London: Bloomsbury, 2021), 145–148; Kaitlyn Ugoretz, "Digital Shinto Communities," The Database of Religious History, https://religiondatabase.org/browse/1071.

[8] For publications on the globalization and environmental turn of Japanese religions, particularly Shinto, see: Nobutaka Inoue, "Globalization and Religion: The Cases of Japan and Korea," in *Religion, Globalization, and Culture*, ed. Peter Beyer and Lori Beaman (Leiden: Brill, 2007), 453–471; Aike Rots, "Worldwide Kami, Global Shinto: the Invention and Spread of a 'Nature Religion'," *Czech and Slovak Journal of Humanities* 3 (2015): 31–48; Aike Rots, *Shinto, Nature and Ideology in Contemporary Japan: Making Sacred Forests* (London: Bloomsbury, 2017); Ugo Dessì, *The Global Repositioning of Japanese Religions: An integrated approach* (London: Taylor and Francis, 2017). Two unpublished master's theses provide useful historical and ethnographic data of the American Shinto community at Tsubaki Grand Shrine of America. See: Sarah S. Ishida, "The making of an American Shinto community," Master's thesis (University of Florida, 2008.); Craig Rodrigue, "American Shinto Community of Practice: Community formation outside original context," Master's thesis (University of Nevada, Reno, 2017).

of Web 2.0.⁹ This development quickly snowballed into the ubiquitous online networks hosting billions of users a day which we now call "social media."

Digital archival research reveals that online groups explicitly interested in the Japanese religious tradition known as Shinto can be traced all the way back to the advent of Web 2.0, with the creation of the Shinto Mailing List (ShintoML) Yahoo! Group in 2000. ShintoML connected over one thousand members, who were extremely active from 2000 to 2011. The volume of posts peaked between 2002 to 2009, with several hundred to over one thousand messages shared per year. Beginning in 2010, activity dropped precipitously, with only a few dozen messages being posted each year from 2015 to 2020.¹⁰ Similarly, the mailing list for members of the Tsubaki America Grand Shrine (later Tsubaki Grand Shrine of America, hereafter TGSA), located in Granite Falls, WA, was founded on Yahoo! in 2004 and included nearly nine hundred members at its peak. It exhibits the same drop in activity starting in 2011.¹¹

This striking change in the activity of the two largest Shinto mailing list networks can be attributed to the rise of social media and its greater technological affordances for communication and community building. Popular forum sites such as Yahoo! were soon eclipsed by the creation of social networking sites (SNS), culminating in the creation of Facebook, the current dominant social media platform, in 2006. Facebook was the first social network to reach one billion registered accounts in 2013 and reports 2.85 billion monthly users as of July 2021.¹² According to a Pew Research Center study, 70% of American adults polled in 2021 reported using

---

9 For more on the history of Web 2.0, see: Sam Han, *Web 2.0* (London: Routledge, 2011).
10 Yahoo! shut down its Yahoo Groups network on December 15, 2020, citing a steady decline in usage over the previous several years and the platform's unsuitability for the company's "long-term strategy." See: "Yahoo Groups has shut down," Yahoo, https://web.archive.org/web/20210410030354/https://help.yahoo.com/kb/SLN35505.html.
11 Tsubaki Grand Shrine of America was a branch shrine of Tsubaki Grand Shrine (Tsubaki Ōkami Yashiro), a Jinja Shinto shrine located in Mie Prefecture and established according to shrine records in the third century BCE. TGSA was founded in 2001 as the result of the merging of Tsubaki Grand Shrine of America in Stockton, CA (est. 1986) and Kannagara Jinja in Granite Falls, WA (est. 1992). The shrine was officially closed on June 30, 2023. The public Facebook group continues under the new name "SHINTO / Kannagara no Michi." See: Ishida, "The making of an American Shinto community"; Rots, "Worldwide Kami"; Rodrigue, "American Shinto Community of Practice."
12 "Most popular social networks worldwide as of July 2021, ranked by number of active users (in millions)," Statista, https://web.archive.org/web/20210805222822/https://www.statista.com/statistics/272014/global-social-networks-ranked-by-number-of-users/; "Global Social Media Stats," DataReportal, https://web.archive.org/web/20210804100237/https://datareportal.com/social-media-users.

Facebook.[13] The drop in ShintoML activity on Yahoo Groups corresponds with the release of Facebook's updated group features in 2010, the same year that Facebook first overtook its competitors and claimed the number one spot in terms of popularity. The oldest groups among the largest and active DSCs on Facebook were created between 2010 and 2011, and early posts within these DSCs reference the ShintoML, suggesting that members of the mailing list migrated to and formed part of the early membership of Facebook DSCs.

Today, more than seven thousand individuals—potentially as many as twelve thousand—are members of an active digital Shinto community hosted on Facebook.[14] Exact membership is difficult to calculate without access to backend logs for three reasons: 1) many of the more active DSC members hold membership in more than one DSC; 2) users may join DSCs using multiple accounts; and 3) there is little trace of the activity of members who do not regularly interact with other members through posts, comments, and reactions (often referred to by netizens as "lurkers"). However, we can conclude through comparison of membership data from Facebook and Yahoo Groups that membership in DSCs has multiplied six times over the last twenty years, demonstrating a significant increase in global interest, if not active participation, in Shinto practice.

Membership within the seven largest and most active DSCs ranges from a few hundred to over seven thousand accounts. Among the public groups, Facebook groups created by Shinto shrines based in the mainland United States lead the pack. "SHINTO/ Tsubaki America Grand Shrine" created by the priest of TGSA in 2011 includes some 7,600 members, and the new "Shinto Inari/Shinto Shrine of Shusse Inari in America" group created in 2020 by the priest of Shinto Shrine of Shusse Inari in America (Los Angeles, CA) already includes five hundred members at the time of writing. The other four DSCs are private, and their numbers similarly range between five hundred and over four thousand members.

As mentioned, two of the seven DSCs included in this study are managed by Shinto shrines located outside of Japan. Another private group is organized by Kyoto's famous Fushimi Inari Grand Shrine. These three shrine groups were created primarily for the maintenance of transnational confraternities (*kō* 講) of lay devotees.[15] Thus, shrine-led DSCs provide more than just a forum for people to share

---

13 Brooke Auxier and Monica Anderson, "Social Media Use in 2021," Pew Research Center, April 7, 2021, https://www.pewresearch.org/internet/2021/04/07/social-media-use-in-2021/.
14 These numbers are based on the public membership counts for two of the largest and distinct digital Shinto communities at the time of writing, which report 4,200 members and 7,600 members respectively. The author expects there is a good deal of overlap between the two.
15 For more on the history of *kō*, see: Lucy S. Itō, "Kō 講: Japanese Confraternities," *Monumenta Nipponica* 8, no. 1–2 (1952): 412–415.

information and ask questions about Shinto; they also outline membership requirements for interested individuals, fundraise for shrine events and renovations, and distribute informational and ritual materials meant specifically for their confraternity members. The other four are general Shinto interest groups, some of which are targeted toward the veneration of particular *kami* such as Inari or practitioners living in certain regions (e.g., the United Kingdom, the US East Coast).

Members of these DSCs tend to be non-Japanese individuals with surface-level knowledge of Japanese history and culture gleaned from popular Japanese media, local news outlets, blogs, and brief visits to Japanese shrines.[16] However, some of the most active members in these groups have extensive knowledge of Shinto gained through personal study, lived experience in Japan, and several years of membership in DSCs, and they often play a crucial role in welcoming and integrating new members into the community. As such, these senior members may be considered stakeholders or "committed elites" who wield considerable authority in the community by virtue of their claims to access to specialized knowledge,[17] firsthand experience of life in Japan and Japanese culture, and ritual material and textual resources such as prayers and domestic altars.

While further research is required to fully understand the demographics of DSC members, a rough picture of active membership may be extrapolated from survey data regarding DSC members' domestic Shinto practice, centered on rituals conducted at their *kamidana*, gathered by the author in February 2019.[18] With the permission of group "admins" or "mods" (short for "administrator" and "moderator" respectively), I employed voluntary sampling by posting an explanation of the survey and a link in three of the private general interest DSCs. I received a representative sample of fifty survey responses, including all admins/mods and committed elites identified prior to the survey, as well as a good number of active members, less active members, and lurkers.

In terms of nationality, the survey responses indicate that the majority of active DSC members live in the United States (70%), followed by the United Kingdom (20%), although membership spans the globe, including members from Poland, Sweden, Australia, and India. The majority of DSC members disclosed that they grew up in

---

16 The recent increase in non-Japanese Shinto practitioners online mirrors trends other researchers have observed in-person at Tsubaki Grand Shrine of America. See: Ishida, "The making of an American Shinto community"; Rodrigue, "American Shinto Community of Practice."
17 Roy Wallis, "The social construction of charisma," *Social Compass* 29, no. 1 (1982): 33.
18 One product of the author's survey was the creation of a gallery of images of transnational Shinto practitioners' *kamidana*, with their owners' permission, on the "Kami Shelf" page of the author's research website: "Digital Shinto." See: Kaitlyn Ugoretz, "The Kami Shelf," Digital Shinto, https://www.digitalshinto.com/wall-of-kamidana.

nominally Christian households; however, some members grew up in Atheist and Buddhist families. Most DSC members who own a *kamidana* currently identify as Shinto practitioners, Shinto-Buddhists, or Neopagans who have incorporated elements of Shinto worship into their eclectic practices. Judging by this cross-section of DSC membership, members join DSCs in order to learn more about Shinto—a tradition that they are not familiar with due to their upbringing in non-practicing families outside of Japan—and connect with like-minded individuals.

Official group leadership, on the other hand, is populated by a mix of Japanese, Japanese diaspora (*nikkei*), and non-Japanese admins/mods with varying levels of Shinto ordination, ranging from fully ordained priest to lay shrine caretaker. For example, the admin of TGSA is Rev. Lawrence "Koichi" Barrish, the head priest of the physical Tsubaki Grand Shrine of America who claims to be "in two thousand years of Shinto history [...] the first Shinto priest who is not Japanese."[19] The admin of the largest private group is a Canadian-born associate priest of Japanese heritage at a Konkokyō sectarian Shinto shrine in Japan. Meanwhile, the admins of the Fushimi Inari confraternity group, include Brittany, a non-Japanese lay devotee of the *kami* Inari from the United States, and Ms. Morimoto, a Japanese instructor who holds rank and teaching qualification from Fushimi Inari Grand Shrine.

Defining the Field: A Bourdieusian Analysis of the Internet

Having briefly outlined the development and present character of DSCs hosted on Facebook, we may now situate them in Bourdieusian terms. In his influential theorization of distinction and taste, sociologist Pierre Bourdieu argues that practices are produced through the complex and dynamic dialectical relationship between habitus, the social field, and capital. Thus, in order to understand the creation of new practices within digital Shinto communities such as the regular posting of digital

---

[19] "First Non-Japanese Shinto Priest Rev. Koichi Barrish Discusses His Faith," World Religion News, June 5, 2015, https://www.worldreligionnews.com/religion-news/first-non-japanese-shinto-priest-rev-koichi-barrish-discusses-his-faith. According to literature and religion scholar John Dougill, Rev. Barrish was ordained in the 1990s. Contrary to Ishida, Rodrigue, and Barrish himself, while it is possible that Barrish is the first licensed non-Japanese American Shinto priest, the author's research to date suggests that the certification of Rev. Paul de Leeuw of the Japanese Dutch Shinzen Foundation in Amsterdam by the Yamakage school predates his by a decade. Austrian Florian Wiltschko was the first non-Japanese Shinto priest to be licensed through a Shinto seminary (Kokugakuin University) and appointed by Jinja Honchō in 2012. See: Rots, "Worldwide Kami."

artefacts relating to the materiality of members' home altars, we must undertake a "triple coordinated elucidation" of these three variables as they pertain to DSCs.[20]

According to Bourdieu, the habitus is "a system of durable and transposable dispositions which, integrating all past experiences, functions at every moment as a matrix of perceptions, appreciations, and actions, and makes it possible to accomplish infinitely differentiated tasks, thanks to the analogical transfer of schemata acquired in prior practice."[21] In other words, the habitus is an internalized and embodied system of cultivated dispositions which mediates between the agency and creativity of the agent and the structure and principles of the group or society in which they are socialized.[22] Scholars across a number of fields have contributed to the theorization of the "digital habitus," extending Bourdieusian theory into the technologically mediated social spaces of social media.[23] This understanding of habitus resonates with Birgit Meyer's conceptualization of "aesthetic formations," which highlights the role that media and material culture play in the formation of religious subjectivity and community.[24] Drawing upon the work of Michel Maffesoli,[25] Meyer observes how the sharing of images mobilizes and generates particular modes of thinking and feeling which in turn produce communities. Loïc Wacquant notes that the strategies, dispositions, or schemata that form the habitus are "transferable to various domains of practice [...] and realms of consumption," a phenomenon we will return to shortly.[26]

A field is generally a social arena which has its own specific logics ("doxa") that influence individuals' practices and in which individuals, according to their social position within the field, struggle in power relations to appropriate different types

---

[20] Loïc Wacquant, "A Concise Genealogy and Anatomy of Habitus," *Sociological Review* 64, no. 1 (2016): 64–72.
[21] Pierre Bourdieu, *Outline of a Theory of Practice*, trans. Richard Nice (Cambridge: Cambridge University Press, 1977), 72.
[22] Wacquant, "A Concise Genealogy and Anatomy of Habitus," 67.
[23] See: Gabe Ignatow and Laura Robinson, "Pierre Bourdieu: Theorizing the digital," *Information, Communication & Society* 20, no. 7 (2017): 950–966.; Alberto Romele and Dario Rodighiero, "Digital Habitus or Personalization without Personality," *HUMANA.MENTE Journal of Philosophical Studies* 13, no. 37 (2020): 98–126.; Rosella Gambetti, "Netnography, Digital Habitus, and Technocultural Capital," in *Netnography Unlimited: Understanding Technoculture Using Qualitative Social Media Research*, ed. Robert V. Kozinets and Rossella Gambetti (London: Routledge, 2020), 293–319.
[24] Birgit Meyer, "Introduction: From Imagined Communities to Aesthetic Formations: Religious Mediations, Sensational Forms, and Styles of Binding," in *Aesthetic Formations: Media, Religion, and the Senses*, ed. Birgit Meyer (New York, NY: Palgrave Macmillan, 2009), 7.
[25] Michel Maffesoli, *The Contemplation of the World: Figures of Community Style* (Minneapolis, MN: University of Minnesota Press, 1996).
[26] Wacquant, "A Concise Genealogy and Anatomy of Habitus," 66.

of capital.[27] Sociologists and scholars of digital media have recognized the Internet, or more specifically social media, as one such social field,[28] which encompasses an innumerable, proliferating variety of nested sub-fields such as "Facebook," "Facebook group," "Facebook religious groups," and "Shinto Facebook group."[29] I would argue, however, that the Internet is more productively conceptualized as a web or network that connects many overlapping, intersecting, and differentiated fields and sub-fields. This argument should not come as a surprise; after all, it describes the literal definition of the portmanteau of "Internet," meaning "interconnected networks." Still, if we take a particular web-based platform like Facebook and its inhabitants as our primary site and community of study, it becomes clear that the structures, interests, and practices of Facebook are quite different from another platform such as WordPress, Instagram, or LinkedIn. For example, long texts are out of place on Instagram, which is primarily populated by images with little to no accompanying text, whereas personal photographs other than professional headshots are typically deemed inappropriate on LinkedIn. Thus, the digital habitus of users, their practices, and the types of capital at stake also differ depending on the social media in question.[30] Discrete communities on Facebook, labelled as "groups," may then be considered subfields, as they share the same general social and technological infrastructure of Facebook, but distinguish themselves from other groups even further in terms of interests and practices.

As a field, the Internet generates its own forms of interest and gives rise to a "new digitally oriented habitus" in its inhabitants, whom we might call "netizens" (a popular portmanteau of "Internet citizen").[31] This digital habitus "not only is structured by the field or social forces that produced it, but [. . .] is also structuring."[32] It encompasses a host of new sensibilities, interpretive frameworks, and practices within this field which are rarely reflected upon consciously. A few representative examples include the posting of multimedia content, the impulse to stay up to date and routinely check one's notifications of new content, and the desire for

---

27 Bourdieu, *Outline of a Theory of Practice*.
28 See: Johan Lindell, "Bringing Field Theory to Social Media, and Vice-Versa: Network-Crawling an Economy of Recognition on Facebook," *Social Media + Society* 3, no. 4 (2017): 1–11; Chris Julien, "Bourdieu, Social Capital and Online Interaction," *Sociology* 49, no. 2 (2015): 356–373.
29 For more on the relationship between fields and subfields, see: Pierre Bourdieu, "The Political Field, the Social Field, and the Journalistic Field," in *Bourdieu and the Journalistic Field*, ed. Rodney Bensen and Erik Neveu (Cambridge: Polity Press, 2005), 29–47.
30 Zizi Papacharissi and Emily Easton, "In the Habitus of the New: Structure, Agency, and the Social Media Habitus," in *A Companion to New Media Dynamics*, ed. John Hartley, Jean Burgess, and Axel Bruns (Oxford: Blackwell Publishing Ltd, 2013), 172.
31 Julien, "Bourdieu, Social Capital and Online Interaction," 368.
32 Ibid.

and sense of gratification derived from engaging with content through comments and expressions of agreement ("likes") or emotion ("reactions").[33] Julien notes that although such competencies might seem unnecessary or a waste of time for people who do not spend a significant amount of time on the internet, they are vital for those that do. And the more time that one spends online, the more important and "natural" they become.[34]

We now have a general understanding of the digital fields in which netizens such as members of digital Shinto communities interact and the digital habitus which they collectively cultivate. What shape does capital take in this digital realm? Bourdieu defines capital as follows:

> Capital is a social relation, i.e., an energy which only exists and only produces its effects in the field in which it is produced and reproduced, each of the properties attached to class is given its value and efficacy by the specific laws of each field [...] the specific logic of the field determines those which are valid in this market, which are pertinent and active in the game in question, and which, in the relationship with this field, function as specific capital — and, consequently, as a factor explaining practices. This means, concretely, that the social rank and specific power which agents are assigned in a particular field depend firstly on the specific capital they can mobilize.[35]

Thus, as netizens develop a digital habitus and position themselves within various Internet fields, they both determine and have determined for them the properties and types of capital available to and valued by their peers. In the case of DSCs, Shinto capital may include material goods such as ritual objects (e.g., *kamidana*), books on Shinto, or other Japanese cultural artifacts, as well as immaterial privileges including personal conversations or relationships with Shinto priests, experience of living or traveling in Japan, and proximity to Shinto shrines. As we will see

---

[33] In 2016, Facebook was one of the first social media platforms to allow for a greater range affective communication beyond "liking" a post. At the time of writing, there are six other "reactions" that Facebook users may choose from: love, care (added as of March 2020 in response to the global COVID-19 pandemic), haha, wow, sad, and angry. These reactions are visually depicted as animated emojis. Below a given post, users can see a list of all other users' reactions to it, ranked in order of most popular reaction. In the past, Facebook has added additional temporary reactions to mark a special occasion, such as "thankful" (Mother's Day) and "pride" (LGBTQ+ Pride Month). Facebook discontinued temporary reactions in 2018. For more information, see: Liz Stinson, "Facebook Reactions, the Totally Redesigned Like Button, Is Here," Wired, February 24, 2016, https://www.wired.com/2016/02/facebook-reactions-totally-redesigned-like-button/; Andrew Liptak, "Facebook is no longer releasing temporary reaction buttons," The Verge, June 3, 2018, https://www.theverge.com/2018/6/3/17422500/facebook-no-longer-creating-custom-pride-mothers-day-like-reactions.
[34] Julien, "Bourdieu, Social Capital and Online Interaction," 368.
[35] Pierre Bourdieu, *Distinction: A Social Critique of the Judgment of Taste*, trans. Richard Nice (Cambridge, MA: Harvard University Press, 1984), 113.

below, DSC members also seek forms of "technocultural capital," which Gambetti defines as "a set of embodied knowledges, skills, competencies and dispositions that individuals mobilize in social media platforms and objectify in the form of textual, visual and symbolic cultural artifacts."[36] As we will see, in this case, technocultural capital within DSCs often takes the form of digital artifacts such as images of material objects, namely *kamidana*. With this Bourdieusian understanding of social media as fields, netizens as having a digital habitus when engaging these fields, and capital as defined according to the structure and interests thereof, we may begin to qualitatively examine these phenomena in the concrete terms of the Facebook platform and the digital Shinto communities that call them home.

Seeking the Facebook Algorithm

There is one agency at work across all of Facebook's subfields, what Bourdieu might call a "structuring force," and in the development of the digital habitus that we must account for: the Facebook algorithm. While the minute workings of the Facebook algorithm continue to change and are largely invisible to users, it has a clear preference for visuality. In what follows, I trace how this preference has developed and how it impacts the digital habitus of Facebook users, including global Shinto practitioners.

Descriptions of computer algorithms ironically highlight their indescribability. While we can simply say that algorithms are "a sequence of instructions telling a computer what to do,"[37] operating under the conditions of AND, OR, and NOT, the fact of the matter is that we do not fully understand the impact that the complex algorithms which form the basis of our relationship with the Internet. Scholars in software studies liken algorithms to a "black box:" we know that processes are going on in there, but we cannot fully know what they are.[38] In other words, algorithms are a known unknown. The opaqueness of technology is especially evident in the neural networks employed by machine learning algorithms on social media

---

36 Gambetti, "Netnography, Digital Habitus, and Technocultural Capital," 309.
37 Pedro Domingos, *The Master Algorithm: How the Quest for the Ultimate Learning Machine Will Remake Our World* (New York, NY: Basic Books, 2015), 1.
38 See: Wendy Hui Kyong Chun, *Programmed Visions: Software and Memory* (Cambridge, MA: The MIT Press, 2011); Taina Bucher, "Want to be on the top? Algorithmic power and the threat of invisibility on Facebook," *new media & society* 14, no. 7 (2012): 1164–1180; Rob Kitchin and Martin Dodge, *Code/Space: Software and Everyday Life* (Cambridge, MA: The MIT Press, 2011).

sites like Facebook.[39] At its core, the Facebook algorithm determines what posts a user sees from the people within their social network on their "news feed," a seemingly inexhaustible timeline of status updates, comments, photos, questions, and articles located in the center of one's home page. That is, because there are billions of accounts posting content on Facebook daily, users cannot and do not see everything that their Facebook "friends" or pages and groups that they choose to "follow" post on their news feed. While the computational filtering of news feed content is very practical, if not a necessity, the reasoning behind the Facebook algorithm's choices is unclear and often unpredictable. Launched in 2006, the earliest iteration of the Facebook algorithm was simply referred to as a "news feed algorithm," and the parameters for the algorithm's operations during this time are not well-known due to a lack of transparency in terms of the metrics and back-end analytics made available to users. Facebook's VP of Product Chris Cox described the development of the news feed ranking algorithm as "turning knobs [. . .] Turn up photos a little bit, turn down platform stories a little bit."[40]

In 2010, at the annual meeting of the F8 Facebook conference, Facebook announced the second major iteration of the news feed algorithm dubbed "EdgeRank."[41] This time, the developers provided a clear explanation of some of the ways in which EdgeRank makes decisions. Each item that could possibly appear on a user's news feed is called an "Object," and the EdgeRank algorithm evaluates Objects based on three main criteria, called "Edges:" affinity, weight, and time decay (Fig. 3). An Object's affinity score depends upon the history of interaction between the user and the Object's creator. Interactions cover a wide range of practices including clicks, likes, comments, and sharing. Each of these modes of interaction carry their own "edge weight" score. For example, commenting on a post is weighted more heavily than liking a post. The type of media embedded in an Object also factors into its weight. Currently, posts featuring photos and videos rank above those with just text. Finally, the timing or the recency of a post plays a role. An Object's time edge decays over time, so that newer posts are prioritized. The average time of day and frequency that a given user logs into Facebook and checks their news feed may also play a role in an Object's time score.[42]

---

39 Simone Natali, "Amazon Can Read Your Mind: A Media Archaeology of the Algorithmic Imaginary," in *Believing in Bits: Digital Media and the Supernatural*, ed. Simone Natali and D. W. Pasulka (New York, NY: Oxford University Press, 2020), 28.
40 Cox made these comments while discussing the evolution of the Facebook algorithm beyond EdgeRank in a News Feed media event on August 6, 2013. See: Matt McGee, "EdgeRank Is Dead: Facebook's News Feed Algorithm Now Has Close To 100K Weight Factors," MarTech, August 16, 2013, https://martech.org/edgerank-is-dead-facebooks-news-feed-algorithm-now-has-close-to-100k-weight-factors/.
41 McGee, "EdgeRank Is Dead."
42 Jeff Widman, "EdgeRank: A Guide to Facebook's Newsfeed Algorithm," EdgeRank.net, http://edgerank.net/.

EdgeRank's operations were certainly not limited to just these three factors, but they provide some insight into how the algorithm's developers approached the issue of personalizing and constantly updating a user's news feed with the kind of content they were most likely to engage with.

u_e ~ affinity score between viewing user & edge creator

w_e ~ weight for this edge type (create, connect, like, tag, etc.)

d_e ~ time decay factor based on how long ago the edge was created

Fig. 3: EdgeRank formula. (EdgeRank.net).

As soon as users might have felt they had a handle on how the Facebook algorithm works, it changed again. In 2011, Facebook quietly retired EdgeRank and adopted a new, nameless algorithm based on machine learning.[43] As the term "machine learning" suggests, this third iteration of the algorithm is capable of learning from the ever-increasing amount of data that it is fed and making predictions and decisions without being specifically programmed how to interpret a given condition. In 2013, Engineering Manager for News Feed Ranking Lars Backstrom reported that the algorithm took into account more than 100,000 factors, which included the EdgeRank factors of affinity, weight score, and time decay alongside many other equally important metrics.[44] With the post-EdgeRank algorithm constantly growing and changing, it is virtually impossible to completely understand it.

Still, Facebook made some effort to announce major sea changes in how the algorithm operates. In 2018, Facebook co-founder and CEO Mark Zuckerberg explained that the algorithm would be tweaked in order to better match his vision and users' reported desire for the platform to "encourage meaningful social interaction" and multidirectional communication over one-way broadcasting (the previous reigning social media marketing strategy). This update was dubbed "Facebook Zero," and in practice it meant that the algorithm would favor person-to-person interaction (i.e., posts with high engagement from friends and Groups), over those from Pages run by businesses and other organizations.

---

43 McGee, "EdgeRank is Dead."
44 Ibid.

The fact that the Facebook algorithm remains largely unknown and invisible after fifteen years only adds to its power. As Wendy Chun argues, "our media matter most when they seem not to matter at all, that is, when they have moved from the new to the habitual."[45] Similarly, Bourdieu notes that the internalization and sublimation of social schemata into the body and the unconscious mind as habitus are fundamental to the reproduction of the social and political world and hierarchical structures of power as "natural."[46] Though we do not entirely comprehend the algorithm's inner workings on a conscious level, they continue to work on us. Just as a machine learning algorithm learns from the data produced by our behavior, users gain expertise (or data) as to what the algorithm prefers through experimentation and repetition over time. As we click, post, like, comment, and share, our bodies become archives which (re)produce ourselves and the media that mediate us.

What habits does the Facebook algorithm specifically inculcate? In her research into mediated modalities of visibility, Taina Bucher argues that the Facebook algorithm silently exercises power over users through the production of a "threat of invisibility."[47] Unlike Bentham's panopticon, which disciplines the imprisoned to behave as if they are constantly under surveillance, Facebook's regime of (in)visibility disciplines users to actively pursue visibility in order to avoid obscurity. Lindell describes the resulting social field as operating according to an "economy of recognition."[48] This visibility or recognition is bestowed as a reward when the algorithm recognizes a user as creating or interacting with content on the platform in certain preferred ways, practices often described as "feeding" the algorithm. Visibility, then, represents a fundamental type of social capital that Facebook users are trained to seek by both producing and consuming ("presuming") ever more visual content.[49] Moreover, as "the dynamics of new media are founded upon the

---

[45] Wendy Hui Kyong Chun, *Updating to Remain the Same: Habitual New Media* (Cambridge, MA: The MIT Press, 2016), 1.
[46] Bourdieu, *Outline of a Theory of Practice*, 165–166.
[47] Bucher, "Want to be on the top?" 1171.
[48] Lindell, "Bringing Field Theory to Social Media."
[49] In 1980, Alvin Toffler coined the terms "prosumer" and "presumption" to describe the "progressive blurring of the line that separates producer from consumer" (267). The concept of presumption is a topic of great discussion in various fields, including technology, business and marketing, media studies, and fan studies. For example, Axel Bruns argued along similar lines that social media encourages a "participatory culture" based on "produsage," the combination of production and use that in turn generates value for consumption. Presumption often entails uncompensated labor which is then converted into a commodity by corporations. This dynamic is clearly present within Facebook communities. While DSC members create content for themselves and for each other, they are simultaneously value for Facebook and its associate advertisers by contributing

premise and the promise of constant change and permanent evolution," a "habitus of the new" has emerged to structure engagement within social media fields.[50] According to Papacharissi and Easton, the habitus of the new encourages practices of authorship and disclosure (posting), listening (reading and otherwise engaging with posts), and redaction (editing, remixing, and moderating).[51] The Facebook field, feed algorithm, and digital habitus then work together to drive users to continuously post new, highly visual content in which they mobilize technocultural capital to construct the digital social self.

We now have some understanding of how Facebook users and the algorithm come to comprehend and co-constitute each other through habitual use. What effects do these encounters between people and software have on religion? I argue that the Facebook algorithm's preference for visual content influences not only DSC members' posting practices on social media, but also their personal and collective relationships with Shinto material culture, namely the domestic *kamidana* altar.

Material Access to Shinto Capital

Douglas Cowan's heuristic framework for online religious community members is useful for understanding how DSC members' socialization into the community impacts their posting practices. Cowan defines five levels of identification, interaction, and investment from least to greatest: lurker, inquirer, stakeholder, authority, and innovator.[52] As mentioned above, it is difficult to measure the engagement of lurkers in online communities. As such, this paper will necessarily focus on the engagement of active members. While there are a few notable innovators associated with DSCs, they tend to assert their views outside of well-established DSCs — either by creating their own Facebook group or page or an independent website. Therefore, I will primarily refer to DSC members as inquirers, stakeholders, and authorities.

Posting practices within DSC groups typically fall into four broad categories: self-introductions, inquiries, acquisitions, and testaments. It is customary in online communities to post a self-introduction in order to make one's presence known to

---

to user engagement on the platform. See: Alvin Toffler, *The Third Wave* (New York, NY: Bantam, 1980); Axel Bruns, *Blogs, Wikipedia, Second Life, and Beyond: From Production to Produsage* (New York, NY: Peter Lang, 2008); Christian Fuchs, *Social Media: A Critical Introduction* (London: SAGE Publications, 2014).
50 Papacharissi and Easton, "In the Habitus of the New," 171–184.
51 Ibid., 177–180.
52 Douglas Cowan, *Cyberhenge: Modern Pagans on the Internet* (London: Routledge, 2004).

the community — thereby proving that one is a serious member, not a lurker — and express gratitude for being granted entry into the group. At this point, "authorities," typically admins and/or Shinto clergy, and "stakeholders," generally knowledgeable and active members with a significant amount of experience in the community, will often comment on the post, welcoming the newcomer and directing them to the group resources link. After introductions are made, new members will typically ask for more information, inquiring about how to begin to practice Shinto and where to get the necessary materials, core Shinto beliefs and textual resources, or particular Shinto deities and shrines, hence their categorization as "inquirers." Once inquirers find the resources they are searching for, they often post images to display their acquisition and demonstrate their proficiency to the rest of the community. Finally, DSC members post testaments to personal experiences which have led them to Shinto and encounters with the kami which affirm their chosen spiritual path. The accumulation of posts in these four rhetorical genres effectively create over time an archive of community resources for understanding and practicing Shinto.

Thanks to the networking of social fields, DSCs are constructing their own aesthetic formations or sense of taste informed by but distinct from both other online communities in general and Shinto tradition. The conditioning of this digital Shinto taste is achieved not only through human agents, but also through technological agents imbedded in the structure of Facebook such as the newsfeed algorithm.[53] According to the logic of the DSC field, the performance of the acquisition of Shinto cultural capital, in the form of ritual materials such as *kamidana*, becomes a key practice signifying access. We will see that, as access to Shinto capital among DSC members increases, authenticity emerges as a distinguishing property, hierarchically valuing certain modes of access and acquisition above others. Finally, the desire for greater appropriation of capital — and by extension recognition and authority — and distance from necessity drives the ongoing accumulation of Shinto "cultural goods."[54] This process of the generation and subsequent conditioning of digital Shinto taste and mobilization of Shinto technocultural capital primarily plays out in a specifically visual medium, which is shaped by the structure of the field, namely the feed.

---

53 For more on the agency of algorithms, see: Paul Kockelmann, "The anthropology of an equation: Sieves, spam filters, agentive algorithms, and ontologies of transformation," *HAU: Journal of Ethnographic Theory* 3, no. 3 (2013): 3–61.
54 Bourdieu, *Distinction*, 1.

Accessing Shinto Capital

Once new DSC members have posted their self-introductions and inquired as to what ritual materials at minimum are necessary for practice, they begin to document their acquisition of such materials through the posting of digital images of their ritual objects. The community agrees that some form of *kamidana* is ideal, if not required, for the veneration of the *kami*. At a minimum, this home altar includes an *ofuda*. Ideally, a *kamidana* will also include some sort of housing, vases for sacred *sakaki* branches and small containers for offerings of rice, water, salt, and sometimes sake. One inquirer Marie shared a photo of her *kamidana* in typical DSC fashion with the caption:

> So far, this is what I have for my kamidana. It's not fancy, and I don't have an ofuda yet, but I'm still making small offerings. A family member gave me the kamidana as a gift. I got the stone fox at a local indigenous community's gathering. The vase for the omiki [sake] came from family too. I hope this is acceptable for now. :)

Though she discloses that she does not yet have an *ofuda* enshrined in her *kamidana*, which is technically necessary in order to ritually encounter kami, Marie's post is in fact very typical in a number of ways. First, Marie makes it clear in her caption that she has access to information about Shinto—she knows that she needs a *kamidana* as well as the ritual role of the ofuda, despite not yet having the latter, and she has command of Japanese terminology for various implements. In addition, Marie demonstrates her access to Shinto materials; she has successfully acquired a *kamidana* through a family member from an online store. Marie has taken her first step toward constructing her identity as a Shinto practitioner and gaining recognition as one within the community. The attached image is crucial to the post achieving these goals by showing "receipts" (i.e., objective proof or evidence, often in the form of photographs or screenshots) of Marie's capital. As forum users often challenge in response to unverified claims, "pics or it didn't happen," Marie includes this digital image of her *kamidana* in likely anticipation of the question, "Are you a serious Shinto practitioner?"[55]

---

55 For more on the growing necessity of visual evidence for life on the internet, see: Adam Schrag, "'Pics, or it didn't happen': On Visual Evidence in the Age of Ubiquitous Photography," *Pacific Journal* 10 (2015): 1–16.

Authenticating Shinto Capital

As DSC members share images of ritual materials and information about how they acquired them, Shinto capital has effectively become more accessible to more people. Both survey data on home altar practices and observational data from DSC Facebook groups illustrate that while new members like Marie often have an adaptive, "by any means possible" attitude and frequently purchase cultural goods from online stores like Amazon and eBay, authorities and stakeholders within the community tend to make prescriptive comments when it comes to acquisitional practices. For example, Leo posted a photo of a metal object with a green patina and the name of Fushimi Inari Grand Shrine inscribed on it (Fig. 4), asking the community, "I found this Inari item online. Does anyone know what it is and where I can get one? Thanks!"

Fig. 4: A Fushimi Inari bell (*juyosho*). (Found on eBay).

A few members identified the object as a bell called a *juyosho* usually given to Inari devotees by a shrine in exchange for a donation, with one person adding that they had bought one from a Kyoto-based vendor on eBay. Soon enough, two active members, one an admin and the other a prominent stakeholder, stepped in. Brittany, the admin, cautions, "Please don't purchase items from online resellers. It's not allowed." Brittany's comment prompted a lengthy discussion between several members on ethical consumption. They explained that receiving goods from a shrine in exchange for a donation is not technically a purchase; goods received from a shrine through the mail are ritually protected by special packaging; and the act of purchasing from a mediator between the shrine and the devotee generates ritual pollution which harms the efficacy of the ritual material. Thus, authorities within DSCs claim that only cultural goods obtained directly through a shrine are authentic and efficacious. Apart from authorities and stakeholders, who are often either clergy themselves or have close relationships with clergy, very few members have awareness of and direct access to Shinto shrines, even those located in the United States. As a result, DSC members with such social and cultural capital position themselves above those who do not, creating an implicit hierarchy of both access and authenticity through the regulation of the "material economy of the sacred."[56]

Another case is noteworthy within this web of distinctions as an example of how members with knowledge of the "appropriate" way to acquire Shinto but inadequate access are still able to mobilize their own reserve of capital through the posting of images of ritual materials. Shortly after the intense discussion sparked by Leo's post, Joe posts a picture of an *omamori* (Fig. 5) — a protective talisman — from Fushimi Inari Grand Shrine with a lengthy confession:

> I received this today. I messed up. I saw this on Amazon and got excited. I purchased it out of ignorance. I use the word purchase here purposefully because it really was a commercial transaction. I learned from the Shinto groups that I obtained it incorrectly when it was already in the mail. I regret this mistake and I hope Inari Okami will forgive me, but I'll also treat this item with the respect it deserves even if it has become polluted and lost its virtue.

This event is interesting because there was no obvious need for Joe to disclose that he had bought ritual materials "incorrectly" or to post an image. However, Joe is able to both mobilize and recuperate his Shinto capital by demonstrating his access to Shinto goods, even if somewhat "inauthentic," his new knowledge of the property of authenticity, and his devotion to the *kami* Inari. For Joe, posting a picture of illicit goods is still better than posting no picture at all, and some access is better than no access. These two related events and the struggle between agents over authenticity illustrate the power of the feed's demand for visual posts to continuously elicit them from users. In response, the digital Shinto judgment of taste is developing and becoming more complex through the generation of distinctions.

---

56 David Morgan, "The Material Culture of Lived Religion: Visuality and Embodiment," In *Mind and Matter*, ed. Johanna Vakkari (Helsinki: Taidehistorian seura, 2010), 27.

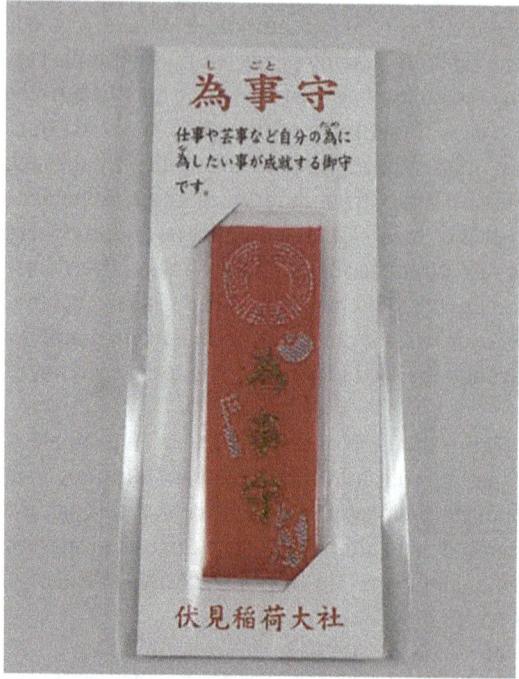

Fig. 5: Joe's problematic Fushimi Inari omamori from an online vendor.

Accumulating Shinto Capital

If one has acquired the necessary materials and practical knowledge for ritual practice and has done so as authentically as possible, how can one further distinguish themself from their peers in DSCs? Neither Bourdieu nor Marx would be surprised to find that the prescription is the further accumulation of Shinto capital. A diachronic analysis of DSC members' socialization into the community and their posting practices demonstrates that once a Shinto practitioner has set up their *kamidana*, they often seek to add additional elements and embellishments. Survey and interview data show that DSC members sometimes speak in terms of "upgrading" their *kamidana*, often referring to the replacement of a single-door *miyagata* with a three-door *miyagata* or the addition of more *miyagata* to accommodate more *ofuda* and thus more *kami*.

Dave, a veteran DSC member and extremely active stakeholder, has documented the growth of his *kamidana* through Facebook posts over the last six years. Recently, he posted a series of thirteen pictures documenting his unpacking of goods he received from a Shinto priest step-by-step, an Internet-based practice known as "unboxing." Unboxing, typically performed through the medium of video, draws its popularity from allowing the viewer to get a sense of a product before they buy, as well as to vicariously experience the thrill of consuming a product in advance of purchase or without having to purchase it themself.[57] In this case, Dave produced (and the audience consumed) images of a set of twin guardian fox statues handmade by a Shinto priest and administrator of the DSC. He also provides a picture of the statues installed on his elaborate *kamidana*,[58] laden with various paraphernalia, including several votive plaques (*ema*), lucky arrows (*hama-ya*), protective charms (*omamori*), several small fox figurines, paper lanterns, and a large vermillion banner printed with an image of Fushimi Inari Grand Shrine. He laments that he will need to reinforce the altar shelf due to the added weight and comments, "[it's] almost complete," suggesting future additions or reconfigurations.

Influenced by the Facebook algorithm's regime of visibility and the habitus of the new, DSC members must continue to post novel images in order for their religious identity to continue to be rendered visible to the community. Even well-established stakeholders and authorities within DSCs find reasons to post new pictures of their *kamidana*, perhaps with new additions, special offerings, or a different arrangement. In the increasingly differentiated development of a digital Shinto habitus and taste, *kamidana* thus undergo a transformation from relatively simple domestic altar to a work-in-progress, an ongoing personal project of creative assemblage. Each new addition is broadcast by the individual to the community through some sort of image post, prompting admiration and questions concerning the material's properties and provenance, to gain recognition as a Shinto practitioner and increase one's social capital and position within the community.

---

57 Research on unboxing videos to date has primarily focused on the subject in terms of marketing media, as well as children's digital literacies and practices, particularly the popular YouTube channel EvanHD. See: Jackie Marsh, "'Unboxing' videos: Co-construction of the Child as Cyberflâneur," *Discourse: Studies in the Cultural Politics of Education* 37, no. 3 (2015): 359–380; Marina Ramos-Serrano and Paula Herrero-Diz, "Unboxing and Brands: YouTubers Phenomenon Through the Case Study of EvanTubeHD," *Prisma Social* 1 (May 2016): 90–120; David Craig and Stuart Cunningham, "Toy unboxing: living in a(n unregulated) material world," *Media International Australia* 163, no. 1 (2017): 77–86. However, Leander Kahney (2004) and Anja Pogačnik and Aleš Črnič (2014) have examined the private unboxing of products made by the technology company Apple as a kind of ritualistic practice. See: Leander Kahney, *The Cult of Macintosh* (San Francisco, CA: No Starch Press, 2004); Anja Pogačnik and Aleš Črnič, "iReligion: Religious Elements of the Apple Phenomenon," *The Journal of Religion and Popular Culture* 26, no. 3 (Fall 2014): 353–364.

58 A photograph of this particular *kamidana* may be viewed on the Digital Shinto Project website. See: Ugoretz, "The Kami Shelf."

Conclusion

In this chapter, I have shown that digital Shinto communities are developing a distinct taste for and relationship with Japanese religious material culture through the practice of sharing images of physical ritual objects such as *kamidana* altars. Though these digital artifacts are formed by pixels and bits, their production and consumption are fundamentally material. This form of technocultural capital is made possible by the global manufacturing and movement of *kamidana*, their physical handling and positioning, the taps, clicks, and other bodily motions involved in their photographing and posting, and the feeling of recognition and rush of serotonin when seeing these images and other people's engagement with them. I suggested that there is another material agent at work in the ongoing formation of a global Shinto habitus: the Facebook algorithm. Transnational Shinto practitioners recognize and are recognized by others as such through their displays of photos documenting their access to, authentication, and accumulation of Shinto capital thanks to the Facebook algorithm recognizing their posts as valuable to the social media platform and its users.

Scholars of religion are particularly attentive to the power that invisible, intangible forces may exert over people's lived experiences. Yet there is relatively little scholarship focusing on the religious implications of algorithms.[59] Further research is necessary to determine how the Facebook algorithm's desire for visual media and other aspects such as personalized advertisements may influence consumption of religious material and the creation of sacred space within the home. In addition, there is much to be said about how the algorithm influences structures of authority within online communities. Scholars of Asian religions have an opportunity to bring our considerable expertise to bear on the question of how algorithms — quietly running in the background of our social lives — participate in the material economy of the sacred and mediate lived religious thought, feeling, and identity.

---

[59] See: Sasha A. Q. Scott, "Algorithmic Absolution: The Case of Catholic Confession Apps," *Online – Heidelberg Journal of Religions on the Internet* 11 (2016): 254–275; Natali, "Amazon Can Read Your Mind."

Bibliography

Auxier, Brooke and Monica Anderson. "Social Media Use in 2021," Pew Research Center, April 7, 2021, https://www.pewresearch.org/internet/2021/04/07/social-media-use-in-2021/.
Bourdieu, Pierre. *Distinction: A Social Critique of the Judgment of Taste*. Translated by Richard Nice. Cambridge, MA: Harvard University Press, 1984.
Bourdieu, Pierre. *Outline of a Theory of Practice*. Translated by Richard Nice. Cambridge, MA: Cambridge University Press, 1977.
Bourdieu, Pierre. "The Political Field, the Social Field, and the Journalistic Field." In *Bourdieu and the Journalistic Field*, edited by Rodney Bensen and Erik Neveu, 29–47. Cambridge: Polity Press, 2005.
Bruns, Axel. *Blogs, Wikipedia, Second Life, and Beyond: From Production to Produsage*. New York, NY: Peter Lang, 2008.
Bucher, Taina. "The algorithmic imaginary: exploring the ordinary affects of Facebook algorithms." *Information, Communication & Society* 20, no. 1 (2017): 30–44.
Bucher, Taina. "Want to be on the top? Algorithmic power and the threat of invisibility on Facebook." *new media & society* 14, no. 7 (2012): 1164–1180.
Chun, Wendy Hui Kyong. *Programmed Visions: Software and Memory*. Cambridge, MA: The MIT Press, 2011.
Chun, Wendy Hui Kyong. *Updating to Remain the Same: Habitual New Media*. Cambridge, MA: The MIT Press, 2016.
Cowan, Douglas. *Cyberhenge: Modern Pagans on the Internet*. London: Routledge, 2004.
Craig, David and Stuart Cunningham. "Toy unboxing: living in a(n unregulated) material world." *Media International Australia* 163, no. 1 (2017): 77–86.
Dessì, Ugo. *The Global Repositioning of Japanese Religions: An integrated approach*. London: Routledge, 2017.
Domingos, Pedro. *The Master Algorithm: How the Quest for the Ultimate Learning Machine Will Remake Our World*. New York, NY: Basic Books, 2015.
"First Non-Japanese Shinto Priest Rev. Koichi Barrish Discusses His Faith," World Religion News, June 5, 2015, https://www.worldreligionnews.com/religion-news/first-non-japanese-shinto-priest-rev-koichi-barrish-discusses-his-faith.
Fuchs, Christian. *Social Media: A Critical Introduction*. London: SAGE Publications, 2014.
Gambetti, Rosella. "Netnography, Digital Habitus, and Technocultural Capital." In *Netnography Unlimited: Understanding Technoculture Using Qualitative Social Media Research*, edited by Robert V. Kozinets and Rossella Gambetti, 293–319. London: Routledge, 2020.
"Global Social Media Stats," DataReportal, https://web.archive.org/web/20210804100237/https://datareportal.com/social-media-users [Accessed August 6, 2021].
Gould, Hannah. "Domesticating Buddha: making a place for Buddhist altars (butsudan) in western homes." *Material Religion* 14, no. 4 (2019): 488–510.
Gould, Hannah, Tamara Kohn and Martin Gibbs. "Uploading the ancestors: Experiments with digital Buddhist altars in contemporary Japan." *Death Studies* 43, no. 7 (2019): 456–465.
Han, Sam. *Web 2.0*. London: Routledge, 2011.
Ignatow, Gabe and Laura Robinson. "Pierre Bourdieu: Theorizing the digital." *Information, Communication & Society* 20, no. 7 (2017): 950–966.
Inoue, Nobutaka. "Globalization and Religion: The Cases of Japan and Korea." In *Religion, Globalization, and Culture*, edited by Peter Beyer and Lori Beaman, 453–471. Leiden: Brill, 2007.

Ishida, Sarah S. "The making of an American Shinto community." Master's thesis, University of Florida, 2008.
Itō, Lucy S. "Kō 講: Japanese Confraternities." *Monumenta Nipponica* 8, no. 1–2 (1952): 412–415.
Iwamura, Jane Naomi. "Altared States: Exploring the Legacy of Japanese American Butsudan Practice." *Pacific World: Journal of the Institute of Buddhist Studies* 3, no. 5 (2003): 275–291.
Julien, Chris. "Bourdieu, Social Capital and Online Interaction." *Sociology* 49, no. 2 (2015): 356–373.
Kahney, Leander. *The Cult of Macintosh*. San Francisco, CA: No Starch Press, 2004.
Kitchin, Rob and Martin Dodge. *Code/Space: Software and Everyday Life*. Cambridge, MA: The MIT Press, 2011.
Kockelmann, Paul. "The anthropology of an equation: Sieves, spam filters, agentive algorithms, and ontologies of transformation." *HAU: Journal of Ethnographic Theory* 3, no. 3 (2013): 3–61.
Lindell, Johan. "Bringing Field Theory to Social Media, and Vice-Versa: Network-Crawling an Economy of Recognition on Facebook." *Social Media + Society* 3, no. 4 (2017): 1–11.
Liptak, Andrew. "Facebook is no longer releasing temporary reaction buttons," The Verge, June 3, 2018, https://www.theverge.com/2018/6/3/17422500/facebook-no-longer-creating-custom-pride-mothers-day-like-reactions.
Maffesoli, Michel. *The Contemplation of the World: Figures of Community Style*. Minneapolis, MN: University of Minnesota Press, 1996.
Marsh, Jackie. "'Unboxing' videos: Co-construction of the Child as Cyberflâneur." *Discourse: Studies in the Cultural Politics of Education* 37, no. 3 (2015): 359–380.
McGee, Matt. "EdgeRank is Dead: Facebook's News Feed Algorithm Now Has Close to 100K Weight Factors," MarTech, August 16, 2013, https://martech.org/edgerank-is-dead-facebooks-news-feed-algorithm-now-has-close-to-100k-weight-factors.
Meyer, Birgit. "Introduction: From Imagined Communities to Aesthetic Formations: Religious Mediations, Sensational Forms, and Styles of Binding." In *Aesthetic Formations: Media, Religion, and the Senses*, edited by Birgit Meyer, 1–30. New York, NY: Palgrave Macmillan, 2009.
Morgan, David. "The Material Culture of Lived Religion: Visuality and Embodiment." In *Mind and Matter*, edited by Johanna Vakkari, 14–31. Helsinki: Taidehistorian seura, 2010.
"Most popular social networks worldwide as of July 2021, ranked by number of active users (in millions)," Statista, https://web.archive.org/web/20210805222822/https://www.statista.com/statistics/272014/global-social-networks-ranked-by-number-of-users/ [Accessed August 6, 2021].
Natali, Simone. "Amazon Can Read Your Mind: A Media Archaeology of the Algorithmic Imaginary." In *Believing in Bits: Digital Media and the Supernatural*, edited by Simone Natali and D. W. Pasulka, 19–34. New York, NY: Oxford University Press, 2020.
Nelson, John. "Home Altars in Contemporary Japan: Rectifying Buddhist "Ancestor Worship" with Home Décor and Consumer Choice." *Japanese Journal of Religious Studies* 35, no. 2 (2008): 305–330.
Okada, Yoshiyuki. "Kamidana," Encyclopedia of Shinto, https://d-museum.kokugakuin.ac.jp/eos/detail/?id=9666 [Accessed August 30, 2021].
Papacharissi, Zizi and Emily Easton. "In the Habitus of the New: Structure, Agency, and the Social Media Habitus." In *A Companion to New Media Dynamics*, edited by John Hartley, Jean Burgess, and Axel Bruns, 171–184. Oxford: Blackwell Publishing Ltd, 2013.
Pogačnik, Anja and Aleš Črnič. "iReligion: Religious Elements of the Apple Phenomenon." *The Journal of Religion and Popular Culture* 26, no. 3 (Fall 2014): 353–364.
Rambelli, Fabio. "Home Buddhas: Historical Processes and Modes of Representation of the Sacred in the Japanese Buddhist Family Altar (Butsudan)." *Japanese Religions* 35, no. 1/2 (2010): 63–86.

Ramos-Serrano, Marina and Paula Herrero-Diz. "Unboxing and Brands: YouTubers Phenomenon Through the Case Study of EvanTubeHD." *Prisma Social* 1 (May 2016): 90–120.

Rocha, Christina. "'Can I put this Jizō together with the Virgin Mary in the altar?': Creolizing Zen Buddhism in Brazil." In *Issei Buddhism in the Americas*, edited by Duncan Ryūken Williams and Tomoe Moriya, 5–26. Urbana, IL: University of Illinois Press, 2010.

Rodrigue, Craig. "American Shinto Community of Practice: Community formation outside original context." Master's thesis, University of Nevada, Reno, 2017.

Romele, Alberto and Dario Rodighiero. "Digital Habitus or Personalization without Personality." *HUMANA.MENTE Journal of Philosophical Studies* 13, no. 37 (2020): 98–126.

Rots, Aike. *Shinto, Nature and Ideology in Contemporary Japan: Making Sacred Forests*. London: Bloomsbury, 2017.

Rots, Aike. "Worldwide Kami, Global Shinto: the Invention and Spread of a 'Nature Religion.'" *Czech and Slovak Journal of Humanities* 3 (2015): 31–48.

Schrag, Adam. "'Pics, or it didn't happen': On Visual Evidence in the Age of Ubiquitous Photography." *Pacific Journal* 10 (2015): 1–16.

Scott, Sasha A. Q. "Algorithmic Absolution: The Case of Catholic Confession Apps." *Online – Heidelberg Journal of Religions on the Internet* 11 (2016): 254–275.

Stinson, Liz. "Facebook Reactions, the Totally Redesigned Like Button, Is Here," Wired, February 24, 2016, https://www.wired.com/2016/02/facebook-reactions-totally-redesigned-like-button/.

Toffler, Alvin. *The Third Wave*. New York, NY: Bantam, 1980.

Turner, Kay. *Beautiful Necessity: The art and Meaning of Women's Altars*. New York, NY: Thames & Hudson, 1999.

Ugoretz, Kaitlyn. "Case Study — World-Wide Shintō: The Globalization of 'Japanese' Religion." In *Bloomsbury Handbook of Japanese Religions*, edited by Erica Baffelli, Andrea Castiglioni, and Fabio Rambelli, pp 145–148. London: Bloomsbury, 2021a.

Ugoretz, Kaitlyn. "Digital Shinto Communities." The Database of Religious History, https://religiondatabase.org/browse/1071 [accessed January 10, 2022].

Ugoretz, Kaitlyn. "Do Kentucky Kami Drink Bourbon? Exploring Parallel Glocalization in Global Shinto Offerings." *Religions* 13, no. 257 (2022): 1–15.

Ugoretz, Kaitlyn. "The Kami Shelf," Digital Shinto, https://www.digitalshinto.com/wall-of-kamidana. [Last modified June 2019].

Wacquant, Loïc. "A concise genealogy and anatomy of habitus." *Sociological Review* 64, no. 1 (2016): 64–72.

Wallis, Roy. "The construction of charisma." *Social Compass* XXIX, no. 1 (1982): 25–39.

Widman, Jeff. "EdgeRank: A Guide to Facebook's Newsfeed Algorithm," EdgeRank.net, http://edgerank.net/ [accessed August 6, 2021].

"Yahoo Groups has shut down," Yahoo Help, https://web.archive.org/web/20210410030354/https://help.yahoo.com/kb/SLN35505.html [accessed August 6, 2021].

L.W.C. van Lit and J.H. Morris
Conclusion: Surprising Effects of the Digital Turn

Between the proposal we wrote for this volume and the actual submissions we received, lies a stark difference. In hindsight, we editors were relying too much on the assumption that we can do the same old work that our fields have been doing for decades, but this time digitally. Thus, we had initially emphasized the study of premodern religion through digital surrogates of its usual evidence of manuscripts, art, and architecture. The problems we thought we would be facing were those in the digitization process. But as it turns out, a variety of things change drastically, once you investigate religion (ancient as it may be) in a digital world. We can group those surprising differences into three points. One has to do with a resurfacing of Orientalism as a critical inflection point. Another is the modernity or vitality of ancient religions which become partly digital themselves. Lastly we notice a struggle about which details we need to capture digitally. We shall discuss them here in turn.

Orientalism

Perhaps most eye-catching is the re-emergence of Orientalism as an important theoretical framework. Plau specifically invokes the term in his reflections, but we think he is not the only one who is struggling with it. Orientalism is usually understood as an entrenched, stereotypical representation of religion that supports or encourages a colonial power dynamic. We think a broader definition is useful here: an oppositional, one-sided representation of a religious expression that forces an epistemological paradigm or power relationship onto an interlocutor. The problem is, of course, that other aspects of the religious expression are under-emphasized and since this is done in some form of conversation with someone else, there is an element of coercion or negotiation. Fact finding and value judging start to overlap, and their boundaries become blurry. At worst, facts are weaponized. At best, values impede any further mingling.

We see the problem emerge in six contributions, in different shapes and forms, some more obvious than others. The two most obvious ones are Plau and Curtis.

Plau gives a detailed discussion on inherent biases in digital tools when working on manuscripts. He points out that the clarity or neatness of technology can mask reality. For example, placing manuscripts on a map seems like a clean solution to investigate dissemination. Until we notice that only 19 out of 180 manuscripts mention a location in the colophon. And even then, as Plau argues, what are we looking at? Can the map say something about dissemination or does it actually say something about the purchase strategy of Henry Wellcome in the nineteenth century? Similarly, transcribing the manuscripts digitally allows for easy encoding of variants. But a lot of variants are merely differences in spelling or other kinds of regional differences based on differences in vernacular. The technology, however, demands us to display only one at a time, driving us towards selecting the best among all variants. But isn't this the age-old Orientalist view of Sanskrit as the high language and vernacular as a mere obstacle to reach the original? Plau, in short, reconsiders our entire endeavor. He concludes we should at every step of the way be aware that we do not produce accurate representations and that our research should not be an endpoint, but rather an appendix, in our continued pursuit to engage with religious texts from the past. Plau's carefulness can be explained as an awareness of inherently being the "aggressor," as what he works with are texts written by people who have been dead for hundreds of years. Then again, we would concur that scholarship also needs courage to make a decision and take a stance. Without it, we do not move the needle. Plau is afraid that "having passed through my hands, the material, now digital, is not without my conceptual fingerprints." We would say that every interaction, especially with a historical artifact, is an editorial decision. And any editorial decision purposely emphasizes some aspects over others, based on our understanding of what makes something truly interesting. These fingerprints are therefore unavoidable, indeed they are good, as long as we contextualize ourselves and keep exercising the uncomfortable questions that Plau uncovers.

The situation is quite different in Curtis' contribution. While for Plau, Orientalism is a problem that hides within the unspoken assumptions of one's own work, for Curtis it is as clear as day, forcefully pushed onto her, in the form of a barrage of messages coming from a specific account on Twitter. These messages contain all sorts of Orientalist tropes that are presented matter-of-factly, and because they address scholars directly they demand a response. While scholars of ancient religions usually have all the time in the world to come up with the correct response, since their sources won't talk back and their colleagues discuss matters through peer-reviewed journals, in the age of social media all of a sudden the pressure is on to immediately come up with the right response. A complicating factor is that such Orientalist remarks could be favorably received by practitioners of the religions in question themselves, if it meets some purpose. Oftentimes, this purpose has to do with strife between religious groups over national identity and political power. This jolts us back to the question who we are to say, as outsiders, what a religion ought or ought not to be. In this regard, Curtis is a lot more forceful than Plau. "We must be prepared to support all that it means to be a public intellectual," she writes. While Plau is careful not to force a biased interpretation of the facts onto a wider audience, as though reigning from an ivory tower, Curtis is convinced that not saying anything in the situations she finds herself in, would exactly be an ivory tower attitude.

We can notice, then, different dimensions to this new problem of Orientalism. One dimension is how certain people are in rightfulness of their actions. Curtis, Flügel and Van der Meij and Van der Putten veer towards being very certain about their representation of religious phenomena that they encounter. Plau, Ugoretz, and Datta are seen to go back and forth on the normative impact their findings have and the objective possibilities their values have. Flügel's chapter is an interesting contrast to Plau's. They both work on early modern Jainism, but Flügel writes about his prosopography database project with a commanding sense of purpose. The design decisions they made in the project are geared towards integrating different historical sources. The reasons why these sources should be leading are taken for granted: this is how we did things, so this is how we do things. That both scholarly works and confessional works are sourced towards the same database is seen as unproblematic. Facts are, after all, facts, no matter where you find them (or are they?). Van der Meij and Van der Putten's chapter is equally interesting to interrogate on this question. Their work, just like Flügel's, is part of a project. The DREAMSEA project digitizes manuscripts from Southeast Asia, especially from private collections. At all levels of the organization, there are people and institutions involved from both the region itself as well as from Europe and North America. Plau expresses his wish that his work contributes to a repatriation of cultural heritage to people from the region (in his case the Indian subcontinent), "to the communities to whom they matter the most." Van der Meij and Van der Putten dryly state that they routinely find the manuscripts they digitize in very poor storage condition, as the owners see their possessions as nothing more than "relics of the past." They cannot use it because they do not understand the script nor, sometimes, the language. Should we, then, also dismiss these manuscripts as worthless? Or are Van der Meij and Van der Putten right in feeling a sense of urgency to preserve them digitally?

Another axis is how much they are themselves starting this interaction ("aggressor"), or how much they are on the receiving end ("victim"). Plau, Flügel, and Van der Meij and Van der Putten have a more active role, while Curtis, Ugoretz, and Datta are more on the reactive end of the spectrum. The reactive side is especially interesting. Ugoretz looks at online religious communities, specifically those that attract followers who live outside of Asia. It could be argued that this is a form of cultural appropriation, committed oftentimes in an ill-conceived or half-informed manner. An important question of her chapter is "If domestic altars in Japanese traditions are a deeply private and personal matter, why then do transnational Shinto practitioners make a habit of sharing photos of their *kamidana* online?" She opts for a soft approach. Rather than seeing it as a bad practice, she sees it as a new practice. Datta has a different kind of online community as her subject; the loose alliance of protests spread across different platforms and constantly weaving in and out the digital and real world (related to the 2013 Shahbag Protests). A recurring theme in her chapter is how people make religious-normative decisions based on misunderstandings of technology they are using for the first time. She calls this "misconceptions" and a "vicarious religion," thereby attempting to strike a compromise between retaining a correct understanding of what religions ought to be (historically) and the actual behavior online and in the real world (in the present).

Perhaps we ought to have expected the theme of Orientalism to appear in the volume — we are known as the editors of *The Digital Orientalist* after all, though we have been careful to distinguish between the Saidian Orientalism (colonialist biases underpinned popular and scholarly representations of Asia) and digital Orientalism (i.e. the digital study of the orient) as a potentially useful descriptor (homogenizing though it may be) of attempts to apply digital methods and tools to Asian studies.[1] Nevertheless, the term "digital Orientalism" has also entered scholarship quite separately and with quite different connotations than within our own work. We see the term adopted by Mahsa Alimardani and Mona Elswah to refer to the continued use of "the stereotypical and discriminatory lens by which western nations view the Middle East and North African region. . .to assert dominance and colonialism"[2] within the digital sphere and particularly how this shapes the approaches of Western social media companies vis-à-vis users in the Arabic world. Maximilian Mayer employs the term in reference to negative stereotypes about China's internet revolution and authoritarianism,[3] and Esperanza Miyake uses digital orientalism as a framework to understand how digital culture perpetuates the racialized and gendered Othering of the Japanese virtually.[4] Similar discourses previously adopted the term "Techno-Orientalism" which focused on the technological "emasculation" of Europe and North America by nations such

---

[1] L. W. Cornelis van Lit, James H. Morris and Deniz Çevik, "A Digital Revival of Oriental Studies," *Revue de l'Institut des langues et cultures d'Europe, Amérique, Afrique, Asie et Australie* 39 (2020): 1–14.
[2] Mahsa Alimardani and Mona Elswah, "Digital Orientalism: #SaveSheikhJarrah and Arabic Content Moderation," *POMEPS Studies* 43, *Digital Activism and Authoritarian Adaptation in the Middle East* (2021): 69.
[3] Maximilian Mayer, "China's Authoritarian Internet and Digital Orientalism," in *Redesigning Organizations: Concepts for the Connected Society*, ed. Denise Feldner (Cham: Springer, 2020), 177–192.
[4] Esperanza Miyake, "I am a virtual girl from Tokyo: Virtual influencers, digital orientalism and the immateriality of race and gender," *Journal of Consumer Culture*. DOI: https://doi.org/10.1177/14695405221111719.

as Japan and how this shapes Orientalist discourses and Othering.[5] In any case, it should be clear that for some scholars Orientalism in the digital world has emerged as the successor of Orientalist discourses of old. However, as the foregoing discussions indicate it should be equally clear that we are seeing a much more complex interaction with Orientalism as a theoretical framework in this volume and beyond. It is neither simply the digital study of the orient nor simply the successor of Saidian Orientalism, it can represent both, but also many more things — the biases of digital tools and our use of them, responses on social media, the positionality and action of the scholar and their project etc.

Vitality

The wide-reaching, real-world influence of the interaction between religion and the digital is encapsulated particularly well in Datta's contribution. She illustrates the often intertwined nature of politics and religion in the Bangladeshi movements that she discusses. This exploration provides an important record of the country's emergence from technological inequality with a focus on how Bangladesh's rural-urban divide has influenced this emergence, showing us how users can engage with religio-political discourse and protest through social media. We are likely familiar with using social media for voicing protest, but our own experience does not necessarily translate well to the situation in Bangladesh. Both the ephemeral and the emergent character of the rise in digital religio-political discourse are captured well by Datta, showing the evolution by which people adapt and readapt digital means to reach their real-life goals. The ephemeral nature of digital media means that as easy it is to participate, as difficult it is to get the entire picture of it. Because digital media obtains its importance by being shared, often in private or semi-private digital spaces, it is not the static state but rather the dynamic flow of information that is important. For example, a digital statement by an established politician or

---

5 The following explorations are particularly important or accessible: David Morley and Kevin Robins, *Spaces of Identity: Global Media, Electronic Landscapes, and Cultural Boundaries* (London: Routledge, 1995), digital version with no page numbers; Toshiya Ueno, "Japanimation and Techno-Orientalism," in *The Uncanny: Experiments in Cyborg Culture*, ed. Bruce Grenville (Vancouver: Vancouver Art Gallery, 2001), 223–231; Toshiya Ueno, "The Shock Projected onto the Other: Notes on *Japanimation and Techno-Orientalism*," in *The Uncanny: Experiments in Cyborg Culture*, ed. Bruce Grenville (Vancouver: Vancouver Art Gallery, 2001), 232–236; Masanori Oda, "Welcoming the Libido of the Technoids who haunt the junkyard of the Techno-Orient, or the Uncanny Experience of the Post-Techno-Orientalist Moment," in *The Uncanny: Experiments in Cyborg Culture*, ed. Bruce Grenville (Vancouver: Vancouver Art Gallery, 2001), 249–273.

religious leader with little to no engagement is less important than a digital statement by a random supporter of a movement which is shared, liked, commented, and reposted many times. For people in digital studies or cultural analytics, this is no news. But for us, experts in religions from Asia, it requires an entirely different approach. We cannot continue to rely on a canon or institutional importance. Datta prefers to take a sample of texts, photos, pictures, videos, and audio from various platforms, and study its contents and the context from which it emerges (or, more often, is shared), to get a grip on this. In effect, what she captures is the shifting nature of religious practice and identity making, showing that digital tools are virtually immediately incorporated into this shift, once they become available. As such, while the consequences manifest prominently in real life (through protests, sometimes even violence), the process that led to it cannot be understood without analyzing people's digital lives. Datta's approach is convincing but what remains is to ask ourselves if we should do this ourselves or leave it to others more well-versed in such an approach. After all, this is digital culture, which is best discussed by those researchers who have made digital media their homestead. Datta does not address this question specifically, but implicitly does make a case that this could be alright when the issues are merely economic, political or social, but not when it is religious. Ancient elements of religion are creatively reused in subtle ways. Even in cases where an element is incorrectly used, such an observation is interesting to make, and nearly impossible to make without a deep understanding of the religion. It will be easier for us to adapt methods from fields such as digital studies, than it is to rely on those researchers learning enough about the religions to correctly interpret the evidence. When we, the editors, initiated this volume, we did not think it would be our business to investigate contemporary, digital culture. But Datta and other contributors convincingly show we better get ourselves involved in it. The interaction between real life political struggle and online religious practices shows that the stakes are high, making it very important that a correct understanding is provided. Further, because of the global nature of online events, the possibility becomes much higher that someone completely removed from the local context starts interpreting these online events. Misinterpretation is therefore much more common than before.

Correctly understanding the religious significance of digital practices is displayed in the chapter by Ugoretz as well. Ugoretz captures the reverse: real life events and norms have their influence on people's digital behavior where they terminate to form a truly digital alternative to traditional religion. Her work is mostly centered around photos of domestic Shinto altars. This could have been seen as a form of digitization: a normal, real life religious phenomenon is digitally captured through a photo merely to be analyzed as the normal religious phenomenon that it is. But instead, her analysis of online Shinto communities identifies new practices, new types of leaders, new rites of initiation, and all kinds of other customs that together make up a (new) religion. And not just that, but she shows how aspects of the digital fabric (such as Facebook's algorithm which favors certain kinds of postings over others) practically influence these customs. Ancient religions are not just digitized, but their digital versions are fundamentally different in form and in practice. Ugoretz's starting observation is that such domestic altars are normally a private affair, not to be shared with others let alone brag about, which makes photographing and discussing the photos an inherently conflicting practice, and yet no conflict about the practice itself is witnessed on these forums. Ugoretz's intervention is to not measure this practice against old customs, but instead see it as an emergent new system of customs with religious meaning. It is not a yearning to old customs that makes people come together to discuss Shinto altars, but it is a genuine desire to do something new. Old religion and its materiality is respected, but only as a foundation on which to build a new digital religious performance. Ugoretz adopts a semi-participant observation approach explaining this new system of customs as much as possible in their own words. As remarkable as the vibrancy of these communities is, a cautionary note is in place as well. In terms of absolute numbers, the number of participants is very small compared to the total number of Shinto practitioners and the people that do constitute these communities are of a very specific demographic. It shows traces of being a platform for the diaspora but in fact it goes even further out from the religious center, drawing in people who were born outside of it and who do not wish to become full converts but rather enjoy only parts of it. A "light" version. Perhaps a westernized version? Perhaps this is a digital equivalent of the "yoga" that is used as fitness training in Europe and North America. Might we even dare to say that (digital) Orientalism rears its head once again? But here we are neither aggressors nor victims, simply bystanders. Could we take a more antagonistic stance as Curtis describes, or is that not the spirit in which she argues for it? A lot of question marks, and we like to leave it at that. We think that us scholars can have, on certain topics, a better understanding of what the meaning is of ancient religions and we do think that this comes with some sort of duty to explain this meaning. While we are used to do so in scholarly publications, with the creative reuse of ancient religions in the digital world, we are challenged to extend our work towards this domain. How far this goes and under what circumstances it is most stringent, remains an open discussion.

Another aspect of the vitality of ancient religions, pertaining to us scholars primarily, is touched on in Van der Meij and Van der Putten's chapter. The project they describe digitizes manuscripts that very few people seem to care about, and in this sense the old materiality of religion is not accepted in its own right. From an emic perspective, the materials have lost their value to which digitization adds nothing. But for an entirely different group of people, the digital repository blows new life into them: from obscurity they are ushered into the spotlight to be reflected upon with new eyes. So many hurdles are taken away that the group of potentially interested grows exponentially. So, here too ancient religious texts are not simply digitized, but they start an entirely new life. It is fascinating to see how these four scholars put a spotlight on this new life and provide us with different ways to capture and describe it. A final note we wish to make is that in all three cases, it is digital photography that plays an important role. We do not see the full implications of this, but we do suspect that it is a notable aspect of this remarkable vitality that ancient religions show.

Level of Detail

A typical problem for the study of religion in Asia is the dearth of usable datasets and the difficulty in making them. Morris's chapter engages the most with the problem, in his discussion of using digital tools to digitize and begin to analyze texts related to Christianity in Japan. Even the most basic of functions such as segmentation into words proved impossible for off-the-shelf products. Issues arise because written texts from Asia are often not left-to-right, they can be written in multiple scripts and languages within the same document, and can contain uncommon vocabulary. In Morris's case, even Latinized texts, typeset in modern typography, were incorrectly processed by OCR software. As Lee dryly states in her chapter: "Digital models are only as complete as the datasets they reference." This may sound like stating the obvious, but as it turns out one can quickly identify unknown variables that greatly influence the outcome of one's analysis. Of course, as Lee also states, "no amount of data will be able to describe a historical circumstance with complete fidelity." This is of course the art of the scholar: to present those pieces of evidence which convincingly depict a historical event, without the need for more information. But as Plau alludes to, and Lee makes note of as well: digital datasets and their visualizations can have a veneer of accuracy and completeness.

Robker is another key chapter for understanding the importance of this theme of level of detail. This is something we somewhat anticipated, as we wished to include the Bible since its level of complexity (textually and historically) is as complex as it gets, while the amount of attention it has been given is unmatched. The problems pertaining to textual studies are therefore most visible for the Bible. Central to Robker's discussion is the observation that despite all the scholarly attention, many important issues are simply undecided. The indecision is of such a nature that a more complex and flexible methodology such as computer technology can provide, could truly shed new and definitive light on these undecided points.

The promise of digitization is there, Robker shows. However, as Robker shows as well, this potential remains largely untapped. His discussion of the state of the art in digitization of manuscripts and texts of the Hebrew Bible arrives at the conclusion that both more witnesses need to be digitized, and deeper work needs to happen on each of them including machine- and human-readable text and metadata such as paratexts and on its origin. Some of this work seems obvious to the point that one may wonder why it has not been executed. This is an observation that will hold true, we think, of much work on ancient, religious texts across all of Asia. We think it is simply and merely due to the relative low number of scholars capable of such work, and not because of some inherent restraint. In this sense, with new tools at our disposal, there is all kinds of exciting, groundbreaking work to be done. However, some of this work that Robker describes, such as the transcription on manuscript level of large sets of manuscripts, is not so obvious. Its execution is much harder to imagine, simply because it transcends the work load of a single scholar. This does not preclude a prevailing positive attitude among our contributors. Robker explicitly states it thus: "there has never been a more auspicious time to advance this work." A similar attitude is visible in Flügel's and Van der Meij and Van der Putten's chapters. Flügel is very direct in his ambition: to create a database with 100,000 recorded names of historical Jaina personalities. He sets this goal and simply gets to work. Similarly, Van der Meij and Van der Putten are very certain about their project, even though the 7353 manuscripts so far digitized can only be a drop in the bucket of available material: "We are convinced that this is the way forward." Even for Morris, there is hope. He ends his chapter noting that his object of study "provide the opportunity to collaborate...[and] to explore new questions."

What We Expected

We consciously delineated this book project from *The Digital Orientalist*, an online magazine that was founded by Van Lit in 2013 and which Morris has also served in various capacities since 2018, despite some crossover in contributorship. Nevertheless, our experience working on *The Digital Orientalist* did shape our expectations for this collection. In our proposal, we noted our expectation to be able to produce a handbook of the "very best practices and wisest lessons...that can kickstart any newcomer to the conversation." Such a statement encapsulated the patterns that we had both observed over the decade of *The Digital Orientalist*'s existence — growing interest in the digital humanities and their relation to Asian studies, and an increasing interest in practical, user-friendly guidance for both elementary and more advanced tasks. Indeed, at the time we were receiving fairly frequent requests to increase the number of articles targeting those just setting out on their journey in the digital humanities and how we should increase the accessibility of the platform to those with little experience in the digital humanities was being discussed at meetings of the magazine's editorial board. We were also undoubtedly influenced by the fact that *The Digital Orientalist* has always aimed to focus on "practical examples" as captured in the website's tagline: "Practical examples and theoretical reflections on the do's and don'ts of using digital tools for your study and research in African and Asian Studies." However, these joint foci on newcomers and practice potentially caused us to overlook much wider debates happening amongst those active in the field (which we discussed above) and which are perhaps excluded from the more practice-based *Digital Orientalist*. What we expected then was a book on what has been described as the first and second waves of the digital humanities — a mixture of material on the creation and running of projects and their usage — what we got was something more, though not necessarily the third wave proposed by David M. Berry (exploring "the *digital* component of the digital humanities in the light of its medium specificity").[6]

And there is still plenty to be found, for those who simply want to get experienced in the practice. For GIS, one can look at contributions by Gonzalez and Lee. Gonzalez shows what to do if you wish to create and view a database, while Lee goes a step further showing what to do computationally. To reinforce a computational approach, one needs to read Zorkina's chapter. Zorkina does not show the specific code she used, but discusses her approach on a detailed level that really helps to understand how to translate scholarly questions into technological answers. Setting up networks, in preparation for network analysis, is covered in Flügel's chapter. Unicode and TEI, the two major principles of scholarly editing, are discussed in our introduction and by Plau. Digitization is discussed at length in Van Lit, Robker, and Van der Meij and Van der Putten. The latter especially give detailed practical insights into how to actually do it. Lastly, handling social media can be deduced from the chapters by Ugoretz, Curtis, and Datta, although they do not speak of it in a computational or programmatic manner. Perhaps many of the practices can be learned, too, from more general introductions to digital humanities. The very specific, odd and sometimes downright problematic issues that arise when applying these techniques to historical, religious material from Asia have been catalogued in this volume. We hope the reader has been inspired to go out there and break digital new grounds in their own field.

---

[6] David M. Berry, "Introduction: Understanding the Digital Humanities," in *Understanding the Digital Humanities*, ed. David M. Berry (Houndmills: Palgrave MacMillan, 2012), 4.

Bibliography

Alimardani, Mahsa and Mona Elswah. "Digital Orientalism: #SaveSheikhJarrah and Arabic Content Moderation." *POMEPS Studies* 43, *Digital Activism and Authoritarian Adaptation in the Middle East* (2021): 69–75.

Berry, David M. "Introduction: Understanding the Digital Humanities." In *Understanding the Digital Humanities*, edited by David M. Berry, 1–20. Houndmills: Palgrave MacMillan, 2012.

Lit, L. W. Cornelis van, James H. Morris and Deniz Çevik. "A Digital Revival of Oriental Studies." *Revue de l'Institut des langues et cultures d'Europe, Amérique, Afrique, Asie et Australie* 39 (2020): 1–15.

Mayer, Maximilian. "China's Authoritarian Internet and Digital Orientalism." In *Redesigning Organizations: Concepts for the Connected Society*, edited by Denise Feldner, 177–192. Cham: Springer, 2020.

Miyake, Esperanza. "I am a virtual girl from Tokyo: Virtual influencers, digital orientalism and the immateriality of race and gender." *Journal of Consumer Culture*. DOI: https://doi.org/10.1177/1469540522111719.

Morley, David and Kevin Robins. *Spaces of Identity: Global Media, Electronic Landscapes, and Cultural Boundaries*. London: Routledge, 1995.

Oda, Masanori. "Welcoming the Libido of the Technoids who haunt the junkyard of the Techno-Orient, or the Uncanny Experience of the Post-Techno-Orientalist Moment." In *The Uncanny: Experiments in Cyborg Culture*, edited by Bruce Grenville, 249–273. Vancouver: Vancouver Art Gallery, 2001.

Ueno, Toshiya. "Japanimation and Techno-Orientalism." In *The Uncanny: Experiments in Cyborg Culture*, edited by Bruce Grenville, 223–231. Vancouver: Vancouver Art Gallery, 2001.

Ueno, Toshiya. "The Shock Projected onto the Other: Notes on *Japanimation and Techno-Orientalism*." In *The Uncanny: Experiments in Cyborg Culture*, edited by Bruce Grenville, 232–236. Vancouver: Vancouver Art Gallery, 2001.

Subject index

abjad 9, 11, 14
accuracy 5, 35, 50, 67, 86, 127, 133–135, 142, 150, 213, 215–216, 220–222, 224–225, 281, 318, 324
algorithm 21, 57, 99, 133, 180, 191, 199, 293, 301–306, 311–312, 323
alphabet. See script
altar 214, 289–293, 296–298, 300–301, 305–308, 310–312, 319
Anglocentrism 12–14
API: application programming interface 102–103
Arabic 8, 10, 13–14, 78, 85, 91, 246, 320
archive 74, 81, 91, 98, 106–107, 122, 150, 217–220, 247, 294, 304, 306. See *also* library; museum
archiving. See archive
atheism 239–240, 248–249, 252, 297

Bangla 242, 244–245, 251–252
Bangladesh 21, 233, 235–239, 241, 244–249, 251–252, 321
Bible 19, 73, 111–136, 324–325
bibliography 101, 122, 157–158, 171, 207, 218, 220
blog 233, 235, 237–239, 241, 248–250, 252, 296
blogger. See blog
Bodhisattva 48, 59–60, 62, 64–67
Buddha 48, 50, 53–56, 59–61, 64, 66–67, 263
Buddhism 15, 17–18, 27–29, 32–38, 40–41, 44, 47–50, 52, 61–62, 66, 68, 73, 260–263, 266–267, 275, 292, 297
butsudan. See altar

calendar 2, 15, 83, 206
calligraphy. See handwriting
canon 106, 112, 116, 322
catalog 48, 85–86, 88, 101–102, 125, 142, 144, 150–151, 159, 161, 163, 167–168, 170, 326
cataloging. See catalog
Catholicism 74, 207, 291
China 13, 28, 179, 182, 187
Chinese 8–10, 12, 14–15, 31–32, 178–180, 183, 189, 192, 206–207
Chinese characters 7–8, 10–11, 31–32, 206–207, 211, 224

Christianity 15, 20, 112, 205, 207–208, 217–220, 222, 226–227, 297, 324
CJK: Chinese, Japanese, Korean characters 8, 10, 12, 31–32, 206–207. See also Chinese; Chinese characters; Hanja; Japanese; Korean
clergy 187, 292, 306, 309. See also missionary; monk; nun; priest
coding 38, 108, 126, 132, 158–161, 165, 171, 184, 192–193, 214, 326
collaboration 9, 20, 33, 39, 44, 123, 131–133, 162, 172–173, 227, 276, 325
collocation 180–192, 194, 196–200
colonialism 3–7, 40, 139, 144–147, 149–150, 152, 258, 265, 272–273, 317, 320. See also orientalism
colophon 84–85, 87–89, 144, 158, 161–162, 167–171, 318
commentaries 91, 113
community 19, 21, 28, 33, 39, 75, 141, 152, 182, 207, 247–248, 258–259, 263, 265, 269–270, 272, 275, 277, 280, 289, 291–301, 305–208, 310–312, 319–320, 322–323
computational linguistics 20, 128, 159, 178, 181–182, 216, 302, 326
computer vision 18, 97, 99–100, 102–103, 107, 109–110
Confucianism 73, 187
copyright 125, 222, 224
coronavirus. See COVID-19
corpus (corpora) 20, 27, 105–107, 161, 178–180, 182–186, 191–193, 205, 226
COVID-19 74, 94, 257, 263, 278, 280
crowd-sourcing 131–133, 234, 240–242
CSS: cascading style sheets 36, 38
cursive. See handwriting

Daoism 47, 177, 187–189, 195–196, 198
data 17, 18, 28–29, 31, 33–39, 41, 43–44, 48–49, 56–57, 67–68, 73, 75, 82–90, 92–94, 97, 100–103, 107–108, 110, 113, 115, 118, 124, 126–128, 130–136, 140, 142, 144, 147, 150, 157–167, 171–173, 213, 216–217, 222–224, 226, 276, 278, 280, 295–296, 303–304, 308, 310, 324–326. See also dataset; metadata

https://doi.org/10.1515/9783110747607-015

database 20, 29, 34, 73–75, 82, 92–93, 98, 150, 157–164, 172–173, 217–220, 319, 325–326
datafiction 241. See also fiction
dataset 29, 31, 33, 35, 38, 41, 67, 108, 113, 135–136, 158, 161–162, 166, 172, 222, 234, 324. See also data; metadata
deities 48, 59–64, 141, 261, 263, 272–273, 289–292, 296–297, 306–307, 309–310
democracy 242–244
democratization 129, 252
diachrony 111–112, 114–119, 124, 128, 130, 133, 134–136, 160, 310
dictionary 11, 78, 85, 180, 199, 205–206, 212–216, 218, 225–227
digital humanities, waves of 326
The Digital Orientalist 1, 320, 325–326
digitization 15, 17–19, 73–75, 77, 81–94, 99–102, 105, 107, 110, 112, 121–124, 129, 131, 133–134, 149–150, 216–222, 226, 245, 257, 317, 319, 322–326. See also photograph; photography; transcription
disinformation 251–252, 259
distant reading 104, 106, 109
divine 16, 291
divination 73, 82–83

eBay 308
ethnocentrism 277. See also eurocentrism
empire. See colonialism
encoding 8, 12, 17, 97, 132, 139, 318
eurocentrism 2–6, 16, 147

Facebook 21, 233–237, 239–243, 245, 247–248, 251, 259, 277, 290, 293–295, 297, 299–306, 308, 310–312, 323
facsimile 119–125, 128–130, 132–134
fiction 187, 241, 248–250. See also datafiction
folio 103, 119–120, 122–124, 128, 167–168
font 8, 12–13, 210–211

GIS: geographic information system 17–18, 36, 38, 47–50, 57, 60–61, 63, 67, 326. See also map; mapping
GitHub 29–30, 33, 38, 179–180, 184, 192–193, 211
geomapping. See GIS: geographic information system

Global South 7, 10
Google 14, 101, 173, 212, 218, 225
goddess. See deities
gods. See deities

handwriting 11, 13–14, 16, 77, 79–80, 114, 206–208, 220
Hanja 31–32, 35, 48. See also Chinese characters
Hanzi. See Chinese characters
heritage 34, 40, 74, 79, 164, 260, 263, 272–273, 275, 319
Hinduism 73, 141, 236, 262–263, 267, 275
hiragana. See kana
HTML: hypertext markup language 36, 38
HTR: handwritten text recognition. See OCR: optical character recognition

IIIF: International Image Interoperability Framework 220
India 9, 19, 139–147, 150, 162–166, 262–263, 275, 292, 319
Indonesia 18, 73–75, 79, 81–82, 84–89, 91, 93
inscription 49, 64–65, 157–158, 161–163, 165–167, 171, 179
Instagram 259, 299
interface. See UI: user interface
Islam 9, 16, 73–74, 82, 86, 89, 91, 95, 141, 233, 236–240, 244, 246, 249
Islamophobia 146

Jainism 20, 140–141, 157–173, 319, 325
Japan 6–7, 10, 13, 14–16, 20, 40, 205–227, 258–282, 291–297, 300, 312
Japanese 1, 7–8, 11–12, 14–16, 206–227, 307
Javanese 78, 81, 85
JavaScript 99

kami. See deities
kamidana. See altar
kana 10, 208, 211, 224–225
kanji. See Chinese characters
katakana. See kana
keyword 104
Korea 6, 13, 17, 27–29, 31–36, 38, 40–41, 44, 48–67
Korean 12, 29, 31–32, 34–36, 39, 48

Subject index — 331

Laos 75, 83, 86, 93. See also Southeast Asia
LTR: left to right 14, 85, 113, 324. See also RTL: right to left
local 5-6, 34, 48, 66, 73, 78-79, 81-83, 85-89, 91, 233-234, 238, 240-241, 243-244, 246, 248-250, 279, 296, 307, 322
localization 12, 18, 39, 258
lexicon 85, 122-123, 125, 127-128, 180, 184
librarians. See library
library 74-76, 83-86, 91-92, 99-103,105, 121-122, 124, 130-132, 142, 144, 150, 163, 171, 173, 177, 218-220, 257
LinkedIn 299

machine learning 99, 301, 303-304
magazine 1, 249, 325-326
manuscript 2, 18-19, 73-94, 98-110, 111-125, 128-135, 139-145, 149-152, 157, 162-163, 167-171, 206-208, 217, 219, 317-319, 323, 325
map 17, 29, 31, 33, 36, 38, 48-49, 55, 57, 67, 142-145, 172, 206, 317-318. See also GIS: geographic information system; mapping
mapping 36, 47, 142-145, 166
metadata 18, 39, 47, 73, 75, 82-89, 92-93, 103, 130, 142, 144, 150, 171, 217, 276, 325. See also data; dataset
missionary 15-16, 20, 207-208. See also clergy; monk; nun; priest
monk 28, 32, 47, 52, 58, 64, 157, 165-166, 170. See also clergy; missionary; nun; priest
multilingual 1, 208-209, 212, 216, 227
museum 47, 74-75, 86, 89-90, 92, 102, 173, 276. See also archive

network analysis 33, 38, 41, 43-44, 47, 68, 157-158, 160, 172, 191
non-Latin scripts 2, 9, 12. See also abjad; Chinese characters; CJK: Chinese, Japanese, Korean characters; Hanja; kana; script
nun 171. See also missionary; monk; priest

OCR: optical character recognition 9-10, 13-14, 98, 106, 113, 133, 220, 222-226, 324
orientalism 19, 22, 139, 147, 149, 151-152, 260, 317-321, 323. See also colonialism

paleography 134
patronage 50-52, 62, 66, 157, 159-161, 242
philology 85, 104-105, 106, 109-110, 143, 145-150, 164
pilgrimage 59, 68, 260
photograph 18, 89, 93, 98-103, 107, 119-124, 129-130, 132-134, 217, 221, 226, 234, 236, 242-245, 259, 277, 289, 291-292, 299, 302, 307-308, 312, 320, 322-323. See also digitization
photography 86, 88, 131, 312, 323-324. See also digitization
photoshop 250
poetry 177-179, 182-193, 196-198, 206, 238, 245-246
preservation 32, 34, 55, 74-76, 79, 81, 83, 91, 94, 115-116, 164-165, 178-179, 248, 260, 278, 319. See also preservation
priest 196, 295, 297, 300, 310-311. See also clergy; missionary; monk; nun
protest 233-234, 236-240, 242-245, 248-249, 251
repository 31, 37-38, 52, 74, 76, 83-84, 93, 159, 218-220, 323. See also database; GitHub
ritual 21, 47, 50-52, 73, 87-88, 238-240, 289-290, 293, 296, 300, 306-310, 312
romanization 32, 35-36, 215-216
RTL: right to left 14, 85, 113, 206. See also LTR: left to right

sacred 47, 50-52, 54, 64, 66, 90, 244, 248, 251, 289-291, 307, 309, 312
Sanskrit 92, 143, 145-147, 151, 159, 165, 266, 318. See also Siddhaṃ
script 1-2, 8-15, 32, 78-79, 82, 85-86, 88-89, 91, 113, 205-206, 208-209, 211-212, 215-216, 218, 225-226, 319, 324. See also abjad; Chinese characters; CJK: Chinese, Japanese, Korean characters; Hanja; kana
segmentation 13-14, 179-180, 192, 199, 212-216, 227, 324
Shahbag 21, 233-252, 320
Shinto 21, 260-262, 275, 289-301, 305-312
shrine 17, 260, 262, 289-290, 292-297, 306-311. See also kamidana
Siddhaṃ 15. See also Sanskrit

social network 21, 81, 234, 239, 257, 259, 274–275, 289, 293–294, 299, 302, 306
Somewhereinblog 239, 249–250
SoundCloud 235, 244, 251
Southeast Asia 73–79, 82–83, 85–86, 91, 93–94
statue 18, 48, 50, 53, 56, 165–166, 258, 311
stop list 182–184, 216

tagging 113, 120, 183, 235, 239, 243, 245, 259
taxonomy 158–159, 161, 164
teaching 257, 282, 297
TEI: text encoding initiative 17, 19–20, 98, 132, 139, 142–143, 150–151, 173, 326
Telegram 244
Thailand 75, 79, 82, 85–86, 88, 93. See also Southeast Asia
timeline 142–144, 302
token. See segmentation
tokenization. See segmentation
training 20, 84, 86–87, 108, 132, 163–164, 205, 226, 265, 271, 276, 278, 282, 304, 323
transcription 12, 15, 85, 89, 129, 132–134, 142, 150–151, 210, 217, 219–226, 318, 325. See also digitization; photograph; photography
transliteration. See romanization

travel 51, 53, 55, 57–59, 64, 67–68, 91, 94, 144, 146–147, 186, 190, 192, 198, 300
troll 263, 268, 274–275, 281
Twitter 21, 235, 239, 244–245, 258–265, 269, 275–277, 279–281, 318

UI: user interface 98–99, 102–103, 108, 120, 122–123, 125–127, 217, 227, 244.
unboxing 310–311
unicode 12–13, 326

vernacular 91, 140, 143–145, 147, 151, 318

weblog. See blog
website 33–34, 39, 73–75, 89, 91–93, 101–103, 120, 123, 216, 234, 280, 305
the West 1–7, 82–84, 112–113, 152, 261
Wikipedia 281
woodblock printing 11, 14, 16, 207–208

X. See Twitter
XML: extensible markup language 20, 97, 123, 128, 131

YouTube 89, 235, 237–238, 245–246, 248, 275

www.ingramcontent.com/pod-product-compliance
Lightning Source LLC
Chambersburg PA
CBHW071400300426
44114CB00016B/2126